Escape From Excel® Hell:
Fixing Problems in Excel
2003, 2002, and 2000

Escape From Excel® Hell: Fixing Problems in Excel 2003, 2002, and 2000

Loren Abdulezer

Wiley Publishing, Inc.

Escape From Excel® Hell: Fixing Problems in Excel 2003, 2002, and 2000

Published by
Wiley Publishing, Inc.
10475 Crosspoint Boulevard
Indianapolis, IN 46256
www.wiley.com

WILEY

About the Author

Loren Abdulezer is CEO and President of Evolving Technologies Corporation, a New York–based technology consulting firm. He is an experienced IT professional serving major Fortune 500 companies, including Citigroup, JP Morgan Chase, IBM, Procter & Gamble Pharmaceuticals, and Pfizer. He has consulted on strategic technology and Internet product design, data analysis, mathematical modeling, visual modeling, and simulation, MIS/Web reporting, Java and object-oriented programming, Internet security, and business continuity planning.

Loren is a world acknowledged expert on spreadsheets, visual modeling, and dashboard technology. He is the author of *Excel Best Practices for Business* (www.ExcelBestPractices.com), also published by Wiley, and is a Crystal Xcelsius Consulting Partner for Business Objects S.A. (www.XcelsiusBestPractices.com). You can find out more information about Loren and the book *Escape From Excel Hell* at www.EscapeFromExcelHell.com.

To my wife, Susan; without her encouragement and enthusiasm,
this book would not be a reality.

Acquisitions, Editorial, and Media Development

Executive Editor: Gregory S. Croy

Development Editor: Susan Christophersen

Technical Editor: William Good

Copy Editor: Susan Christophersen

Editorial Manager: Jodi Jensen

Media Development Project Supervisor: Laura Moss

Media Development Specialist: Kit Malone

Media Development Coordinator: Laura Atkinson

Composition Services

Project Coordinator: Adrienne Martinez

Graphics and Production Specialists: Beth Brooks, Lauren Goddard, Denny Hager, Joyce Haughey, Heather Ryan, Amanda Spagnuolo

Quality Control Technician: Dwight Ramsey

Proofreader: Tricia Liebig

Indexer: Ty Koontz

Publishing and Editorial for Technology Dummies

Richard Swadley, Vice President and Executive Group Publisher

Andy Cummings, Vice President and Publisher

Mary C. Corder, Editorial Director

Publishing for Consumer Dummies

Diane Graves Steele, Vice President and Publisher

Joyce Pepple, Acquisitions Director

Composition Services

Gerry Fahey, Vice President of Production Services

Debbie Stailey, Director of Composition Services

Contents at a Glance

Table of Contents

Part II: Escape in Under Two Minutes

Part III: More Elaborate Escapes

Preface

Spreadsheets are among the most widely used and useful programs on the planet. Despite the popularity of spreadsheets, people face constant challenges in using them. *Escape From Excel Hell* is your guide to troubleshooting them.

The problems I have selected for *Escape From Excel Hell* are based on commonly encountered problems that appear on community bulletin boards, listservs, and newsgroups. I researched well over 10,000 of them. Although there is a wide diversity of problems, a great many of them are repeatedly asked.

I have organized the material in *Escape From Excel Hell* so that it is most convenient for you, the reader and, presumably, a person who has experienced "Excel Hell." I group the easy and quick problems in the early chapters (Part I: Escape in Under 30 Seconds), the ones that require a little thinking or effort in the middle (Part II: Escape in Under Two Minutes), and the most challenging ones for the last (Part III: More Elaborate Escapes). Many of the spreadsheet solutions outlined in *Escape From Excel Hell* are included on the book's CD-ROM. Updates and other relevant information can be found on www.EscapeFromExcelHell.com.

By definition, a book on troubleshooting and escaping spreadsheet problems cannot be a typical spreadsheet book. It has to address the very kinds of things you deal with when you get into a jam. Some of these solutions, which I call 30-second escapes, provide immediate and quick fixes. They don't depend on theory; you just need to be armed with a few facts. These, along with some basic information, make up the first several chapters.

I would be drastically shortchanging you if I only gave "lookup answers" without providing guidance on how to diagnose problems. If you add a trendline to an Excel chart, what will you do when you realize that missing data points are interpreted as zero values and totally throw off the trend? Chapter 8 includes this problem, what happens, and what to do about it. Other chapters do the same: that is, try to anticipate the associated issues so that the answer you sought doesn't lead you to new frustrations.

In working in the business and corporate environment, I find that people who need to work with spreadsheets sooner or later are bound to veer off the well-paved path. When they do, they get stuck with problems such as a skewed trendline or a formula that produces the wrong results. All too often, people don't have the means to adequately deal with the problem and have to resort to a stop-gap or patchwork solution. And too often, these don't work well. They certainly don't provide that comfort zone you would like to have.

You need effective strategies to avoid falling into spreadsheet ditches, and effective tools to get yourself out of them when you are stuck. This is the essence of what *Escape From Excel Hell* is all about.

Loren Abdulezer

January 2006

Acknowledgments

During my writing *Escape From Excel Hell* I have had the good fortune of crossing paths with Howard Dammond, a colleague I had known only peripherally. After I spoke to him about *Escape From Excel Hell*, all that changed. Throughout the course of my writing, we engaged in a wonderful dialog, making Howard an incredible resource who substantially enhanced the quality of this book.

In writing this book I have benefited from the many thousands of online questions and answers. The people both asking questions and providing answers have allowed me to better discern what is important in the minds of people, brilliant insights, and clever techniques. To both communities of users and experts alike, I am grateful for the open dialogue you have placed into numerous public forums.

I would also like to thank the following people, many of whom have contributed ideas in public and online forums (appearing in order of first name):

Chip Pearon, Dana DeLouis, Dann Stayskal, Dave Peterson, David Billigmeier, David Geen, David McRitchie, Debra Dalgleish, Dermot Balson, Don Guillett, Gord Dibben, Harlan Grove, Harry Butler, JE McGimpsey, John Picard, John Tassopoulos, John Walkenbach, Jon Peltier, Kevin Gordon, Martin Los, Mike Alexander, Norman Harker, Norman Jones, Patrick O'Beirne, Peo Sjoblom, Steve Newbern, and Tom Ogilvy.

I feel that it's a privilege to work with Greg Croy and Susan Christophersen, and the whole team at Wiley. Their professionalism and dedication truly typifies best practices. I want to thank John Walkenbach for his feedback during the early stages of writing, which helped shape the book. Bill Good is an amazingly talented individual who knows how to think outside and in the box. This makes him an ideal technical editor. From the Wiley team, I also want to thank the following people (appearing in order of first name): Andy Cummings, Kit Malone, Laura Moss, Leah Cameron, and Mary Bednarek.

Special thanks go to the folks at Business Objects, and in particular to Kirk Cunningham, who has been instrumental in making resources available to me so that I could write about Crystal Xcelsius. I want to thank the following individuals at Business Objects who played a significant role in getting me on the fast track to using Crystal Xcelsius (appearing in order of first name): Charles Rudolph, Gerrit Neve, Jaime Zuluaga, Jason Hardy, Mary Brigden, Rick Dendy, Ryan Camoras, Santi Becerra, and Santiago Becerra.

Introduction

Thank you for buying this book. I am hoping you will make excellent use of it. For many of you, I expect the book to follow the "20:80 rule" (and yes, I said 20:80 instead of the usual "80:20 rule"). By this I mean that you may already know 80 percent of the information in the book, but the content in the remaining 20 percent more than justifies the purchase you just made.

I had the good fortune of having the editors from Wiley ask me to write this book. I think one of the reasons they asked me is because of a very special requirement and because of how I value the importance of it. And that most important requirement is you, the reader. There are at least 300 million Excel users out there. If one in three hundred already possesses a wealth of technical knowledge, it means that some 1 million people are, so to speak, black-belt experts. This book is written for the 299 million of you who have daily tasks and priorities that typically are not centered on spreadsheets (except when problematic spreadsheets would make you want to pull your hair out), hence the title, *Escape From Excel Hell*.

How This Book Is Organized

I've spent a great many years working in corporate America where people live and die by spreadsheets. I've seen how they use spreadsheets: sometimes terribly inventive, sometimes terribly inefficient, sometimes elegantly, and all too often, with incomplete spreadsheet knowledge. Although I stress best practices (some of you may be familiar with my book, *Excel Best Practices for Business*, also published by Wiley), it is equally important to have in your hip pocket those little tricks and tidbits of knowledge that will make you proficient with spreadsheets. An important distinction should be drawn between spreadsheet trivia and spreadsheet knowledge. The latter will give you some agility, and that's exactly what I want to arm you with.

If I were writing a military manual I might write about two things: strategy and tactics. My book *Excel Best Practices for Business* covers the strategy portion. *Escape From Excel Hell* covers the tactical portion. This book is designed to allow you to pick your problems and, with surgical precision, strike the problem, solve it, and move on.

I've broken out the problems and organized the book into three basic categories:

- Part I: Problems you can solve in less than 30 seconds
- Part II: Problems that would take you a few minutes to solve
- Part III: Problems that could easily take you more than 10 minutes to solve

I chose this organization in order to introduce ideas to problem solving as you come across them while you use spreadsheets. The under-30-seconds problems in Part I are easy ones if you already know the fix. If you have only recently begun to use spreadsheets, you'll find the solutions in this part valuable as they help you to fill gaps in your knowledge and put you on the road to building practical skills.

The problems that involve several minutes to solve (Part II) are not necessarily more difficult. You might be constructing some spreadsheet formula involving subtle logic. Knowing the approach won't give you the immediate solution. You will have to work through the problem, but it shouldn't require a great deal of effort.

Finally, there are the "How do I slay the dragon?" problems (Part III) that are more involved, but may have an elegant solution. You might, for instance, be receiving a not-so-pretty computer run and have to make sense of the numbers within Excel. If the computer run is small, say, a page or so, you might slog your way through the document to characterize the essential information. This form of electronic pencil pushing may work for small files, but it will quickly become unwieldy as file size grows. For these more challenging problems, I provide you with ready-made spreadsheets that are designed to be easily modified by you. I also give you instructions on how to use and extend these examples.

The overwhelming majority of the devilish Excel problems I bring up are based on many thousands of commonly encountered spreadsheet problems (I researched more than 10,000 of them). So the problems selected for this book are directly connected to the spreadsheet user community of people like you. In fact, user questions phrased similarly to the ones I researched appear frequently throughout the book, styled just like this one from Chapter 1:

> *"When I enter the value 12, Excel turns it into 0.12, but when I enter 12.24, Excel keeps it the way I entered it. How can I prevent this from happening?"*

The solutions I provide are the ones I believe will give you the agility to solve these problems and similar ones on your own. At the end of the day, no book can give you all the spreadsheet solutions. You need a blend of hip pocket tips and some basic skills. I've aimed to provide both.

Also, as much as possible, I provide you with already complete "take-aways" that you can immediately use (they're discussed in the book, and you'll find the actual files on the book's CD-ROM), without spending much time or having to learn much. These are composed of snippets of Excel formulas, cheat sheets, and completed spreadsheets. They are easy to use, don't require much thought, and are thorough (those of you who have read my prior book know that I pay very careful attention to details).

What Do You Need to Know?

Obviously, the more experience and knowledge you have in working with spreadsheets, the better off you'll be.

You won't need much to get started. Part II (Escape in under Two Minutes) helps to build up your core competency with spreadsheets. Macros are used in this book. If you're not exactly sure what a macro is, don't worry. The macros I use in *Escape From Excel Hell* are principally for convenience. For instance, I give you a spreadsheet that allows you to click a button to switch back and forth between column labels displayed as letters or numbers. Alternatively, you could do this manually by changing a setting in the Tools⇨Options menu.

Those of you a little more fluent with spreadsheets will appreciate the numerous examples of spreadsheet formulas and completed spreadsheets. I hope the book will contribute to your sense of outside-the-box thinking. Experimentation works great when you have well-designed spreadsheets that can accommodate your personal preferences. It also helps to have real-world examples similar to the kinds you encounter daily.

Forget the theory: If you have good examples to try out, and you tag team (with me), you'll have plenty of opportunity to hone your instincts for getting things done with spreadsheets. If I can have my way, Excel will no longer be that troublesome software that occupies too much of your valuable time.

Those of you who have become black belts in Excel have done so by applying yourselves with great diligence. You've achieved your level by constantly pushing the boundaries of your knowledge. Chances are, you are not going to want to stop learning and improving your foundations. I will assure you that there's a thing or two for you to learn (possibly more!). And you may want to pick up several copies of this book, if for no other reason than to stanch the flow of questions from colleagues wounded from their battle with Excel.

By now, you should be itching to start using the book, mostly because it is going to be rewarding (or because you are allergic to Excel and this book is a soothing balm). For most of you, that reward is freedom from much of the drudgery of plowing through spreadsheets. Isn't it great when that same effort gives rise to improved skills, is interesting, and, perhaps to your astonishment, fun?!

How to Get the Most out of This Book

Basically, the problems I address in this book are the ones that are likely to trip you up. There are plenty of problems that experienced spreadsheet users treat as common knowledge and don't bother explaining or bringing them up to their less experienced colleagues. These are the kinds of problems largely discussed in Part I (Escape in Under 30 Seconds).

For those of you who feel you already know this material, press on further into the book. Before making a hasty jump past the first few of chapters, take a look at what you're skipping. Because Excel is so feature rich, there may be something you didn't think about doing.

As you go through Part II (Escape in Two Minutes), you will quickly find two things:

- You will have to roll up your shirt sleeves to solve the problem.
- There is often more than one way to solve the problem.

Sometimes I'll point out different ways to solve the exact same problem. Other times you'll be creative and devise approaches of your own. If my approach is different than the one you would come up with on your own, then at least I am giving you some new ideas.

Part III (More Elaborate Escapes) contains problems that are either more involved or open-ended. Aside from worked out examples, I provide best practices to help you apply them to your own situations.

One final word: Associated with this book is an online site at `http://www. EscapeFromExcelHell.com`.

Conventions Used in This Book

Following are the various conventions used in the book.

Spreadsheet Functions and Cells

The built-in Excel worksheet functions (such as SUM or RAND), as well as standard Excel add-in functions (such as RANDBETWEEN), all appear in UPPERCASE format. User-defined names assigned to cell ranges appear in mixed case and monofont (for example, `SomeValueDefinedForACell`).

Using Keystroke Sequences and Menu Command Sequences

Isolated keystrokes are identified by the name as it appears on the keyboard: Alt, Ctrl, and so on. Keystroke combinations are signified by a plus sign, as in Ctrl+Alt+Del (the DOS reboot sequence).

Menu command sequences, such as clicking File to open that menu and then clicking Save to save a document, are signified as follows: File⇨Save.

Macintosh users should consult Appendixes A, B, and D to better map actual experiences with the book description.

Icons Used in the Book

Following are descriptions of some visual cues used throughout this book to draw your attention to specific issues.

TIP
Practical techniques to get in the habit of using regularly to promote effective and efficient spreadsheet preparation and maintenance.

NOTE
Ideas or issues that require some special awareness or workaround.

CAUTION
When you see this icon, read carefully. Some actions you might be about to take could be disastrous. Some things you may not know could hurt you. In cases such as these, ignorance is definitely not bliss.

WARNING
An even stronger version of the Caution.

Part  1

Escape in Under 30 Seconds

Chapter 1

Spreadsheet Basics

In This Chapter

◆ Learning things about spreadsheets you don't typically find in manuals and classes

◆ Fixing up odd behavior in your spreadsheets

◆ Setting Excel macro security

◆ Getting the most out of an Excel menu

◆ Understanding Excel templates

◆ Taming your Excel toolbars

◆ Alleviating window "pains" in Excel

A Good Place to Begin

Have you ever wanted to individually format different words in a sentence or phrase appearing in a spreadsheet, such as those appearing in Figure 1-1? If you haven't thought about or attempted to do so, put the book down and try it now. It's a simple enough task, but it's not so obvious if you haven't done it before.

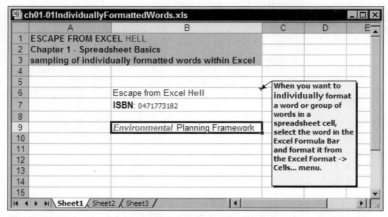

Figure 1-1: Spreadsheet cells with individually formatted words

Here is how you do it. Select the spreadsheet cell containing the text you want to format. In the Excel Formula Bar (see Figure 1-2), select the word(s) you want to change.

Figure 1-2: Edit individually selected words in the Excel Formula Bar.

With the text selected in the Formula Bar, click Format⇨Cells and you will be presented with a dialog box like that shown in Figure 1-3.

NOTE

I should point out that if you are used to entering and adjusting your spreadsheet formulas and content *inside the spreadsheet cell* and are able to select text within the cell, you can go ahead and format the content of your selected text.

Now, isn't this easy to do? It is easy but not obvious, because you have to use a Format "Cells" menu to change a piece of text *inside a cell*. Unless you happen to know about this *hidden* feature, it may never occur to you to that you can use a cell feature for a subcell element!

This book is filled with techniques that "may never occur" to you during your normal use of spreadsheets. Most of these techniques are in Part I ("Escape in Under 30 Seconds").

This chapter and the ones to follow outline some commonly encountered problems and challenges, and some easy fixes.

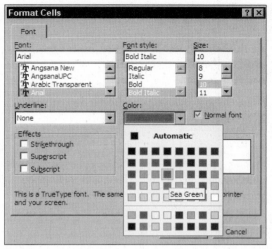

Figure 1-3: Format the selected word as you would regularly format a spreadsheet cell.

My Spreadsheets Have Gone Haywire — Help!!

Every now and then, it looks as though something with Excel is totally messed up. These "haywire" moments are typically caused by Excel having the wrong settings. In this section, I outline a few issues relating to settings and show some easy fixes.

"When I enter the value 12, Excel turns it into 0.12, but when I enter 12.24, Excel keeps it the way I entered it. How can I prevent this from happening?"

The very first time this problem is encountered, it must be bewildering. Fortunately, it is easy to fix. Choose Tools⇨Options and click the Edit tab. You will notice that Excel allows you to set fixed decimals. If there is a checkmark next to this setting, uncheck it (see Figure 1-4) and then click the OK button.

In some cases, it may be easier to enter a long list of numbers using fixed decimals, but generally this causes more confusion than it avoids.

"My spreadsheet columns are labeled using numbers instead of letters. I want to change it back."

Sometimes you'll be given a spreadsheet in which the columns appear with numbers instead of letters. This is referred to as the "R1C1" style. The usual display of column letters is known as the "A1" style. Excel supports both ways of displaying spreadsheets. That's because the underlying formulas and values used by Excel have nothing to do with how they are displayed.

To change your setting, choose Tools⇨Options and click the General tab. You will notice that Excel allows you to set R1C1. Uncheck this setting (see Figure 1-5) and then click the OK button to get back the A1 style.

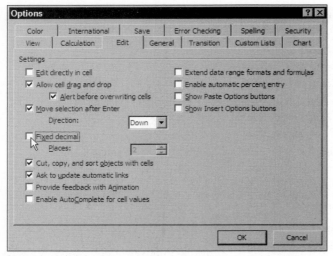

Figure 1-4: Disable (uncheck) the "Fixed decimal" setting.

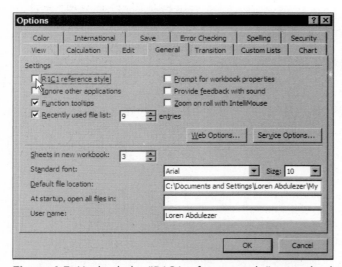

Figure 1-5: Uncheck the "R1C1 reference style" to get back the A1 style.

NOTE

There is a spreadsheet on your CD-ROM called `ch01_02SwitchTool.xls`. When you open this spreadsheet you will see two buttons labeled R1C1 and A1. Clicking the appropriate button will allow you to switch back and forth between the two reference styles without having to go through the Excel menus.

Understanding the R1C1 reference style

There are two ways to represent rows and columns in Excel spreadsheets. One of these is to label them with row and column numbers, and the other uses row numbers and column letters. These labels, whether in the "R1C1" style or "A1" style, are just a way to display and specify cell locations on a spreadsheet. Because Excel gives you the option of switching back and forth between these two modes, it doesn't matter which one you prefer using.

I want to explain some features of using the R1C1 style. Several things are worth mentioning.

- Absolute cell references don't require any "$" symbols. They are just the row number and column number. For instance, $D$10 is the same thing as R10C4.

- Relative cell references are shown with brackets around the respective row or column number offset. For example, using the A1 style, if you copy the formula =K2+U2+AE2 from cell A2 and paste it into cell D7, the resulting formula will be =N7+X7+AH7. In the R1C1 style, the exact same formula would be =RC[10]+RC[20]+RC[30]. The formula is saying, "add the sum of the cells appearing 10 columns to the right plus 20 columns to the right plus 30 columns to the right."

  In this sense the formula is visual, that is, it is not too difficult to visualize a formula grabbing the values of the cells 10, 20, and 30 columns to the right. When I copy and paste this formula from A2 to D7, the resulting formula (in R1C1 notation) is still =RC[10]+RC[20]+RC[30].

  Notice one thing else: The R1C1 style formula isn't tied to which cell the formula is written in. The formula =$A2+B3 appearing in D6 will not match the results of the formula =$A2+B3 appearing in G17. You have two identical-looking formulas meaning different things!

By now it should be obvious that I have a personal preference for using the R1C1 style over A1. However, because most of the world is used to the A1 style, I have kept just about all the examples in this book in the A1 style. I am also providing you with a spreadsheet on the book's CD-ROM that will allow you to go back and forth between the two styles at the click of a button. If you are curious to find out more about putting the R1C1 style to good use, see my book, Excel Best Practices for Business (Wiley Publishing, Inc., 2004).

"My spreadsheets are all backward!"

Spreadsheets can display labels in reverse order as shown in Figure 1-6 (and no, you haven't been abducted by aliens and transported to some parallel universe).

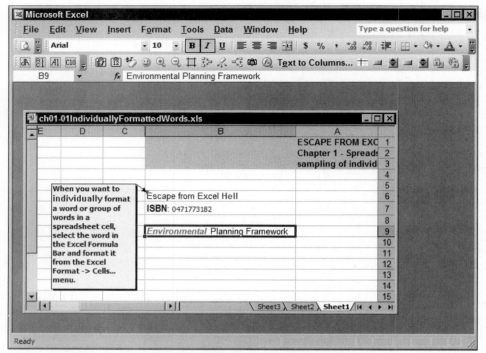

Figure 1-6: This spreadsheet is reversed (column labels all go in the wrong order and rows appear on the right instead of the left side).

So, how does this situation come about and why would Excel allow you to do this? It's very simple (see Figure 1-7). Excel is used in many countries and many languages. In some languages, the order of text flows from right to left, in contrast to English. If the natural orientation for a language is from right to left, wouldn't it be more natural if you could start the column and row labels from the top-right corner? Excel allows you to make this kind of customization. From the Excel menu, click Tool⇨Options and click the International tab, as shown in Figure 1-7.

To return the orientation to the usual left to right, *uncheck* the View Current Sheet Right-to-left setting. Also make sure that the Default direction is set Left-to-right (refer to Figure 1-7).

So, how might these settings all get changed? I'll give you one way. One member in my family tends to click any button without realizing what he's changing. My mother affectionately refers to him as "having pepper in his fingers." Maybe there is someone in your family with pepper in his fingers!

I am willing to bet that some of you who try to navigate to the Excel Options window are stumped by another problem: Excel won't allow you to go to the Tools menu and select Options. It's grayed out!

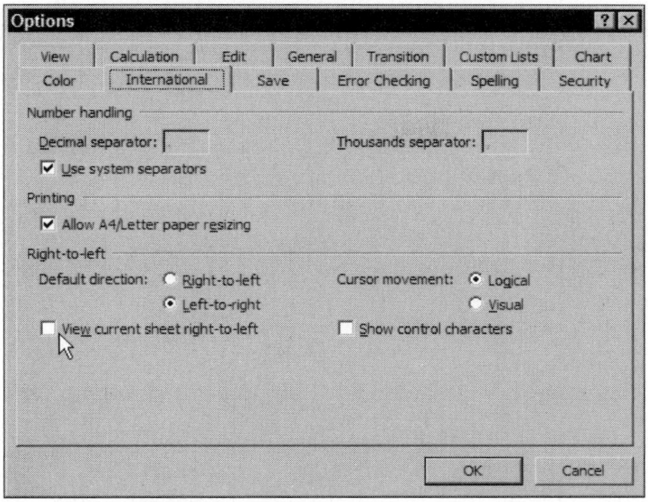

Figure 1-7: You can adjust settings to go from right to left or from left to right.

Excel allows you to set options that tell the software how it should behave at any time. To be able to set your options (such as the International setting), you need to have a spreadsheet already open. It doesn't matter which one, and the settings you choose don't apply to any specific spreadsheet. If you try to get to the Options menu item while no spreadsheets are open, you will see the Options menu item grayed out (see Figure 1-8).

Figure 1-8: The Options item on the Excel Tools menu is grayed out when no spreadsheet is open.

To fix this situation, simply make sure that a spreadsheet file is open first. It doesn't matter which spreadsheet file is open. If you haven't created any or can't find a spreadsheet, simply click New from the Excel File menu (or press Ctrl+N). If Excel doesn't create a file but displays a bunch of possible files on a panel on the right (see Figure 1-9), select Blank Workbook.

Part I

Figure 1-9: Options for New Workbook

After you have a spreadsheet or workbook open, you should have no problem changing the options. Try it.

If you are new to Excel, some of the terminology may be confusing. The sidebar "Excel workbooks, worksheets, and templates," later in this chapter, may clarify a few points.

"My Formula Bar disappeared."

I once downloaded a very interesting spreadsheet from the Department of Energy. Unfortunately, the spreadsheet had an interesting side effect. The macros used in the spreadsheet tried to make the spreadsheet behave like a traditional software application and removed the Formula Bar. After the spreadsheet was closed, the Formula Bar did not reappear. Though this kind of problem is annoying, it's solved with another quick fix. From the Excel menu, click Tools⇨Options, click the View tab, as shown in Figure 1-10, and then click the OK button.

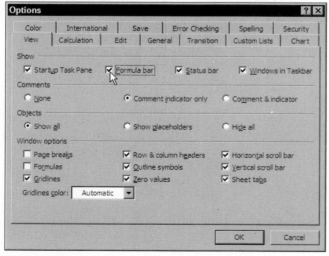

Figure 1-10: Check the setting for the Formula Bar in the View tab.

Macro Security

"Excel won't let me run any spreadsheets that have macros. What can I do?"

Figure 1-11 shows the kind of warning error you will get if you open a spreadsheet containing a macro and your security settings in Excel are set to High.

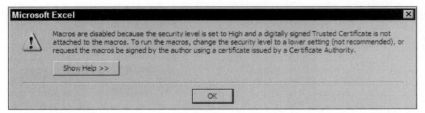

Figure 1-11: Warning message presented by Excel that tells you it disabled the spreadsheet macros

NOTE

Unlike the rest of Excel, which contains numbers and calculation formulas, macros contain programming code. Macros can extend the capability of a spreadsheet to do more than straight computations. They can add interactivity and intelligence in a way that formulas by themselves cannot. This capability is good, but it also presents some dangers. For this reason, Microsoft sets the security settings for Excel macros to High, thereby disabling macros unless they come from a trusted source.

Unless the spreadsheet containing a macro has been digitally signed and that signature can be verified, you will be unable to run the macros as long as your security settings are set to High or Very High. Incidentally, when Excel is first installed on your computer, the default setting is High. This means that if you never touched your security settings, you would not be able to run any Excel spreadsheet containing macros unless it was digitally signed and specifically trusted by you.

Although this is surely the safest way of configuring your software at the time of your install, having a high security setting can get in the way if you are frequently receiving spreadsheets with macros from people you trust but the spreadsheets lack the needed digital signatures. Even then, you have no guarantee that the macros will be safe. All you are doing is saying that you trust the source that is providing you with the spreadsheet, and you trust that it hasn't been altered in some way by a potentially malicious third party.

Let me give you the quick and practical solution. Set your security setting to Medium. You can do this by clicking Tools⇨Macro⇨Security and, in the Security Level tab, click the button next to Medium (see Figure 1-12).

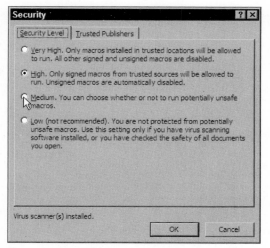

Figure 1-12: Adjusting your Security Level setting to Medium

Here is what this accomplishes. Anytime you open a spreadsheet that contains macro code, Excel will ask whether you want to enable or disable macros. This setting gives you maximum flexibility. Instead of unilaterally disabling macros, it allows you to decide whether to enable the macros at the time you open the spreadsheet file.

 CAUTION
Disabling the macros doesn't mean that the macros are disabled for all time. They are just disabled at the time you happen to open the spreadsheet file. If you close the file and e-mail it to a friend, the file will still contain the macros. Unless your friend also does something to disable the macros, the macros will be enabled.

If you want to play it safe, just select Disable Macros with the Medium Security Level settings. Later in the book (see Chapters 4 and 10), I show you how to inspect the macros for yourself. If you plan on working with spreadsheets you trust but that have macros, then setting your macro Security Level to Medium is recommended.

Excel Menus

"Excel never shows a full menu unless I click the double arrow at the bottom of the menu or wait a few seconds for the menu to expand. If I select an item on the expanded list, it then gets added to the short list. As a result, my menus are constantly changing in appearance! How can I once and for all get the menus to be fully expanded and unchanging?"

The accordion pull-down menu system (see Figure 1-13) used in Excel is a classic over-engineered solution that many people find annoying but don't know how to fix.

Figure 1-13: Abbreviated menu with double arrow

Here's how to fix it:

1. Click the Customize feature from the Tools menu.

   The Customize window with its three tabs appears.

2. Click the tab labeled Options.

3. The second checkbox, Always Show Full Menus, is not selected. Click this checkbox to make sure that full menus are enabled.

4. Click the Close button to accept the changes you made.

Excel workbooks, worksheets, and templates

While we're at it, let's get the terminology straight. When a spreadsheet file in Excel is being opened or referred to, it is called a workbook. Within each workbook you will see tabs appearing along the bottom. These tabs may have generic names such as Sheet1 or Sheet2. When you click any of these tabs, a sheet appears that corresponds to the tab name. Not surprisingly, these sheets are referred to as worksheets.

When you open a new workbook (do so by clicking File⇨New from the Excel menu), you typically see multiple worksheets, which are named Sheet1, Sheet2, and so forth. The individual worksheets are all empty initially; when you move between worksheets, you see no differences between them. After you start populating them with data or formulas, you will easily know which worksheet you are looking at. You have several ways to move between worksheets. You can click the tab appearing at the bottom of the worksheet. Or press Ctrl+PgDn or Ctrl+PgUp. Notice that to the bottom left of the worksheet, tabs appear as a bunch of triangular arrows. These help you to navigate through the list of worksheets.

From time to time you may hear about Excel templates. An Excel template is not a generic term but is actually a specific type of spreadsheet file that you can create and use. The filename suffix for a template file is .xlt instead of the usual .xls.

continued

continued

Excel templates are well suited for finely tuned spreadsheets that you will use repeatedly. A good example is a time sheet that could be distributed to a group of people. Perhaps, instead of using a template, you could commandeer an already populated spreadsheet and clean out the data. Would this be a good idea? What if you accidentally miss clearing out all the data or inadvertently clobber a spreadsheet formula? These are reasons that you may want to think about using template files.

Creating a template is easy. When you save your spreadsheet, click File⇨Save As (see the following figure).

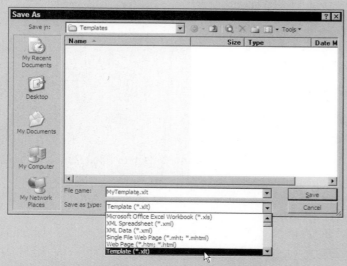

Saving a file as an .XLT template

Keep in mind that the .xlt file is typically stored in the Documents and Setting directory, usually inside the Application Data\Microsoft\Templates directory of your Application Data folder (see the next figure).

Typical location of Excel Templates

Thankfully, you don't have to search for the directory in which to save the templates. Excel takes care of that for you automatically.

To open a template, click File⇨New and then, in the Templates list, click On my computer (see the first figure that follows) and select the template (as shown in the second figure that follows).

Standard location of Excel Templates you create

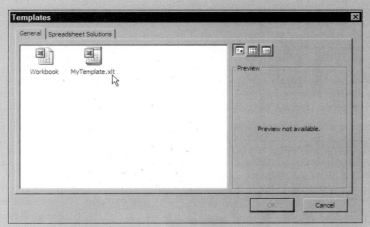

Templates located in the General tab

Your template will open as a regular .xls file, but when you save it, Excel will try to save it in the Templates folder and not the usual location where you keep your regular spreadsheet files. You need to navigate to your preferred directory; otherwise, you will end up with a lot of clutter and misplaced files!

Toolbars and Toolbar Icons

"My toolbar is missing some icons that it used to have! What happened?"

Just underneath your Excel menu is a series of icons placed on a set of toolbars. Clicking each of these icons causes Excel to perform a particular task. There are benefits of using toolbar icons: They are very accessible (except when hidden!) and are often quicker than trying to do the equivalent through the Excel menu.

Here is the problem and what you can do about it. If you have more toolbar icons than there is space across your Excel application window to hold them, Excel will try to park these icons somewhere. Out of the box, Excel will hide some of them, but it doesn't do a very good job of letting you know that there are hidden icons. It gives a visual signal, but it's subtle: Look for a couple of extra "notches" on the right side of the toolbar. When you click these notches, the hidden toolbars become visible (see Figure 1-14) and you can click the icon you want.

This method works, but having to find hidden icons sort of defeats a chief benefit—their immediate accessibility.

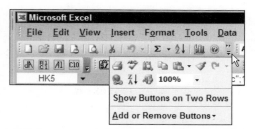

Figure 1-14: Click the toolbar notch to make hidden icons visible.

There is a second solution, but it may not be what you want. Look back at Figure 1-14. You'll notice an option called Show Buttons on Two Rows. If you select this option, your toolbar icons will be visible, but they will occupy multiple rows (see Figure 1-15). If you don't happen to have a gigantic screen, you'll pay dearly for valuable screen real estate.

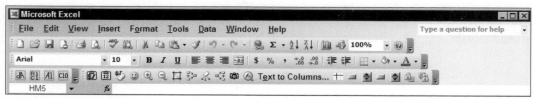

Figure 1-15: Toolbar icons are visible but there is a lot of wasted space.

A third solution is available. It entails customizing your toolbars to contain only the icons you need. This is likely to be your best approach, but it involves more than a 30-second point-and-click escape. The next section, "Customizing Your Excel Software with Toolbars," outlines the steps.

"A toolbar that I don't need is on my screen. How do I make it go away?"

The answer is easy if your toolbar happens to be free floating. Simply click the X at the top-right of your toolbar. However, toolbars that are nestled directly under the Excel menu do not have that X. For these, click Tools⇨Customize and click the Toolbars tab. You will see a list of toolbars. The ones that are visible have a checkmark next to them. Uncheck the ones you no longer wish to see. If you want to experiment with some of the toolbars that are not visible, simply place a checkmark next to their names and they'll be instantly visible.

Customizing Your Excel Software with Toolbars

At this point I would like you to define some custom toolbars of your own. Ultimately, the ones you choose are up to you. Just keep in mind that you'll quickly run out of screen space if you activate too many toolbars. I show you some useful ones you may want to keep as part of your standard arsenal.

If you have never customized your toolbars, they may appear similar to those in Figure 1-16.

Figure 1-16: Excel default settings

You can add to the existing slate of toolbars on your screen, but I would like you to construct your own custom group. First, go to the Excel menu and click Customize. Notice the three tabs running across the top of your Customize window. Make sure that the Toolbars tab is the frontmost tab showing. If it's not, click it. When you see the checklist of predefined toolbars, click the New button to create your own custom toolbar (see Figure 1-17).

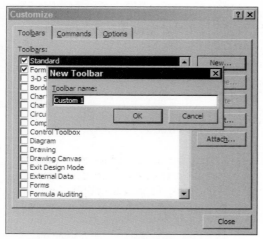

Figure 1-17: Give your custom toolbar a name.

The name can be any descriptive name of your choosing. For now, you can call it Group1. I use the Group1 toolbar that's set up here throughout the book. You are free to create additional groups. You can also mix and match icons among the different groups.

Click the Commands tab. You will notice a variety of categories, including File, Edit, View, and so forth. Click the Edit category. To the right of the Categories list are the various commands. Scroll down on the right till you see Paste Formatting (see Figure 1-18). Click Paste Formatting to select it.

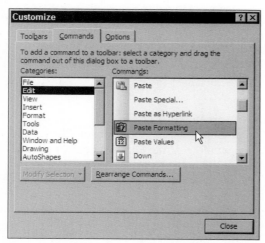

Figure 1-18: Select a toolbar icon to add to your custom group.

To add the feature to your toolbar, simply click the feature you desire to add. Notice that when you hold the mouse button down, the arrow pointer displays a small box with a plus sign (+) in it. While you have your mouse button held down, drag the icon onto your empty Group1 toolbar. When you drag the icon onto the Group1 toolbar, two things happen:

1. The + changes to an x.

2. A vertical insertion point indicates where the icon will be positioned.

When you release the mouse button inside the Group1 toolbar, you see the icon deposited there.

For the Edit Category, add the toolbar commands for Paste Values and Clear Formatting. You may have noticed that in addition to Clear Formatting, there is a feature for Clear Contents. Although you could also add this icon to your toolbar, it won't really benefit you to do so, because you can clear the contents of any cells on the spreadsheet that happen to be selected just by pressing the Del key.

Feel free to experiment and try adding any variety of command icons to your toolbar that you want. Whatever helps you to be productive is great. Also keep in mind that unless you have a super-gigantic screen, the real estate space on your computer display can be a precious commodity. After you've had a chance to experiment with the different toolbar icons, pick the ones that are most useful to you (that is, the ones you will use on a regular basis).

To get off to a good start and have in place the icons that will be used throughout the book, add the following to your toolbar:

- From the View category: Zoom In and Zoom Out

- From the Insert category: Diagram

- From the Format category: Light Shading

- From the Tools category: Trace Precedents, Trace Dependents, Remove All Arrows

- From the Data category: Text To Columns

- From Window and Help Freeze Panes

Your Group1 toolbar should now appear similar to Figure 1-19.

Figure 1-19: Group1 custom toolbar

There are "space saving" icons that combine the benefits of several toolbar icons. The Diagram icon is one. Icons and menu options that have the ellipsis (...) following them often have this feature. When you click the Diagram icon, you will be able to choose among Cycle diagrams, Radial diagrams, Pyramid diagrams, and so forth. Unless you have a specific favorite and use it constantly, you won't really need all the different options in your custom toolbar.

Sometimes you will want specific toolbar icons even though you can access the feature through one of the space-saving icons. The Paste Values and Paste Formatting are such icons. Being able to paste pure values that are devoid of formulas and formatting information is an important feature to have. Likewise, being able to paste formats will facilitate your ability to manage spreadsheet information.

Some of you who are already used to using the Format Painter may be wondering, "Why bother at all with the Paste Formatting when I have the Format Painter?" The Format Painter just clones the format of a selected region of cells at a new location. If, in addition to formatting, you also want to paste the values, then you'll need to do more than just use the Format Painter. You'll have to go back to your original selection of cells and then copy and paste the values. This adds to the number of steps you need to perform and will slow you down. If you feel tightly wedded to the Format Painter, do not fret. Continue using what you're already adept at. Old habits die hard. Some of them are important to keep. Others should be shed. Ultimately, you're the best person to make that call.

Keep in mind that all of the facilities of these toolbars are generally accessible through the Excel menus.

The Freeze Pane is particularly practical. I can't tell you how often I see spreadsheets in a split mode, as in Figure 1-20. Sometimes I think the split-pane feature of spreadsheets should really be called the "Split Pain" feature. This problem is easily corrected if you use the Freeze Pane icon (see Figure 1-21). The Freeze Pane icon acts as a toggle switch, enabling you to quickly switch back and forth. You can find the Freeze/Unfreeze Pane feature in the Excel Window menu, but using the toolbar icon is much quicker.

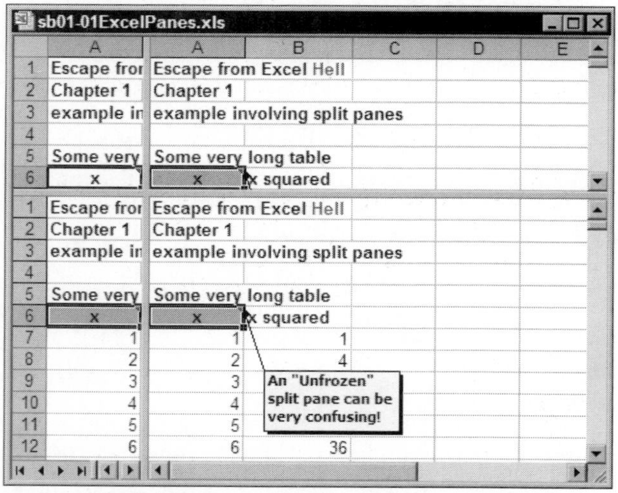

Figure 1-20: Confusing use of split-pane

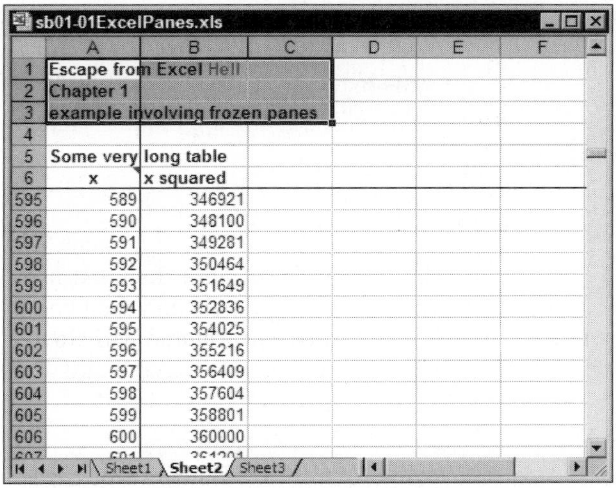

	A	B	C	D	E	F
	sb01-01ExcelPanes.xls					
1	Escape from Excel Hell					
2	Chapter 1					
3	example involving frozen panes					
4						
5	Some very	long table				
6	x	x squared				
595	589	346921				
596	590	348100				
597	591	349281				
598	592	350464				
599	593	351649				
600	594	352836				
601	595	354025				
602	596	355216				
603	597	356409				
604	598	357604				
605	599	358801				
606	600	360000				
607	601	361201				

Figure 1-21: After you click the Freeze Pane icon, the confusing split-pane is gone and the spreadsheet scrolls naturally with a split screen.

Text to Column is a feature that is particularly handy if you're going to be working with data files that are provided from third-party sources, such as government-published information pulled off the Internet.

Here's the last bit of configuration and I'll be done with toolbars. Right now, your Group1 toolbar (refer to Figure 1-19) is floating somewhere on your screen, because I haven't told you to anchor it to the standard Excel toolbars. Just click the Group1 toolbar anywhere on the title bar and the mouse point will take on a compass-like appearance. Holding the mouse button down, drag the toolbar over to the other toolbars and the Group1 toolbar will snap into place (see Figure 1-22).

Figure 1-22: Three rows of toolbars

Be careful not to unintentionally park the toolbar above the menu or over to one of the edges of your Excel application window. If a toolbar does get too close to the top, bottom, left, or right, it will snap to that edge. To unglue the toolbar from the edge, place your mouse over the top-left corner of the toolbar (there should be series of textured vertical dots), click your mouse to grab the toolbar, and move it away.

Notice that the toolbars take up three rows and there's a fair amount of empty space. Unless you're using a really large screen, you may want to consolidate all the toolbars into two rows. They can be shoved onto the second row, but there is not quite enough space to simultaneously display all of them on a straight horizontal line.

I don't know about you, but I don't particularly like the idea of using second-class icons. If they're out of sight, they're out of mind. Also, what's the purpose of having hidden icons when you already have their underlying capabilities in the Excel menus?

My first way of fixing this is to effectively remove the icons I don't expect to be using. There are a number of strategies. You can keep the Group1 toolbar at its full length and try resizing the formatting toolbar on its left to be a shorter width. This will relegate some of the Formatting icons to second class. Somehow this is not so palatable.

You could whisk away some of the icons to never-never land, dragging and dropping them to the desktop area. By doing so, you would be modifying an Excel standard feature, which I'm not sure you would want to do.

There's another way that's quite safe. Construct a new toolbar called Formatting2 (or whatever name you want to give it). Add to this toolbar the formatting facilities you need and exclude the rest. In the Customize Options menu, deselect the Formatting toolbar and check the newly created Formatting2 toolbar. Now there are no second-class icons and they all fit on two rows.

Nothing forces you to keep toolbars at the top of the spreadsheet. Aside from having them hover somewhere around, you can park them off to the side.

Closing Thoughts

This chapter's main purpose is to get out of the way those annoying particulars that routinely hamper spreadsheet productivity. With luck, most of you haven't come across a significant number of problems like the kind outlined here. If you do, you will find some easy fixes here. Also, you can find additional material at
http://www.EscapeFromExcelHell.com.

Chapter 2

A Few Good Functions

In This Chapter

- ◆ Formula essentials
- ◆ Excel can process text, too!
- ◆ Characterizing data with statistics
- ◆ Picking from among the crowd using selectors
- ◆ Cell references available upon request
- ◆ Excel Math function bootcamp
- ◆ Following the logic up and down the formula tree
- ◆ Using calendar arithmetic

In some sense spreadsheets are like a game of chess. It doesn't take very long to learn the basic moves of the game, but it can certainly take time to acquire a keen sense of how the game should be played. Likewise, spreadsheets are easy to learn but it can take time to get the hang of them.

There is a fundamental difference. In chess you are playing against an opponent, and the moves you make can be tied into what your opponent is doing. As a result, you can often focus your attention to a specific area or topic.

Unlike in chess, with spreadsheets there is no opponent. Your spreadsheet "board" is open ended. As long as you're not putting in invalid formulas, Excel is not going tell you what to do. Sure, it has wizards, and can guess some things when you type in incorrect or incomplete formulas; but it's not going to be your mentor.

You can always learn an extra Excel function or two, or find a way to squeeze your report onto a single printed page, but nailing down that keen sense of how to build spreadsheets and work those formulas will multiply your abilities. It will also increase your ability to put to use the little tidbits of information all the more easily.

The rest of Part I focuses on these issues in their simplest form. This chapter covers a number of useful Excel functions, but really focuses on issues faced by the beginning spreadsheet user. In particular, the effort is concentrated on getting you to be adept at handling spreadsheet formulas (and not on the basics of Excel). Intermediate spreadsheet users will also find plenty of value in this chapter.

The remainder of the chapter is a reference on Excel functions. It is not meant to be comprehensive but is intended to give you what you need when you face difficult problems in Excel and you're not sure which functions to use, let alone how to use them. When possible, I try to convey the subtleties and hidden wrinkles. Use this chapter's material on Excel functions as a reference for whenever you have questions.

Formula Basics

"Anything but the simplest of formulas are too complex to handle in a spreadsheet. I understand some of the functions used in Excel, but I am too often clueless about how to put them together."

Any person's first experience or foray into constructing spreadsheets can be daunting. You have to juggle several things simultaneously:

- You have to organize and arrange the information that goes into your spreadsheet.
- You need to specify the basic results you're going to get out of it, and how you want it presented.
- You have to construct those dreaded formulas. Arrrgh!

In case all that isn't enough, you may also need to validate the correctness of your spreadsheet and figure in some room for growth. As with anything else that's successful, a good spreadsheet tends to be used, and increasing demands and requirements will find their way to your spreadsheet.

Divide and Conquer

This is all too much to do in one step, so we'll take it a piece at a time. Even then, you can break it further into manageable slices. My goal right now is to get you to shed that spreadsheet anxiety by explaining a few good techniques that are easy to learn and to use. Later, I show you how to flex some of those spreadsheet muscles.

SIMPLE FORMULAS

The first technique you can put to use immediately so that you can start using formulas in a way that makes sense and gets results you expect. Common sense will tell you what the average of 100, 200, and 300 is. This is easy enough to type into an Excel formula.

```
=AVERAGE(100,200,300)                    returns 200
```

There are several observations worth noting. The result makes sense and the formula is intuitive. You can easily start changing the numbers 100, 200, 300 to see what the results are. What happens if you change 300 to –300? Does AVERAGE work if you try to enter four or five numbers instead of only three?

What happens if you want to change the value of one of the numbers to something like 999999999999999999999? You will see a number like 3.33333E+20. There is not enough space in the spreadsheet cell to display the complete number with all the decimal places. So, Excel automatically uses a shorthand notation to handle very large or very small numbers. That E+20 is telling us that the number 3.33333 is to be multiplied by 1 with twenty zeros after it.

When you look at the number, you know that Excel has to be storing this number with an internal accuracy that's greater than the six digits displayed. That is in fact the case. The actual number stored inside Excel is 333333333333333000000. That's a good deal more precise than the displayed six digits, but what are all those zeros at the end? It turns out that Excel's maximum precision is 15 digits. If you look carefully and count the digits, you will see 15 significant digits.

For the most part, 15 digits of precision are plenty to work with, but that limit can trip you up in a number of situations. Frequently, such situations arise when you're trying to represent credit card numbers or bar code scan data. The way around the limit is to treat the data as a sequence of letters and find ways to analyze the information.

Although it is quick and easy to embed hardwired numbers inside a spreadsheet formula, it is not a good practice in general to do so. Here's why:

1. Every time you change your test number, you'll have to manually edit it. This method will slow you down and is prone to error.

2. You'll be creating a very choppy spreadsheet because none of the numbers will be connected to one another. One of the chief benefits of spreadsheets is that changing a number in a formula in one place can instantly cascade through to other parts of the spreadsheet. Somehow, I don't think you want to forego this kind of benefit.

3. When a formula contains a hardwired number, unless you specifically know where to find all the hardwired numbers within formulas—their values—you will have difficulty updating every single instance of the hardwired value.

Item three could be the devil lurking in your formulas. If it's out of sight, it's out of mind, and it can totally compromise your spreadsheet.

TIP

In a pinch, you can use hardwired values in a formula as a quick-and-dirty approach, but as a practice, you should avoid it.

FEED TWO BIRDS WITH ONE SEED

If you shouldn't be using hardwired values inside formulas, where can you park them? You should place them in isolated spreadsheet cells so that they are easily identified and a quick visual glance will let you know what their values are.

Your formula in the previous locations could be modified to something like:

```
=AVERAGE(A6,B6,C6)
```

This formula will return the average value of whatever is in the spreadsheet cells A6, B6, and C6. And if the values of any of these spreadsheet cells change, so will the average value computed by this formula. That's an important advantage, and the benefits don't stop there. If you cut the cell A6 and decide to paste it to cell D17, all the formulas that referenced A6 will be automatically revised to reflect the change. For instance, Excel will automatically revise your formula for computing averages so that it would become:

```
=AVERAGE(D17,B6,C6)
```

The key factor to keep in mind is that if you build spreadsheets using certain effective practices, you'll be able to make changes in your spreadsheet design without fear of retribution.

You can get a little more sophisticated with your formulas. You can use user-defined names and cell ranges.

You can define a range of cells rather than just a single cell. Suppose that you have a series of values listed in the column of cells A8:A18. Your formula would be

```
=AVERAGE(A8:A18,B6,C6)
```

Excel allows you to create user-defined names for specific ranges of cells. You can, for instance, select the range of cells A8:A18 and, from the Excel menu, click Insert⇨Name⇨ Define and give your range the name GroupA. You might have a set of values in other ranges, and you may want to define names for them as well. They might be names such as GroupB and GroupC. You can then rewrite your formulas to be something like the following:

```
=AVERAGE(GroupA,GroupB,GroupC)
```

These names can be pretty much anything you need them to be so that the formulas are easy for *you* to understand.

"I need to show some simple descriptive statistics over a range of cells located in different parts of my spreadsheet."

You can get a little more mileage out of the formula you use to define cell ranges. To find out the total over your range of cells, you could do it the hard way:

```
=SUM(A8:A18)+SUM(B8:B18)+SUM(C8:C18)
```

If you have given names to each of these blocks of cells as GroupA, GroupB, and GroupC, respectively (as described previously), you could use the formula:

```
=SUM(GroupA)+SUM(GroupB)+SUM(GroupC)
```

or better yet:

```
=SUM(GroupA,GroupB,GroupC)
```

What if you want to find the largest value over the entire range of cell? You could use:

```
=MAX(GroupA,GroupB,GroupC)
```

For the minimum value, it would be:

```
=MIN(GroupA,GroupB,GroupC)
```

Excel also sports a standard deviation function called STDEV and a median function called MEDIAN. Need I tell you tell you how to construct these formulas?

```
=STDEV(GroupA,GroupB,GroupC)
=MEDIAN(GroupA,GroupB,GroupC)
```

The point I am getting at is not what's involved in the use of specific Excel functions but rather how you go about building increasingly sophisticated spreadsheets without breaking your stride.

Now it's time to reap some of the benefits of this spreadsheet construction style. If you've been keeping this book alongside your computer and have been entering this example or have opened the sample spreadsheet file from your book's CD-ROM, you will have a formula for computing averages, as well as others for computing the sum, maximum, minimum, standard deviation, and median values. What if your requirements change at some future date, or you realize that you need to account for data for additional cells over the range: A19:A22? If you specified your formulas using cell coordinates instead of cell names, you'd have to go back and manually revise each of your formulas. This is not only time consuming but also prone to error. You can instead just redefine your user name, GroupA, as A8:A22. Do this by clicking Insert⇨Name⇨Define and clicking the GroupA item in your list of user-defined names. Change the cell coordinates in the Refers To portion at the bottom of the Define Name dialog box; then, click the OK button.

Now that you've revised GroupA to mean A8:A22, is your formula for computing averages still going to be the following?

```
=AVERAGE(GroupA,GroupB,GroupC)
```

The answer is yes. This is also true for your formulas for computing maximum, minimum, standard deviation, and median! There are no formulas to rework, which is certainly a good thing. Is it time to bring out the champagne bottle and glasses? Perhaps not yet, but you're on the right track.

Relative, Absolute, and Hybrid Cell References and Replicating Formulas

One of the chief benefits of having spreadsheets is that it is easy to copy and paste a formula across the spreadsheet, at least when the formula is not giving you trouble.

"When I try to copy and paste a formula into multiple cells, the numbers come out wrong."

Consider three quantities, 100, 200, and 300, and a discount rate of, say, 15%. It should be evident that the discount amounts would be 100*15%, 200*15%, and 300*15% (or 15, 30, and 45, respectively). You know from the previous discussion to hardwire the numbers into the individual spreadsheet cells. You could place the three quantities 100, 200, and 300 in a vertical column, such as in cells A8, A9, and A10. You could place the discount percentage somewhere in column B, say, B5. It should be straightforward to just multiply the quantities in column A times the discount percentage in column B and then place the result alongside each quantity in cells B8, B9, and B10.

The first of the three formulas would be:

```
=A8*B5
```

It would be nice to copy and paste it to the two cells below it. If you do so, you will get something like Figure 2-1, which, of course, isn't what you want.

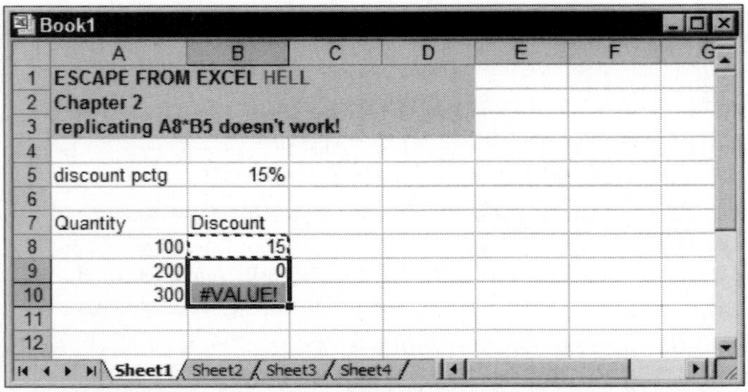

Figure 2-1: Replicated formulas are not correct!

What *would* work would be a set of formulas like this:

```
=A8*B5
=A9*B5
=A10*B5
```

Straight copying the first cell at B8 and pasting it into the two below gives you:

```
=A8*B5
=A9*B6
=A10*B7
```

You can see what's going on. You want the row number in column B to be kept constant (that is, you want all the formulas to be using B5 and not change over to B6 or B7). The way you can do this in Excel is to embed a special blocking symbol in front of the row number or column letter. The $ character is the blocking symbol. If you start with the formula:

```
=A8*B$5
```

and replicate it to the two cells below it, you will get the following (see Figure 2-2):

```
=A9*B$5
=A10*B$5
```

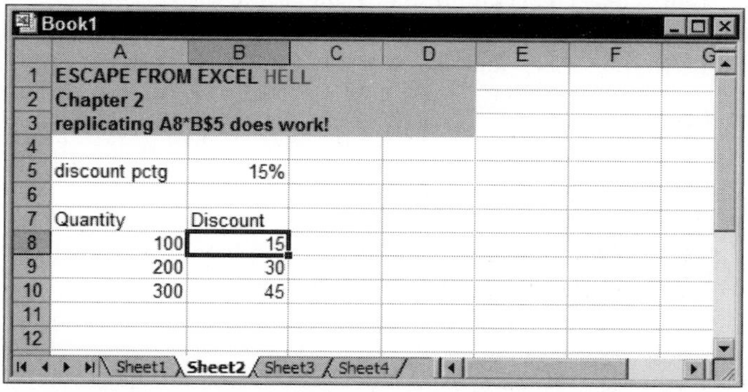

Figure 2-2: Replicating a fixed row down the column is a formula that works.

The embedded $ blocking symbol is just an annotation that tells Excel how a formula is allowed to be replicated. It doesn't affect the actual computation result. The value returned by A10*B$5 and A10*B5 is exactly the same, but the two formulas replicate differently.

Admittedly, use of the $ symbols inside a spreadsheet formula makes the formula appear clumsy, but it gets the job done. To make your life a little easier, you can add or remove the $ symbols by selecting the *appropriate portion in your formula*, that is, the portion that you want to change, and then repeatedly pressing the F4 key (Macintosh users can press ⌘T) to cycle through B5, $B$5, B$5, and $B5.

This method is fine, but you need to be aware of a few more subtleties. Suppose that you have more than one discount rate. They may be 15%, 20%, and 25%. You might just want to place the 20% and 25% figures to the immediate right (columns C and D) and populate the discount amounts in the rows below (cells C8 through D10).

Your first instinct might be to copy the column of cells B8:B10 and paste them into C8:D10. The result you get is shown in Figure 2-3.

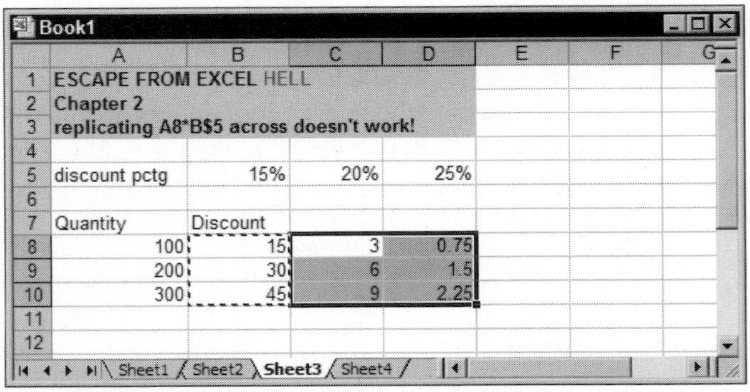

Figure 2-3: Formulas in column B do not replicate correctly to columns C and D.

As you replicate A8*B$5 across, the column for the discount percentage changes correctly while the row is held constant. This is what you want, so what is still wrong with the formula? Quick inspection of the formulas in column D will show you that they are no longer picking up the quantities in column A but instead are referencing the column to their immediate left. This is because there is no blocking dollar symbol in front of column A. Your formula should be $A8*B$5 so that by the time it is replicated to cell D8, it should be $A8*D5 (see Figure 2-4).

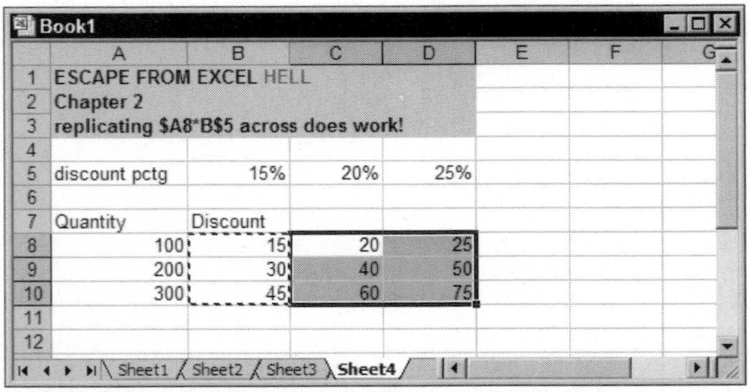

Figure 2-4: Replicating $A8*B$5 correctly holds the top row fixed and the left column fixed for all cells in your table.

The formula used back in Figure 2-2 didn't reference a fixed column A because you had no need to replicate across multiple columns, so it didn't make a difference whether or not column A was fixed.

Constructing a Lookup Style Table

The type of table you just created is a lookup table. You may recall addition and multiplication tables from your days in elementary school. These are lookup style tables.

TIP

The basic rule of thumb when building a lookup style of tables with values based on the extreme left column and top row is to block the column letters for lookup values on the left and to block row numbers for lookup values at the top of the table.

I want to give you the easy way to create a lookup style table. In the example you've been working with, select the quantities in column A (cells A8:A10) and give these cells the name Quantity (that is, select cells A8:A10; then, from the Excel menu click Insert⇨ Name⇨Define, type the name **Quantity**, and press OK). Do the same for the percentages appearing in cells B5:D5, but give that selection of cells the name DiscountPctg.

Now type the following formula in cell B8:

```
=Quantity*DiscountPctg
```

Replicate this cell for all the cells in B8:D10.

All the formulas are easily set up and even easier to read. If it's this easy, why go through all the heartache with the $ symbols? There are several answers to that question:

- Over the course of time, you will come across spreadsheets created by other people who will be using formulas with all the $ symbols embedded in them. You'll have to read and understand those formulas and, on occasion, fix them. Unless you have the ability to pull apart a formula, you will feel lost or dependent upon others. Somehow, I don't think you want that to happen.

- It may not always be possible to use defined names in such a simple manner.

- Sometimes you may want to experiment with formulas. Creating and juggling a bunch of names serves only to slow you down, not to mention all the clutter that comes along with user-defined names.

- User-defined names are basically fixed cell references. The example discussed previously contains three values for quantities and three values for the discount percentage. This may be good for your lookup table today, but a month from now you may want to consider six or 16 quantities instead of just three. To make your formula work, you will have to redefine the cell range for quantity. Doing so creates extra work. It may just be easier to create user-defined names and incorporate them into your formulas at the last stages.

Using Capitalization to Locate Errors

"The error message #NAME? in my formula is cryptic. Why am I getting this message?"

You may have noticed that Excel always displays its standard cell coordinates and that Excel functions such as SUM and AVERAGE appear in all-UPPERCASE form. This is true even if you enter the functions or cell coordinates in lowercase form.

There are reasons that this fact is good for you. To see why, go ahead and try entering the formula in lowercase form:

```
=random()+average(2,3)
```

Notice that you get a #NAME? message when you type this formula. It has nothing to do with typing your formula in lowercase form. The reason is simply that there is no RANDOM function in Excel. It doesn't exist. Excel doesn't know what to do with this, so it throws back a cryptic #NAME? message. The message will not help you figure out what is wrong with your formula. If you view the formula you just entered in the Excel Formula Bar, you will see that it altered your formula by converting every standard Excel function into UPPERCASE form. Your formula appears as:

```
=random()+AVERAGE(2,3)
```

This format serves as a dead give-away that the offending function is RANDOM and not AVERAGE. Incidentally, the Excel function for generating uniform random numbers between 0 and 1 is RAND. The corrected formula is as follows:

```
=RAND()+AVERAGE(2,3)
```

The technique of typing formulas in lowercase form and allowing Excel to convert it will help you to spot errors in your formulas when they do occur. It also makes for easier typing.

The same is true concerning user-defined names. It is a good rule to create user-defined names using a MixedCase representation, such as Quantity or DiscountPctg. Excel converts the user-defined names in your formulas to the MixedCase form. This format makes it easy for you to distinguish between Excel functions and your names and simultaneously spot errors if they involve your defined names.

Introduction to Excel Functions

The rest of this chapter is largely for quick reference concerning Excel functions such as AVERAGE. In contrast to the rest of the book, the coverage here doesn't necessarily focus on the typical Excel Hell types of problems. When you're constructing your formulas, you can easily get tripped up by some subtleties. This section introduces a variety of Excel functions, outlines their syntax, and illustrates how they can be used. Of course, I will try to point out some things to watch out for. I am hoping that this section will serve you well both as a quick reference guide and to help you quickly and easily construct Excel formulas.

You can find all the examples for these functions on the book's CD-ROM. You should be able to copy and paste these examples directly into your spreadsheets. Additionally, many of the examples use hardwired values instead of cell references or user-defined names as inputs. For instance, you might see something like

```
=MAX(2,3,SQRT(5))
```

instead of

```
=MAX(B1,B2,B3)
```

There are two reasons for a formula to appear this way:

1. The compact representation is easier to read and grasp.
2. It matches the examples on your CD-ROM. Having the formulas self-contained will make it easier for you to copy and paste them directly into your spreadsheets.

Although this book shuns the practice of using hardwired values in formulas and Excel functions, it is used here to facilitate a clearer explanation.

What follows is a list of Excel functions relating to text manipulation, statistical- and aggregation-related functions, selectors, math, Boolean and conditional functions, cell referencing functions, date/time related functions, and some miscellaneous functions.

The list is not comprehensive, but achieving basic competence with these functions will give you much mileage in working with spreadsheets. I hope this will help to smooth (or should I say "soothe") the rougher edges in your work with spreadsheets.

Word and Text Manipulation

Though Excel is a powerful number cruncher, it also can be used to manipulate words and text. In this section, I outline some of the text manipulation functions, as well as their usage and subtleties. The Excel functions covered in this section include:

& (the joining operator)	SUBSTITUTE
CONCATENATE	LOWER
EXACT	UPPER
FIND	PROPER
SEARCH	LEN
LEFT	TRIM
MID	CODE
RIGHT	CHAR
REPLACE	CLEAN
REPT	TEXT

Each of the following sections begins with the syntax usage for the function. Notice that some Excel functions support optional arguments. This is signified by the bracketed expression in the argument list. For instance, the FIND function has a syntax listed as:

```
FIND(find_text,within_text[,start_num])
```

The optional argument is `start_num`. As an example, the following two formulas are identical:

```
=FIND("e","spreadsheet")
=FIND("e","spreadsheet",1)
```

They both start searching from the beginning of the `within_text` expression.

THE & JOINING OPERATOR AND CONCATENATE

```
CONCATENATE(text1,text2,...)
```

The `&` operator and the CONCATENATE function join strings of text together. Here are some simple examples that should make its usage clear.

```
="Tax"&"Rate"                          returns 'TaxRate'
=CONCATENATE("Tax","Rate")             returns 'TaxRate'
```

The CONCATENATE function can accept optional "arguments" as its input. You can construct something like

```
=CONCATENATE("John"," A. ","Doe")
=CONCATENATE(FirstName,MidInit,SurName)
=CONCATENATE(A6,B6,C6)
=CONCATENATE("John",MidInit,C6)
```

Notice that the first formula uses hardwired values. The second uses user-defined names, the third uses cell references, and the last uses a combination of all three types.

Both the CONCATENATE and joining operator (`&`) are useful in constructing expressions. A realistic example is something like this:

```
="The amount you owe is $"&VLOOKUP(CustomerID,aDataTable,2)
```

In this case, a lookup is performed on a data table based on the customer ID. The value found in the second column of that table is then appended to the string.

STRING EQUALITY AND CASE SENSITIVITY

```
EXACT(text1,text2)
FIND(find_text,within_text[,start_num])
SEARCH(find_text,within_text[,start_num])
```

Every now and then, you will need to look at different string expressions and see whether they are equal. Look at the following:

```
John A. Doe
john a. doe
John A  doe
```

Are the three expressions equal? The answer is, it depends. If you want to get strict about case sensitivity, you can say that they are not equal. Let me ask you this, though. Do you think they refer to the same person? Now what is your answer?

Okay, let's not worry about case sensitivity. Are they equal? The first two are, but there is a missing period next to the middle initial in the last line, and that expression has an extra space after the middle initial. Therefore, it doesn't match the first two.

In contrast to what is typical for a relational database, a spreadsheet can be accommodating and allow for variations on the data entered or imported. On one hand, this makes for great freedom in gathering and assembling data. On the other, it makes for an Excel Hell nightmare when you try to consolidate duplicate or almost duplicate data. Excel is not the culprit; the data is. You would do well to arm yourself with a few good functions.

Outlined in Table 2-1 is a comparison of Excel functions used with text.

TABLE 2-1   CASE SENSITIVITY COMPARISON OF VARIOUS EXCEL FUNCTIONS

Excel Formula or Operation	Value Displayed	Comments
=EXACT("John A Doe","john a doe")	FALSE	EXACT function is case sensitive.
="John A Doe"="john a doe"	TRUE	The equality operator is not case sensitive. Also note that = appearing inside a formula is not the same as the = that starts off the formula.
=VLOOKUP("jOhN a DoE",SomeDataset,2) =VLOOKUP("john a doe",SomeDataset,2)	Returns the same results with either formula.	VLOOKUP is not case sensitive.
Using the Excel sorting feature		Sorting is not case sensitive unless it is enabled from the Options button from the Sort dialog box.

continued

TABLE 2-1   CASE SENSITIVITY COMPARISON OF VARIOUS EXCEL FUNCTIONS (continued)

Excel Formula or Operation	Value Displayed	Comments
=SUBSTITUTE("aBbB","B","x")	axbx	SUBSTITUTE is case sensitive.
=FIND("b","BBBbbb")	4	FIND is case sensitive. Note that finding an empty string does not return an error.
=FIND("B","BBBbbb")	1	
=FIND("","BBBbbb")	1	
=SEARCH("b","BBBbbb")	1	SEARCH is not case sensitive.

LEFT, MID, AND RIGHT

```
LEFT(text,num_chars)
MID(text,start_num,num_chars)
RIGHT(text,num_chars)
```

These examples illustrate the syntax usage and show you the computed results.

No doubt you can guess what LEFT, MID, and RIGHT do. Representative examples include:

```
=LEFT("Escape from Excel Hell",6)       returns 'Escape'
=MID("Escape from Excel Hell",8,4)      returns 'from'
=RIGHT("Escape from Excel Hell",10)     returns 'Excel Hell'
```

REPT, REPLACE, AND SUBSTITUTE

```
REPT(text,number_times)
REPLACE(old_text,start_num,num_chars,new_text)
SUBSTITUTE(text,old_text,new_text[,instance_num])
```

These three functions are used for placing specific string sequences within a string of characters. Here are some representative examples of these functions:

```
=REPT("*",3)&"Header"&REPT("*",3)        returns '***Header***'
=REPLACE("Now is the time.",5,2,"was")   returns 'Now was the time.'
```

The SUBSTITUTE function is case sensitive. If the optional argument of the occurrence number is provided, it will substitute only that for that occurrence.

The syntax for SUBSTITUTE is

```
=SUBSTITUTE (text,old_text,new_text[,instance_num])
```

Here are a couple of examples:

```
=SUBSTITUTE("AbAbcA","A","x")          returns 'xbxbcx'
=SUBSTITUTE("AbAbcA","A","x",2)        returns 'AbxbcA'
```

LOWER, UPPER, AND PROPER

```
LOWER(text)
UPPER(text)
PROPER(text)
```

You use these functions to adjust the capitalization of characters in a string. Here are some representative examples of these functions:

```
=LOWER("A Tale of two Cities")        returns 'a tale of two cities'
=PROPER("A Tale of two Cities")       returns 'A Tale Of Two Cities'
=UPPER("A Tale of two Cities")        returns 'A TALE OF TWO CITIES'
```

Notice that PROPER forces the phrase into uppercase for the first letter of *every* word and into lowercase for all others. This may not be your intended effect. Do you necessarily want the first letter in *of* to be capitalized?

LEN AND TRIM

```
LEN(text)
TRIM(text)
```

These unassuming functions are among the most practical Excel functions for working with text.

LEN allows you to determine the length of a string of characters. TRIM allows you to remove excess character spaces between words as well as remove the leading and trailing spaces for the phrase. Here are some representative examples of these functions:

```
=LEN("Now is the time.")             returns 16
=TRIM("   Too    many    spaces   ") returns 'Too many spaces'
```

The function LEN is very useful. It can help you determine whether a particular spreadsheet cell is empty. You might, for instance, want to count how many rows of empty space there are between two entries. A sample of this is provided on the book's CD-ROM.

CHAR, CODE, AND CLEAN

CHAR(number)
CLEAN(text)
CODE(text)

If you receive data from third-party sources and bring it into Excel, you may have seen some "gremlins" interspersed in the data. Typically, they appear as hollow little boxes sandwiched between words of text. Nowadays, databases and programs that export data that's ultimately used inside a spreadsheet can prevent these gremlins from appearing. When you do come across them, it is often easy to manually edit them out of a spreadsheet cell. If this happens once in a blue moon, that's fine. But what if you have to constantly import new data from the same source and they always have these nonprinting characters? What if there is just too much data for you to go through and spot where they occur? A special function, CLEAN, was created to get around this problem (see Figure 2-5).

	A	B	C	D	E	F
	ch02-02Examples.xls					
1	ESCAPE FROM EXCEL HELL					
2	Chapter 2					
3	text manipulation examples					
4						
5	Result	Function/Task				
65	hollow box --> 〖 <-- hollow box	="hollow box --> "&CHAR(26)&" <-- hollow box"				
66	hollow box --> <-- hollow box	=CLEAN(A65)				
67						

Sheet1 / CompleteAsciiTable / AdditionalData / Sheet3 /

Figure 2-5: Gremlins and how to zap 'em.

I should point out that sometimes you may want to insert these nonprinting characters into your text. You might, for instance, be generating an outline in Excel that gets copied into Word or some other application. Excel can generate multiple tabs for the appropriate level of indenting.

What's in a character?

The Excel function CHAR returns the ASCII character that corresponds to a specific number code. These codes were developed so that computers and telecommunication devices could transfer information digitally. There are 26 letters in the English alphabet. If you wanted to transmit information between devices using letters, you'd have to come up with 26 distinct signals. What about if you want to distinguish between upper- and lowercase letters? You would have to double the number of potentially distinct signals. Okay, what about punctuations and other symbols such as $, %, @, or #? You can see that your alphabet soup is growing. At this point you haven't even put the digits 0, 1, 2, 3, 4, 5, 6, 7, 8, and 9 into the mix (not to mention +, –, *, /). Rather than worry about the bewildering and growing spectrum of symbols, it is far easier to store, send, and receive numerical codes.

Excel has functions that map an ordered structure of characters to a number sequence and will produce the character symbol that corresponds to the known number code. Here are some sample computations:

```
=CHAR(65)                              returns 'A'
=CHAR(66)                              returns 'B'
=CHAR(67)                              returns 'C'
=CHAR(97)                              returns 'a'
=CHAR(98)                              returns 'b'
=CHAR(99)                              returns 'c'
=CHAR(32)                              returns ' '
=CODE("a")                             returns 97
=CODE("A")                             returns 65
=CODE(" ")                             returns 32
```

In the `ch02_02Examples.xls` file, you will find a complete table showing all the CODE values and their CHAR symbols. In terms of special symbols, the ones you'll likely need to know about the most are spaces, tabs, carriage returns, and linefeeds.

A character space that normally separates words can be generated using CHAR(32). To generate a tab character, you use CHAR(9). A carriage return can be generated using CHAR(13), a linefeed by using CHAR(10). Generating tabs, carriage returns, and linefeeds may not be all that beneficial inside the spreadsheet. However, when a spreadsheet file is saved as text or its contents are exported, the appearance of this character encoding could be relevant to other programs.

You should be aware of some cross-platform issues. If you are using your spreadsheet to generate text for use in other programs, you will find that lines are separated differently depending on whether the system you are exporting to is Windows based, Macintosh, or Unix/Linux. On a Windows platform, lines end with a carriage return followed by a linefeed. On the Mac it is just a carriage return, and on Unix/Linux it is just a linefeed.

TIP

Excel will often autoformat your cell as you enter text. For instance, you can enter something such as

first
time

into a single spreadsheet cell and have the text take up two lines inside the cell. Simply type **first**, press Alt+Enter, and then type **time**. Pressing the Alt+Enter keys accomplishes two things simultaneously. It alters the appearance of the cell so that a second line of text appears immediately below where you were just typing. Excel also inserts an invisible linefeed character (actually, a CHAR(10) symbol) into the text.

TEXT

TEXT(value, format_text)

The function TEXT takes a value and converts it into hard-coded text according to the type of format you specify. For instance, it may be important to represent five-digit ZIP Codes with their leading zeros. If you type a number for a ZIP Code just as 08872, Excel converts this to the number 8872. This may not be what you want.

There are several ways to fix this problem. One is to insert an apostrophe symbol (a single quotation mark) in front of the leading zero. This action accomplishes two things. The apostrophe blocks Excel's evaluation engine, so Excel won't treat it as a number and try to strip out the leading zero. Additionally, Excel treats it as text. As you may recall, numbers in spreadsheets are generally aligned right (that is, they are always aligned with the right side of the spreadsheet cell). Text, as with a name or address, is generally aligned left. If you have a list of ZIP Codes in the spreadsheet with only a few of the ZIP Codes having a leading zero, and you use the apostrophe to preserve the leading zeros, then these manually edited ZIP Codes will appear out of alignment. You can always format the whole column of ZIP Codes to be either right aligned, left aligned, or centered, to make that problem go away. You may have others to contend with. When you try to sort your column, Excel will pick up on the fact that some of the cells are numbers and others are text. It will ask you whether you want it want to treat anything that looks like a number as a number. In the simplest of scenarios, saying yes will work fine. Real life has a tendency to get more complicated. So, there may be reasons to avoid the single apostrophe.

Here's another approach you can take; this one involves the Excel function TEXT. You can enter a formula like this:

```
=TEXT(8872,"00000")
```

This formula converts the number to a text format, much the same way you would by using an apostrophe. So why might you want to use the TEXT function when you have the simpler mechanism of the apostrophe? You may want to use a *compound formula*. The ZIP Code might be a value that is retrieved from some list. You might have a formula like this:

```
=TEXT(VLOOKUP(SomeCustomerID,CustList,2),"00000")
```

where the customer ID is in the first column of CustList and the ZIP Code is in the second column. Also, nothing says that you have to be glued to using only five-digit numbers.

The TEXT function is very flexible. Its use recurs throughout this book; you can find a good deal of it in Chapter 5, "Getting Correct Results with Excel Formulas."

NOTE

Note that another way is available to treat the ZIP Code with leading zeros. You leave it as a number but tell Excel to format this cell so that it always displays five digits, including the leading zeros. This approach works great. When you print your spreadsheets or view them on-screen, you will see the leading zeros. If you have a list of five-digit ZIP Codes and need to sort them, they will sort nicely in ascending (or, if you specify, descending) order. If you save your file as a tab-delimited text or a .csv file (comma-separated variables), then Excel will save them with the leading zero.

The scenario gets more complex when you're combining five- and nine-digit ZIP Codes. More is said about ZIP Codes and sorting in Chapter 8, "Involved Data Analysis."

Aggregation and Statistical Functions

Excel has many functions that summarize data contained over a range of cells. Representative functions of this kind include:

MAX	RANDBETWEEN
MIN	SUBTOTAL
AVERAGE	SUM
MEDIAN	SUMPRODUCT
COUNT	SUMIF
COUNTA	STDEV
COUNTIF	VAR
RAND	

MAX, MIN, AVERAGE, MEDIAN

```
MAX(number1,number2,...)
MIN(number1,number2,...)
AVERAGE(number1,number2,...)
MEDIAN(number1,number2,...)
```

MAX returns the *greatest* value found in the list of numbers or ranges of cells. MIN returns the *lowest* value found in the list of numbers or ranges of cells.

NOTE

Negative values are *always lower* than any positive value, however small. Positive values are always *greater* than any negative value.

Here are some sample calculations:

```
=MAX(1,2,3)                    returns 3
=MAX(1,2,SQRT(100))            returns 10
=MIN(-500,0.0001,6400,0)       returns -500
=MIN(500,-0.0001,6400,0)       returns -0.0001
```

AVERAGE returns the statistical mean or average value over a set of numbers or range of cells (see Figure 2-6).

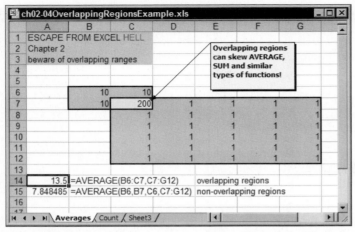

Figure 2-6: Be sure to take into account overlapping ranges when working with functions such as AVERAGE.

NOTE

Be aware that overlapping ranges of cells can skew the AVERAGE returned.

Sample calculation:

```
=AVERAGE(100, 900)                         returns 500
```

In the file ch02_03FStatisticalExamples.xls on the book's CD-ROM, I show how to compute average values, standard deviations, and variances when frequency counts are involved. I leave you to explore this file on your own.

MEDIAN is an interesting kind of function and is fairly easy to visualize. Think about taking all your sample data and arranging all the data points in order from lowest to highest. Now simultaneously pluck out the very highest and very lowest data point. Continue repeating this removal of the highest and lowest data point till only one member or data point is standing. The value of that data point is the median of your dataset.

Note that the order in which you feed the data into the Excel MEDIAN function doesn't change the outcome. MEDIAN(1,2,3) = MEDIAN(2,3,1).

Sample calculations:

```
=MEDIAN(1,2,3,4,5)                         returns 3
=MEDIAN(1,4,5,2,3)                         returns 3
=MEDIAN(1,2,500,501,502)                   returns 500
=MEDIAN(1,2,10,10)                         returns 6
```

COUNT, COUNTA, COUNTIF

```
COUNT(value1,value2,...)
COUNTA(value1,value2,...)
COUNTIF(range,criteria)
```

COUNT tallies the number of numerical entries for the listed cells or cell ranges. The file `ch02_04OverlappingRegionsExample.xls` on the book's CD-ROM has multiple entries, one of which is an example using COUNT (see Figure 2-7).

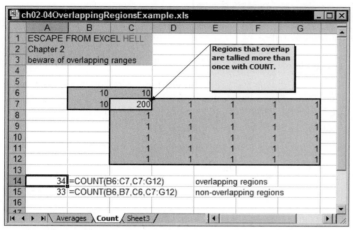

Figure 2-7: Overlapping regions are tallied more than once when using COUNT.

Sample calculations:

```
=COUNT(B6:C7,C7:G12)                  returns 34
=COUNT(B6,B7,C6,C7:G12)               returns 33
```

COUNT tallies numeric entries only.

COUNTA is similar to COUNT except that it tallies any "nonblank" cells. It doesn't have to be numeric only. Any cell with text, a number, or a formula will contribute to the tally. Open a new spreadsheet and enter the following in the cells A1, A2, and A3:

```
1                                      (cell A1)
=IF(A1>345,"A1 is bigger than 345","") (cell A2)
A3 has text in it                      (cell A3)
```

Leave the cell A4 blank. You will find the following:

```
=COUNTA(A1:A4)                         returns 3
=COUNT(A1:A4)                          returns 1
```

It may be worth your while to reflect upon the issue of counting ZIP Code entries. Which function will you use to perform the count when some of the ZIP Codes have apostrophes in front of them to preserve the leading zeros? I'll leave you to ponder this one for yourself.

COUNTIF takes a region of cells and tells you how many of the cells match a specific criterion. If you look back at either Figure 2-6 or 2-7, you will see three cells with a value of 10 and one cell with a value of 200. You can use COUNTIF to find out how many of a range of cells match a particular criterion:

```
=COUNTIF(B6:C7,"<=200")                    returns 4
=COUNTIF(B6:C7,"<200")                     returns 3
```

A more realistic use of COUNTIF might be something like this:

```
=COUNTIF(YourDataset,">="&OverTheCreditLimit)
```

Here you're asking Excel to tell you how many cells have a value that matches or exceeds OverTheCreditLimit. Both the COUNTIF function and its cousin SUMIF are worth getting to know. They will solve a variety of Excel Hell–type problems.

RAND AND RANDBETWEEN

```
RAND()
RANDBETWEEN(bottom,top)
```

Chances are, if you're doing anything that's probability and statistics related, sooner or later you will come across the functions RAND or RANDBETWEEN. You might as well learn a couple of things about them now.

RAND is a *pseudo* random number generator. Every time your spreadsheet is recalculated, RAND will return a number that is between 0 and 1. What value will it return? Well, that's just about anybody's guess. That's the idea. It is not supposed to be predictable. This makes it great for generating small random samples.

On average, you would find that 20 percent of the time, RAND will produce a value between 0.8 and 1. Fifty percent of the time, it would produce a value between 0.5 and 1. Also 50 percent of the time, it would produce a value within the range of 0.25 to 0.75. This should lead you to the idea that the probability distribution associated with RAND is *uniform*. Again, that's the idea behind RAND.

One word of caution about the use of RAND: Although it *simulates* a uniform distribution pretty well, it is not suitable for commercial cryptographic applications. If you need to generate a million or so numbers, you will get gaps and bunching up in the distribution. However, if you generate hundreds or several thousand numbers, the effect will be virtually undetectable. I plan to post some statistics about the accuracy of RAND for large samples on my Web site, www.EscapeFromExcelHell.com.

Part I

If I ask you to "pick a number between 1 and 100" and you give me an arbitrary number, you are doing exactly what the function RANDBETWEEN does. In Excel, such a formula is written as

```
=RANDBETWEEN(1,100)
```

 NOTE
RANDBETWEEN requires the Excel Analysis ToolPak Add-In to be loaded. The Analysis ToolPak is a standard part of the Excel install but is not automatically loaded. To make sure that you have it installed and loaded, go to Excel menu and click Tools⇨Add-Ins. You should see a list of Add-Ins. If the Analysis ToolPak has no checkmark next to it, check it now. Also do the same for Analysis ToolPak - VBA. Click OK. If for some reason you don't see these in the list of add-ins, follow the general instructions for loading add-ins in Appendix B, "Installing the Escape Excel Hell Utility Pak."

"I have a problem distributing my spreadsheets that use RANDBETWEEN. I have the Analysis ToolPak installed and running on my computer, but not everybody else does. I can't tell the whole world to load it. What should I do?"

Do not fret. Here are some substitute formulas that will work the same way as RANDBE-TWEEN does:

```
=ROUND(RAND()*(Top-Bottom),0)+Bottom
=ROUND(RAND()*(100-1),0)+1
=ROUND(RAND()*(C3-B3),0)+B3
```

The first formula uses user-defined names such as Top and Bottom. These might have values such as 100 and 1, respectively. You can actually put the numbers inside your formula, as is shown in the second of the three examples. The third example uses cell coordinates.

SUBTOTAL

```
SUBTOTAL(function_num,ref1,...)
```

The SUBTOTAL function could aptly be called the "Swiss Army Knife of Excel functions." In a single formula, you can choose to take a set of data and get its AVERAGE, COUNT, COUNTA, MAX, MIN, PRODUCT, STDEV, STDEVP, SUM, VAR, or VARP computations.

Here is how SUBTOTAL works. Say that you have the numbers 10, 10, 10, and 100 appearing in cells B6:C7 (as was displayed in Figures 2-6 and 2-7). To get the AVERAGE value, you enter

```
=SUBTOTAL(1,B6:C7)                    returns 57.5
```

To get the COUNT, you enter

```
=SUBTOTAL(2,B6:C7)                          returns 4
```

For COUNTA, you would replace the function_num with 3. For MAX, you would use 4 for the function_num. There's a little wrinkle here, however.

"When I use the SUBTOTAL function, I get a different result, depending on whether I open the spreadsheet in Excel 2003 or an earlier version."

When Microsoft introduced Excel 2003, it added new functionality to SUBTOTAL and, in the process, introduced some problems for Excel users.

The pre-2003 versions of Excel would use a function_num ranging from 1 through 11, and SUBTOTAL would work only on "visible" cells. Excel allows you to collapse rows or columns to make cells hidden. In Excel 2003, Microsoft changed the behavior of SUBTOTAL to include both visible and hidden cells in computation results. Microsoft also decided to restore the visible-only mode by giving you an additional range of numbers for function_num, 101 – 111. So, SUBTOTAL(101,B6:C7) in Excel 2003 works the same as SUBTOTAL(1,B6:C7) in pre-2003 versions of Excel.

It is perfectly understandable and desirable to add in new functionality. It seems that Microsoft's reassignment of the function_num parameter has created an artificial problem if your cell ranges in SUBTOTAL has hidden cells.

I can give you a quick workaround for this:

```
=IF(LEFT(INFO("release"),2)="11",SUBTOTAL(Val+100,Range),SUBSTOTAL(Val,Range))
```

Val can be a number between 1 and 11 depending on whether you want AVERAGE, COUNT, or any of the other functions supported by SUBTOTAL. The Range can be any range of cells you want (for example, B6:C7).

INFO("release") tells you the version of Excel that is running the spreadsheet. In Excel 2003, the value returned is the string "11.0"; in Excel 2004 for the Macintosh, it is "11.1". As new releases of Excel are introduced, you may need to work out new variations on the workaround formula.

SUM

```
SUM(number1,number2,...)
```

Almost anybody who uses Excel is already familiar with SUM. There are several things you may want to know. If SUM sees text that resembles a number; it will convert it to a number. SUM will convert TRUE to the number 1, and will convert FALSE to the number 0. When SUM sees a date appearing as text, it will convert it to its serial number representation.

```
=SUM(1,2,3,4)                               returns 10
=SUM(1,2,"3","4")                           returns 10
=SUM(1.25,TRUE)                             returns 2.25
```

```
=SUM(1.25,4=2*2)                                        returns 2.25
=SUM("4/10/2006")                                       returns 38817
```

SUM accepts a range of cells for its "arguments." You can have formulas like these:

```
=SUM(B1:B12)
=SUM($B$1:D14)
=SUM(DailySalesForTheMonthOfJuly)
=SUM(DailySalesForTheMonthOfJuly,DailySalesForTheMonthOfAugust)
```

SUM, as is true of essentially all Excel functions, evaluates its arguments before passing them to the function. Translated into plain English: If you have an expression like this:

```
=SUM(1,2,100+200+300)
```

Excel will first calculate the 100+200+300 and turn it into 600 and then compute SUM(1,2,600).

You can use this fact to your advantage. You may have noticed that each of the arguments in a function is separated by commas. When an Excel function accepts a list of arguments as it does with SUM, it caps the maximum number of arguments to 30. You'll have no problem entering something like:

```
=SUM(1,2,3,4,5,6,7,8,9,0,1,2,3,4,5,6,7,8,9,0,1,2,3,4,5,6,7,8,9,0)
```

which will return the value 135. If you try to slip in one more argument:

```
=SUM(1,2,3,4,5,6,7,8,9,0,1,2,3,4,5,6,7,8,9,0,1,2,3,4,5,6,7,8,9,0,1)
```

Excel will complain. To get around this problem, you can split your arguments and have SUM evaluate each of them separately. Here are some examples of doing so:

```
=SUM(1,2,3,4,5,6,7,8,9,0)+SUM(1,2,3,4,5,6,7,8,9,0)+SUM(1,2,3,4,5,6,7,8,9,0)+1
=SUM(SUM(1,2,3,4,5,6,7,8,9,0),SUM(1,2,3,4,5,6,7,8,9,0),SUM(1,2,3,4,5,6,7,8,9,0),1)
=SUM(D1:D31)       where the data resides in D1:D31
```

TIP

SUM has the capability to add up values across multiple worksheets. Here are a couple of examples:

```
=SUM(Sheet2:Sheet3!D4)
=SUM(Sheet1:Sheet3!D4:G24)
```

In the first example, the value of D4 in each of Sheet2 and Sheet3 are being summed. In the second example, the values appearing in D4:G24 for each of Sheet1, Sheet2, and Sheet3 are summed. You might find this technique useful for situations in which you have the same kind of data recurring every week or every month, as may be the case with a timesheet.

TIP

SUM has the capability to add ranges that intersect. There is a special reference operator called the Intersection Operator, which is represented as a space character between ranges. An example of the sum of the overlapping cells can be found in the Intersection worksheet tab of ch02_04OverlappingRegionsExample.xls.

```
=SUM(B6:C7 C7:G12)                    returns 200
```

In and of itself, this feature is not so noteworthy, but when it's combined with functions such as OFFSET and INDIRECT, it becomes interesting. I will post some examples on my Web site at www.EscapeFromExcelHell.com.

SUMPRODUCT

```
SUMPRODUCT(array1,array2,array3,...)
```

Many a spreadsheet involves taking the numbers in one column, multiplying them by numbers in another, and summing up all the individual multiplications. This is exactly what SUMPRODUCT does. With SUMPRODUCT, you won't need extra columns or rows for tabulating intermediate calculations.

If you have two lists, ItemsOnHand (located in cells C10:C35) and AssetValue (located in cells D10:D35), then you can use either of the following two formulas to determine the total value of the merchandise:

```
=SUMPRODUCT(A10:A35,B10:B35)
=SUMPRODUCT(ItemsOnHand,WholesaleValue)
```

For the second formula to work, the user-defined names ItemsOnHand and WholesaleValue must have the same number of rows and columns.

SUMPRODUCT is allowed to have more than just two arguments. You might have a MarkUpRatio located in C10:C35. To get your retail value, you can use formulas like:

```
=SUMPRODUCT(A10:A35,B10:B35,C10:C35)
=SUMPRODUCT(ItemsOnHand,WholesaleValue,MarkUpRatio)
```

By the way, there is nothing in SUMPRODUCT that says you can use it only with columns of data. Had the ItemsOnHand, WholesaleValue, and MarkUpValue data been transposed so that they start from A10 and A11, respectively, and move over to the right, your formula would be

```
=SUMPRODUCT(A10:Z10,A11:Z11,A12:Z12)
```

There is one thing you should note: SUMPRODUCT will not tolerate data whose rows and columns do not line up. For instance, you cannot quadruple your product by doing something like:

Related functions and array formulas

There are some related functions you may want to know about:

- SUMSQ returns the sum of the squares of items in an array.

- PRODUCT multiplies every item in an array of cell values.

- MMULT performs a matrix multiplication.

I'll leave you to look these up on your own.

One more word about calculations involving arrays: You may come across formulas that have curly braces in them, such as:

```
{=SQRT(SUMSQ(Unit_Costs_Uncertainties*Units_Shipped))}
```

These are known as array formulas and are often found with formulas involving matrix multiplication, or the sum of the squares of products (such as the preceding formula).

They have some curious (and annoying) properties. The formula displayed in the Excel Formula Bar shows the curly braces, but when you click inside the Formula Bar to edit them, the braces disappear. Additionally, if you just press Enter, the curly braces disappear altogether and you may get an error such as #VALUE!. The reason you may get an error of this kind is that Excel needs to be explicitly told that the formula is an array formula. You tell Excel this by editing the formula and, *while in the edit mode*, pressing Ctrl+Shift+Enter rather than just Enter. For the Macintosh platform, use ⌘+Shift+Enter.

```
=SUMPRODUCT(4,A10:Z10,A11:Z11,A12:Z12)
```

But it is perfectly fine to bring the single number outside SUMPRODUCT, like so:

```
=4*SUMPRODUCT(A10:Z10,A11:Z11,A12:Z12)
```

SUMIF

```
SUMIF(range,criteria,[sum_range])
```

Conditional sums, if used properly, can be very elegant and powerful. Figure 2-8 shows a schedule of items detailing their quantity, price, and amount. There will be some price threshold that caps your purchase. In the example, it is set to $11.50. If you purchase all items costing $11.50 or less, then there will be only 13 items and the total purchase amount will be $60.52. The function SUMIF sets some range you are going to look at (namely, Price), a criteria including in the sum (less than or equal to Threshold), and what to return (depending on which of the two formulas you are looking at, it could be Quantity or Amount).

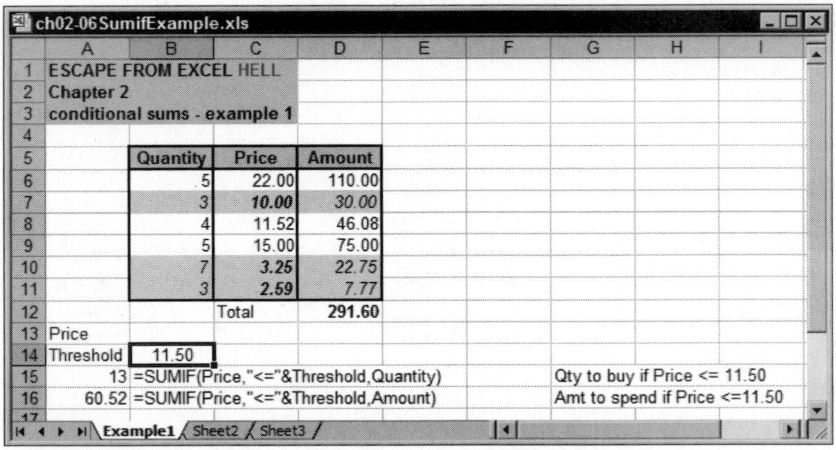

ch02-06SumifExample.xls

	A	B	C	D	E	F	G	H	I
1	ESCAPE FROM EXCEL HELL								
2	Chapter 2								
3	conditional sums - example 1								
4									
5		Quantity	Price	Amount					
6		5	22.00	110.00					
7		3	***10.00***	*30.00*					
8		4	11.52	46.08					
9		5	15.00	75.00					
10		7	***3.25***	*22.75*					
11		3	***2.59***	*7.77*					
12			Total	**291.60**					
13	Price								
14	Threshold	11.50							
15	13	=SUMIF(Price,"<="&Threshold,Quantity)					Qty to buy if Price <= 11.50		
16	60.52	=SUMIF(Price,"<="&Threshold,Amount)					Amt to spend if Price <=11.50		

Example1 / Sheet2 / Sheet3

Figure 2-8: Conditional sum based on a price threshold

Note one other point: All lines in which Price is less than or equal to `Threshold` are colorized, and `Price` is in ***bold italics***. This spreadsheet (`ch02_06SumifExample.xls`, which can be found on the book's CD-ROM) makes use of conditional formatting. The topic of conditional formatting is discussed at length in Chapter 5.

STDEV

```
STDEV(number1,number2,...)
```

The standard deviation (computed using the STDEV function) is a measure of the extent of difference between the mean (computed using the AVERAGE function) value and each of the individual data points. The more coherently aligned the data points are to your mean value, the lower the standard deviation will be. If you have many data points, then typically about two-thirds of them will be within one standard deviation from the mean value, and close to 95 percent will be within two standard deviations from the mean value.

I discuss more about probability distributions in later chapters, particularly in Chapter 9.

VAR

```
VAR(number1,number2,...)
```

Variance and standard deviation are both collective measures of how far each of the data points in a sample is from its average value. Loosely speaking, these two quantities are flip sides of the same coin. Rather than bore you with the mathematical details, I'll let it suffice to give you some sample calculations and some observations.

If you have a set of data starting in `B2` and going down through `B6`, with the values `12`, `9`, `13`, `14`, and `11`, you can compute the variance of the sample using this formula:

```
=VAR(B2:B6)                          returns 3.7
```

Interestingly, you can embed an array inside a formula without having to press Ctrl+Shift+Enter. Quite literally, you can enter the curly braces into the formula as follows:

`=VAR({12,9,13,14,11})`   returns 3.7

TIP

There's a little known trick for lifting values from a single of cells in a spreadsheet and placing them, separated by commas, directly into the Formula Bar. Using the current example of calculating variances, here's what you do. While entering:

`=VAR(B2:B6)`

select the text `B2:B6` directly inside the Formula Bar and press the F9 key. Your formula will instantly turn in to:

`=VAR({12,9,13,14,11})`   returns 3.7

The curly braces are automatically included.

This technique doubles as a great shortcut if you want to pick up a large list of numbers and automatically have them separated by commas. All you need to do is copy the text inside the curly braces, and voilà! You have comma-separated text.

Note that if the region of cells takes up multiple rows, there will be a semicolon (;) instead of a comma as the separator.

Some properties of VAR

There is an interesting mathematical relationship that is known and used by actuaries in the analysis of risk:

`VAR(aX+b) = a² VAR(X)`

What this is really saying is that if all your data is shifted by a constant amount `b`, the variance of your new data will be the same as before. For example, if you add the value 4 to each element of {12, 9, 13, 14, 11}, the dataset will become `{16,13,17,18,15}`; the variance, however, remains unchanged.

`=VAR({16,13,17,18,15})`   returns 3.7

If you multiply each value in your data by 3, the variance of your new data will increase by a factor of 3 squared, or will be 9 times bigger than your original data:

`=VAR({36,27,39,42,33})`   returns 33.3

and 9*3.7 is 33.3.

What if you combine the multiply and shift factors simultaneously? Your variance changes by the a² factor, the same as before. So, if you multiply your original data by 3 and then add the value 4, Excel will compute your variance as:

`=VAR({40,31,43,46,37})`   returns 33.3

Math

The Excel math functions and operators covered in this section include:

+	INT
–	MOD
*	QUOTIENT
/	ROUND
^ (exponentiation)	SQRT
ABS	DEC2HEX
CEILING	HEX2DEC
FLOOR	

Although I could have a field day discussing logarithms, exponents, trigonometric functions and the like, I'll leave you to explore these functions on your own.

ADDITION, SUBTRACTION, MULTIPLICATION, AND DIVISION

Adding (+), subtracting (–), multiplying (*), and dividing (/) are very much standard operations in Excel. My focus here is on the order in which Excel calculates formulas. When possible, Excel tries to calculate items in a formula from left to right, but there is a pecking order in which some operators have a higher priority even though they may be further to the right. Read on for more explanation.

```
=2+2*2/2                          returns 4
=2*2+2/2                          returns 5
```

EXPONENTIATION

Exponentiation is fairly straightforward. Two to the third power (a.k.a., 2 cubed, or 2 * 2 * 2) is expressed as:

```
=2^3                              returns 8
```

You need to be aware of several useful math rules when working with exponents:

```
(A^m)^n = A^(m*n)
A^(-x) = 1/(A^x)
(A^m)*(A^n) = A (m+n)
1^n = 1
```

These relationships may help you to simplify a knotty formula like:

```
=(A1^2*A1^4)^(2/6)
```

Applying the first exponentiation rule reduces this expression to `(A1^6)^(2/6)`, and it can be further reduced to `A1^(12/6)` and simplified to `A1^2`. I think you will agree that

```
=A1^2
```

is a simpler formula.

OPERATOR PRECEDENCE

If you combine several operators in a single formula, Excel performs the operations in the order shown in Table 2-2. If a formula contains operators with the same precedence—for example, if a formula contains both a multiplication and division operator—Excel evaluates the operators from left to right.

TABLE 2-2   OPERATOR PRECEDENCE IN EXCEL

Priority and Type	Operator Symbol	Description or Examples
1st Reference Operators	: ,	(colon) (single space) (comma)
2nd Negation	–	for example: −1
3rd Percentage	%	20%
4th Exponentiation	^	2^3 which returns 8
5th Multiplication and Division	* and /	2*3 4/5
6th Addition and Subtraction	+ and –	2+3 2−3
7th Concatenation	&	"Tax"&"Rate"
8th Comparison Operators	= < > <= >= <>	1=2 returns FALSE 2<3 returns TRUE 3>4 returns FALSE 4<=5 returns TRUE 5>=6 returns FALSE 6<>7 returns TRUE

Two additional rules apply to the interpretation of Table 2-2.

1. The order in which Excel evaluates an expression can be altered by inserting left and right parentheses at desired locations in the expression. For example:

   =2^1+2   returns 4

   but, with the parentheses, it becomes:

   =2^(1+2)   returns 8

2. Whenever operators of the same priority level are found, the order of evaluation is strictly from left to right. For example:

   =6+5+4+3^2+1

   really gets treated as if it were:

   =6+5+4+(3^2)+1

   which is 11+4+(3^2)+1, and which evaluates to 15+(3^2)+1, and then to 15+9+1, and then to 24+1, and finally 25.

ABSOLUTE NUMBERS

ABS(number)

An absolute number is very easy to understand. The following examples should make it clear:

=ABS(-30)	returns 30
=ABS(-3)	returns 3
=ABS(0)	returns 0
=ABS(3)	returns 3
=ABS(30)	returns 30

This insipid-looking function can be used innovatively. You will see a rather clever and unexpected use of it in Appendix A involving approximations.

CEILING AND FLOOR

CEILING(number,significance)
FLOOR(number,significance)

CEILING and FLOOR are useful because they round up and round down to a precise level of significance. This makes them useful for constructing spreadsheet tables such as the one shown in Figure 2-9.

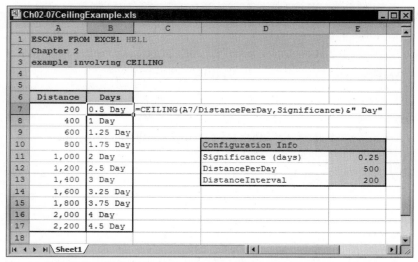

Figure 2-9: Using CEILING to construct a distance table

The formula in Figure 2-9 is

```
=CEILING(A7/DistancePerDay,Significance)&" Day"
```

The formula is very useful in that it can create a schedule based on the level of signifi-cance. This is something you can enter in one place and have the whole spreadsheet sched-ule updated.

ROUND AND INT

```
ROUND(number,num_digits)
INT(number)
```

ROUND is a commonly used function and is easy to understand. The following examples will make its use clear.

```
=ROUND(6325.1252,3)                    returns 6325.125
=ROUND(6325.1252,2)                    returns 6325.13
=ROUND(6325.1252,1)                    returns 6325.1
=ROUND(6325.1252,0)                    returns 6325
```

ROUND can work with numbers larger than decimal fractions.

"I need my financial estimates rounded to the nearest thousand dollars."

```
=ROUND(6325.1252,-3)                   returns 6000
```

If you want the number rounded to the nearest 100, you use:

```
=ROUND(6325.1252,-2)                        returns 6300
```

and for the nearest 10, you use:

```
=ROUND(6325.1252,-1)                        returns 6330
```

INT simply lops off the decimal portion of a number for positive numbers but doesn't quite work the same for negative numbers.

```
=INT(6.0000001)                  returns 6
=INT(6)                          returns 6
=INT(5.9999999)                  returns 5
=INT(-6.0000001)                 returns -7
=INT(-6)                         returns -6
=INT(-5.9999999)                 returns -6
```

 CAUTION

INT on negative values may work differently than you expect. For negative numbers, it will return the next lower number. For example, INT(-3.9) will return -4.

MOD AND QUOTIENT

```
MOD(number,divisor)
QUOTIENT(numerator,denominator)
```

I first learned about Modulo Arithmetic when I was in elementary school. The teachers who taught us didn't seem to have any good ideas how it's useful other than to predict what the time would be if you advanced your clock by, say 32 hours.

Thinking about clocks on a 12- or 24-hour cycle captures the essence of what the Excel MOD function does, but that doesn't convey that MOD can be used in a practical and versatile way. When you think about clocks, you realize that the cycle is pegged to a static number such as 12 hours.

Figure 2-10 shows the effective use of MOD. Notice that you can easily adjust the ReminderInterval.

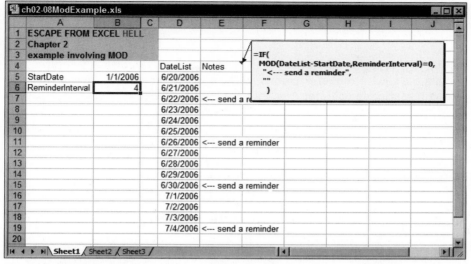

Figure 2-10: MOD function with variable reminder interval integrated into calendar

Sample calculations:

=MOD(35,11)	returns 2
=MOD(34,11)	returns 1
=MOD(33,11)	returns 0
=MOD(32,11)	returns 10
=MOD(-5.9,1)	returns 0.1
=MOD(-1.9,1)	returns 0.1
=MOD(-0.9,1)	returns 0.1
=MOD(0.9,1)	returns 0.1

QUOTIENT returns the integer portion of a division. There are some important subtleties you should be aware of.

You need to have the Analysis ToolPak loaded for Excel to recognize the QUOTIENT function. As a quick stand-in, you could replace QUOTIENT(a,b) with INT(a/b), *provided that both a and b are of the **same** sign* (that is, they are both positive or both negative). If they are of opposite signs so that the ratio will return a negative number, QUOTIENT(a,b) and INT(a/b) will return different results! The following calculations should make this clear:

=22.75/2	returns 11.375
=QUOTIENT(22.75,2)	returns 11
=QUOTIENT(-22.75,2)	returns -11
=INT(22.75/2)	returns 11
=INT(-22.75/2)	returns -12

SQUARE ROOTS AND CUBE ROOTS

```
SQRT(number)
```

The SQRT function is just as you might imagine it to be. For example, SQRT(9) returns 3. You can also obtain the square root of a number by raising it to the one-half power. You can do this with the exponentiation operator ^ or with the POWER function.

```
=SQRT(9)                                    returns 3
=9^0.5                                      returns 3
=9^(1/2)                                    returns 3
=POWER(9,0.5)                               returns 3
=POWER(9,1/2)                               returns 3
```

You can obtain cube roots by raising a number to the one-third power; for example, 5*5*5 is 125, so the cube root of 125 is 5.

```
=POWER(125,1/3)                             returns 5
```

You can't directly get the square root of a negative number. You will get a #NUM! error. Excel does have a bunch of specialized functions for dealing with complex numbers (numbers constructed from square roots of negative numbers and real numbers). These specialized functions require the use of the Analysis ToolPak.

Incidentally, you can use the SQRT function inside an array formula like this:

```
{=SQRT(SUMSQ(Unit_Costs_Uncertainties*Units_Shipped))}
```

DEC2HEX AND HEX2DEC

```
DEC2HEX(number,[places])
HEX2DEC(number)
```

In a world that's increasingly Web-centric, the need for converting between HEX-coded numbers and their decimal representation is becoming more prevalent. You may have the occasion to edit some HTML pages and you might come across a fragment like

```
bgcolor="#e2ac10"
```

This code is a little cryptic, but basically the first two characters after the # symbol are the red component in hexadecimal form. The next two characters specify the green component. The last two specify the blue component. If this sounds a little perplexing, well, that's because it is. A hexadecimal number is something that is easy for a computer to understand. The triplet of colors is combined into a single number.

Rather than scratch your head, you can write an Excel formula to extract the value for each color. So, if the cell A1 has an expression like #e2ac10, you can get the value of each color using formulas like

```
="Red is: "&HEX2DEC(MID(A1,2,2))          returns 'Red is: 226'
="Green is: "&HEX2DEC(MID(A1,4,2))        returns 'Green is: 172'
="Blue is: "&HEX2DEC(MID(A1,6,2))         returns Blue is: 16
```

Going in the reverse direction, you can use something like:

```
=DEC2HEX(B1+256*B2+256*256*B3)
```

If B1 has the value 226, B2 has the value 172, and B3 has the value 16, the value returned by your formula will be E2AC10.

NOTE

DEC2HEX and HEX2DEC require the Analysis ToolPak to be loaded.

Boolean and Conditional Functions

One of the features that distinguish a spreadsheet from many of the hand-held calculators is the capability to encode some kind of programming logic inside its formulas. These are Boolean operators or conditional functions and include AND, FALSE, IF, =, >, <, >= ,<= , <> , OR, and TRUE.

CONDITIONAL OPERATORS

```
=, >, <, >=, <=, <>
```

Conditional operators are binary Boolean operators, which evaluate two expressions and then compares the values of these two expressions according to some criteria, such as greater than or lesser than. It then reports a TRUE/FALSE value. There are a few things to note:

- These conditional operators aren't restricted to operations on numbers. It is perfectly legal to construct formulas like the following:

  ```
  =IF("Paula">"Paul","Paula comes after Paul","software bug")
  ```

- The operator <> stands for "not equal."

- Although you can have a greater than or equal to operator (>=), or a less than or equal to operator (<=), Excel will not accept =>, =<, or >< operators in any formula.

Sample calculations:

```
=2=3                                      returns FALSE
=2<3                                      returns TRUE
=2>3                                      returns FALSE
=2>=3                                     returns FALSE
=2<=3                                     returns TRUE
=2<>3                                     returns TRUE
```

NOTE

Conditional operators generally return TRUE/FALSE values, but sometimes they can't, depending on the expressions they operate on. Here is an example:

One or both expressions evaluates to an improper value. For instance, when one of the expressions involves an HLOOKUP computation, it is easily possible that it is trying to retrieve an out-of-range value such as:

```
=HLOOKUP(2,{1,2,3;4,5,6},2)>6
```

This returns an #N/A.

LOGIC COMBINERS

```
AND(logical1,logical2,...)
OR(logical1,logical2,...)
```

You will often find combinations of logical tests. The AND function returns TRUE only if every logical test returns a TRUE. For instance:

```
=AND(3>1,SQRT(64)<9,"Paula">"Paul")        returns TRUE
=AND(3>1,SQRT(64)<9,"Paula"="Paul")        returns FALSE
```

The OR function returns TRUE any time at least one of the tests results in a TRUE. For instance:

```
=OR(2<1,5-2=SQRT(250000),ROW(A25)=25)       returns TRUE
=OR(2<1,5-2=SQRT(250000),ROW(A25)=255999)   returns FALSE
```

TRUE AND FALSE

```
FALSE()
TRUE()
```

Excel has the functions TRUE and FALSE, which bear the same names as the value each produces (TRUE and FALSE, respectively).

"I need to convert TRUE into 1 and FALSE into 0."

The following examples show you how to do this conversion:

```
=N(TRUE)                                    returns 1
=N(FALSE)                                   returns 0
=1*TRUE                                     returns 1
=1*(325>12)                                 returns 1
=--TRUE                                     returns 1
=--(2<3)                                     returns 1
```

The use of the double minus can be a bit perplexing. Its use is discussed in Chapter 9.

"I need to convert a 0 into a FALSE and a 1 into a TRUE."

You can do this conversion like so:

```
=and(0)                              returns FALSE
=and(1)                              returns TRUE
=and(0.02)                           returns TRUE
=and(AnyNonZeroValue)                returns TRUE
```

EXCEL LOGIC SWITCHES

"I need to turn a TRUE into FALSE and a FALSE into TRUE."

Every now and then you may need to apply various kinds of logic switches in Excel, such as turning a TRUE into a FALSE or vice versa.

Excel has a NOT function that reverses the polarity of the logic. The following examples illustrate how it works:

```
=NOT(TRUE)                           returns FALSE
=NOT(SQRT(100)+SQRT(25)=15)          returns FALSE
=NOT(0)                              returns TRUE
=NOT(-0.00002)                       returns FALSE
```

*"I need an Exclusive Or (XOR) switch that returns a TRUE if either ConditionA is TRUE or ConditionB is TRUE, but **not both at the same time**."*

Here's how:

```
=NOT(ConditionA=ConditionB)
```

CONSTRUCTING LOGIC TREES WITH IF

```
IF(logical_test,value_if_true,value_if_false)
```

In contrast to the other Boolean and conditional operators, the function IF is not obligated to return a TRUE or a FALSE. Instead, it performs a test that must evaluate to either a TRUE or a FALSE, and based on the result of this test, you tell it what to return if it is true, and what to return if it is false. Here are some examples:

```
=IF(A1>RedAlert,"Too risky since "&A1&" exceeds "&RedAlert,"")
=IF(TODAY()>DATEVALUE("12/31/1999"),"21st Century","20th Century")
```

There is nothing to stop you from nesting IF statements.

```
=IF(A1>55,IF(A1>75,"Well over the speed limit!","Over the speed
limit."),"Within the speed limit.")
```

If your formula involves nesting several layers deep, it is usually better to split the formula into multiple cells or find a simplification of it.

Selectors

What good would a spreadsheet be if you couldn't find information you are looking for? One benefit of a spreadsheet is that formulas and data can co-exist as one entity. This section explains the fundamentals of CHOOSE, HLOOKUP, INDEX, MATCH, and VLOOKUP, and illustrates how they can be used.

VLOOKUP AND HLOOKUP

```
HLOOKUP(lookup_value,table_array,row_index_num[,range_lookup])
VLOOKUP(lookup_value,table_array,col_index_num[,range_lookup])
```

VLOOKUP is popular among many spreadsheet users, so I describe it here in some detail.

VLOOKUP takes a value it is searching for, looks down the first column of a data range, finds the closest match, and retrieves the item from a specific column of that data range. There are some subtleties you'll want to know about (look at Figure 2-11 or open the file ch02_09VlookupExample.xls on the book's CD-ROM).

Figure 2-11 shows two datasets containing the same data, but one is in ascending order and the other is not. Rows 12–23 show various computations involving VLOOKUP. You can supply an optional TRUE or FALSE parameter at the end of the VLOOKUP formula. If you omit this optional value, Excel will treat the formula as though you entered the value TRUE.

Whenever the TRUE parameter is specified (or implied), the first column of the dataset you are searching needs to be in ascending order. In this case, VLOOKUP will find the last known match with your search term. In your OrderedDataset, the term 10 appears twice. The one returned by VLOOKUP (with the range_lookup being TRUE) is the 1940. If you want to get the very first match instead of the last good match, you will need to supply VLOOKUP with the FALSE range_lookup option. This is shown in row 23.

What happens if you search for something that is not in your list? If you use the TRUE parameter (or don't specify it at all), you will get the closest value that is *less than* your search term.

```
=VLOOKUP(15,OrderedDataset,2,TRUE)        returns 1940
```

The number 15 is not in the dataset. The closest search value under 15 that has a good match is 10, and VLOOKUP picks up its search result.

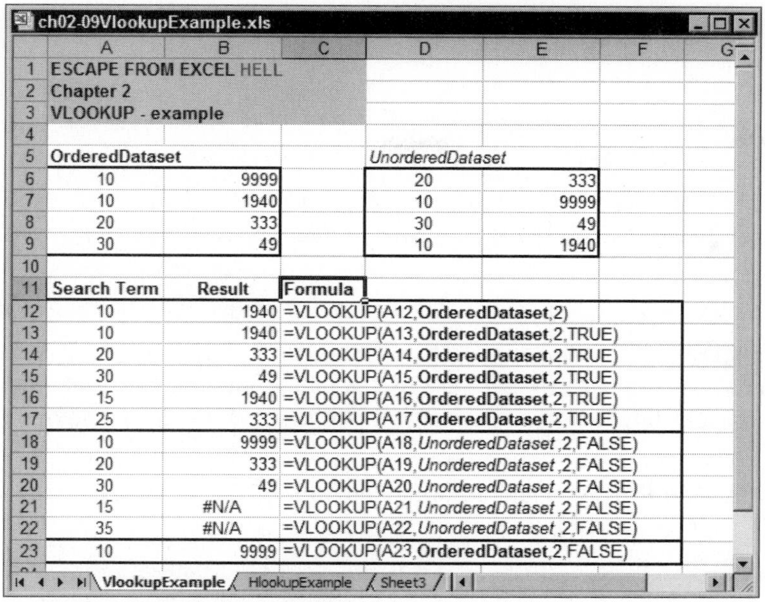

ch02-09VlookupExample.xls

	A	B	C	D	E
1	ESCAPE FROM EXCEL HELL				
2	Chapter 2				
3	VLOOKUP - example				
4					
5	OrderedDataset			*UnorderedDataset*	
6	10	9999		20	333
7	10	1940		10	9999
8	20	333		30	49
9	30	49		10	1940
10					
11	Search Term	Result	Formula		
12	10	1940	=VLOOKUP(A12,**OrderedDataset**,2)		
13	10	1940	=VLOOKUP(A13,**OrderedDataset**,2,TRUE)		
14	20	333	=VLOOKUP(A14,**OrderedDataset**,2,TRUE)		
15	30	49	=VLOOKUP(A15,**OrderedDataset**,2,TRUE)		
16	15	1940	=VLOOKUP(A16,**OrderedDataset**,2,TRUE)		
17	25	333	=VLOOKUP(A17,**OrderedDataset**,2,TRUE)		
18	10	9999	=VLOOKUP(A18,*UnorderedDataset*,2,FALSE)		
19	20	333	=VLOOKUP(A19,*UnorderedDataset*,2,FALSE)		
20	30	49	=VLOOKUP(A20,*UnorderedDataset*,2,FALSE)		
21	15	#N/A	=VLOOKUP(A21,*UnorderedDataset*,2,FALSE)		
22	35	#N/A	=VLOOKUP(A22,*UnorderedDataset*,2,FALSE)		
23	10	9999	=VLOOKUP(A23,**OrderedDataset**,2,FALSE)		

VlookupExample / HlookupExample / Sheet3

Figure 2-11: VLOOKUP examples

As a practical matter, it is often necessary to specify the `FALSE` parameter in VLOOKUP for one of the following reasons:

- The dataset being searched is not in ascending order.
- A match that doesn't correspond to what's exactly in your lookup table would be erroneous.
- You want to pick up the first matching occurrence rather than the last one when multiple lines correspond to your search criterion.

The function HLOOKUP is just VLOOKUP flipped on its side. In the spreadsheet file `ch02_09VlookupExample.xls` on the book's CD-ROM, look at the second worksheet tab called `HlookupExample`.

CHOOSE AND MATCH

```
CHOOSE(index_num,value1,value2,...)
MATCH(lookup_value,lookup_array[,match_type])
```

CHOOSE and MATCH make a very effective tag team. Think about a project that may have some amount associated with it; call it `UnitsSold`. You may want to classify the level of `UnitsSold` as `Low`, `Medium`, or `High` based on the thresholds of `0`, `50`, and `275`.

To find out what classification the level of `UnitsSold` is, you can use a formula like the following:

```
=CHOOSE(MATCH(UnitsSold,A1:A3),"Low","Medium","High")
where A1:A3 holds the values 0, 50, and 275, respectively.
```

The formula is telling Excel to match `UnitsSold` to the first, second, or third group. It then passes on the value of `1`, `2`, or `3` to CHOOSE; indicating which of `Low`, `Medium`, or `High` is to be returned.

There are several caveats for you to know about.

Generally, MATCH finds the largest value that is less than or equal to `lookup_value`. The lookup array or list (such as `A1:A3` in the example) needs to be in ascending order, with numbers appearing before any text (alphabetically arranged) and the text appearing before FALSE, TRUE.

Valid sequences of data in the lookup array would be the following:

```
0,50,275
-100,0,2500
3.14,"Pie",TRUE
```

The following sequences would not be valid:

```
50,0,275
"Pie",3.14,FALSE
TRUE,3.14,"Pie"
```

If your data is unordered, you can specify an optional `match_type` parameter to be `0`. In this case, MATCH finds the first value that is exactly equal to `lookup_value`.

If your data is in descending order following a TRUE, FALSE, Z–A descending numbers pattern, you can specify an optional `match_type` parameter to be `-1`. MATCH finds the smallest value that is greater than or equal to `lookup_value`.

INDEX

```
INDEX(array,row_num,column_num)
INDEX(reference,row_num,column_num,area_num)
```

INDEX is easy to understand. Think of a table populated with values, flanked on the top and left by index values. It may be a table showing per capita income level by industry sector versus geographic region (see Figure 2-12).

If you want to know what value is in both the second column and third row, you enter something like

```
=INDEX(MyEconomicTable,2,3)              returns 275
```

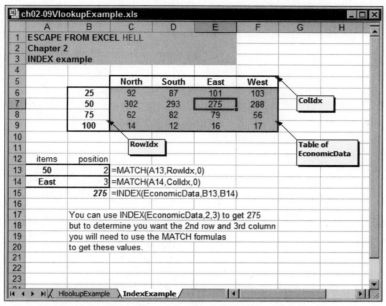

Figure 2-12: Retrieving values from a table using INDEX and MATCH

INDEX enlists the aid of the helper function MATCH to retrieve the correct row and column index. Make note of the fact that MATCH sets the optional `match_type` parameter to 0 so that exact matches are performed.

Constructing Cell References

The four functions COLUMN, ROW, INDIRECT, and OFFSET add considerable power and flexibility to spreadsheets you can create. They are often called into use to solve Excel Hell problems, so they are worthy of some discussion. You will find that COLUMN and ROW are easy to understand, learn, and apply. You should make them part of your standard formula arsenal.

COLUMN AND ROW

```
COLUMN([reference])
ROW([reference])
```

ROW does just what it says. It reads out the row number of the cell it resides in. If reference to another cell is provided in its argument, it returns the row number of the top-left corner of that reference. For instance, for a cell in B6:

```
=ROW()                                    returns 6
```

If you supply a cell reference, ROW provides the appropriate information:

```
=ROW(G25)                                    returns 25
=ROW(K22:AZ311)                              returns 22
```

COLUMN works the exact same way as ROW, except that column information is returned. For instance, for a cell in B6:

```
=COLUMN()                                    returns 2
```

If you supply a cell reference, ROW provides the appropriate information:

```
=COLUMN(G25)                                 returns 7
=COLUMN(K22:AZ311)                           returns 10
```

In addition to ROW and COLUMN are the related functions ROWS and COLUMNS. They report how many rows or columns stretch across a range. For instance:

```
=ROWS(K22:AZ311)                             returns 290
=COLUMNS(K22:AZ311)                          returns 42
```

ROW AND COLUMN COUNTING

A spreadsheet does a great job in letting you increment a bunch of dates or numbers across a row or column. It's great until you start inserting rows and columns. Now you have to rework the formulas where you spliced in some new rows. You may now end up with a bunch of formulas like:

```
=A1+1
=A2+1
                         an empty cell in this row
=A3+1
...
```

To fix this, you have to copy the A2+1 formula into the empty cell and the one below it. Now that's just for this single column. You may have formulas in other cells to fix. If you're careful and adept with formulas, this will be easy enough to fix. Have you ever deleted a row and suddenly found a thousand #REF! errors populating your screen? All this happens because the formula references are altered and possibly compromised when you insert and delete data.

A good way to get around this problem is to make use of a technique called Spreadsheet "Inlining." This technique simply counts the number of rows (or columns) apart the current cells from some starting location and uses this measure in its calculation. Figure 2-13 shows how to automatically decrement or increment a value based on row positions. Now you won't have to worry about altered formulas. Just fill in the empty cell and go about your merry way.

Chapter

Easy Formatting Fixes

In This Chapter

◆ Getting the most out of spreadsheet layout and organization

◆ Version tracking and documenting your spreadsheets

◆ Worksheet layout and formatting

◆ Finding and moving data in your spreadsheet

◆ Aligning text

◆ Merged cells and the problems they cause

◆ Cell shading and colorization

◆ Managing fonts

◆ Managing the appearance of text and numbers

◆ Managing Comments

The focus of this chapter is to help you get your spreadsheets in order. There are plenty of easy steps you can perform. I show how you can improve readability of your spreadsheets through adjusting your spreadsheet layout and formatting. And for when your spreadsheets grow and get more complex, I describe some facilities to help track the changes. There are common problems people encounter in spreadsheet formulas. I show some of the easy fixes for these, too (I save the harder ones for the later chapters, though).

Basic Spreadsheet Layout and Organization

The topic of spreadsheet layout and organization needs to be addressed on two levels: the layout and organization inside individual worksheets, and the organization of the whole workbook. Believe it or not, organizing the workbook can make a major difference in the manageability of your spreadsheet, especially when it gets large and complex. I have plenty to say about this in later chapters and refer to it as a *Layering Approach*. For now, I want to leave you with the thought that as your spreadsheets increase in complexity, it makes sense to separate the different parts of your spreadsheet into separate worksheets, as follows:

- Keep all your source data on one worksheet without any complicated formulas. Keep all your analyses and formulas on another. (In Chapters 6 and 9, I show you how to shuttle the data so that only the piece you need to look at gets analyzed.)

- Maintain your presentation of the analysis on a third worksheet. Your presentation layer (or layers) won't be riddled with complex formulas, because all the hard work is already done in the analysis layer. This approach leaves you free to be creative in designing an attractive and sensible-looking presentation report without worrying about messing up a complicated formula.

Perhaps all this seems obvious. But I've seen too many spreadsheets that have literally everything jumbled together.

Essential Spreadsheet Information Should be Up Front

"When I open a spreadsheet, I can't tell what it's being used for."

Needless to say, when you open a spreadsheet it can be a challenge to figure out what's going on in it, or specific details on how it is designed to work. It can also be a point of embarrassment when that spreadsheet happens to be one created by you, too long ago to remember any of the details.

As a matter of standard practice, it is always good to start off your spreadsheet by placing answers to the following three questions at the top of every spreadsheet:

1. Who?

2. What?

3. When (where, how, or why)?

Doing so (and in the order listed) enables people to know, at a glance, exactly what they're looking at, even if they don't look at the rest of the spreadsheet. It will save you and other people time. Imagine submitting a spreadsheet as part of a competitive bid or proposal.

Your spreadsheet immediately identifies your organization, what exactly is being presented in the spreadsheet, and further specifics such as date, time, or other relevant information. Now imagine that your competitors omit some of this up-front information. Forgetting about the numbers, whose spreadsheet will be easier to grasp? Who gains the competitive edge?

Now, back to the question of what the spreadsheet is being used for. Sometimes this may not be so easy to state in the form of a one-line answer for a worksheet banner or header. The question is complicated by the fact that it could simultaneously be used for multiple purposes instead of just one. Also, the spreadsheet may have been created by someone else in your organization. When you're not the original author of the spreadsheet, there are several easy things you can do to decipher what is happening in the spreadsheet:

- Create a disposable copy of the spreadsheet so that you can freely tinker with it.

- If the entire spreadsheet is located on a single worksheet and it is too busy, you may want to reorganize the spreadsheet. Possibly you can offload identifiable portions of the spreadsheet onto individual worksheets (remember, this is your disposable copy, so you can be indiscriminate about such things). You'll find more information on organizing spreadsheets into separate, identifiable layers in Chapter 9.

Before tinkering with a spreadsheet, it is a good practice to preserve it in its original form and make a copy that you can freely alter. Do this by going to the Excel menu and clicking File⇨Save As; then, save it with a new filename of your choosing. Now you can freely make changes to that file, tinker with formulas, reorganize information, and annotate it as you see fit.

I am hoping that in the spreadsheet you are examining, you have some notion of what it contains. It might be something that looks like a Balance Sheet or Income Statement, but that the organization or subsidiary may not be clearly identified. You might see information by month but not know whether the data pertains to last year or the year before.

As you start peeling away the layers of obscurity, annotate the spreadsheet. All the details may be fresh in your mind, but time has a way of eroding clarity. Also, there is bound to be turnover in a company, so it is best if usable documentation persists.

Version Tracking

"I've created so many versions of the same spreadsheet that I don't even know which one is the latest. How can I keep track of the different versions of my spreadsheet?"

There are a number of different ways you can track versions of your software. At the most rudimentary level, you can look at the file modification date from Windows Explorer. This is simple, but there is no revision tracking. You'll have no idea how many prior versions were created, not to mention whether your file modification date is reliable. It is very easy for a spreadsheet to be resaved long after any significant changes.

There is another approach, one that utilizes Excel's File Properties feature. In any open workbook, click File⇨Properties and then click the Custom tab (see Figure 3-1). Within the Custom tab is a list of attributes that you can supply with specific values. These include Completion date, Department, and Project. You can populate these attributes with text, dates, numbers, and Yes/No values. Though you can manually set the values, it is better to link them to your spreadsheet. To make your work easier, I provide an already prepared spreadsheet (open file `ch03-01FileProperties.xls` on the CD-ROM with this book). When you check the box for Link to Content, you will be able to associate these attributes with any of the user-defined names in your spreadsheet.

Notice that the file I just mentioned contains four fields starting with `MyField`. These are fields that are not prebuilt in Excel. When you type in a new name in the Name: input box (see Figure 3-1) and associate it with the appropriate user-defined name, the button above the Delete button will change from Modify to Add. Click the Add button. Now your new custom field will be added to the list.

This is a nice facility, but to use it effectively, you need to pay attention to the following:

- Excel will not police you when you're updating values. For instance, there is nothing to stop you from placing a completion date of `12/7/1932`.

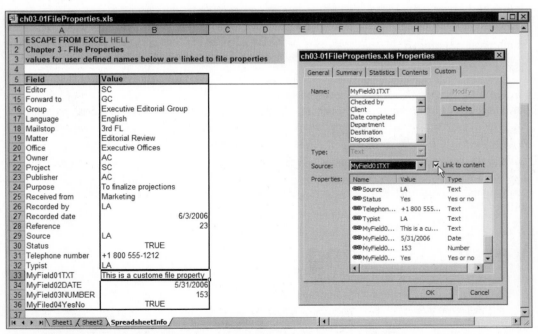

Figure 3-1: Custom fields can be maintained in the file properties of your spreadsheet.

- It would not be practical to use all the fields available. If you use all 25-plus fields, you will suffer from "clutteritis," not to mention the burden of constantly updating all this information! My strong recommendation is that you track four or at most a half-dozen items. Because you are free to create your own fields, you can make this facility well-suited for your needs.

- The File Properties feature of Excel doesn't track the history of changes made to your spreadsheet.

Saving Multiple Versions of a File Is Not Enough

"I need to document changes to my spreadsheet as it evolves. And it would be helpful to date/time stamp these."

One way to keep track of key changes to your spreadsheet is to create multiple versions of the file and vary the filename slightly. Instead of calling a file `MySpreadsheet.xls`, you might start with the name `MySpreadsheet01.xls`. After you make a sufficient number of changes, you might save it as `MySpreadsheet02.xls`, and continue making filename revisions as necessary.

The advantage of this approach is that you have something to fall back on in case your latest version is compromised. I heartily recommend that you adopt this practice. However, it is not informative enough to tell you what is being changed. In addition to filename revisions or serializing, you need to document changes.

There is no facility built into Excel that directly supports documenting your revisions. For this reason, I provide you with a template file (`RevisonHistory.xlt`) on the book's CD-ROM that takes care of all this for you. Figure 3-2 shows a typical spreadsheet using the Revision History template. When you click the New Entry button, a new line will be inserted at the top of your list of changes, it will be date/time stamped, and you can directly enter your initials and your most recent changes on the immediate right. As you advance through different versions or revisions of your spreadsheet, you can click the New Revision button to advance the `asOfDate` and the `revNum` revision number. So, your revision number will advance from 1 to 2 to 3 and so on. If you place a letter after it, such as 1A, it will advance to 2A.

When you use this tracking tool, I suggest you do the following:

- Synchronize your filename with the revision number. Doing so will make it easy to identify what changes or enhancements have been introduced since previously revised files.

- After you date/time stamp an entry with your comments, *do not alter* the entry. Instead, add entries to clarify, supplement, or redact a previous entry. Adding new entries rather than altering previous ones is central to the integrity of your documentation trail. It is what adds the credibility to your spreadsheet.

	A	B	C	D
	DocumentedProjection.xls			
1	YOUR OGANIZATION NAME			
2	Revision History for: [please fill in]			
3	as of 5/10/2006		[New Entry] [New Revision] Revision 2A	
4				
5				
6		Change made		
7	Date	or entered by	Description	
8				
9	5/05/2006 12:24 PM	LA Rev. 2A	Restated quarterly periods so that timeline starts from Q4'2006.	
10	5/03/2006 12:05 PM	LA	Integrated results into financial statement summary.	
11	5/01/2006 12:05 PM	LA	Computed total shipping requirements, calculated cost of sales and selling expense.	
12	4/27/2006 12:02 PM	LA	Extended forecast for 4 quarters.	
13	4/25/2006 5:46 PM	LA	Implemented time phased intro for specific segements	
14	4/24/2006 9:58 PM	LA	Computed gross number of passengers to and from primary cities.	
15	4/24/2006 2:55 PM	LA	Assembled lookup data for historical records dating from during Q1'2005. Also contains initial estimate pricing estimate.	
16	9/09/2005 10:46 PM	LA	Copyright notice and Software License Agreement appears in the macro portion of this spreadsheet.	
17	11/15/2002 12:21 AM	LA	©2002-2006 Evolving Technologies Corporation	
18				
19				
20				
21				

IncomeStmt / BalanceSheet / **RevisionHistory**

Press ALT+F11 keys. The notice is on Module1 for this spreadsheet and has been digitally signed.

Figure 3-2: Tracking tool to document changes to your spreadsheet

The use of macros is required to make all this work. These macros, as is true of all the macros provided in this book, have been digitally signed. After you identify the digital certificates for this book as being trusted, Excel will load them without requiring your permission every time. As you make changes to the files, the digital certificates remain perfectly valid as long as you don't alter the macros.

NOTE

You are free to modify the macros for this template. Simply press Alt+F11 and modify or save the macros in the spreadsheet's module. After you alter the macro in any way, the digital signature attached to the file will be obliterated. Thereafter, every time you open the file, if your security level is Medium or higher (it should *never* be set to Low!), Excel will warn you that the macros can be altered by anyone without any trail.

Even if you are the only person who has access to your files, Excel will still give you the warning each and every time you open the file. Your only way around this, should you modify the macros, is to obtain your own digital certificates.

Incidentally, the revision history template links the asOfDate and revNum values to attributes stored in the Custom File Properties.

NOTE

Excel has a facility for tracking changes (Tools⇨Track Changes⇨Highlight Changes), but it is a good deal more involved (see Figure 3-3). Typically, this is useful when spreadsheets are shared by multiple users, and it is best to use when the spreadsheets are highly refined and the changes being made are subtle, are last-minute changes, or having a precise audit trail is critical.

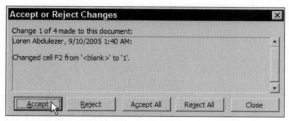

Figure 3-3: Tracking changes

Worksheet Layout and Formatting

Excel can assist you in formatting your spreadsheet content. This section explains how.

You can use auto format features. Sometimes Excel is too aggressive in formatting your content and may need to be tamed. Headers and footers are easily customizable. I show you how to turn spreadsheet gridlines off and on. Finally, I explain how to utilize Excel .xlt templates.

AutoFormat and AutoCorrect Features

"I would like to liven up my spreadsheet reports with a consistent look and feel. Is there a quick and easy way to do so?"

Excel has an Auto Format facility that allows you to enhance the readability of your spreadsheets. Select the cells in your spreadsheet that you want formatted; then, from the Excel menu, click Format⇨Auto Format (see Figure 3-4).

A dialog box pops up that shows you different sample formats. The Auto Format facility will automatically allow you to highlight totals, place underscores at the appropriate places in a report, insert currency symbols, and so on.

 NOTE

If you want to experiment with each of these settings and tell Auto Format whether to enable changes to number formats, fonts, alignment, borders, patterns, or adjust width/height, be sure to click the Options button to display the individual checkboxes.

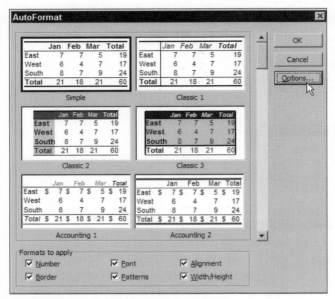

Figure 3-4: Using the Auto Format facility.

The AutoFormat dialog box presents quite a few formats. To make things easier to view (and print), I provide you with a sample file, `ch03-02AutoFormatSample1.xls`, on the CD-ROM. You can adjust the individual items in the "Simple" report that appears in the spreadsheet. As you make changes to this report, the values automatically carry over to the other reports while keeping all the distinct formats. In this way you can use your own data to instantly see how each formatted report looks and prints.

NOTE

The format List 1 highlights every other row of data in your report, which is typical of the way mainframe computer runs might appear (basically following an AB AB pattern).

The format List 2 highlights row in pairs, following an AA BB AA BB pattern.

"Every time I type in CNA, Excel decides to change it to CAN. What gives?"

Excel is configured to AutoCorrect your entries. Microsoft has a reputation for designing software that tries to relieve the user from having to think through everything. Relieving users of clerical burdens can be useful, but sometimes too much of a good thing is not good. I personally don't like to shut off my mind and run in autopilot mode.

To fix this, click Tools⇨AutoCorrect Options and, in the dialog box, uncheck Replace Text As You Type (see Figure 3-5).

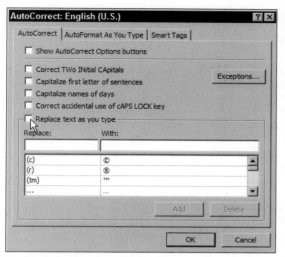

Figure 3-5: Deselect Replace Text As You Type and other AutoCorrect options to give yourself more control.

While you're at it, you may want to uncheck the other AutoCorrect options that you don't need.

My suggestion is that you turn off these extra help features and, one by one, add them back as you need them. This way you can be more in control and will have a more finely tuned expectation of what you do and what Excel does.

Managing Headers and Footers

"I have a spreadsheet with quite a few worksheets. Is there any way I can set the worksheet headers and footers all at one time, instead of having to set them individually?"

You can easily set all your worksheet headers and footers simultaneously. The technique is to "group select" the worksheets. You hold down the Ctrl key and click each of the worksheet tabs you want to select. As the worksheets become grouped, the worksheet tabs change from gray to white.

But you might find it too slow to click each individual worksheet tab. A quicker way to group select the worksheets is to hold down the Ctrl+Shift+PgDn keys. If your keyboard is set to auto-repeat, after a brief delay, sheet after sheet will be group selected. You can adjust your keyboard auto-repeat properties in the Windows Keyboard Control Panel.

If you want to deselect a few of the many worksheet tabs, simply Ctrl+click the worksheet tab you want deselected.

With your worksheets group selected, you can go ahead and set your headers and footers all in just one step.

NOTE

When you're done selecting your group of worksheets, remember to deselect your worksheet tabs. Otherwise, changes you make to an individual worksheet will apply to all the group-selected worksheets!

Later, you'll see how this aspect can be put to use.

Toggling the Row and Column Gridlines

"Some of the worksheets I prepare are used for polished-looking reports. I don't want to see gridlines on these worksheets. How can I remove them so that they don't appear, the way it is with my printed reports?"

In your Excel menu, click Tools➪Customize and, in the Customize dialog box (see Figure 3-6), click the Commands tab. On the left panel, select Forms and find the Toggle Grid button on the right panel. Click and drag this onto one of your toolbars (preferably one of the custom toolbars you created, as described in the section "Customizing Your Excel Software with Toolbars," in Chapter 1, "Spreadsheet Basics").

Now you can just click the Toggle Grid toolbar icon to switch the row and column gridlines on and off. There are several things to note about this feature:

- The Toggle Grid toolbar icon alters the state of only the current worksheet.
- Toggling in this manner won't affect any of your print settings.
- Toggling in this manner won't alter any of the cell borders you create.

Figure 3-6: Adding a Gridlines toggle switch to your suite of toolbar icons.

Removing the Gridlines

"I want to permanently remove gridlines from my spreadsheets whenever I create them. I am able to change my Excel Options by unchecking the Gridlines box in the View tab. This works fine for the current worksheet, but the option is wiped out whenever I open a new workbook. What should I do?"

As explained in Chapter 1, whenever Excel opens a new workbook, it constructs it from a template file. The default template is called `Book.xlt`. You can modify this file so that it has the gridlines removed, and resave it as a template file. Rather than overwrite the default template, it is far safer to create the spreadsheet template the way you want and save it under a different filename, such as `MyFavoriteTemplate.xlt`. Here are the steps:

1. Create a template spreadsheet the way you want, such as with the gridlines removed.

2. From the Excel menu, click File⇨Save As and give the file a name of your choosing. It is generally a good practice to avoid using spaces in the middle of your filenames. For example, using `MyTemplate.xls` or `My_Template.xls` is better than `My Template.xls`, the latter with the space between "My" and "Template." Because spaces are invisible, it is possible to type two spaces and not realize they are not together. This can cause confusion. You can easily end up with two files, one with a single space between "My" and "Template.xls," another with two spaces. How will you tell which one is which?

3. Before clicking the Save button, change the file type to Template (*.xlt) in the Save as Type option. This action will automatically change the suffix of your filename from `.xls` to `.xlt`. Additionally, Excel should switch the directory in which the template file is saved to the Excel template directory. On the Windows platform, this is typically

   ```
   C:\Documents and Settings\User Name\Application Data\Microsoft\
   Templates\
   ```

   Of course, the `User Name` will correspond to the user name for your computer.

After you save the template file, you will be able to open new spreadsheet files using File⇨New and, over on the panel on the right, select Templates in My Computer.

There is one further annoyance that Microsoft Windows or Excel might throw at you. When you attempt to save your regular spreadsheets, Excel may be looking in the Templates directory instead of your usual location for spreadsheet files. Just navigate back to the directory in which you always save your spreadsheet files. Excel will quickly forget about saving to the Templates directory. Just one further piece of advice: Do not save your regular `.xls` files in the Templates directory. Doing so will make file access very messy, cluttered, and problematic.

Previewing Your New Template

"When I open a template file, I see the option to show a preview of the template. None of the templates I create have previews. How do I get Excel to show the preview?"

Before saving your spreadsheet template, click File⇨Properties and click the Summaries tab. In the bottom-left portion of this window is a checkbox for Save preview picture. If it is unchecked, check it.

Incidentally, this will work for all spreadsheet files, not just template files. It just works better with templates, because when you select a template you are about to open, Excel displays its preview in a second panel (that is, provided that you haven't changed the default settings for Excel). When you click File⇨Open for a regular spreadsheet, you will have to tell Excel to show the Preview of files you select. You may want instead to choose Details, which shows the file size modification date. Though you can switch back and forth between Details, Preview, and Properties, doing so is not nearly as convenient as setting previews with template files.

"When I open spreadsheet files, I am not seeing the kind of information I should expect to see in the Open dialog box. All I seem to be getting are icons. What can I do?"

When you're about to open files by clicking File⇨Open and you have the Open dialog box on-screen, you will see, near the top-right of the window, the Views icon (to the immediate left of the Tools icon). When you click the Views icon, a pull-down menu reveals a variety of viewing options (see Figure 3-7). Feel free to select any of these options. I encourage you to try the Details view. Excel will remember which of these view settings you last used and will keep the setting for the next time you open your Excel files.

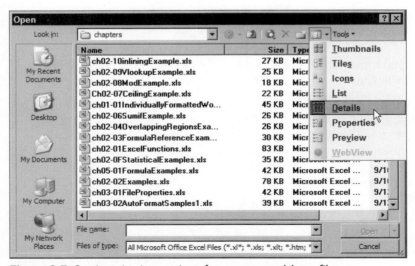

Figure 3-7: Setting viewing options for your spreadsheet files

Grabbing the Data You Want

"How can I select the whole spreadsheet at one time?"

At the top-left corner of your worksheet is a small, empty rectangle immediately above the row numbers and to the left of the column letters. Click this empty box and all the cells in the worksheet will become selected. Now you can format all the cells at one time.

"I want to copy the entire columns H and J and paste them to columns L and M. How do I do this?"

Along the top of your worksheet are the column letters. Click the letter H. You should notice that all of column H is selected. Move your mouse over the letter J, press and hold down the Ctrl key, and click the letter J once to select the J column. Now both columns H and J should be selected. Press Ctrl+C to copy the content. You will see dotted lines appearing around both these columns. Click cell L1 once and press Ctrl+V to paste. Notice that the pasted data has no intervening column, as there was with the original data.

"I have data on a worksheet with many blank cells. How can I remove the blanks?"

Press Ctrl+G and, in the Go To window, click the Special button. You will be presented with a Go To Special window (see Figure 3-8). Click the option Constants. Underneath this option is a series of checkboxes for Numbers, Text, Logicals (true/false values), and Errors (for example, #Name?, or #Value!). Deselect any of these kinds of data you don't want to grab.

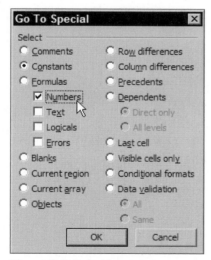

Figure 3-8: Selecting constants on your worksheet

Press OK. All the constants should be selected. Press Ctrl+C to copy your selection, and then press Ctrl+V to paste it your target location. The pasted data should now be consolidated without blanks.

You can copy multiple locations, but you cannot cut multiple locations in one step.

Using the Excel Find Facility

To search for the location of key terms or formulas, you can use Excel's Find facility (Ctrl+F). When the Find dialog box appears, if you see an Options >> button instead of an Options << button, click the button so that the Find dialog box appears as shown in Figure 3-9. You might, for instance, want to find the locations of formulas that use SUM. You can find all instances of its use within a single worksheet or the whole workbook. You may be looking for specific keywords within your spreadsheet or the occurrence of a specific value computed by a formula. In this case, you select Values rather than Formulas in your search options. The Find facility is a great tool for finding a needle in a haystack.

Incidentally, Excel permits you to search and replace (using Ctrl+H). You can not only replace values as you would with a word processor but also perform the search and replace on an Excel formula.

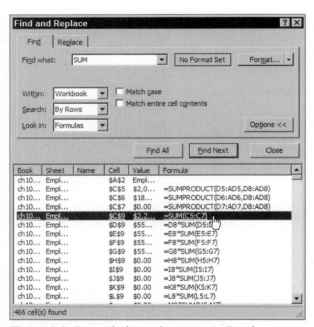

Figure 3-9: Expanded search options in Excel

Go To⇨Special: A Facility for Finding Specific Kinds of Spreadsheet Cells

Another tool that will help you to discern what is going on in a spreadsheet is to click Edit⇨Go To (Ctrl+G) and click the Special button. You can then click the Constants option and shade all the selected cells with one color, perhaps yellow or tan (see Figure 3-10). You can repeat the process but select Formulas instead of Constants, and then shade the cells a light green or blue. The shadings may help you to discern some pattern or structure in the spreadsheet.

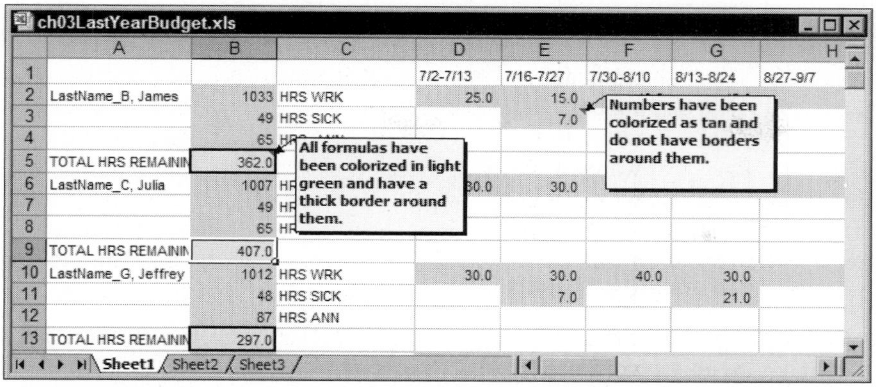

	A	B	C	D	E	F	G	H
1				7/2-7/13	7/16-7/27	7/30-8/10	8/13-8/24	8/27-9/7
2	LastName_B, James	1033	HRS WRK	25.0	15.0			
3		49	HRS SICK		7.0			
4		65	HR					
5	TOTAL HRS REMAININ	362.0						
6	LastName_C, Julia	1007	HR	30.0	30.0			
7		49	HR					
8		65	HR					
9	TOTAL HRS REMAININ	407.0						
10	LastName_G, Jeffrey	1012	HRS WRK	30.0	30.0	40.0	30.0	
11		48	HRS SICK		7.0		21.0	
12		87	HRS ANN					
13	TOTAL HRS REMAININ	297.0						

ch03LastYearBudget.xls

Sheet1 / Sheet2 / Sheet3 /

All formulas have been colorized in light green and have a thick border around them.

Numbers have been colorized as tan and do not have borders around them.

Figure 3-10: Go To⇨Special allows you to locate and mark formulas and values.

I have plenty more to say about these features and how to use them later.

Cell Formatting

Excel gridlines and borders are two different kinds of animals. Gridlines apply to worksheets as a whole. Borders apply to individual spreadsheet cells or a range of spreadsheet cells. Of course, a border is not the only type of formatting you can apply to a spreadsheet cell. You can also adjust the cell's alignment, background pattern, font, numeric representation, and the cell protection attributes. You can also make use of conditional formatting, and endow spreadsheet cells with pop-up comments.

Wrapping Text

"When I type a sentence into a spreadsheet cell, it spills over into the adjacent columns. How can I contain the text within the boundaries of the cell?"

There are two ways to keep content within a cell's boundaries. The first is to select your cell and format it (on the Excel menu, click Format⇨Cells and then click the Alignment tab). Within the Text Control portion on the Format Cells dialog box, check the box next to Wrap text. If you see a grayed-out checkbox (as opposed to a checkmark appearing in solid black), this means that some of the cells currently selected have the wrap-text feature turned on and others do not. You can change them all to no wrap (by clicking the checkbox once) or to having wrap text turned on (by clicking once more to go from a pure no wrap to a solid checkmark).

The next method provides an alternative way to enable wrapped text in a single cell.

"I want to control where my line breaks occur when I enable wrap text."

While you're entering text into your spreadsheet cell, press Alt+Enter. This inserts a hard break in the text so that everything else that follows begins on a new line. Note that this forces the cell to turn wrap text on. Depending on how much text you type and the width of the column, there may be other places where the text wraps.

Creating Angled Text

"How do I construct angled text in a table?"

To have angled text, construct a table as you normally would and include borders. The top row will be formatted for angled text. Don't worry if the text overlaps. Select the top row similarly to the way it's done in Figure 3-11.

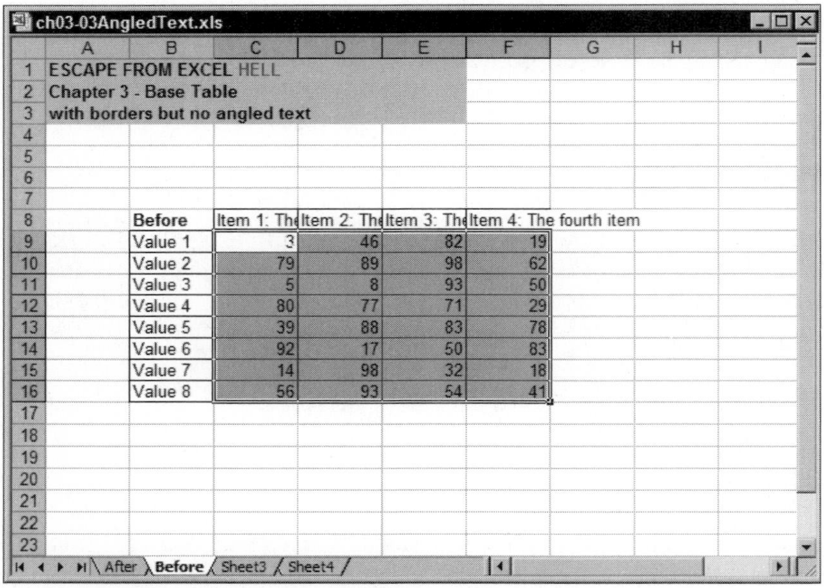

ch03-03AngledText.xls

ESCAPE FROM EXCEL HELL
Chapter 3 - Base Table
with borders but no angled text

Before	Item 1: Th	Item 2: Th	Item 3: Th	Item 4: The fourth item
Value 1	3	46	82	19
Value 2	79	89	98	62
Value 3	5	8	93	50
Value 4	80	77	71	29
Value 5	39	88	83	78
Value 6	92	17	50	83
Value 7	14	98	32	18
Value 8	56	93	54	41

Figure 3-11: Table with borders and no angled text

Format the selected cells (click Format⇨Cells or press Ctrl+1). Then, click the Alignment tab and set the orientation to 45 degrees or some other amount of your choosing. You can do this by grabbing and sliding the orientation dial to 45 or by entering **45**.

When you're creating tables with angled text, you can do some things to improve readability, such as the following:

- Turn worksheet gridlines off because row and column gridlines add "visual noise" to your presentation.
- Colorize individual columns in your table so that the table data is more easily associated with its angled text.

- For cell borders, use thin lines instead of thick outlines.

- The cell data (see, for example, C9:G16 in Figure 3-12) tends to be easier to read when it is centered (as opposed to left or right aligned).

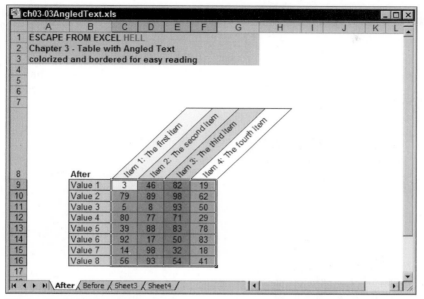

Figure 3-12: Table with angled text

Working with Merged Cells (and Handling the Problems They Cause)

"I was given a spreadsheet to clean up before transferring into a database file. Whenever I try to sort the data, the following message shows up and it won't allow me to sort:

```
The operation requires the merged cells to be identically sized
```

I have spent the better part of a day trying to find the merged cells, but have failed. How can I get around this problem?"

Lurking somewhere in the data you want to sort are merged cells. You could try to find the offending cells, but it's better to do away with merged cells altogether. Here is what you do:

1. Make sure that the cells you want to sort are already selected.

2. Press Ctrl+1 and click the Alignment tab of the Format Cells window.

3. Remove the checkmark next to the Merge cells checkbox (clicking inside the box once should do it).

4. Click OK.

At this stage, you should be able to sort the data as you normally would. I suggest that instead of just removing the merged cell formatting from selected regions of your worksheet, you remove it for the whole worksheet. You can do this by selecting the whole spreadsheet.

Adjusting Cell Background Patterns

When you format cells (using Ctrl+1), you can adjust the cell's shading. These settings can be found in the Patterns tab. Here are a couple of suggestions on the usage of patterns:

- If you have a spreadsheet in which a few pieces of data drive the whole spreadsheet, it is a good practice to colorize those cells.
- Cells with pale color shadings are easier to read than those with dark or primary colors.

"I colorize my patterns and fonts from the toolbar icons. I often notice spreadsheets with other colors that don't appear in my palette. How do I get these colors?"

Press Ctrl+1 and click the Patterns or Font tab. The extra colors will appear there.

In the Patterns tab, you will see solid colors. Select a color. If you want more options, click the Pattern pull-down menu.

The Font tab has a Color pull-down menu that gives you options for font colors other than Automatic.

"I want to colorize the cells on my worksheet in which I can change the numbers. How do I do this?"

Open the Go To Special window (press Ctrl+G and click the Special button) and click the Constants option. Make sure that the checkbox next to Numbers is marked. If you want, you can deselect Text, Logicals, and Errors. Press OK. With all your numbers selected, press Ctrl+1 and click the Patterns tab. Click the color of your choosing and press OK. If you want to remove the background shading for these cells, you can click "No Color" instead of one of the colored swatches.

If need be, you can define additional custom colors. From the Excel menu, click Tools⇨Options and then click the Color tab. Select a color you want to alter and click the Modify button. From here, I'll leave you to explore these features on your own. Although you can create exotic colors, remember that spreadsheets with your custom colors may not render identically when spreadsheets using these colors are open in other people's computers. With the wide range of printers out there, it is almost a foregone conclusion that exotic colors may be troublesome on some of them. Please use custom colors with caution. If you get stuck and want to get back to your original settings, remember the Reset button, which is immediately below the Modify button.

Understanding Fonts and Formatting

"How do I get text inside a spreadsheet to appear with subscripts and superscripts, such as H_2O and mc^2?"

Select the cell you want to edit and then follow these steps:

1. Click inside the Excel Formula Bar and select the specific portion of text you want to turn into a subscript or superscript.

2. Click Format⇨Cells from the Excel menu.

3. In the Effect section, place a checkmark next to Subscript or Superscript and click OK.

 NOTE

Although you can create custom formatting for a portion of plain text, you *cannot* apply subscripts, superscripts, or any other special type of formatting to a portion of a number. You cannot have a number appear like 12^3 unless you are willing to convert the number 123 to text. You can do this by placing a single apostrophe before the number (described in Chapter 2). When Excel treats this as text, you can apply the superscript or other formatting to a portion of the text. Remember, you can still extract the numeric value from the text by using the VALUE function and pointing it to the cell that displays your custom formatted text.

"When I import text into Excel from a computer-generated run, the columns appear to be drunk. They should all line up nice and neatly, but they don't."

The default font in Excel is Arial. This is not a monospace font. With Arial, the characters iii take up much less space than OOO. In a monospace font, all printable characters, including spaces and punctuation marks, are of equal width. Courier and Courier New are examples of monospace fonts.

Monospace fonts are especially useful when you have to count characters or are viewing log files. Though they are not as pretty as other fonts, they help to get everything aligned, and to keep it that way.

As a general practice, I prepare virtually all my spreadsheets using monospace font. I have deviated from this practice in this book because people are not used to seeing spreadsheets with monospace fonts. If you want to standardize using a font other than Arial, click Tools⇨Options and click the General tab. Set your standard font to a font of your choosing. While you have the Options window open, you can adjust some other settings. If you don't see a checkmark next to Function Tooltips, mark that checkbox. Having this feature on will provide you with additional assistance as you enter Excel functions in your Formula Bar. You can increase the number of files appearing on the Recently Used File list up to nine. This will make it easier to retrieve files you recently opened.

The change to a new font may not take effect until you quit Excel and restart it.

Setting Numeric and Text Representation

"How do I set the currency symbol in Excel?"

Currency is handled at the individual cell level. This design is meant to give you the flexibility to display information in multiple currencies on a single worksheet. Of course, you will have to apply any currency exchange rates yourself (or subscribe to some service to provide the information). Here is how you set the currency (see Figure 3-13):

1. Select the cells you want to format for a particular currency.

2. From the Excel menu, click Format⇨Cells.

3. Click the Number tab and select either Currency or Accounting in the Category pane. In the symbol drop-down list, select the currency you desire.

4. In some countries, the practice is to use commas as decimal points and periods as thousands separators. In the Excel menu, click Tools⇨Options and, in the Options dialog box, click the International tab. In the Number handling section, uncheck Use System Separators. In the Decimal Separator and Thousands Separator fields, enter the separator symbols appropriate to your specific country.

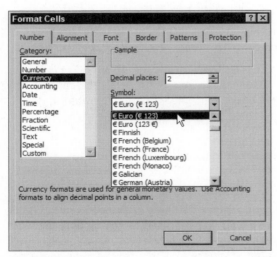

Figure 3-13: Setting the currency for your worksheet selection

"I want to effectively 'hide' some numbers that can be easily changed, but is neither visible nor printed. I have one further complication; I am using Excel in conjunction with other software that does not tolerate protected worksheets. How can I easily achieve this?"

You can use custom formatting. Press Ctrl+1 and click the Number tab. Inside the Category: list, click Custom and, in the Type input box, enter the following:

`;;;`

and then click OK.

NOTE

Anything appearing before the first semicolon provides instructions to Excel on how to format numbers that are positive (greater than zero).

Anything appearing between the first and second semicolon instructs Excel on how to format numbers with a zero value. Between the second and third are instructions for formatting negative numbers. After the third semicolon is just info for non-numeric text. Because nothing is there but the semicolons, there are no formatting instructions and the cell will be left blank!

Scroll through some of the other Custom formats. You'll pick up some ideas on how to format numbers. More is said about custom formats in later chapters.

"When I change a cell's locked or hidden status, nothing happens. I have no idea how to make a cell locked or hidden."

Locking or hiding cells is only the first step. Worksheet protection needs to be turned on. To set this, click Tools⇨Protection⇨Protect Sheet. A Protect Sheet window appears that allows you to activate various protection features for the whole worksheet. I discuss this topic in detail in Chapter 7.

Maximizing the Benefits of the Comments Feature

"I regularly use the pop-up Comments feature of Excel, but what combination of colors and special effects work well, or should be avoided?"

Excel pop-up Comments can be custom formatted to any of a number colorized shades (also known as Patterns), font types, styles, and sizes, and visibility settings. Here are some simple guidelines:

- Select Patterns and font combinations that have good contrast. A light shaded background and dark-colored font typically work well.

- Fonts appearing in **boldface** tend to be easier to read.

- You can have Comments stay always visible (as opposed to being visible only when you pass your mouse over a cell with the Comment). It is nice to have something always visible, but if you overuse this feature, your screen can become too cluttered.

To help make things easier, the file `ch03-04CommentsCatalog.xls` on the book's CD-ROM contains numerous samples of Comments (see Figure 3-14).

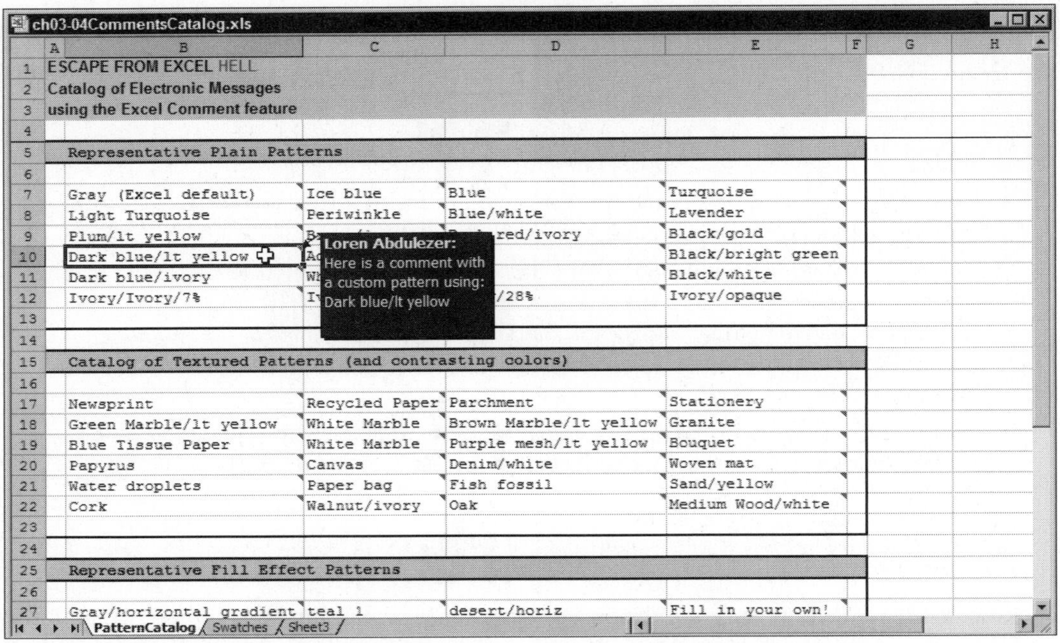

Figure 3-14: Comprehensive sampling of the various Excel Comments formats

It is worth your while to look through these (and look at both worksheet tabs). If you like any one of them, just copy the cell (Ctrl+C) and paste special (Edit⇨Paste Special and then click Comments in the Paste options) to your spreadsheet.

You'll find more information about Comments in Chapter 6 of my book *Excel Best Practices for Business* (published by Wiley).

Closing Thoughts

Part I of this book is meant to quickly put some useful information into your hands. It barely scratches the surface. Sometimes, scratching in the right places can relieve a nagging itch! I hope that this chapter and all the material in Part I can help you solve some real problems and provide some informative discussions and facts.

I discuss many easy fixes in Part II ("Escape in Under Two Minutes"). I've placed them in Part II because they are pieces used to solve harder problems.

This chapter is all about getting your spreadsheets in order. It focuses on the basics. The next chapter ratchets this up a notch by wresting control of your spreadsheet away from Excel and placing it into your hands.

Part II

Escape in Under Two Minutes

Chapter  4

Getting Excel to Behave

In This Chapter

- ◆ Managing worksheets: The more the merrier
- ◆ Hyperlinking and spreadsheet navigation
- ◆ Managing the user experience
- ◆ Using Conditional Formatting to keep formulas and formatting in sync
- ◆ Making worksheet headers and footers dynamic
- ◆ Keeping those pesky macros on their good behavior

It's time to burrow in deeper and put some of Excel's power features to use and at the same time command these features with precision and control.

One topic that almost never gets mentioned is worksheets. The focus relating to spreadsheets tends to be on formulas and formatting, not on managing worksheets. As spreadsheets grow in size and complexity, they tend to have more worksheets. At some point it becomes necessary to manage them. Because methods for dealing with them are usually an afterthought, they are typically unplanned and ad hoc. I give a more systematic treatment here.

Without specific aids to make you nimble, jumping across worksheets and even to other spreadsheets becomes cumbersome. I discuss some navigation aids you can put to use.

Spreadsheets that are large and complex don't start out that way. They grow and evolve organically over time. Every now and then, some midcourse corrections are needed. You may have a lot of worksheets and want to sort the worksheet tabs in some order. I give you tools to automate doing so.

When a spreadsheet gets complicated, managing user experience becomes an important issue. Sometimes this means having a spreadsheet open to a specific worksheet and cell. Imagine having a calendar-like spreadsheet where you have to record an entry for each day of the year. Wouldn't it be nice if the spreadsheet would jump to the cell for today's date anytime you open the file? I show you how to do this, and more.

Headers and footers are not quite as responsive as you may need them to be when you're preparing printed reports. You can put things into a worksheet header or footer, but getting them to adjust dynamically to some computation result is another matter. I give you some tools to facilitate this adjustment.

Give Your Worksheets a Real Workout

"I want to set up my spreadsheet and add a multiple number of worksheets quickly."

Excel makes it easy to add new worksheets. After you open a new spreadsheet, you can insert a worksheet by clicking Insert⇨Worksheet. To insert a group of worksheets in rapid succession, repeatedly press Ctrl+Y right after you insert a worksheet. The Ctrl+Y key combination repeats your most recent action. In this manner you can create a bunch of worksheets quickly and easily.

"My spreadsheet is already developed. I want to add new worksheets, but I want them to come from one of my templates."

An alternative way of inserting worksheets, one that gives you more options, is available. Simply right-click one of the worksheet tabs appearing on the bottom of your Excel workbook. Click Insert and pick a new worksheet, one of the templates, or an Excel chart. If you design your templates to make use of the Preview option, you can quickly decide which template to pick. It is a good practice to design your templates so that they include place-holders for answering the questions who, what, and when in the first three rows of the template.

When you're about to insert a worksheet or template, you will see two tabs in the Insert window, General and Spreadsheet Solutions. When you click the items in the Spreadsheet Solutions tab, you will see a preview, but with the exception of Loan Amortization, nothing meaningful is displayed in the preview. The moral of the story is to build your spreadsheets so that they always convey tangible and meaningful information at first glance.

TIP
If you have a library full of template worksheets, it may help you to store them as individual template files, but with only one worksheet in each template. Doing so will make combining a variety of worksheets within a single workbook easy.

Permanently altering new spreadsheet settings

You can permanently modify the default spreadsheet to have features such as Show Preview Picture. Here's how you do it. Before attempting this, proceed with extreme caution! Remember that these changes are permanent.

Look to see whether you have a `Book.xlt` file in the following location:

`C:\Documents and Settings\{your user name}\Application Data\Microsoft\Excel\XLSTART`

Where `{your user name}` appears, substitute it with the user name that is set on your computer. If a `Book.xlt` file already exists, make a backup copy just in case you need to revert to it at a later date. If you're doing this for the first time, chances are there is no `Book.xlt` file in this directory. The only file you'll see in this directory is `PERSONAL.XLS`. *Leave that file alone!*

If there is no `Book.xlt` file, create one. Open a new spreadsheet as you normally would. Make changes to the spreadsheet the way you want. For instance, you can enable the preview pictures in the file properties, or set it so that gridlines don't appear on the first worksheet. When you are satisfied with your settings, click File⇨Save As and set the Save as Type to Template (*.xlt). There are two small wrinkles to watch for:

- The filename may appear as something like `Book2.xlt`. Change it to `Book.xlt`. There should not be any digit in the middle of the name.

- The file directory may default to something like:

`C:\Documents and Settings\{your user name}\Application Data\Microsoft\Excel\Templates`

In this one instance, the Templates directory is the wrong one to use. You may have to navigate up one directory to locate the `XLSTART` directory. Make sure that you save `Book.xlt` in the `XLSTART` directory.

From this point onward your new workbooks should incorporate the features you built into `Book.xlt`. Should you need to go back to your original settings, you can restore your backup copy of `Book.xlt`. If you want to go back to the Excel defaults, simply remove `Book.xlt` from the `XLSTART` directory.

Managing Multiple Worksheets in a Single Workbook

Accumulating information inside a spreadsheet is easy. One worksheet for each month is very convenient during the first year. By the time you start getting to the second year, you may start wondering whether it's becoming too much of a good thing.

"I inserted a whole bunch of new worksheets into my workbook (using Ctrl+Y to repeat the inserts). Excel is inserting the worksheets to the left, so I end up with something like Sheet9, Sheet8, Sheet7, Sheet6, Sheet5, Sheet4, Sheet1, Sheet2, Sheet3. This is not how I want them ordered. Is there any way I can reorganize them so that they follow a natural order such as Sheet1, Sheet2, Sheet3, Sheet4. . .?"

You can reorder them by clicking the worksheet tab and dragging it to the right or left. There are, however, easier ways to do this reordering, as described next.

MANUALLY MOVING WORKSHEET TABS IS A REAL DRAG!

"I have too many worksheet tabs that have to be arranged alphabetically to drag them manually. Is there some automated way of doing this?"

When you're moving a half-dozen worksheets, it's not so bad, but when you have more worksheets, adjusting them to alphabetical order is time consuming and prone to error. I think you want to minimize this kind of electronic pencil pushing.

Out of the box, Excel does not provide this capability. An add-in prepared especially for this book allows you to do this, however. Appendix B, "Installing the Escape Excel Hell Utility Pak," describes how to install this add-in.

After the add-in is installed, notice the two icons with "WS" symbols. One of them has an arrow pointing to the right. Clicking this arrow will reorganize the worksheets of your active workbook from left to right. Clicking the other icon works in the opposite direction.

 NOTE

Alphabetical order means alphabetical order. So, if you have Sheet8, Sheet9, Sheet10, Sheet81, and Sheet80, when they are sorted alphabetically, the sequence would be Sheet10, Sheet8, Sheet80, Sheet81, Sheet9.

This type of order may not be what you intend. There are two ways you can deal with this problem. One is to rename single-digit sheets with double digits so that Sheet8 is renamed to Sheet08, Sheet9 to Sheet09, and so on. After all the sheets are sorted, you can rename them in their original single-digit form if you want.

Alternatively, if the worksheets with double-digit tabs can be selected as a contiguous group, and then they can be sorted as a group. After doing that, repeat the process for the worksheet tabs with single digits.

You may have many worksheets but want to sort only a certain group of them. As long as you can select them as a contiguous group of worksheets, you can sort them. To select multiple worksheets side by side, press Ctrl+Shift+PgDn or Ctrl+Shift+PgUp.

"I have my worksheets organized with dates like January-2006, August-2005, and so on. I need to sort these worksheets tabs by date, not alphabetical order."

As with the previous worksheet sort facilities, another toolbar icon has a "date" symbol on it. It works the same way as the other two, but with a couple of caveats.

- The Sort facility recognizes fully qualified dates such as 21-Aug-2003 or Feb-2006, but it sees Aug-04 as the fourth day of August.

- To avoid type mismatch errors, do not sort worksheets having names that cannot be resolved to dates. An example of this is a worksheet tab with the name May2006 or 29-Feb2006. Remember, 2006 is not a leap year, so there is no 29th of February in the year 2006.

- Of course, not all your worksheets in a given workbook will necessarily have dates coded into the worksheet tabs. You might, for instance, have a SummarySheet in addition to all the worksheet tabs appearing as dates. As long as you can group select a contiguous group of worksheet tabs, you can arrange them by date.

NOTE

Those of you who want to inspect the macro code in the add-in will find that it is password protected. However, the password for any of the password-protected files in *Escape from Excel Hell* is simply `password`.

OH, I'VE GOT PLENTY OF WORKSHEETS

"I have a whole bunch of worksheets. How do I go to a specific worksheet?"

Your spreadsheet may have plenty of worksheets—so many worksheets that you can't see all the worksheet tabs at one time. You can move the worksheet tabs to the right or left using the tab scrolling buttons. These are located on the bottom-left corner of your workbook and to the left of the worksheet tabs. They appear as "arrowed" or triangular notches. The two inner buttons scroll one worksheet tab in the direction of the arrow. The two outer buttons move the worksheet tabs to the extreme left or extreme right. It is important to note that though the tabs scroll to the left or right, the worksheet that you are viewing doesn't change. The worksheet you are viewing changes only when you click another worksheet tab.

If you right-click any of the tab scrolling buttons, you will see a pop-up list of worksheets with the active worksheet checked (see Figure 4-1). The pop-up list displays 16 worksheets at most. If you have more than 16 worksheets in your workbook, you will see a More Sheets option at the bottom of the list. You can click this option to produce a scrollable list of worksheets.

Here's the quick-and-easy way to navigate to any of the worksheets. Simply press Ctrl+PgUp or Ctrl+PgDn. If your keyboard is set to auto-repeat, you will find that it takes only a few seconds to sift through 50 or 100 worksheets. Believe it or not, people actually use spreadsheets with this many worksheets.

"I have many identically structured worksheets; one for each employee. When I go from the worksheet for EmployeeA to EmployeeB, I would like to keep the cell position from my prior worksheet."

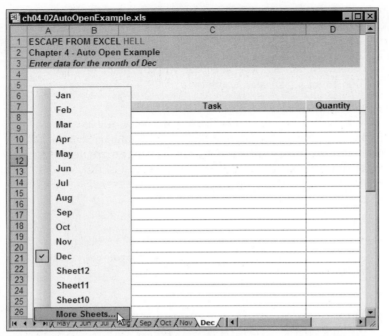

Figure 4-1: Right-clicking worksheet scroll buttons enables you to jump directly to a worksheet.

If you loaded the Escape Excel Hell Utility Pak Add-In, you already possess the means to retain your previous worksheet's cell position through the following keyboard commands: Ctrl+Shift+J and Ctrl+Shift+L. These work the same way as Ctrl+PgUp and Ctrl+PgDn, except that the cell positions are kept the same when going from sheet to sheet. If you select cell H23:H1023 in Sheet2 and press Ctrl+Shift+L, then on the next sheet, H23:H1023 will also be selected.

Controlling the User Experience with Navigation Aids

There are many ways of jumping around to different parts of a spreadsheet, or even among multiple spreadsheets. The simplest way to do so is to give user-defined names to key regions in your spreadsheet. Then you can press Ctrl+G to bring up a Go To window that displays the defined names, select the name, and click the OK button to go to that location.

TIP

If you have a large number of user-defined names, it may take longer to find the name in the list than it would to directly sift through the spreadsheet. There are things you can do to place special key locations at the front of the Go To list so that you don't waste time searching for them.

You may have names like FixedExpenses or VariableExpenses that you need to go to. You can bump these names up to the front of the list by giving them names like AssumptionForFixedExpenses, AssumptionForVariableExpenses, and so forth.

Incidentally, you don't need to alter any of the formulas that use names like FixedExpenses. You can keep the original names and just overlay new names on the same location. For instance, both AssumptionForFixedExpenses and FixedExpenses can have the cell location `A14` of Sheet2.

Go To is useful if you happen to know the names defined in the spreadsheet. Generally, the only people who know these things are the spreadsheet authors. If your spreadsheet is going to third parties, you want to make navigation as easy as possible. In this instance, Go To is not the navigation tool of choice. Better navigation aids are hyperlinks and command buttons, discussed next.

Hyperlinks

Excel provides hyperlink facilities in two forms that shouldn't be confused with one another:

- One of these hyperlink facilities sees any text that looks like a URL and automatically turns it into a Web link, in much the same way that Excel automatically converts text that looks like a date into a serial number. No Excel function is involved.

- Excel has a special HYPERLINK function that can point to a URL, or to a worksheet location within the same workbook or a remote workbook.

TEXT AS A HYPERLINK

"How do I turn off the automatic hyperlink functionality in Excel?"

Excel has the tendency to see anything that starts with a "www" and turn it into a hyperlink. Excel doesn't ask your permission to convert text into a hyperlink; it just automatically does it. This automatic conversion can be problematic if you are revising and editing a mailing list with hundreds of e-mail addresses. Every time you click a cell to edit one of the e-mail addresses, Outlook Express or your e-mail program pops up!

To fix this problem, click Tools⇨AutoCorrect Options and, in the AutoFormat As You Type tab, uncheck Internet and Network Paths with Hyperlinks.

THE EXCEL HYPERLINK FUNCTION

If your spreadsheet gets large and complex, you may want to provide some navigation aids to allow users to quickly jump to different places in the spreadsheet. Conveniently, Excel provides a HYPERLINK function.

The syntax for HYPERLINK is easy:

```
HYPERLINK(link_location[,friendly_name])
```

Here are some examples of HYPERLINK:

```
=HYPERLINK("http://www.EscapeFromExcelHell.com")
=HYPERLINK("http://www.excelbestpractices.com","Link to Excel Best Practices")
=HYPERLINK("A1","Back to top of sheet")
=HYPERLINK("#[SomeRemoteSpreadsheet.xls]ReportSheet3!A1","Link to Quarterly
Summary")
=HYPERLINK("#[ButtonNavigator.xls]IndexSheet2!A5","Back to Index Sheet")
```

HYPERLINK provides the ability to navigate to multiple workbooks, provided that they are open. When you create large and complex spreadsheets, you'll often find it helpful to incorporate a single "index sheet" with links to all the relevant parts of the spreadsheet. If you are using a central navigating page, it is important to provide a "cookie trail" back to the central page.

> *"I use hyperlinks to navigate between worksheets. I constantly have to update the link locations in them every time I change a workbook or worksheet name. Is there any way to do this without having to perform surgery on individual hyperlink formulas?"*

There is an easy fix to this, but the formulas are a bit daunting. The concept is simple. The link location used by HYPERLINK is a piece of text you supply it. This text can be a quoted string such as "A1," or it can be a user-defined name or formula that returns a link location as text.

Generally, the way to do this is to create a user-defined name, give it a value of some cell coordinates, and, in the HYPERLINK formula, reference that name. You can find an example of this in the ch04_01ButtonNavigator.xls file on the book's CD. The Config worksheet contains a user-defined name, IndexSheet.

Essentially, all the worksheets in this spreadsheet have a Back to Index Sheet hyperlink. Rather than use a hardwired value of 'IndexSheet2'!A5, they all point to the user-defined name IndexSheet. Currently, IndexSheet has the value of

```
="'IndexSheet2'!A5"
```

At the drop of a hat, this value can be changed to any other location. As the location described by IndexSheet is changed, all the HYPERLINK formulas are instantly adjusted.

Incidentally, the hyperlink formula used is

```
=HYPERLINK("#"&CELL("address",INDIRECT(IndexSheet)),"Back to Index Sheet")
```

The formula looks scary but is easy to update and maintain. You can change IndexSheet to another name that you may want to use. Also, you can easily adjust the friendly text portion ("Back to Index Sheet").

Managing the User Experience

"My spreadsheet has a group of worksheet tabs labeled Jan, Feb, Mar, ..., Dec. I want the spreadsheet to auto-matically open to the worksheet that corresponds to the current month. Further, I want the spreadsheet to go directly to the current day."

Excel has a `Workbook_Open()` macro that will immediately execute whenever the workbook is opened.

You could hardwire the macro to solve only this problem, but this would not be a good practice. Instead, I recommend that you use a spreadsheet tool (`ch04_02AutoOpenExample.xls`, found on the book's CD) that allows you to customize the behavior without having to touch one line of macro code. Here is how it works: On the Config worksheet of `ch04_02AutoOpenExample.xls`, you will see, on rows eight and nine, the location of where the spreadsheet should open. Rather than hardwire this location inside a macro, compute it as a regular spreadsheet formula. As an example, the worksheet to open to uses the formula:

```
=TEXT(TODAY(),"mmm")
```

This code results in values such as `Jan`, `Feb`, `Mar`..., and these happen to match the worksheet tabs for this file. If your worksheet tabs were sequenced like this: `January-2007`, `February-2007`, and so on, you could use a formula such as this:

```
=TEXT(TODAY("mmmm-yyyy")
```

This formula assumes that you already have worksheets in your workbook that correspond to the current day in your computer system's clock.

> **NOTE**
>
> I've thrown a couple of extra features into this spreadsheet. When the spreadsheet opens, you may want the spreadsheet to take up the full size of the application window so that it's the only spreadsheet visible. Additionally, you may want Excel to be the only application visible. You can control these aspects by adjusting the `TRUE`/`FALSE` values of `ConfigActiveWindowMax` and `ConfigApplWindowMax` (see Figure 4-2).
>
> But wait, there's more! Your spreadsheet, with the calendar dates as is, contains macros. You may want to distribute your spreadsheet without any macros. Rather than have you go through the process of extricating the macros, why not have the spreadsheet without any macros to begin with?! That's right: Place all your data on a remote workbook with absolutely no macros whatsoever.
>
> Have this Auto Open tool perform all the operations on the remote workbook instead of itself. Sound complicated? Simply change the value for the `RemoteWorkbookName` (located in `B13` of your Config worksheet) to an Excel spreadsheet filename of your choosing. Of course, the remote workbook will need to have the worksheet tabs that match the setting in the Auto Open tool.

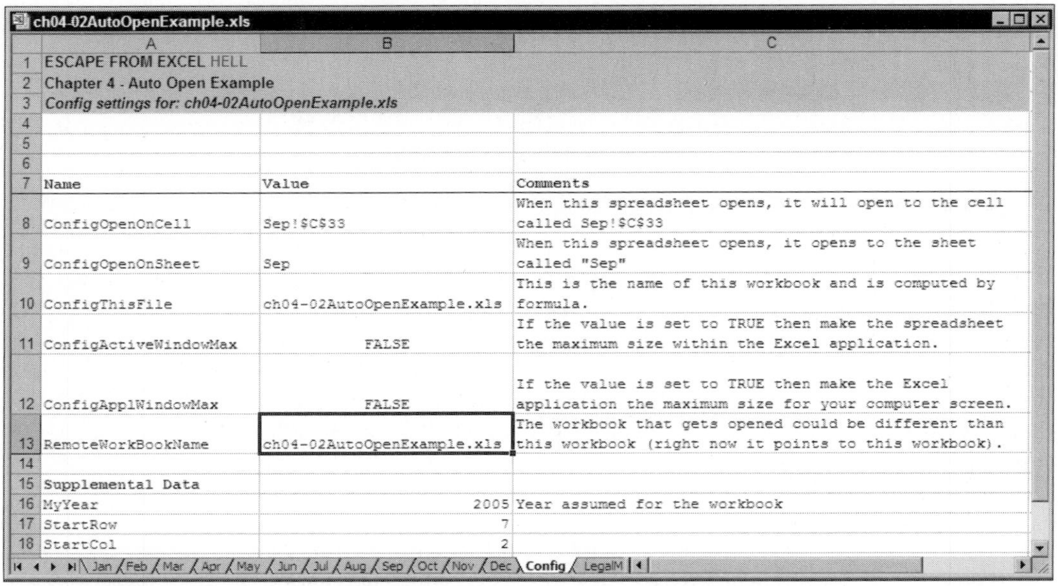

ch04-02AutoOpenExample.xls

	A	B	C
1	ESCAPE FROM EXCEL HELL		
2	Chapter 4 - Auto Open Example		
3	*Config settings for: ch04-02AutoOpenExample.xls*		
4			
5			
6			
7	Name	Value	Comments
8	ConfigOpenOnCell	Sep!$C$33	When this spreadsheet opens, it will open to the cell called Sep!$C$33
9	ConfigOpenOnSheet	Sep	When this spreadsheet opens, it opens to the sheet called "Sep"
10	ConfigThisFile	ch04-02AutoOpenExample.xls	This is the name of this workbook and is computed by formula.
11	ConfigActiveWindowMax	FALSE	If the value is set to TRUE then make the spreadsheet the maximum size within the Excel application.
12	ConfigApplWindowMax	FALSE	If the value is set to TRUE then make the Excel application the maximum size for your computer screen.
13	RemoteWorkBookName	ch04-02AutoOpenExample.xls	The workbook that gets opened could be different than this workbook (right now it points to this workbook).
14			
15	Supplemental Data		
16	MyYear	2005	Year assumed for the workbook
17	StartRow	7	
18	StartCol	2	

Jan / Feb / Mar / Apr / May / Jun / Jul / Aug / Sep / Oct / Nov / Dec / Config / LegalM

Figure 4-2: Auto Open Settings

There are a couple more pearls I want you to harvest from this tool.

In Figure 4-3, you will notice the series of dates that appear in column B. In the Feb worksheet, the date entries range from February 1st to February 28th, unless the year in question happens to be a leap year. So, if the year is 2008, a February 29th entry will automatically appear. For all the other worksheet tabs, you will see the entries automatically going from either 1 to 30, or 1 to 31, depending on how many days there are in the month.

Do you think I'm going to bother with individually preparing each month differently based on having to know exactly how many days (and how many entries to make) occur for each month? Certainly not! Neither you nor I should spend our precious time on electronic pencil pushing.

I want to deconstruct the formulas and explain their logic. I also want to explain how the formatting keeps in synch with the formulas.

Look at what is occurring in Figure 4-3, which shows a sample page for one of the date entry worksheets. The goal is very simple: Prepare the formulas and formatting for all 31 days, regardless of whether that month has 31, 30, 28, or 29 days. Have the formula sense when the day number exceeds the allotment for the month and shut itself off. At the same time, use conditional formatting to also sense this so that the data entry region is resized.

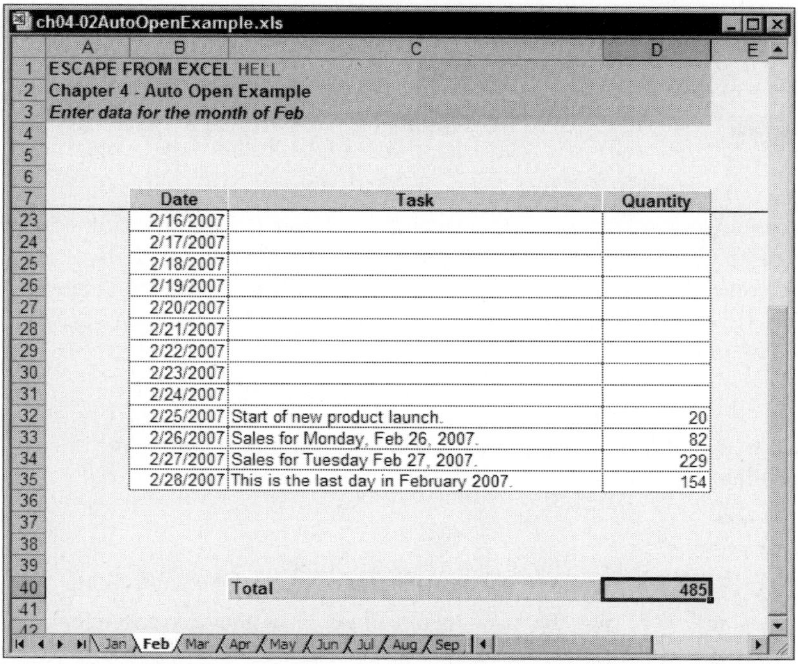

	Date	Task	Quantity
23	2/16/2007		
24	2/17/2007		
25	2/18/2007		
26	2/19/2007		
27	2/20/2007		
28	2/21/2007		
29	2/22/2007		
30	2/23/2007		
31	2/24/2007		
32	2/25/2007	Start of new product launch.	20
33	2/26/2007	Sales for Monday, Feb 26, 2007.	82
34	2/27/2007	Sales for Tuesday Feb 27, 2007.	229
35	2/28/2007	This is the last day in February 2007.	154
40		Total	485

Figure 4-3: Dates in column B are automatically populated for each month.

Here is the basic logic for the serial dates appearing in column B. To get the serial dates to shut themselves off, you have to ask the question, "When do I suddenly switch from one month to the next?" As a formula, this has to be asked in a convoluted way. You have to say something like "Is one day after yesterday's date (which is displayed one row above me) suddenly in the next month?" If it is, you tell it to shut itself off. The actual formula (in B38) that does this is as follows:

```
=IF(B37="","",IF(MONTH(B37+1)>MONTH(B$8),"",B37+1))
```

"I want a formula in general that always gives me my current worksheet name."

Notice that in each of the date worksheets the third row mentions the month or, actually, the name of the current worksheet. This is done by a formula. In essence, here is a formula that you can copy and paste into any spreadsheet to give you the current worksheet name (in cell A1):

```
=MID(CELL("filename",A1),FIND("]",CELL("filename",A1))+1,LEN(CELL("filename",A1)))
```

This formula is employed in the third row of each of the date worksheets of `ch04_02AutoOpenExample.xls`. It is also incorporated into the formula for cell B8 to compute the first date of the month.

"I copied your spreadsheet formula for showing me the worksheet name into a spreadsheet to experiment with it. All I get is a #VALUE! error. Shouldn't your formula work?"

It should, but let me ask a question. Is your spreadsheet saved? If it hasn't been saved, it has not been given a filename. Therefore, there is no filename that can be returned for `CELL("filename")` or `CELL("filename",A1)`. Save your spreadsheet and force a recalc (press F9).

Some further observations are worthy of your attention. Notice that I use a function called CELL. This function enables you to obtain specific information. For instance, `CELL("filename")` tells you the filename along with the complete path all the way up to the current sheet.

 CAUTION

There are two ways of specifying CELL: with and without its optional argument. You can use the formulas either way:

```
=CELL("filename")
=CELL("filename",A1)
```

Both of these will give you the complete filename all the way up to the worksheet.

On the surface, they appear to give the same results. If you have multiple copies of this formula, one on each worksheet, then the results won't match.

Try the following. Open the `takeaway.txt` file, which is located on the book's CD-ROM. You will see the following two formulas:

```
=MID(CELL("filename",A1),FIND("]",CELL("filename",A1))+1,LEN(CELL
("filename",A1)))
=MID(CELL("filename"),FIND("]",CELL("filename"))+1,LEN(CELL("file
name")))
```

In your text editor (probably Notepad), select them both and then copy and paste them into a spreadsheet file. Both formulas should result in the current sheet name, such as Sheet1. Now click another sheet in the *same* workbook and paste the formulas once more. Both of these will display the same results (such as Sheet2). Now comes the weird part: Click back on the first sheet. Remember that they were both Sheet1? One of them has magically changed to Sheet2!

I'm not yet done with this spreadsheet. Notice that the stylish-looking list in columns B, C, and D stop at exactly the end of the month. This is accomplished using conditional formatting. Here are the steps involved:

1. Because the Jan to Dec worksheets are all identically positioned and formatted, you can group select all these worksheets at one time and accomplish the conditional formatting in one step.

   To group them, click the Jan worksheet and then repeatedly press Ctrl+Shift+PgDn until all the worksheets you want are grouped.

2. Select the region of cells you want conditionally formatted. In this case, it is the cells B8:E38. Make note of the cell coordinate in the top-left corner (B8).

3. From the Excel menu, click Format⇨Conditional Formatting.

A Conditional Formatting window pops up (see Figure 4-4).

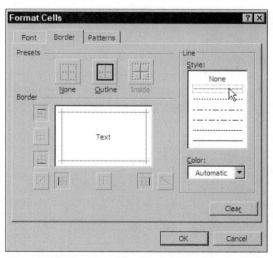

Figure 4-4: Conditional formatting using a formula instead of a cell value

Notice the drop-down list with the options Cell Value Is and Formula Is. Click the Formula Is option. Now place the following in the formula:

=LEN($B8)>0

This formula basically says that if anything is in column B, then apply the special formatting for this condition (Excel gives you up to three conditions to test for).

Now click the Format button (see Figure 4-5) to set the appearance. In this particular spreadsheet, I have set the general background to be an ivory color with no gridlines. I want the data entry area to have a white background and dotted gridlines, so I select a white pattern and a dotted border.

Figure 4-5: Set the appearance of the conditionally formatted cell.

4. Right-click any of the grouped worksheet tabs and select Ungroup Sheets (see Figure 4-6); then, save your file.

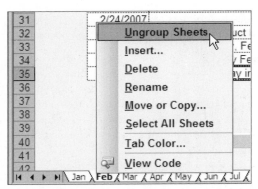

Figure 4-6: Ungroup sheets from the worksheet tabs.

One last point before moving on: Notice that the blue regions, such as C40:E40, have a slightly three-dimensional appearance to them. The use of this technique can give your spreadsheet a professional appearance. The key to having this appearance is to custom format the cell borders. Press Ctrl+1 to format the cells and then click the Borders tab. Give the top and left borders a slightly brighter color than both the cell's background pattern and those of its surrounding cells. Give the bottom and right borders a slightly darker color than both the cell's background pattern and those of its surrounding cells (see Figure 4-7).

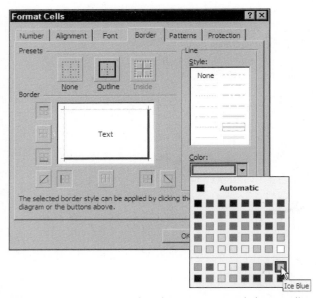

Figure 4-7: Use custom borders to give worksheet cells a subtle 3D appearance.

More Bells and Whistles

Although having a nice-looking spreadsheet is good, I want to show you more features you can use.

"I want to revise my headers and footers in one step and automatically use values computed in the spreadsheet."

The spreadsheet file `ch04_03BellsWhistles.xls` has some additional features built into the previous Auto Open tool. The `ch04_03BellsWhistles.xls` file runs a special Workbook_BeforePrint routine that can update the headers and footers before the worksheet gets printed. It picks up values from spreadsheet computations. Starting in row 20 of the Config worksheet are placeholders for the various page headers and footers. The results of the computations in column B are placed in the corresponding header or footer. You can test this using the print preview feature of Excel.

For example, the left header picks up the value from the spreadsheet formula:

```
="Random value: "&RAND()
```

"I want my headers and footers to make use of custom formatting, such as subscripts and superscripts."

To create a subscript markup code, surround the subscript with &Y. For instance, the chemical description of water (H_2O) would appear as:

```
H&Y&2&YO
```

Superscripts work the same way except that you use the &X markup symbol instead of &Y. More formatting examples are shown in the spreadsheet.

"I want the & symbol to appear in my header or footer."

Enter the **&** symbol twice. As an example, to get the expression `John Wiley & Sons, Inc.`, you enter **John Wiley && Sons, Inc.** Depending on what you are doing, you may want &Y to appear in the header or footer and not be treated as a subscript markup symbol. To accomplish this, enter **&&Y** instead of **&Y**. The same is true of the other kinds of markups involving &.

"I want to be able to individually turn off and on the specific headers and footers."

A simple text switch is used in column C. Type the word **ON** and the respective header/footer will be used when you print. Type the word **OFF** and nothing will appear. If there is anything other than ON or OFF in the column, whatever was used for the header/footer continues to be used.

"I want to print selected worksheets in my workbook in one step without having to print each individual worksheet one at a time."

Group select the worksheet tabs you want printed and then print as you normally would for an individual worksheet. Here are some reminders concerning group selecting worksheets:

- You can add an individual worksheet to the group selection by Ctrl+clicking the worksheet tab. Ctrl+clicking once more will deselect the worksheet tab.

- If you have a contiguous range of sheets that you want selected, you can select the first sheet, hold down the Shift key, and select the last worksheet in the range.

Incidentally, if you want to print all the worksheets in your workbook, right-click any worksheet tab, choose Select All Sheets, and print.

Those Pesky Macros

You may have noticed that I don't shy away from using macros but I do my best to keep you from having to touch macro code. Sometimes, this is unavoidable and you may need to work with macros, even if you're not doing any coding. For this reason, I include some information here.

CAUTION

Making changes in the VB Editor can be dangerous if you are not already experienced in VBA development. It is always wise to get some help from a colleague who does have extensive experience in VBA and macro development. At the very least, consult some of the standard literature references, such as *Excel 2003 Power Programming with VBA* by John Walkenbach (Wiley Publishing, Inc.).

"How do I open a spreadsheet without allowing its autostart macro to run?"

From the Excel menu, click File⇨Open and select the file you're about to open. Before clicking the Open button, hold down the Shift key. This action launches the file without activating any of the macros.

"I have a spreadsheet that I use and want to strip out the macros before giving it to other people. I press Alt+F8 and delete all the macros, but I still get the Security Warning whenever the spreadsheet is open. I know for a fact that I have removed all the macros in the spreadsheet!"

TIP

As a good practice, make a backup copy of your file before making changes to your files with the VB Editor.

Launch the VB Editor (Alt+F11) and look inside the VBA Project Explorer to find your spreadsheet project. If you don't see the VBA Project Explorer window, press Ctrl+R. Locate the Modules folder with your project file. *Make absolutely certain that you are working on the correct spreadsheet project file. You do not want to inadvertently strip out code for another project file!*

 TIP

Before you start the VB Editor, it is a good idea to close all open spreadsheets to which you do not need to make changes. This way, you reduce the chances of making an unintended change to a spreadsheet file.

Inside the folder will be one or more Module files that contain the macro code for your spreadsheet. Even though all the macro code may already be removed from these individual modules, you still have to remove the modules themselves.

Select each module and, from the context menu (right-click to see it), select Remove *ModuleName*. Remove all the modules and save your file (Ctrl+S). Press Alt+F11 to toggle back to your regular Excel mode. Close your file and reopen it.

The macro warning should no longer appear. If it does, you still have some macro code in your spreadsheet. Open the VB Editor once more. There should be no Modules folder associated with your spreadsheet. If there is, remove any modules inside the Modules folder.

If you find no Modules folder, look to see whether there is any macro code with the individual objects inside the Microsoft Excel Objects folder. Locate the `ThisWorkbook` object; there may be one of those auto open routines in it. View the code for this object (click View Code from the context menu), and if it has any macro code, delete auto open code and click Save. There may also be some event macros hidden in one of the Excel "Sheet" objects located in the Microsoft Excel Objects folder. If you are still having trouble eliminating the macros warning, seek the assistance of a professional VBA programmer.

"How do I copy a macro from one workbook to another (such as from your book example to my file)?"

Obviously, you can open a spreadsheet, save it as a new filename, and pare it down to only those elements you need. This is easy to do, but it may not give you enough flexibility. What if you want to mix code from multiple workbooks into one spreadsheet? Assuming that there are no code conflicts, here is how you do it: From the VB Editor, you can export code from individual modules in a spreadsheet. Select the module containing the code you want to export. Press Ctrl+E to export the file. After being exported, it can be imported into another spreadsheet.

You can later import them into other spreadsheet (from VB workbook project, press Ctrl+M and select the module to import).

CAUTION

Make sure that there are no naming or code conflicts. If a macro references a user-defined name from the spreadsheet, you will want the name defined in your target spreadsheet.

If the macro refers to a user-defined name in one of the worksheets, you need to make sure that it also exists in the spreadsheet you are copying the macro to. As an example, a number of macros used in this book make use of user-defined names within the Config worksheet. Here are the steps you can perform to replicate the macros from a source workbook to a target workbook (assuming that the user-defined names all exist within the Config worksheet):

1. Make a backup copy of your target workbook.

2. Within Excel, open both your source and target workbook.

3. Right-click to select the Config worksheet tab of your source workbook; then, click Move or Copy.

4. Within the Move or Copy window, place a checkmark next to Create a Copy. In the To Book pull-down list, select the target workbook. Choose where you want the copied sheet to go to and click OK.

   If for some reason you have a lot of text inside one of the spreadsheet cells, Excel will complain and display a warning message, and will truncate the lengthy text to 255 characters. If you don't want to have truncated text for these cells, individually copy and paste the text content from your source worksheet to the target worksheet.

5. Open your VB Editor (Alt+F11) and export the modules from the source workbooks that you need to replicate. These will be saved as `.bas` files on your hard drive.

6. From the VB Project Editor, select the target workbook and press Ctrl+M to import a file; then, select the file you exported and complete the import. Repeat this process as necessary until you have the required import modules.

7. Before saving the changes to your target workbook, look over the macro code to make sure that it is what you want. When you are satisfied, you can toggle back to your regular Excel mode by pressing Alt+F11. Run your macro to verify that it works as intended, and save your target workbook.

Closing Thoughts

This chapter has a singular focus or aim, and so does much of this book. It's not just to give you a bunch of practical tips and techniques, and it's not just to give you sample tools and spreadsheets you can use. These are things I know you'll derive from the book and through other sources.

I really want you to learn techniques for managing complex spreadsheets. It is very easy for things to get messy and out of control. When they do, the fixes applied are often the wrong ones. Sometimes they work but actually sweep the problem under the rug. Those are the kinds of problems that come back to haunt you big time. And those are the ones I want you to avoid. In the chapters to follow, I continue to harp on this theme.

The next chapter addresses formula problems and fixes.

Part II

Chapter 5

Getting Correct Results with Excel Formulas

In This Chapter

- ◆ Activating Function Tooltips
- ◆ Using Excel aids in constructing formulas
- ◆ Converting dates and time
- ◆ Working with calendar arithmetic
- ◆ Representing angles
- ◆ Converting data involving units and measures

The earlier chapters in this book deal with keeping Excel's behavior in check. It's time to turn your attention to spreadsheet-centric problems as opposed to Excel-centric problems. This shift in focus, though subtle, is important. It gets to the heart of what spreadsheets are about and how to get maximum mileage out of using spreadsheets.

Other than in limited parts of this chapter, I focus on the kinds of problems frequently found when working a spreadsheet application, and not in configuring the software. Rest assured that you will still learn plenty of Excel features and tips along the way.

Entering Formulas

"I get lost when typing in formulas. Does Excel provide any facility to help me?"

Function Tooltips

Several aids are available to you for entering formulas. First, click Tools⇨Options⇨ General and make sure that there is a checkmark next to Function Tooltips. Users of Excel 2000 and earlier may not have the Function Tooltips available to them.

DISPLAYING SYNTAX USAGE

When you have this option enabled, Excel displays the syntax usage for the function you are currently editing immediately below the Formula Bar (see Figure 5-1). There are several things to note:

- In the list of arguments displayed in the Function Tooltips, the one you are currently entering is shown in boldface. (In Figure 5-1, the second argument, OrderedDataset, is currently being entered. The **OrderedDataset** is the table_array portion in the VLOOKUP(lookup_value, **table_array**, col_index_num, [range_lookup]) formula.)

- Arguments that are displayed with square brackets around them are *optional arguments*. Excel will assume certain values if you don't specify the values for the optional argument.

  For instance, notice that the last argument range_lookup in Figure 5-1 has square brackets around it and is treated as an optional argument. The name range_lookup is unfortunately not suggestive of its purpose, nor of the valid kinds of values that it can have. The values for range_lookup can be TRUE or FALSE. Its purpose is to alert Excel of whether the table_array elements are strictly arranged in ascending order.

  Perhaps most important, no hint is generally provided to alert you to what default value Excel assumes. (For the function VLOOKUP, the default value for its optional argument range_lookup is defined to be TRUE.)

- Notice that as you pass the mouse over each argument, the mouse pointer turns into a hand. In Figure 5-1, the mouse is hovering over lookup_value. If you click the lookup_value, the lookup value (A12) will be selected.

Figure 5-1: Function Tooltips display arguments for Excel functions.

This last feature of the Function Tooltips serves an important purpose. It can help you avoid errors when typing a complicated formula.

EDITING NESTED FORMULAS

"I have a complicated formula that tests errors in an expression, and the expression is used later in the formula. I try selecting the expression to copy and paste it within the formula. It's way too easy to make a mistake with all the nested parentheses. Can you give me a surefire way of selecting subexpressions?"

Here is a formula you might be caught with entering:

```
=IF(ISERROR(VLOOKUP($A11,AT$4:AT$46,1,FALSE)),0,VLOOKUP($A11,AT$4:AT$46,1,FALS
E))
```

Basically, the structure of this formula is

```
=IF(logical_test,value_if_true,value_if_false)
```

The `logical_test` happens to be

```
ISERROR(VLOOKUP($A11,AT$4:AT$46,1,FALSE))
```

As shown in Figure 5-2, all that has been typed into the Formula Bar is

```
=IF(ISERROR(VLOOKUP($A11,AT$4:AT$46,1,FALSE)),0,
```

The rest of the formula needs to be entered without typographical errors. What remains to be completed is essentially a repeat of the VLOOKUP function with its arguments.

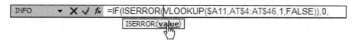

Figure 5-2: Small pieces of a complicated formula can be selected (in this case, the argument for ISERROR).

Place your insertion point between `ISERROR(` and `VLOOKUP`, as shown in Figure 5-2. Doing so displays the `ISERROR(`**value**`)` below that point. When you click **value**, all of `VLOOKUP($A11,AT$4:AT$46,1,FALSE)` is selected in your Formula Bar. Now you can press Ctrl+C to copy it to the clipboard. Click the end of the formula and paste it (Ctrl+V). To complete the formula, you need to add a closing parenthesis at the end.

The skills you develop here in isolating portions of a lengthy formula will come in handy when you are working with extremely hairy formulas.

TIP

If you want to insert the arguments for a function into the Formula Bar, you can press Ctrl+Shift+A. For example, if you are entering a VLOOKUP function and have entered only the following in the Formula Bar:

```
=VLOOKUP(
```

Part II

you can press Ctrl+Shift+A to complete the function. The entered formula in the Formula Bar is now:

```
=VLOOKUP(lookup_value,table_array,col_index_num,range_lookup)
```

Of course, you will have to substitute these argument labels with cell coordinates or user-defined names to get a valid result from your formula. Note that the optional argument label is inserted but is not highlighted with square brackets, as is done with the Function Tooltips. Fortunately, you can still make use of the Function Tooltips here.

Tools That Assist in Constructing Excel Formulas

Excel provides three kinds of tools to assist you in constructing formulas: help information, cell reference handles, and parenthesis matching.

HELP INFORMATION

"I am about to enter a formula, but I am not certain which Excel function to use. How can I find out more information?"

From the Excel menu, click Insert⇨Function. Within the Insert Function window is a pull-down list, as shown in Figure 5-3. It certainly pays to select the All category; when you do, you see the list of every Excel function. As you select any of the functions, you can see that function's syntax and a very brief description (see the left part of Figure 5-4).

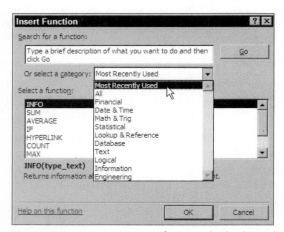

Figure 5-3: You can insert a function by looking through the various categories.

You can also click the `Help on this function` link at the bottom-left corner of the Insert Function window. Clicking this link pops up a Microsoft Excel Help window (the right part of Figure 5-4) on the currently selected function.

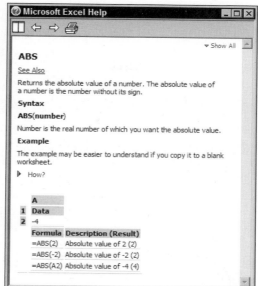

Figure 5-4: Getting information about Excel functions

Close the Microsoft Excel Help window and click the OK button of the Insert Function window (the left window in Figure 5-4). A Function Arguments window appears (see Figure 5-5). You can enter a test value to see what the Excel function returns. Your test value can include other cells from the spreadsheet. Also note that as you type your test value, the Excel Formula Bar is populated with the completed formula (top of Figure 5-5).

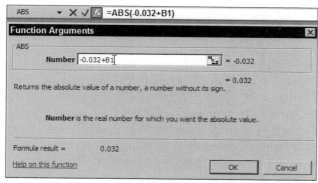

Figure 5-5: Test the results of your formula before you commit to it.

To obtain a cell reference, click the Collapse Dialog icon. This is a red, white, and blue graphic (vaguely resembling an American flag) that appears on the right side of the Number argument in Figure 5-5. When you click the Collapse Dialog icon, the Function Arguments window will collapse, allowing you to select a cell or range of cells in your spreadsheet (see Figure 5-6).

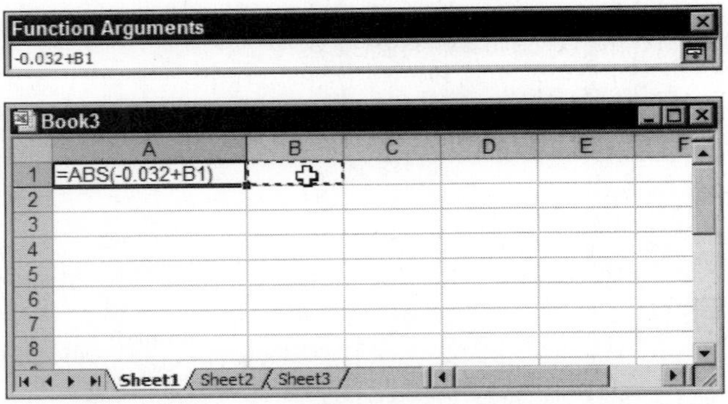

Figure 5-6: Inserting a cell reference in one of the Excel function arguments

When you're finished with assembling the cell reference (by entering + and clicking the B1 cell), you can click the Expand Dialog icon that appears on the top-right corner of Figure 5-6 and kind of resembles a roller-type window shade. To commit your formula, click the OK button of the Function Arguments window.

CELL REFERENCE HANDLES

"I pasted a formula from another cell. It is almost correct, but some of the cell ranges need to be readjusted. Is there any way I can do this quickly and easily?"

Figure 5-7 shows a formula that is supposed to return the sum of the numbers in the shaded area (cells C5:E8). Instead, it is returning the sum of cells C6:E9. If you look at the formula:

=SUM(C6:E9)

you may not spot the error quickly. However, if you click inside the Formula Bar, shown in the top of Figure 5-7, you will see color borders for the argument framing the cells C6:E9. You can not only immediately spot the error but also resize and reposition the borders. Simply click and drag its corner "handle bars." Try repositioning the borders so that they form a tight perimeter around the gray area (cells C5:E8). Guess what—as you resize and reposition the formula reference handles, the formula is automatically readjusted. You will end up with the intended formula of

=SUM(C5:E8)

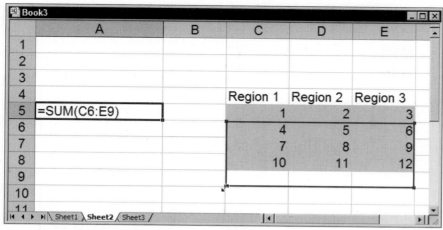

Figure 5-7: Adjusting cell references in a formula visually.

ENTERING FORMULAS WITH PARENTHESIS MATCHING

At some point or another, you will likely write some nested formula that contains layers and layers of opening and closing parentheses. Be aware that as you type your formula, when you enter a closing parenthesis ( )) Excel momentarily highlights the corresponding opening one (see Figure 5-8). This feature helps you to see what your expressions contain as well as to balance the parentheses (that is, ensure that the number of opening parentheses matches the number of closing ones).

Figure 5-8: As you enter a closing parenthesis, the corresponding opening one is momentarily highlighted (in this case, between IF and B5<0).

Unfortunately, the matching balanced parenthesis gets highlighted for just a brief moment. Some Excel formulas can have heavily nested expressions. One technique I often use is to go to the edit line and then backspace or delete one of the closing parentheses and immediately reenter it. Doing so forces the opening parenthesis to be highlighted briefly. Repeatedly deleting and reentering the same closing parenthesis creates a sort of flashing behavior in the matching open parenthesis. This forced flashing behavior helps to overcome the difficulty of identifying matched parentheses.

Part II

Converting and Working with Data

Data exists in many forms, and sometimes not the way we want it. This section shows you a variety of techniques that allow you to transform data.

Date and Time Functions

"I want to take the day of the week as text (such as "Monday") and convert it to a number (such as 1)."

You would want this to work in a manner similar to the Excel WEEKDAY function. WEEKDAY takes a serialized date and returns a number that corresponds to the day of the week. The default convention for Excel is to treat the first day of the week as Sunday and give this the value 1. Hence, Monday is a 2, Tuesday a 3, and so forth.

To reproduce the functionality of WEEKDAY, you need to understand how the optional argument alters its behavior.

WEEKDAY converts a serial date into a weekday number. For instance, you can write something like this:

```
=WEEKDAY("5/2/2007")                    returns 4
                                        (signifying Wednesday).
```

WEEKDAY has an optional second argument, which can be a 1, 2, or 3. The value 1 matches the default convention. The value 2 treats Monday as the first day of the week. Repeating the example with the optional argument as 2, you get:

```
=WEEKDAY("5/2/2007",2)                  returns 3
                                        (signifying Wednesday).
```

 NOTE

If the optional argument is set to 3, Monday is still treated as the first day of the week but is assigned the value of 0. So instead of cycling weekdays from 1 through 7, as with the other two scenarios, you are cycling from 0 through 6.

Unfortunately, the Excel function WEEKDAY requires a serialized date. It has to be pegged to an actual date. It will not be able to convert the word Monday to the number 1, for instance.

A formula must be created that is dependent not on the actual date but rather on the text for the day of week. Depending on the scenario, the following formulas can be used:

Formula that corresponds to WEEDKAY(date,1) — Excel's default

```
=MATCH(A1,{"Sunday","Monday","Tuesday","Wednesday","Thursday","Friday","Saturd
ay"},0)
```

Formula that corresponds to WEEDKAY(date,2) — Monday 1 — Sunday 7

```
=MATCH(A1,{"Monday","Tuesday","Wednesday","Thursday","Friday","Saturday","Sund
ay"},0)
```

Formula that corresponds to WEEDKAY(date,3) — Monday 0 — Sunday 6

```
=MATCH(A1,{"Monday","Tuesday","Wednesday","Thursday","Friday","Saturday","Sund
ay"},0)-1
```

To make things a little easier, the Escape Excel Hell Utility Pak that you loaded as an add-in in Chapter 4 already has a user-defined function called MYWEEKDAY. This function has the following syntax:

```
=MYWEEKDAY(DayOfWeek[,optionalArg=1])
```

Here are some sample computations that you can directly use as a formula if you have the Escape Excel Hell Utility Pak installed:

```
=MYWEEKDAY("Monday",1)                    returns 2
=MYWEEKDAY("Monday")                      returns 2
=MYWEEKDAY("Monday",2)                    returns 1
=MYWEEKDAY("Monday",3)                    returns 0
```

"I have a list of eight-digit numbers in the form of YYYYMMDD that I need to convert into serial dates."

The following formula converts a number such as 20060616 to the date 6/16/2006 (as a serialized date):

```
=DATE(MID(A1,1,4),MID(A1,5,2),MID(A1,7,2))        returns 38884
```

Of course, you will need to format the cell so that it visually appears as the date `6/16/2006` instead of the number `38884`.

TIP

Before entering the date formula, enter a hardwired date. Excel will automatically convert this to a numeric value formatted as a date. After Excel formats the cell to a date structure, overwrite it with the formula, like so:

```
=DATE(MID(A1,1,4),MID(A1,5,2),MID(A1,7,2))
```

The date formatting will be retained when you overwrite the cell value.

You will find these examples in the file `ch05_01FormulaExamples.xls` on the book's CD-ROM.

Using Inlining with calendar arithmetic

Several things are going on in the formula for calculating dates based on column location. Let's deconstruct it. Essentially, you want to take a given start date (1/1/2007) and pair it up with a date five days later (1/6/2007) to get `1/1 - 1/6`. In the next column, you want to add seven days to each of these dates, and keep adding seven days for every column you slide over to the right.

Seven days after January 1st is January 8th, and seven days after that is January 15th. January 1st is just `StartDate`. January 8th is `StartDate+7`. In the second column to the right of `StartDate`, January 15th is `StartDate+2*7`. In the third column to the right of `StartDate`, January 22nd is `Start+3*7`. Basically, all you have to do is increment your `StartDate` by seven times the number of columns you shift over to the right. The easiest way to count the number of columns is to take the difference between the current `COLUMN()` and `COLUMN(StartDate)`, which is the number of weeks:

```
COLUMN()-COLUMN(StartDate)
```

There are seven days in a week, so multiply the number of weeks by 7 and add it to `StartDate` to get the projected date:

```
StartDate+7*(Column()-Column(StartDate)
```

This gives you the numeric value for the date, but you need to format it as text according to an `m/d` or month/day pattern using TEXT:

```
TEXT(StartDate+7*(COLUMN()-COLUMN(StartDate)),"m/d")
```

This computes the left part of the formula. You have to connect each of these dates to a date five days removed.

```
TEXT(StartDate+7*(COLUMN()-COLUMN(StartDate))+5,"m/d")
```

This will give you all the corresponding Friday dates in the sequence, `1/6`, `1/13`,...

You can bring these two together using a construction such as the following:

```
=TEXT(TheMondayDate,"m/d")&" - "&TEXT(TheMatchingFridayDate,"m/d")
```

Counting columns using `COLUMN()-COLUMN(StartDate)` within the formula for projecting dates is an elegant Inlining technique.

"I want to generate across the top of my spreadsheet a range of dates from Monday through Friday starting from 1/1/2007 so that the columns read:

1/1-1/6, 1/8-1/13, 1/15-1/20, 1/22-1/27, 1/29-2/3, 2/5-2/10,...

I also want to be able to adjust the start date and have the list instantly updated."

First I give you the quick solution, and then if you're interested you can peruse what goes on behind the scenes.

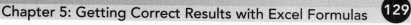

Assuming that you name a cell `StartDate` and place a valid date in it, you can use the following formula:

Formula for Calculating Dates Based on Column Location

```
=TEXT(StartDate+7*(COLUMN()-COLUMN(StartDate)),"m/d")&"-
"&TEXT(StartDate+7*(COLUMN()-COLUMN(StartDate))+5,"m/d")
```

Before worrying about having to enter a complicated formula, you can lift the formula from either of two files on the book's CD-ROM (`takeaway.txt` or `ch05_02CalendarArithmetic.xls`).

"I want to add two years, one month, and 22 days to my StartDate."

Assuming that the `StartDate` happens to be 1/1/2007, here's the quick-and-dirty answer:

```
=DATE(YEAR("1/1/2007")+2,MONTH("1/1/2007")+1,DAY("1/1/2007")+22)
```

This formula returns the date `2/23/2009`. In a spreadsheet, you may have a construction like that shown in Figure 5-9.

Figure 5-9: Incrementing calendar dates

Here is the formula construction (see the IncrementingDates tab of `ch05_02CalendarArithmetic.xls`):

```
=DATE(YEAR(A9)+B9,MONTH(A9)+C9,DAY(A9)+D9)
```

There are a couple of things to note:

- The variable number of days in a month, including leap years, are automatically handled.
- Notice that the quantities for days, months, and years automatically switch from singular to plural form as the respective quantity changes. The following sample formula shows how this automatic switch is done:

  `=IF(B9=1,"Year","Years")`

- The calculations in the spreadsheet also take into account negative quantities, so you can count days, months, and years backward in time.

Be aware that the Excel date arithmetic functions aren't designed to work for dates earlier than Jan 1, 1900, nor will they work for dates after the year 9,999.

"I want to increment my date by 27 hours. I can add 27/24 to the number of days in my DATE formula, but the extra hours get lopped off."

DATE always returns an integer value, and this number is pegged to 12:00 a.m. Because it refuses to handle fractional portions, you can never get the time of day from DATE. To handle that, you need both the DATE and TIME functions together. Figuratively, your formula gets constructed as

`=DATE(year,month,day)+TIME(hour,minute,second)`

The actual formula is

`=DATE(YEAR(A13)+B13,MONTH(A13)+C13,DAY(A13)+D13)+TIME(HOUR(A13)+E13,MINUTE(A13)+F13,SECOND(A13)+G13)`

Notice that the first half of the formula matches exactly what was done in the previous example for incrementing dates. I have also added time factors.

"Whenever I enter a time like 25:10:15, I see that Excel converts it to a value of 1:10:15 and this is not what I want. Also, when I add up a group of hours so that the total exceeds 24 hours, it gets converted to a 24-hour cycle."

You can change the formatting of your cells. In your spreadsheet, enter **25:10:15** and, indeed, you will see it changed to `1:10:15`. Format the cell (press Ctrl+1 and click the Number tab). Select Custom from the list of categories and click the option for `[h]:mm:ss`. If you don't see it in your list of number types, you can enter it in the Type: input field. After you click the OK button, the cell formatted as `1:10:15` should revert back to the original number you entered, `25:10:15`.

"I have a column of hours that are all formatted using the [h]:mm:ss pattern. When I add up these numbers, they are able to display quantities greater than 24 hours, including the totals. I have a problem when I try to deduct time. Negative time quantities always produce a #NUM! error."

You have two strategies available to you. One of these is to change an Excel configuration setting. Select Tools⇨Options and click the Calculation tab. Place a checkmark next to the 1904 date system. This method enables you to enter negative values for time.

NOTE

The 1904 date system encodes different serial numbers for dates than the default settings in Excel. Normally, this should not cause problems if you open the spreadsheet on a computer on which the 1904 date system is not enabled. Though Excel encodes the serialized dates differently in your spreadsheet, it also saves information about the type of date system you are using. When it opens your spreadsheet, the serialized dates will be automatically converted to match your Excel configuration. You can still run into problems when adopting the 1904 date system. Negative time values will not, of course, work properly if the 1904 date system hasn't been enabled. Additionally, your spreadsheet might have some hardwired dependency on the serialized date value.

An alternative is to avoid using serialized time and just use straight algebra to do your computations.

"I want to add up two ranges of time that overlap and eliminate the overlap."

The formula is a little complicated, so I provide it here and ask you to lift it from the book's CD-ROM, in the ch05_02CalendarArithmetic.xls file (on the TimeOverlap worksheet tab).

If you have T1In at B6, T1Out at C6, T2In at E6, and T2Out at F6, the formula for the combined time with overlaps eliminated is the following:

```
=IF(OR($F6<=$B6,$E6>=$C6),($F6-$E6+$C6-$B6),($F6-$E6+$C6-$B6)-(MIN($F6,$C6)-MAX($E6,$B6)))
```

If you use defined names, the formula is

```
=IF(OR(T2Out<=T1In,T2In>=T1Out),(T2Out-T2In+T1Out-T1In),(T2Out-T2In+T1Out-T1In)-(MIN(T2Out,T1Out)-MAX(T2In,T1In)))
```

You may also find the ch05_03TimeSheet.xls file to be of interest (see Figure 5-10). It uses this overlapping feature as well as a host of other features. It is a monthly timesheet. You can update all the dates listed in the worksheet by entering a specific start date. Notice that the spreadsheet stops the entries at the last day of the month.

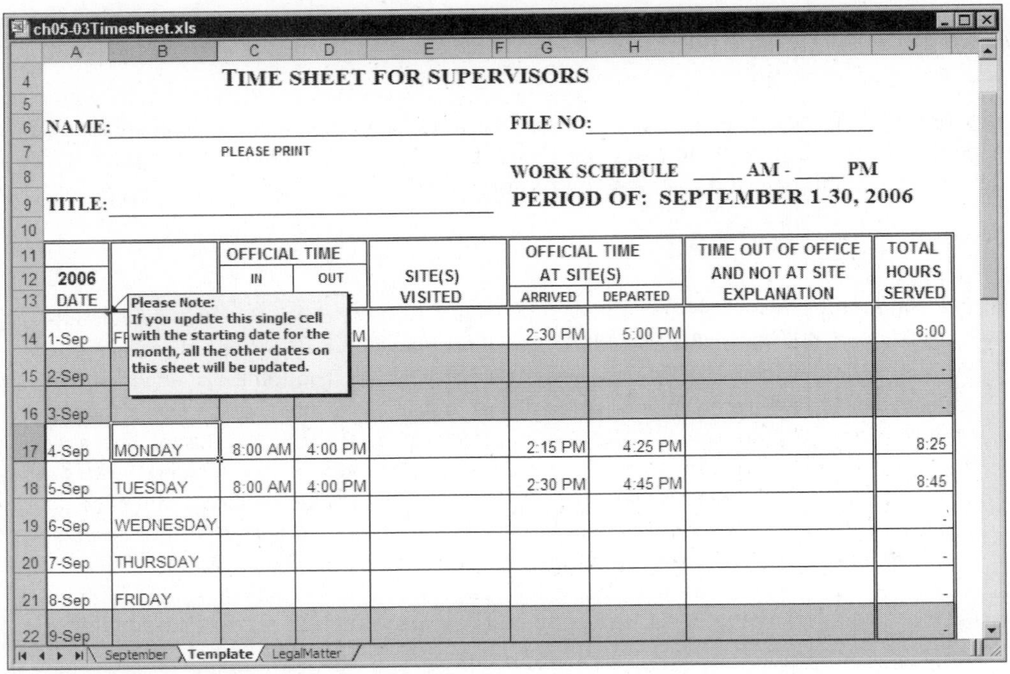

Figure 5-10: Timesheet with overlapping ranges

Though conditional formatting is used to highlight weekends, it uses a formula for the day of the week as its switch. It uses the CHOOSE mechanism for picking out the day of the week:

```
=IF(LEN(A17)=0,"",CHOOSE(WEEKDAY(A17,2),"MONDAY","TUESDAY","WEDNESDAY",
"THURSDAY","FRIDAY","",""))
```

It might have been easier to use the formula:

```
=IF(LEN(A17)=0,"",TEXT(A17,"dddd"))
```

This second formula is more compact. It also displays Saturdays and Sundays. In the CHOOSE formula, notice that the days span from Monday to Friday. Saturday and Sunday are intentionally replaced with empty quotation marks. This feature is used by conditional formatting to highlight those days that are weekends.

These are the kind of trade-offs that you need to think about when constructing spreadsheets. Incidentally, you could have used the formula:

```
=IF(LEN(A17)=0,"",IF((WEEKDAY(A17,2)=1),"MONDAY",IF(WEEKDAY(A17,2)=2,"TUESDAY",
IF(WEEKDAY(A17,2)=3,"WEDNESDAY",IF(WEEKDAY(A17,2)=4,"THURSDAY",IF(WEEKDAY(A17,
2)=5,"FRIDAY","")))))))
```

It works, but it's needlessly verbose. It is very easy to make an error entering a heavily nested formula like this.

Units and Measures

There are several different kinds of measures you may want to use or convert. These can involve angles, compound quantities such as feet and inches or pounds and ounces, or you may have other kinds of conversions in mind.

Representing Angles

"A Google Map URL e-mailed to me has the longitude and latitude embedded in the URL string in their decimal form. I want to extract these as map coordinates and display them in degrees, minutes, and seconds."

Say that the URL happens to be something like the following:

```
http://maps.google.com/maps?ll=32.796537,-117.255996&spn=0.004198,0.007267&t=h&hl=en
```

The task ahead of you is twofold: extract the numbers from the URL string; and represent the decimal numbers in terms of traditional map coordinates.

If someone e-mails this URL to you, you can easily select the text for the decimals and then copy and paste them into your spreadsheet. That might be easy if you're just doing this once. What if you need to do this many times because you are getting URL strings like this all the time? It would be tedious and error prone to manually copy and paste the values. Also, Excel has facilities to extract the data directly from the URL string.

On the MapCoordinates tab of the `ch05_04UnitsMeasures.xls` file (on the book's CD-ROM), you will see the fully worked-out solution (see Figure 5-11).

This worksheet has four parts: the source data or URL, a parse table that identifies boundaries of data you want to extract, the extracted data, and the final results.

If you examine the URL string, you will see that the latitude begins immediately after the first equal (=) sign and ends just before the first comma (,). Similarly, the longitude data begins after the first comma and ends just before the first ampersand (&). You just need to find these positions and use the MID function to extract the portions of text you are interested in. I leave you to explore how MID is used on your own.

NOTE
When you extract text using MID, you may need to convert it to a numeric quantity. You can do so using the function VALUE or just place a double minus sign in the expression. As an example, you can write:

```
=VALUE(MID(MyURL,32,9))
=--MID(MyURL,32,9)
```

Both formulas will produce the same results. The double minus operation is used elsewhere in the book. You will find it to be quite handy.

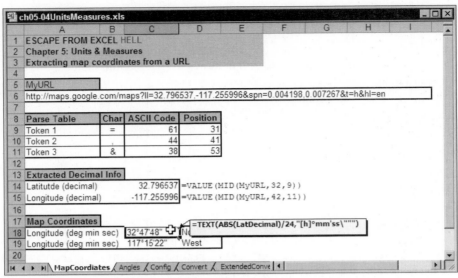

Figure 5-11: Extracting map coordinates from a URL

CONVERTING DECIMAL DEGREES TO DEGREES, MINUTES, AND SECONDS

Continuing with this problem, the task is to convert decimal degrees into traditional map coordinates. In map coordinates, the term *minute* means one-sixtieth of a degree, and the term *seconds of arc* refers to a sixtieth of a sixtieth of a degree. These are the same kind of divisions used to represent time in Excel. In effect, you could commandeer the facilities of Excel to convert decimal degrees. That plan has only one wrinkle: Time is based on a 24-hour cycle, and degrees are not. You will have to use an artificial dividing factor of 24 in your formulas to get them to display correctly.

If you define the name `LatDecimal` to represent the number of degrees of latitude, you can use a formula like the following:

```
=TEXT(ABS(LatDecimal)/24,"[h]°mm'ss\""")
```

Or you can use a simpler formula and apply a custom formatting for time on top of the cell, rather than use TEXT to change its appearance. That formula is

```
=ABS(LatDecimal)/24
```

I would advise against this alternative, however. Why? Because the simpler formula has a value that is off by a factor of 24. You might think you can use it in other computations. To do so, you will have to remultiply by 24 to extract the decimal representation. When you enter other formulas that reference this formatted cell, the other cells will inherit this cell's format, trying to display everything in hours, minutes, and seconds. You'll also have to contend with the factor of 24 to keep the numbers straight. One last piece of this puzzle is sure to cause you confusion. Say that you manage to correctly represent `32.796537` degrees as `32°47'48"`. When you look at the Excel Formula Bar, you'll see:

```
1/1/1900   8:47:48 AM
```

It is far simpler and safer to stay with the original formula that uses TEXT to create a true piece of text showing the latitude in traditional map coordinates. Notice that this formula using TEXT presents no danger of running into negative angles. This is because those are handled separately. You'll have no difficulty determining which quadrant of the globe the map coordinates refer to.

CONVERSION BETWEEN DEGREES AND RADIANS

"I know the sine of 30 degrees is one-half. When I type the formula:
  `=SIN(30)`
I get 0.-0.988031624. I know this can't be correct. How do I fix this?"

Use the formula:

```
=SIN(RADIANS(30))
```

This formula converts 30 degrees into radians. Excel uses units of radians for its trigonometric functions such as SIN, COS, and TAN.

To convert a radian to a degree, use the DEGREES function. For instance:

```
=DEGREES(1)                              returns 57.29577951
```

So, one radian is a little over 57 degrees. If you're curious about converting a quantity of radians into degrees, minutes, and seconds, you can use the following formula:

```
=TEXT(AnAngleInRadians*180/(24*PI()),"[h]°mm'ss\"""")
```

One radian turns out to be about `57°17'45"`.

Converting Measures Using CONVERT

You would think that Excel would provide a systematic way to convert quantities from one type of unit to another. It does; it's called CONVERT. In this section, I show you some sample calculations and explain how you can use CONVERT in a more elaborate and imaginative manner than you may have been aware of. I also provide a tool to extend the capabilities of CONVERT.

CONVERT works in a simple way. If you want to find out how many feet are in 1.25 miles, you can use the following formula:

```
=CONVERT(1.25,"mi","ft")                 returns 6600
```

If you want to know how many inches are in 1.25 miles, you can write:

```
=CONVERT(1.25,"mi","in")                    returns 79200
```

CONVERT transforms quantities from one type of unit to another. It knows about various kinds of units, including weight and mass, distance, time, pressure, force, energy, power, magnetism, temperature, and liquid measure. I don't have the space to go into detail on all these here, but the Excel Help facility provides the basic information.

As powerful as CONVERT is, it has some limitations. The first limitation is that it has to work with pure quantities. So, if you have a problem like this:

"I am told that Abraham Lincoln, our sixteenth President, was 6 feet 4 inches tall. I want to know this in meters."

you'll find that CONVERT cannot, out of the box, handle mixed quantities such as feet and inches. You will have to represent the height purely in terms of either inches or feet before you can use the CONVERT formula. With a foot having 12 inches, 6 feet 4 inches is equivalent to 76 inches (=12*6+4). With everything expressed as inches, you can now use CONVERT to transform the measurement to meters:

```
=CONVERT(76,"in","m")                       returns 1.9304
```

Incidentally, you can represent the measurement in terms of feet:

```
=CONVERT(6+4/12,"ft","m")                   returns 1.9304
```

The second limitation of CONVERT is that it doesn't like to handle derived quantities, as in:

"I need to convert 55 miles per hour to kilometers per day."

Velocity is a derived quantity involving two CONVERT calculations chained together. You can solve the problem of this limitation by setting up a conversion table (see Figure 5-12).

Simply adjust the units on the left and right side of the conversion table.

"I want to convert astronomical units to miles."

This request brings us to the third limitation of CONVERT. The function does not allow you to define units of your own. CONVERT knows about kilometers, meters, statute miles, nautical miles, inches, feet, yards, angstroms, and picas (a pica is 1/72 inch). You can transform a distance from one unit to any of the other units of distance from this list. But the function is totally brain dead when it comes to astronomical units (the approximate distance between the Earth and the Sun).

It would be nice if CONVERT could incorporate new types of units into its rubric of conversion factors. Unfortunately, this is not a design feature of CONVERT. I do have a workaround for you to accomplish this. It is a custom function called MyCONVERT. The function has the following syntax:

```
=MyCONVERT(number,from_unit,to_unit,vlookupTable)
```

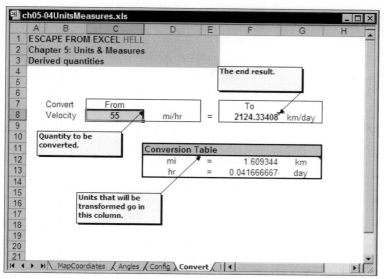

Figure 5-12: Using CONVERT with derived quantities

This works almost the same as CONVERT except that you get to specify a lookup table with your conversion factors. The lookup table is one of your choosing that allows you define your own units and hook them into CONVERT.

The Excel CONVERT function doesn't know anything about furlongs, which are commonly used as a measure in horse racing, so here's an example using furlongs:

1. Define a lookup table of your choosing, with a name like `MyConversionTable`, and give it three columns.

2. In the first column, place labels for the new units you are adding to MyCONVERT.

3. Enter **furlong** in the first column of the table.

4. A furlong is 660 feet, so enter **660** in the second column.

5. In the third column, enter **ft**, to serve as a label.

   Similarly, you can add entries for other kinds of quantities, such as barrels of oil to gallons (see Figure 5-13).

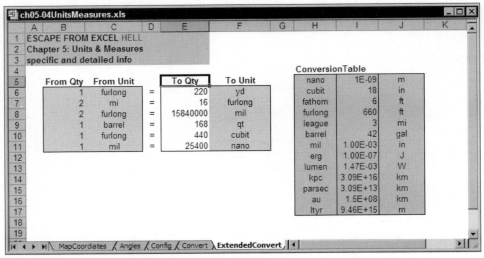

Figure 5-13: MyCONVERT uses an auxiliary table.

Now you can incorporate units such as furlongs into your data conversions.

```
=MyCONVERT(1,"furlong","yd",MyTable)        returns 220
=MyCONVERT(2,"mi","furlong",MyTable)        returns 16
=MyCONVERT(2,"furlong","mil",MyTable)       returns 7920000
=MyCONVERT(1,"barrel","qt",MyTable)         returns 168 (quarts)
```

NOTE

The macro code for MyCONVERT can be found in the VBA code portion of `ch05_04UnitsMeasures.xls`.

MyCONVERT works only if you have the Analysis Toolpak and the Analysis Toolpak - VBA add-ins installed (see Figure 5-14). Depending on how you configured Excel, it may be necessary for you to have your original Excel CD available.

The lookup or conversion table can be a user-defined name, such as `MyTable`, or cell coordinates, such as `H5:J17`. If you use cell coordinates for the table, you should use absolute rather than relative cell coordinates. Using absolute coordinates will make it easier to copy and paste formulas.

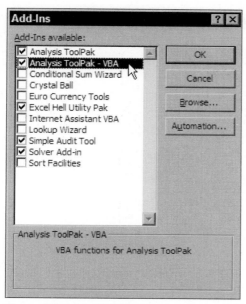

Figure 5-14: MyCONVERT accesses the CONVERT function, a part of the Analysis ToolPak.

Roman Numerals

"I want to turn a regular decimal number into a roman numeral."

You can easily convert numbers to roman numerals. The simplest way is to write something like this:

```
=ROMAN(55)                                    returns LV
```

As is often the case, you need to be aware of a few facts:

- The function ROMAN wants integer values. ROMAN(55.123) returns LV, the same as ROMAN(55).

- The largest number you can convert to a roman numeral is 3999.

- If you try to produce a roman numeral of a negative number, you will get an error.

- ROMAN(0) is just an empty cell.

- There are different forms of roman numerals, with some being more concise than others. These options are detailed in Table 5-1.

TABLE 5-1 DIFFERENT OPTIONS AVAILABLE FOR ROMAN NUMERALS

Form	Type	Example
0 or omitted	Classic	=ROMAN(199) returns CXCIX
1	More concise	=ROMAN(199,1) returns CVCIV
2	More concise	=ROMAN(199,2) returns CIC
3	More concise	=ROMAN(199,3) returns CIC
4	Simplified	=ROMAN(199,4) returns CIC
TRUE	Classic	=ROMAN(199,TRUE) returns CXCIX
FALSE	Simplified	=ROMAN(199,FALSE) returns CIC

Please note that in Excel, 0 normally pairs up with FALSE and 1 with TRUE. For example:

```
=IF(1,"must be true","can't be true")     returns must be true
```

With the ROMAN function, this is not so. ROMAN(199,TRUE) is CXCIX and ROMAN(199,1) is CVCIV. These are not the same. ROMAN(199,0) is CXCIX and ROMAN(199,FALSE) is CIC. If you plan on using a formula to compute the second argument, instead of using a fixed literal value, then be sure that the formula returns a TRUE or FALSE, and not a 1 or 0.

Excel supports converting decimal values to roman numerals, but not the reverse. The spreadsheet ch05_05RomanNumerals.xls on the book's CD-ROM shows how to perform this reverse process. It is particularly instructive to see how this is done with and without arrays.

> *"I want to use VLOOKUP without having a separate lookup table. Is it possible to embed the lookup values directly in the formula?"*

In the WithoutArrays worksheet of ch05_05RomanNumerals.xls, you'll find a lookup table for mapping the letters in the roman numerals with their decimal values. The formulas in column C use this lookup table:

```
=VLOOKUP(MID(RomanNum,Position,1),LookupTable,2,FALSE)
```

Now look at the WithArrays worksheet. Notice that there is no lookup table. The lookup table is embedded as an array inside the formula:

```
=VLOOKUP(MID(RomanNum,Position,1),{"M",1000;"D",500;"C",100;"L",50;"X",10;"V",
5;"I",1},2,FALSE)
```

The curly braces are actually embedded inside the formula. That is, you literally enter { and } as part of the formula. You don't need to press Ctrl+Shift+Enter as you normally would for an array formula.

The use of embedded arrays helps to eliminate some of the visual clutter (there is no separate lookup table). Some consequences of using embedded arrays are the following:

- `C6:C21` have identical copies of the embedded array. If you have to update this array, you need to revise the formulas for all 16 of the cells.

  In general, you have to keep track of where the arrays are used, and you might miss one or two. In the solution without arrays, all the cells are looking up values from a single table. You need to make only one set of changes for the entire spreadsheet.

- You need to keep in mind that Excel formulas have a limited length in the number of characters they will hold. If you are embedding a lookup table as an array, you may need to keep this limitation in mind.

Incidentally, an embedded array can be used with HLOOKUP in the following way:

```
=HLOOKUP(MID(RomanNum,Position,1),{"M","D","C","L","X","V","I";1000,500,100,50
,10,5,1},2,FALSE)
```

Notice that the semicolon symbol in the array occurs only once, resulting in a virtual row of letters, followed by another for numbers. By contrast, the VLOOKUP formula has multiple virtual rows of letters, numbers, and semicolons.

Closing Thoughts

Many people who struggle with spreadsheet formulas don't have to. Though it's easy to get lost in a formula, it's just as easy to use a variety of aides to handle complicated formulas. Features such as Function Tooltips and formula auto complete can be very effective in simplifying a dense formula.

Much of this chapter is consumed with units in all sorts of measures, ranging from dates and times, to angles, to conversions. These kinds of conversions and calculations are, after all, common tasks that are handled with spreadsheets. All too often, they are not approached systematically or in a way that facilitates effective techniques for such problems. An important goal of this chapter is to reinstate this systematic way of thinking.

This chapter is concerned with numbers. In the next chapter I introduce a systematic treatment of visualizing numbers.

Chapter 6

Charts and Data Visualization

In This Chapter

◆ Constructing charts effectively and managing their data

◆ Enhancing a chart's interactive capabilities

◆ Overcoming common chart design challenges

◆ Dynamically updating text appearing in a chart

◆ Understanding worksheet and workbook-level names

◆ Creating conditionally formatted charts

◆ Layering in charts and spreadsheets

◆ Dealing with gaps in your data

◆ Converting and displaying data with error bars

◆ Using trendlines and histograms

◆ Using a full-featured XY Scatter chart

◆ Retrieving loosely coupled data on demand (without link update problems)

Spreadsheets can perform an awesome amount of number crunching and handle complex calculations. One of the main purposes and benefits of using a spreadsheet is to summarize or present that information. This is where data visualization and charting comes in handy. It provides a mechanism for creating a presentation layer, a sort of window into your spreadsheet model.

I address three issues in this chapter:

143

- **Chart construction:** Chart construction techniques and specialized types of charts often present challenges to spreadsheet users. I provide some easy-to-apply techniques and ready-made spreadsheets for you to use.

- **Data management:** A chart can sit on a mountain of data. Getting that data presented visually has its challenges. Sometimes the data has gaps or out-of-range values that skew the graph. Also, if your spreadsheet has years of information or too many kinds of data to view, how will you capture that in a single or a couple of charts? I show you how to structure your spreadsheets into manageable layers.

- **Interactivity:** It often happens that Excel charts are static with little or no interactive capabilities. I show you how to inject some interactivity into your charts.

Common Chart Design Challenges

There are two sets of challenges in constructing charts. One of these deals with subcomponents of a chart, such as a title or specific way to format a component. The other deals with constructing the chart as a whole.

Info for charting newbies

The charting facilities of Excel are well known, but if you're new to Excel or haven't worked with charts, much of what is said and done can be utterly confusing. For this reason, I include some basics, enough to get you started.

Your first step to constructing a chart is to make sure that Excel is displaying the Chart Wizard among the toolbar icons. If you don't see it, it could be for one of two reasons. You have so many toolbar icons in your application window that some of them become hidden. I explain how to deal with "hidden icons" in Chapter 1 (see the section "Toolbars and Toolbar Icons"). If you absolutely do not find the Chart Wizard in your toolbar, you can always add it by selecting Tools⇨Customize and clicking the Commands tab. Within the Charting category you will be able to click and drag the Chart Wizard onto your toolbar.

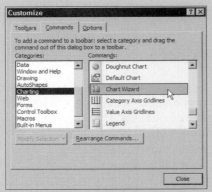

You should find the Chart Wizard by clicking Tools⇨Customize.

If you want to follow the charting example in this chapter, use the `ch06_03Timeline Chart.xls` file, which is on the book's CD-ROM. Open your spreadsheet and select the data you want to place onto a chart.

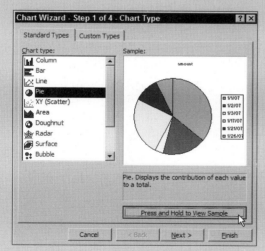

Chart Data	
	amount
1/1/07	10
1/2/07	5
1/3/07	1
1/17/07	7
1/21/07	3
1/26/07	2

Sample data to be shown in a chart

Notice that in addition to the numerical data, I select the category and value labels. Excel will know what to do with this information. After you've selected the desired range of cells, click the Chart Wizard toolbar icon. A Chart Wizard window will pop up. You can select the kind of chart you want to produce in the Chart Type panel. Among the more popular chart types are bar and column charts, line charts, and pie charts. For this example, click Pie. You will see a series of Chart subtypes displayed in miniature panes. To preview how your chart data will appear, click the Press and Hold to View Sample button.

Chart preview of your data and chart type

To proceed, click the Next button. In Step 2 you can specify in greater detail your source data and how Excel should treat this data. For instance, you may be representing separate sets of data (a.k.a. "data series") in individual rows and not by columns. This doesn't apply to the pie chart but is more appropriate for a stacked column chart.

continued

(continued)

Clicking the Next button takes you to Step 3. Here you have the opportunity to decorate your chart with relevant information. As you check and uncheck the various items, Excel displays a running preview.

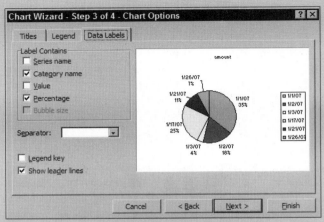

Decorate your chart with the appropriate information.

Be careful not to clutter your chart with too much information. If you are not sure what settings to enable, don't worry; you can adjust the chart settings after it is created.

Click Next. In Step 4 you can specify the chart location. A general practice is to opt for the As Object In option and let the chart be located next to the data range used by your chart.

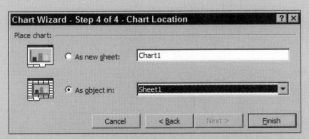

Specify the chart location.

The chart may not appear polished, but you can refine it. The important thing to keep in mind is that the chart is not static but rather is connected to your underlying spreadsheet data and formulas. As the values in your data series change, whether by manual edits or through Excel formulas, so does the corresponding chart.

This explanation about charts and how to use them is barely enough to get started. Further information about Excel charts and techniques can be found in *Excel Charts*, by John Walkenbach, and in my book, *Excel Best Practices for Business*, both published by Wiley.

Chart Components

There are things you can do to easily move around the chart, format components in a visually pleasing way, and control a component's behavior. This section covers each of these topics.

NAVIGATING THROUGH CHART COMPONENTS

"I want to format the x-axis of my chart. Because of the way the chart is constructed, with so many data points, I am having difficulty clicking to select it."

Simply click the chart and press your arrow keys. This will allow you to cycle through the Chart Area, Plot Area, the Legend and its subcomponents, the value and category axes, the Chart title, the gridlines, and series data. After you have your component selected, press Ctrl+1 to format it.

"I have many data points in my chart. I want to highlight three or four of them. Cycling through using the arrow keys takes too long. Is there any simpler way of doing this?"

To quickly highlight a particular data point, click once on the one that you want to format. Notice that this action selects the whole series of data and not just the individual data point. Pause a moment and click once more on that same data point. Now only your intended data point is selected. You can now format it by pressing Ctrl+1. You might want to make it stand out by changing its background color to a bright yellow or something equivalent. If you need to do the same for several other data points, you can immediately select those individual points and press Ctrl+Y, which repeats your last action. In this case, it is repeating your action of formatting your currently selected data point.

 NOTE

If you are not sure what Excel considers your last action to be, select the Excel Edit menu at the top of your application window. You should see something like "Repeat Format Data Point Ctrl+Y" in the pull-down menu. It is always a good idea to verify in this manner the specific action that Excel will repeat.

DYNAMICALLY UPDATED TEXT IN A CHART

"I want my chart title to correspond to the information in my chart data, such as 'Web traffic Activity for April 11.'"

Manually editing a chart title is both cumbersome and error prone. It is certainly a task you don't want to saddle yourself with having to do on a daily basis. Here is how you can construct a dynamic title like the one shown in Figure 6-1. First, construct a formula for your title in your spreadsheet. In the file ch06_01DynamicChartTitle.xls on the book's CD-ROM, you'll find the following formula in cell B6:

```
="Valuation of Portfolios at "&TEXT(OFFSET($A$10,DayNumber,0),"d-mmm")
```

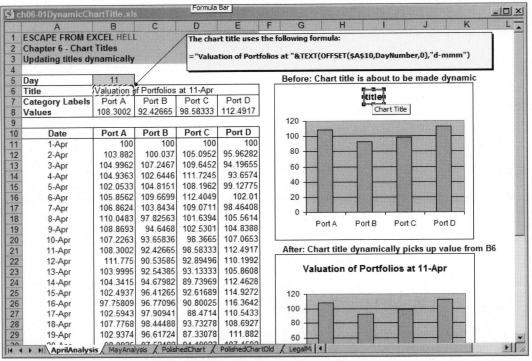

Figure 6-1: The formula inside the spreadsheet is used in the chart table.

The DayNumber is a user-defined name (cell B5). Basically it looks at the column of dates in column A and uses OFFSET to retrieve the day based on the DayNumber. After the date is retrieved, it is formatted using TEXT to match a d-mmm pattern.

To have your chart title use the value from the formula in B6, click the chart title object, as shown in the "Before" chart of Figure 6-1. The cell reference needs to be a fully qualified name referencing the sheet. Next, click the Excel Formula Bar and enter the pseudo-formula (you can just click the cell; Excel automatically inserts the fully qualified cell reference):

```
=AprilAnalysis!B6
```

NOTE

The reference to B6 in the chart title object is not a true formula. The chart title object will not perform a calculation such as

```
=2+3
```

or

```
=TEXT(TODAY(),"d/m/yyyy")
```

The dynamic chart title will have no difficulty using live results from a spreadsheet formula.

"I am trying to reference a named value in my chart title, but Excel complains."

Try using a fully qualified name in your pseudo-formula. This follows the structure of the filename surrounded by single quotation marks, followed by an exclamation mark and then the name value. For instance, if you define cell B6 to be `MyChartTitle`, you can use the following reference in your chart title:

```
='ch06_01DynamicChartTitle.xls'!MyChartTitle
```

"I would like my chart to look a bit more polished. I would like to add more text to the chart, possibly dynamic. I want to see data labels in my chart. I want my chart to have a '3D' relief and make use of shading for a professional appearance."

Figure 6-2 shows how the chart can be structured. In the sections to follow I explain how to introduce some of these features, such as the 3D relief.

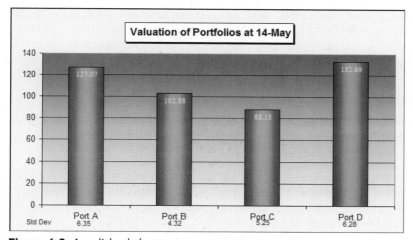

Figure 6-2: A polished chart

"The polished chart you prepared does everything I want. I don't want to go through the process of recreating everything from scratch. Is there any way I can retrofit your chart so that it picks up my data instead of yours?"

It's easy to replace your data with mine. Say that my data resides on columns B through E and yours is on columns G through J. Just click the chart. When you do, the data series will be highlighted with movable handlebars, as shown in Figure 6-3. Position your mouse over the edge of the framed cells. Your mouse will change its appearance to show four compass-like arrows. Click and drag the framed cells to be positioned over your data.

"My data series has more rows and columns than yours."

Not only can you reposition the framed data series, you can also resize them. Click and drag the notches on the corner of the framed data series. Moving these notches will resize the framed data series.

Part II

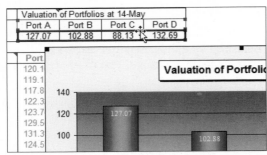

Figure 6-3: Movable handlebars allow you to reposition and resize your chart data series.

When working with charts and to render your data in chart form, you may face a variety of challenges. There are several things you need to think about and issues you will face. You may be vexed by the unintuitive subtleties of worksheet and workbook level names. You may want to add more features to your charts, such as inserting additional text boxes with dynamic content. You may need to have finer control over font sizes and positioning of text and data labels in your charts. You may want to utilize coloration in your charts to make them easier to read and interpret. I take some of these issues up in the following sections.

WORKSHEET AND WORKBOOK-LEVEL NAMES

"I want to replicate my chart for April's data and do the same for May. I select all the cells in my worksheet (using Ctrl+A) and paste what I've selected into an empty worksheet. The chart looks fine but nothing gets updated when I change the data in my new worksheet."

The problem is that the formulas in the pasted cells are still referencing the AprilAnalysis worksheet. There are several ways to deal with this problem. The simplest way is to save your original workbook with the AprilAnalysis worksheet and use Save As to save the workbook under a new name for the May analysis.

You may want a single workbook that holds multiple worksheets, one for each month. In this case, your strategy would be to use the copy worksheet facility. Ctrl+click the AprilAnalysis worksheet tab and select Move or Copy; then, place a checkmark next to Create a Copy in the Move or Copy window. Note that doing so creates a local definition of the user-defined name that is just specific to the new workbook you created.

For instance, the AprilAnalysis workbook has the name DayNumber. When you use the copy worksheet technique just described, you will create a new worksheet called *AprilAnalysis (2)*. Within this newly created worksheet—and only in this worksheet—will exist the locally defined name, 'AprilAnalysis (2)'!DayNumber. Wherever in your formulas on this worksheet you refer to DayNumber, Excel will use the value of DayNumber as specified on this worksheet. In effect, this is a worksheet-level name. Outside of the *AprilAnalysis (2)* worksheet, formulas will use the workbook-level name for DayNumber.

This situation gets very confusing the first time you encounter it. To summarize:

- In general, when you define a name in a spreadsheet, you are creating a workbook-level name. The value is associated with the cell you create it in. This workbook-level name is specific to the actual cell and worksheet.

- If you copy a worksheet that contains workbook-level names, the newly created worksheet will then have matching worksheet-level names.

- You can intentionally create a worksheet-level name by defining a name and specifying the worksheet name, such as *AprilAnalysis (2)*, preceding it in the following manner (see Figure 6-4).

  ```
  'AprilAnalysis (2)'!MyWorksheetLevelName
  ```

- Worksheet and workbook-level names can be the same. You can have a worksheet-level name such as `'AprilAnalysis (2)'!DayNumber` whose value happens to be 14. You can have a workbook-level name such as `DayNumber` whose value happens to be 27. You get the following results:

  ```
  =1+DayNumber        returns 15 (in AprilAnalysis
                      (2) only)

  =1+DayNumber        returns 18 (everywhere else)
  ```

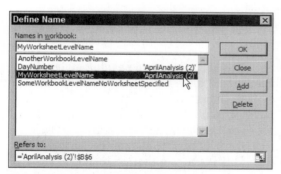

Figure 6-4: Defining a worksheet-level name

INSERTING A TEXT BOX INTO A CHART

"The dynamic chart title is useful. I'd like to insert some additional text into the chart that can be dynamically updated in the same manner."

Click your chart once to activate it. Go straight to the Formula Bar and enter the additional text or a pseudo formula.

You might want to display standard deviation for the whole month under each of the columns. First, create a text box for the word `Std Dev`. Under the category label "Port A," place another text box, but give it the pseudo-formula that specifies the value for the standard deviation. In the PolishedChart worksheet, the formula is

```
=PolishedChart!$B$44
```

NOTE

When you are transferring a value to any kind of text box in a chart, your worksheet has to do all the preparatory work so that it is suitable for the chart. In the case of the standard deviation computations, you may have too many decimal places display and need to round the number to, say, just a couple of decimal places. The formula might be something like this:

```
=ROUND(STDEV(B$11:B$41),2)
```

When you're passing a date value, such as is done in the chart title, it is necessary to use the TEXT function on the serialized date so that it appears in a format like "d-mmm" or "m/d/yyyy."

CREATING 2.5 DIMENSIONS

"I would like the bars in my column chart to have a 3D relief."

In your column chart, right-click your series data and select Format Data Series from the context menu. In the Patterns tab, click Fill Effects.

The Gradient tab gives you options for various color combinations and shading styles. To create the 3D (or, as I like to think of it, 2.5 dimensional) style vertical bar, select One Color. You can experiment with Two Colors or Preset, though you will lose the ability to adjust the shading from Dark to Light. Pick a color of your choosing from the pull-down menu for Color 1. The color I use in this example is called Periwinkle. Set the shading style to Vertical. You will see four shaded squares or variants. The one on the bottom-right corner is light in the center and dark on the sides. This is the one that corresponds most closely to the appearance of a 3D cylindrical bar.

Note that the chart title is formatted with a custom border and has a `Shadow` attribute enabled. You can set these attributes in the Patterns tab of the Format Chart Title window (click the title and press Ctrl+1). When the border surrounds the text, such as the chart title, it tends to hug the text very tightly. You can insert an extra space in the beginning of your chart title formula.

"I want to display values in my column chart."

Right-click your data series in the chart and select Format Data Series from the context menu. In the Data Labels tab, place a checkmark next to Value. If you need to specify the category or series name (or both) in addition to the value, be sure to specify the kind of Separator in the pull-down menu when you're setting the `Data Labels`.

"I want to adjust the appearance of my data labels, but I can't find any settings to adjust the data labels I just created!"

You can see your values for your series data hovering above the cylindrical columns. You click your series data but find that you have no way to format the numbers. This is because when you make the values appear, the values are embodied separately. Simply click the data values in the chart and not the column cylinders. With the data selected, you can right-click to choose Format Data Labels.

There are four tabs in Format Data Labels: Patterns, Font, Number, and Alignment. Click the Number tab and adjust the formatting. For instance, you may want to show the values to two decimal places rather than six or seven.

 NOTE

In contrast to the chart text box previously described (which displayed text data for the standard deviation), the Excel chart knows enough about the series data values to allow you to format the data inside the chart rather than beforehand.

You can format the appearance of the data values by clicking the Number tab and formatting numbers as you regularly would for a range of cells in a worksheet.

 TIP

Spreadsheets have a way of evolving more rapidly than you might anticipate. Rather than have to manually adjust the number formatting of your values as your spreadsheet evolves, you can have the chart values match the worksheet format by placing a checkmark next to Linked to Source within the Number tab.

Next, click the Alignment tab (see Figure 6-5). Notice the options available for the label position. In this particular worksheet, the label position for the values is set to Inside End.

After your data values are placed directly on top of the custom shaded cylindrical bars, the automatic colors chosen by Excel may not be what you want. Click the Font tab and set the Color to a contrasting color for your column or bar chart. Bright yellow text against a darker blue or black background tends to be easier to read than other combinations.

One more point is worth mentioning. Excel wants to automatically scale the font size. All too often this results in charts that appear cluttered. The text and numbers tend to be oversized when the Auto Scale option is enabled. If you're creating a chart, let the visualization of the graphical information dominate the chart. It shouldn't have to compete with numbers; they're already in the worksheet.

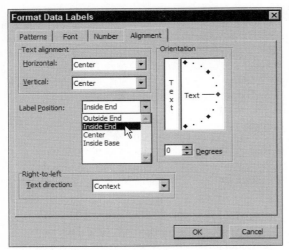

Figure 6-5: Setting the alignment attributes for the series data.

My suggestion is, if you want complete control, turn off the Auto Scale for font size wherever it occurs in your chart and set it yourself. Of course, make the sizing consistent across the board. I personally tend to use the smaller 8- or 9-point font size so that I can pack more information into a chart without making it too distracting.

SOME FURTHER GUIDELINES ON CHART FORMATTING

Colors can be used for great effect in Excel charts. Notice that in my examples I try not to go into overdrive on chart colorization and features.

If you want your charts to look professional, it may be necessary to turn off many of the "auto" attributes of the Excel charts, such as font sizing and colorization of chart components. Turning these off means that you're on your own. But in this case, being able to control the chart attributes is what you want.

I offer some thoughts and suggestions, mostly to give you an organized way to approach your charts. Ultimately, you need to trust your preferences and instincts on combining artistic presentation with quantitative information.

I personally find that soft, shaded colors based on pastels tend to work better than putting everything in heavy, solid colors. Let the heavy and strong colors be used for alerts. A little later, I show you how to do conditional formatting for charts.

Apply shaded/single colors to the series data and save the two color-customized fills for the chart's Plot Area.

In your series data, you have the option of formatting your components to be transparent. This appearance can be advantageous in creating "floating" components, particularly with stacked charts. It is often used for simplified Gantt Charts (timeline charts used in project management). Later I present some examples using transparent graphical components.

Conditionally Formatted Charts

In your spreadsheet you have the ability to use conditional formatting. Out of the box, graphical components don't seem to share these capabilities. It would be nice to have a chart whose graphical components can change their color or appearance to draw attention to something happening in the chart.

These steps are needed to make this conditional formatting work:

1. You need to organize your worksheet so that the "conditional features" are picked up from the worksheets. This calls for separating your spreadsheet functionality into individual worksheets: one for holding the data, one for analyzing it, and one for a dedicated presentation layer.

2. Consider having three streams of data: your regular data and two kinds of exceptions that you need to flag. Because these three situations are mutually exclusive, you can use a stacked chart to combine them. The stacked chart gives the illusion of having a single data series with multiple colors depending on the value displayed; hence, a conditionally formatted chart (see Figure 6-6).

I leave you to explore the `ch06_02ConditionalChart.xls` file on the book's CD-ROM; however, there are some very important things you need to be aware of. They relate to handling missing data and formatting the chart series data, as with the problem described next.

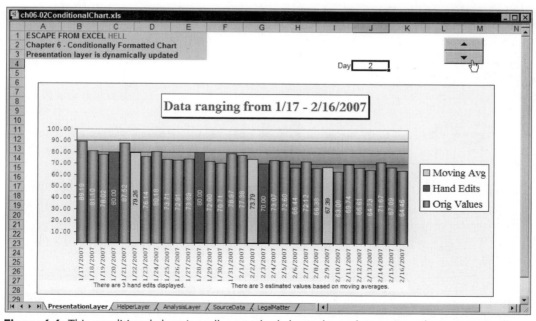

Figure 6-6: This conditional chart is really a stacked chart whose data series values are mutually exclusive.

Part II

"I have a few missing data points in my data. The points more or less follow a predictable pattern, so I should be able to use a moving average to fill in the gaps. How do I combine the data to present a chart without holes?"

This problem reveals two complications:

1. Most people construct moving average formulas with lagging or leading trends. Also, adjusting the period of the moving average is not something that everybody immediately knows how to do.

2. A moving average should be "balanced" so that the period you are averaging stems as far back in time as it does going forward. For a seven-day moving average, you would compute the average of your data for a given day with the next three days and the prior three days. What do you do if there is a gap in your current day?

Here is the solution. Your moving average period, previous period, and next period are defined in the AnalysisLayer worksheet (see Figure 6-7) as:

```
MovAvgPeriod is a defined value (which is set to 7 in this example)
PreviousPeriod is defined as =-INT(MovAvgPeriod/2)
NextPeriod is defined as =MovAvgPeriod+PreviousPeriod-1
```

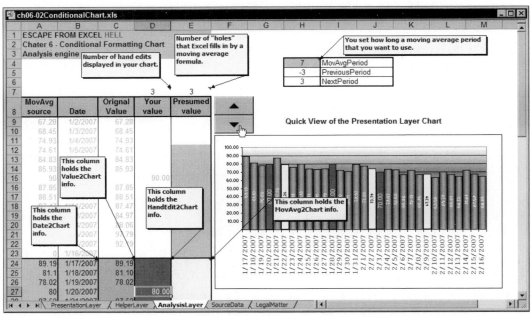

Figure 6-7: The AnalysisLayer worksheet does all the hard work, but only on a sliver of data.

The formula for the moving average is essentially (in cell E27):

```
=AVERAGE(OFFSET(A27,PreviousPeriod,0,MovAvgPeriod,1))*(MovAvgPeriod/(MovAvgPer
iod-1))
```

Notice that the formula contains a multiplying factor of (MovAvgPeriod/(MovAvgPeriod-1)). If you take just the straight moving average without this factor, the value returned will be underestimated.

"It is very clever to use a stacked chart by creating separate data series. My alert values are colorized differently. I can display their values directly on the cylindrical bars. My only problem is that I need the zero values to disappear (see Figure 6-8)."

Zero artifact (a zero on its side at top of each bar)

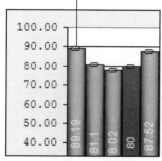

Figure 6-8: Get rid of the zero artifact (hovering at the top of the columns)!

You can handle this situation by formatting the series data labels. Right-click each of the series data labels (for the regular data values, the manual edits, and the moving average estimates) to format them. In the Number tab for the Format Data Labels window, make sure that the option for Linked to Source is checked. In your source data, set the custom format for your numbers as something like the following:

```
#,##0.00;"-"#,##0.00;;
```

This format will cause the data used for your chart to hide the zero values. The format pattern in front of the first semicolon instructs Excel on how to display positive numbers. Between the first and second semicolon is the pattern for displaying negative numbers. The pattern for zero values is specified between the second and third semicolons. Notice that no pattern is present there, so zero values are suppressed!

NOTE

Your source data could conceivably hold thousands of records. I told you to make sure that Linked to Source is checked. If you adopt the layered approach, as is done in this spreadsheet, you need to set the formatting only for the 31 rows in the AnalysisLayer worksheet that make their way into the chart. You don't need to worry about formatting the numbers in your source data.

Miscellaneous Chart Construction Issues

This section covers a variety of chart construction issues. All too often, charts don't incorporate certain kinds of constructions because it is not realized that options and solutions are available.

TO GAP OR NOT TO GAP

"I have data over a range of dates. There is no data for most of the dates. I want to show this data in two different ways. In one of these, I want to see it in strict chronological time with the empty values. In the other one, I want to see the same chart with no gaps in the values."

Most of the time Excel correctly decides whether gaps in the timeline should be explicitly shown. Sometimes, though, you won't want to give Excel "automatic" control in this way. Figure 6-9 shows two different ways to display the exact same data. You'll also find this side-by-side comparison in the ch06_03TimelineChart.xls file on the book's CD-ROM.

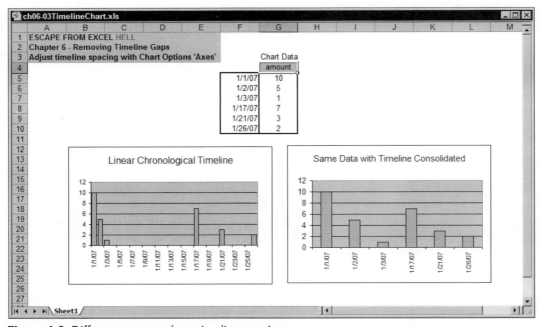

Figure 6-9: Different ways to show timeline spacing

Figure 6-10 shows you how to set timeline options. When you're creating a chart or modifying an existing one, right-click the chart and select Chart Options.

In the Axes tab, you can select from three radio buttons:

- Automatic
- Category
- Time-scale

Instead of Automatic, choose either Category or Time-scale.

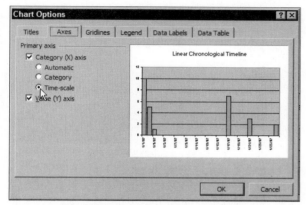

Figure 6-10: Category and Time-scale options are used to adjust timeline.

NOTE

When you select Time-scale, the graphical components for the series data tend to be very narrow, approaching pencil thin. You can adjust the thickness by formatting the data series, clicking the Options tab, and setting the Gap width to a low value such as 0 or 20 (see Figure 6-11).

As you adjust the gap width setting, the chart is visually adjusted to show you how it will appear.

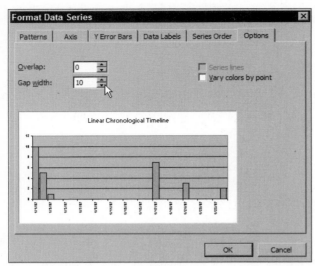

Figure 6-11: Adjusting the gap width determines the bar thickness.

REPRESENTING DATA

"I just went to the Internet and retrieved some stock price info for a public company. I got everything I wanted and more. I got the date, close, high, low, open, adjusted closing, and volume. I really want to see just the closing and high/low prices. There are a few problems. The data was supplied to me in reverse chronological order. The trends in the data plot are in the wrong direction [see Figure 6-12]. To make matters worse, I can barely distinguish between the high, low, and closing values."

Let's work through these issues one problem at a time. Upon being presented with reverse chronological data (that is, the earliest data appears last in the list) for the first time, the data may appear in the chart in the wrong order, as shown in Figure 6-12.

Click the Chart Category Axis (the axis with the dates), press Ctrl+1, and go to the Scale tab. Look for the Dates in Reverse Order setting and change it.

You've now reversed the sequence of dates in your line plot, but the values may still be difficult to read. It would be nice to display the closing prices as a line and see high and low as error bars. Start by plotting the closing stock price as a line chart. After you've created the chart, you can click the data series and press Ctrl+1 to format it. Go to the Y Error Bars tab, click the Custom option, and set the range of cells you want for the upper and lower values in the error bars (see Figure 6-13).

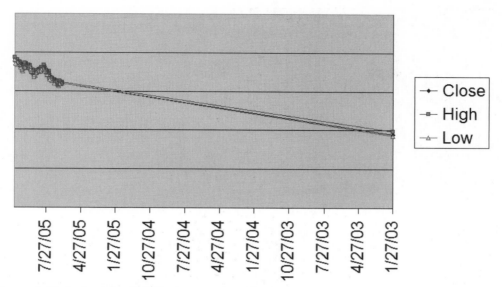

Figure 6-12: A chart that is difficult to read and interpret

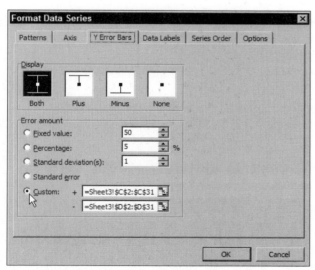

Figure 6-13: Error bars in your data series can be mapped to cell ranges.

"My high and low prices are no good for depicting error bars! I get a ridiculous-looking chart [see Figure 6-14]. *"*

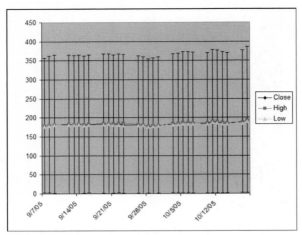

Figure 6-14: High and low values are no good for displaying error bars.

You need to use the "deltas" or numerical difference between the closing price and its high (or low) price. If your dates appear in column A, closing price in column B, high in column C, and low in column D; then, place in column E formulas like these:

```
=C2-B2                              Formulas for the "High" delta
=C3-B3
. . .
```

and in column F:

```
=B2-D2                              Formulas for the "Low" delta
=B3-D3
. . .
```

Instead of the range of cells shown in Figure 6-13, use the range of cells that point to columns E and F (the delta values).

You can format the line thickness and appearance of the data and chart appearance so that you wind up getting something like what appears in Figure 6-15. You can find a completed workbook with the error bar plots in ch06_04StockPriceLinePlot.xls on the book's CD-ROM.

NOTE

Your data may have gaps in your data despite the fact that you download information over a contiguous range of dates. Stock prices, for instance, are not going to have prices for dates on Saturdays, Sundays, and legal holidays. If these gaps pose an issue to you, you can set your Chart Options for Axes to Category, instead of Automatic or Time-scale.

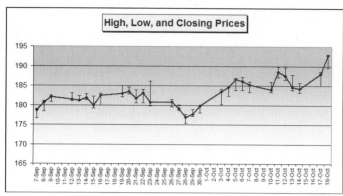

Figure 6-15: Stock price with error bars displayed properly

ADDING A TRENDLINE

"I want to add a trendline to my chart."

Right-click the data series of your chart and select Add Trendline.

Figure 6-16 shows the type of trend you can create.

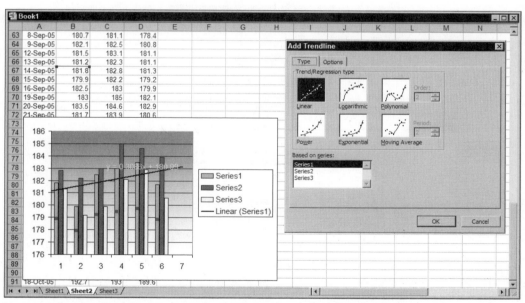

Figure 6-16: Trendlines and moving averages can be superimposed on your charts.

NOTE

Trendlines can be thrown off with zero values in the chart data. A good way to eliminate this problem is to insert #N/A in its place. This technique is described in detail in the "Testing for Data Types and Cell Properties" section of Chapter 8. Figure 8-13 shows this graphically.

CREATING HISTOGRAMS

"I want a simple histogram that allows me to redefine the intervals at any time and have the chart redrawn."

Figure 6-17 shows this; it also displays the key formula for computing the frequency counts.

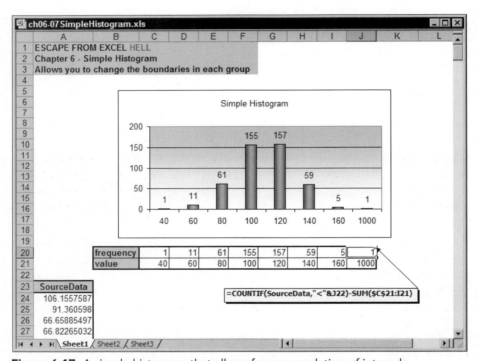

Figure 6-17: A simple histogram that allows for easy updating of intervals

Basically, the technique is to count the cumulative number of occurrences in the dataset below a certain value and subtract from it the sum of the previous values. Here is the formula:

```
=COUNTIF(SourceData,"<"&J22)-SUM($C$21:I21)
```

You can try adjusting the intervals in the histogram with the ch06_07SimpleHistogram.xls file on the book's CD-ROM.

A Useful Chart

What follows is a ready-made XY Scatter chart with all the bells and whistles. You can use it right away. It has a wealth of features to harvest and incorporate into spreadsheets of your own.

A Slightly Enhanced XY Scatter Chart

"I need an XY Scatter chart that allows me to display the data in quadrants, places text labels next to selected data points, and allows me to pick data from a combination of datasets. I also want to annotate the various data points on the fly. Oh, one more thing: I don't want to distribute this with any macros."

Sounds like a tall order? Well, it is, but you have it as a finished tool (file `ch06_05XYScatterTool.xls`) that you can use right away.

I encourage you to spend a little time understanding how this tool works so that you can customize it and harvest some of its techniques in your own spreadsheets.

XY Scatter plots are easy to create in Excel but not so easy to build in some custom features.

QUADRANT SCALING

A typical XY Scatter plot shows the values of various points of data along an XY plane. You might be performing some kind of risk analysis, comparing frequencies of various kinds of hazards versus level of exposure. An XY Scatter chart is an excellent mechanism for visualizing such quantitative information. It is natural to take your data and break it up into four quadrants or sectors.

There's a hidden problem here. If you'll be dividing your data into quadrants, how do you classify where the dividing line goes? If you are doing statistical sampling, an average value could be used as your threshold. That typically won't work outside statistical sampling. You might be evaluating the cost of installing various security devices in your organization versus the potential exposure your business faces if you don't install the devices. What amount of loss might be deemed acceptable? Obviously, you'll have to come up with your own criteria to use to classify your data.

The Scatter Plot tool (shown in Figure 6-18) can be found on the book's CD-ROM (file `ch06_05XYScatterTool.xls`).

The key to using this tool lies in understanding that everything works in layers. Your data that you want to plot is one layer. Your configuration information that tells the spreadsheet how everything is organized is in another layer. You have a presentation layer in which you interactively choose what you want to see and can annotate the XY Scatter chart. Of course, some computations are going on behind the scenes in an analysis layer.

THE SOURCE DATA

The XY Scatter tool has a sample set of source data (see Figure 6-19).

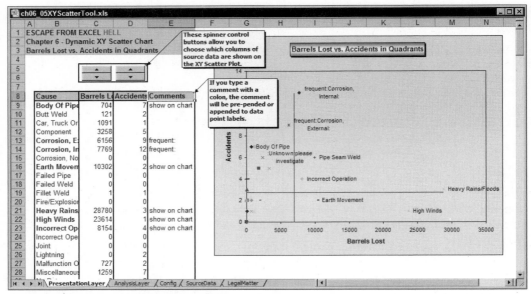

Figure 6-18: Configurable XY Scatter Plot tool

ch06_05XYScatterTool.xls

ESCAPE FROM EXCEL HELL
Chapter 6 - XY Scatter Tool Sample Source Data
Hazardous Liquid Pipeline Accident Summary by Cause 1/1/2005 - 10/06/2005
US Department of Transportation - Office of Pipeline Safety
Source Data
http://ops.dot.gov/stats/LQ05_CS.HTM
(generated 10/18/2005)

The Source Data Location should be referencing the user defined name located here. In this case, it happens to be:
MySourceDataLocation

Cause	Accidents	Barrels Lost	Property Damages	Fatalities	Injuries	Prop Damages (Log Base 10)
Body Of Pipe	7	704	1049087	0	0	6.02
Butt Weld	2	121	66556	0	0	4.82
Car, Truck Or Other Vehicle Not Related To Excavation Activity	1	1091	100757	0	0	5
Component	5	3258	429926	0	0	5.63
Corrosion, External	9	6156	2291564	0	1	6.36
Corrosion, Internal	12	7769	592531	0	0	5.77
Corrosion, Not Specified	0	0	0	0	0	0
Earth Movement	2	10302	22000550	0	0	7.34
Failed Pipe	0	0	0	0	0	0
Failed Weld	0	0	0	0	0	0
Fillet Weld	1	1	51982	0	0	4.72
Fire/Explosion As Primary Cause	0	0	0	0	0	0
Heavy Rains/Floods	3	28780	1230500	0	0	6.09
High Winds	1	23614	0	0	0	0
Incorrect Operation	4	8154	460803	0	0	5.66
Incorrect Operation By Operator Personnel	0	0	0	0	0	0
Joint	0	0	0	0	0	0

PresentationLayer / AnalysisLayer / Config / SourceData / LegalMatter

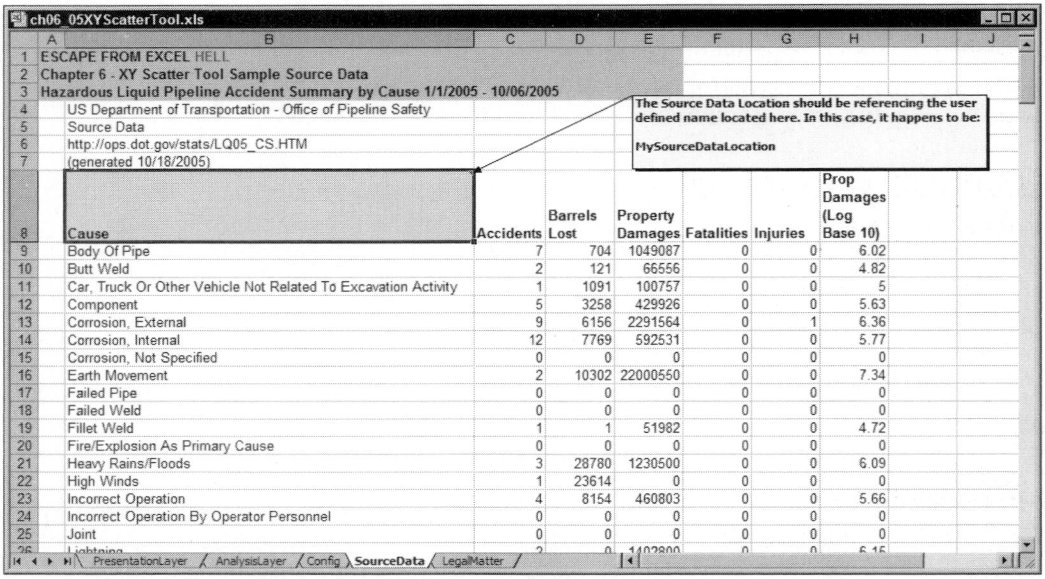

Figure 6-19: Sample source data used by the XY Scatter tool

A little info about the source data used in this example

Throughout this book I try, where possible, to use real-world data. I think it's important that the book's examples reflect the kinds of obstacles that arise when working with actual data. As an example, how do you handle a chart when some of the data stretches over many orders of magnitude? These kinds to situations arise often enough that contrived examples aren't needed.

In the XY Scatter tool, I include hazardous liquid pipeline accident information reported by the U.S. Department of Transportation—Office of Pipeline Safety. It details counts of reported accidents, barrels lost, property damages, fatalities, and injuries published on 10/18/2005. The data covers accidents reported in the first three quarters of 2005 (you can go to `http://ops.dot.gov/stats/LQ05_CS.HTM` to get the data). I suspect that the impact of Katrina and other hurricanes of the season are not fully accounted for in this dataset. As I get updated data, I will post it to the book's Web site: `www.EscapeFromExcelHell.com`.

"My data stretches over many orders of magnitude. This makes it difficult to place onto a chart. How do I handle this?"

There are several ways to deal with this. One of them is to use facilities already built into Excel. When using the Chart Wizard, you can you can specify a Custom Type and select Logarithmic.

An easier way to do this is to take one of your existing charts and set the Value Axis to a logarithmic scale (see Figure 6-20).

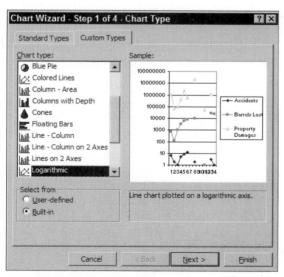

Figure 6-20: Setting the Logarithmic scale option and the resulting chart

"It is nice to convert everything into a logarithmic scale, but not all my data series need to be represented as a logarithm. I've often seen a secondary axis on Excel charts, but I'm not sure how to make it appear and use it."

One of your data series may be dominating your spreadsheet. In the case of the pipeline accident data, the property damage could number into the millions of dollars whereas the number of accidents might be only several dozen. In this case, you may want to shunt the property damages data series onto a secondary axis. Click the data series. If it's truly dominating the chart (such as in the left window in Figure 6-21), you shouldn't have any difficulty picking it out. With the data series selected, press Ctrl+1 to format the series. In the Axis tab (in the window to the right in Figure 6-21), select Secondary Axis.

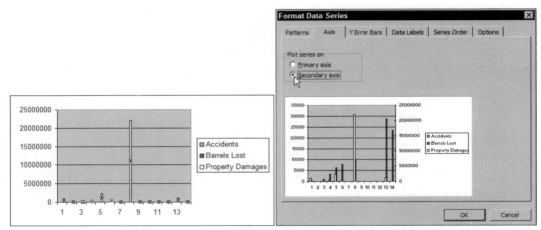

Figure 6-21: Resizing the spike in a data series by using a Secondary Y Axis

Because the data series is represented separately, using a logarithmic scale may not even be necessary.

"I got my Secondary Y Axis showing on the right side of my chart, but I can't seem to get a Secondary X Axis!"

Logic and common sense would seem to dictate that if you enable the Secondary Y Axis by formatting a data series, you should be able to do the same for a Secondary X Axis. After you get the Secondary Y Axis to appear, you can get a Secondary X Axis to appear by setting the Chart Options (and not by formatting the series data; see Figure 6-22)!

After all this, I'm sure your head must be spinning from all the varied and bewildering chart options. But there's one more approach to understand, and it's important. It gets away from all the charting headaches. The strategy you need to think about is to manage the data *before* it makes its way into the chart. This what is done in the last column of source data in the file `ch06_05XYScatterTool.xls`. The formula uses a pseudo-logarithm so that it avoids the problems with negative and zero values. If property damages are listed in column E, then the `Prop Damages (Log Base 10)` are

```
=IF(E9<1,0,ROUND(LOG(E9),2))
```

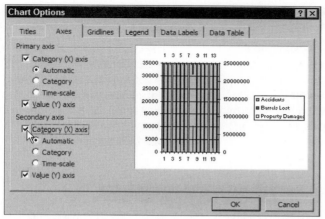

Figure 6-22: To enable the Secondary X Axis (after Secondary Y Axis is enabled), you need to change Category (X) Axis on the Chart Options.

THE CONFIG WORKSHEET

Although this worksheet resides on the XY Scatter Tool spreadsheet, you can point the tool to retrieve data from any other spreadsheet file, and you can do so *without any hard links*. Quite literally, just place the name and location of the source data on the Config worksheet (see Figure 6-23).

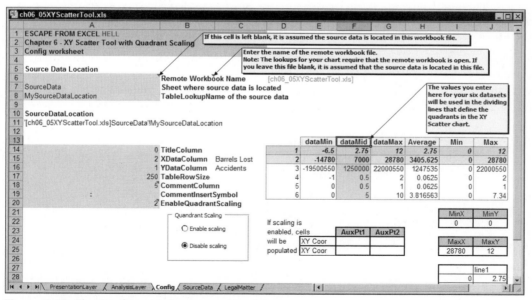

Figure 6-23: The Config worksheet maps the data.

"I would like to link data from another spreadsheet and not have to worry about link updates. Is there any clean way to do this? I know macros could be used, but that's way over my head, and I don't want to manually copy and paste every time my data changes."

The XY Scatter tool has its own SourceData worksheet for holding the original data. For maximum flexibility, it would be nice to use data directly from another spreadsheet without having it hardwired. The XY Scatter tool does this, but there is a lot happening in that spreadsheet that isn't specifically tied to retrieving remote data. You could take the time to isolate the retrieval component; however, it is not necessary, because I have done it for you. On the book's CD-ROM, I provide a spreadsheet you can use for this purpose (ch06_06LooselyCoupledLinks.xls; see Figure 6-24).

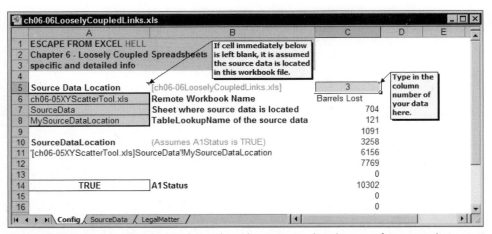

Figure 6-24: Loosely Coupled Links tool easily retrieves data by specifying just the remote workbook and lookup locations

Notice that if you enter the name of another open spreadsheet file, you can retrieve the data from the remote workbook. In Figure 6-24, the remote workbook name is ch06_05XYScatterTool.xls, the file that contains the accident data. The third column of the accident dataset is labeled Barrels Lost. Entering the number 3 in cell C5 retrieves that third column. If you enter 4, you retrieve the fourth column of data, which happens to be Property Damages. There are several advantages to linking data in this manner.

- There is no hardwiring of spreadsheets, so you will not get the link update problems when you update filenames.

- Absolutely no macros or programming is involved.

- As your source data changes, so does your spreadsheet that retrieves the data.

To use this facility, you can replicate the formulas from column C and adjust the column number.

NOTE

As a technical aside, here is the lookup formula and how it works:

```
=OFFSET(INDIRECT(SourceDataLocation,A1Status),ROW()-ROW(C$5)-
1,C$5-1)
```

Basically, the formula is saying to find the spreadsheet cell represented by the SourceDataLocation. From this location, do a lookup for the value of a cell a certain number of rows and columns away.

That column number or selector can be adjusted by manual editing or through a conventional Excel formula. In fact, this is how the XY Scatter tool allows you to switch the data that is shown in the XY Scatter tool (see Figure 6-18).

Now I want you to turn your attention to the presentation layer of the XY Scatter tool. You may have many data points to plot. Displaying labels for all of these data points will make for a very cluttered and hard to read chart. Instead, you may want the data description such as High Winds or Heavy Rains/Flooding to be displayed on the XY Scatter chart. Typing anything in the Comments column (column E) will make the label appear next to the data point on the Excel chart. If your comment has a colon in it, the comment will be prepended or appended at the end of the data label depending on whether the text appears before or after the colon. You can combine the types of annotations in one. For example, you might enter the comment Risky:Must Verify for the Cause described as Component. In this XY Scatter chart, the data label will appear as follows:

Risky:Component:Must Verify

The colon delimiter can be changed to any symbol of your choosing (adjust cell A19 in the Config worksheet).

I have a few final points to mention about the Config worksheet. The purpose of this XY Scatter tool is to give you precise control over how to set the dividing lines when you're splitting your XY chart into the four quadrants. The place you set this is highlighted in Figure 6-25. The rows in this portion of the Config worksheet signify the six datasets or columns in your source data. Conditional formatting is used to help identify which datasets are being displayed in the XY chart. These are highlighted in the green and blue colors on the Config worksheet (not discernible in the book, but you can see the colors in the ch06_05XYScatterTool.xls file on the book's CD-ROM).

The values you enter here for your six datasets will be used in the dividing lines that define the quadrants in the XY Scatter chart.

	dataMin	dataMid	dataMax	Average	Min	Max
1	-6.5	2.75	12	2.75	0	12
2	-14780	7000	28780	3405.625	0	28780
3	-19500550	1250000	22000550	1247535	0	22000550
4	-1	0.5	2	0.0625	0	2
5	0	0.5	1	0.0625	0	1
6	0	5	10	3.816563	0	7.34

Figure 6-25: The `dataMid` column allows you to specify the dividing lines that split the XY chart into four quadrants.

Closing Thoughts

In some ways this chapter is thorough and replete with details; in other regards it is necessarily incomplete. There are far too many topics related to charting and data visualization to cover in a single chapter. My goal was to show you some real problems, the kinds that get you quickly into trouble, such as with gaps in the data. My other goal was to provide practical solutions while arming you with the skill and agility to solve similar problems on your own.

The chapter on data visualization is not closed. I have more to say about this topic in the remaining chapters.

Part III

More Elaborate Escapes

Chapter 7

Common Issues with Excel Components

In This Chapter

◆ Putting conditional formatting to practical use

◆ Understanding spreadsheet calculation

◆ Facilitating data entry through Excel's validation facilities

◆ Protecting workbooks, worksheets, and files

◆ Harnessing Auto and Advanced Filters

Overview

This chapter addresses some important techniques and issues. Though conditional formatting is used from time to time, it generally comes in as an afterthought. One reason is that the methodology for using formulas to control formatting is not generally well understood. Techniques of conditional formatting are easy to learn. They facilitate communicating information in a spreadsheet in a very useful and tangible manner. When you acquire the essential skills, you will find that conditional formatting weaves quite naturally into the fabric of your spreadsheets. This use is illustrated very clearly when it is integrated with Excel's data validation facilities. Moreover, these facilities greatly enhance user experience.

In this chapter, other interesting topics are addressed as well. You'll find a good deal of discussion about spreadsheet protection and how it works, and security issues and vulnerabilities. The chapter finishes with essential techniques in using Auto and Advanced Filters.

Conditional Formatting

One of my favorite topics concerning spreadsheets is conditional formatting. I'm especially delighted that the role of conditional formatting is being greatly expanded on in Excel 12.

From my perspective, spreadsheets behave as living, breathing, dynamic entities. When something goes wrong or conditions change, your spreadsheet should be actively communicating something about this. Profitability may be way off, or the spreadsheet may need to alert you of some inconsistency in your data or formulas. Whatever the case may be, conditional formatting can greatly enhance the design, readability, and effectiveness of your spreadsheets.

I explain some basic concepts about conditional formatting and show how to put them to use.

You may recall that number values can change their appearance based on their value. You can, for instance, make a number in a cell appear green if it is positive and red if it is negative. You can do this by setting the Number format of a cell to Custom and specifying it as something like this:

```
[Green]#,##0_);[Red]#,##0
```

Controlling how a cell is formatted based on its value or according to some formula is a powerful capability. This custom number formatting is nice but there are other number formatting effects you may want to use in tandem. These effects may include, for example, making the text boldface or italicized. You may want to alter the background pattern of a cell or adjust its borders. The key point is that Excel does provide a facility to do all this in one step. Further, it allows you to specify multiple criteria or conditional tests to determine a cell's behavior. With Excel version 11.x and earlier, you can specify three conditional tests for any spreadsheet cell. Excel 12 ups the number of conditional tests considerably.

Regardless of which version of Excel you use, the conditional tests get applied one at a time in a strict sequential order. As soon as one of the tests succeeds, the corresponding formatting rule is immediately applied and all the others are forgotten. A test always returns a TRUE or FALSE value. If for some reason the conditional test or formula returns something other than TRUE or FALSE, it is treated as though it were FALSE. A conditional test might be useful in determining, for example, whether a value of a cell falls between two values.

To summon conditional formatting, select a spreadsheet cell or group of cell and then, from the Excel menu, click Format⇨Conditional Formatting.

There is a sequence of testing you may want to think about, as illustrated in the following situation:

"I am trying to use conditional formatting to highlight a spreadsheet cell in a color indicated by its value. Basically, I am trying to mimic the states of water based on temperature. If the water is boiling it is red. If it is liquid, it should be colored blue. If it is at the frozen state, it should be gray. The temperature scale I am using is Fahrenheit (for which water boils at 212 and freezes at 32 degrees). I am not sure how to set up the tests using the Cell Value Is option."

Forgetting about the fact that it would make more sense to use the Celsius temperature scale, here is what you might do. There are two approaches. The first is to use the `Cell Value Is` technique; the second is to use `Formula Is`. I show you how to do each of these in the following sections.

Using a Cell Value for Conditional Formatting

When you select `Cell Value Is`, you have a variety of options for testing whether the cell value is

- `between a minimum and maximum value`

- `not between a minimum and maximum value`

- `equal to a value`

- `not equal to a value`

- `greater than a value`

- `less than a value`

- `greater than or equal to a value`

- `less than or equal to a value`

NOTE
The "between" range includes the minimum and maximum endpoints. The "not between" range excludes the minimum and maximum endpoints.

You can choose to use a set of conditional tests such as:

```
Condition1: Cell Value Is greater than or equal to 212
Condition2: Cell Value Is greater than 32
Condition3: Cell Value Is less than or equal to 32
```

Notice that the `Condition2` test overlaps with the `Condition1` test. This is perfectly fine because the only way that `Condition2` is being tested is if the `Condition1` test was run and already failed. As a result, the test of the middle temperature range (`Condition2`) doesn't need to test for its upper limit.

Part III

NOTE
The values appearing in the test can be literal numbers such as 212 or 32, or they can alternatively be spreadsheet cell references that contain the values.

Using Formulas for Conditional Formatting

When you select Formula Is, you must rely on using formulas that return only a TRUE or FALSE value. These formulas reside in the conditional tests. They can use values of other spreadsheet cells, as is shown in Figure 7-1 (you can find the ch07_06Conditional Formatting.xls file on the book's CD-ROM). Notice that the conditional formulas for cell D6 reference the contents of another cell, B6.

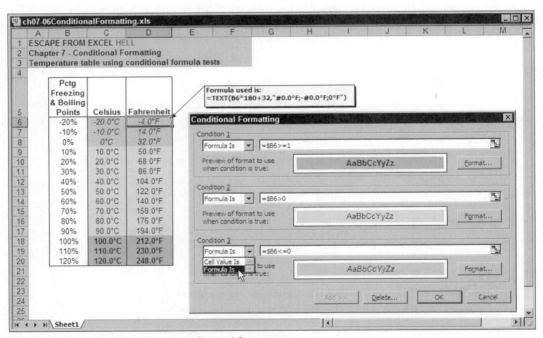

Figure 7-1: Using a formula in conditional formatting

Conditional Formatting Using Content from Another Worksheet or Workbook

"I want to apply conditional formatting using criteria from another worksheet."

Normally when you're applying conditional formatting, you cannot directly reference another worksheet or, for that matter, another workbook (see Figure 7-2).

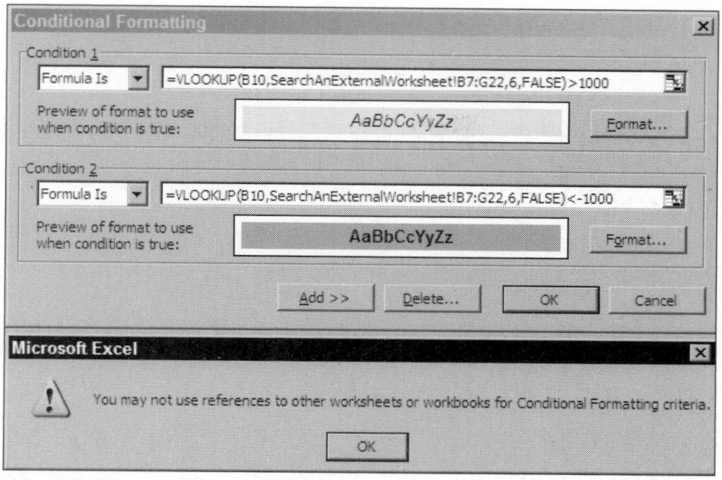

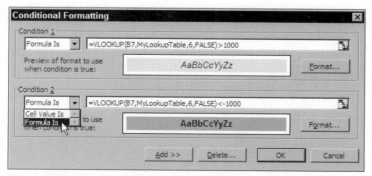

Figure 7-2: Conditional formatting does not want you to use references to external worksheets.

The good news is that you actually can. The key is to employ user-defined names. This allows you to enable conditional formatting based on an external worksheet reference. I show you how to accomplish this, and at the same time, show you how to use the same mechanism for dynamic data validation.

To follow this example, you need to open the spreadsheet ch07_01OffWorksheetCondFormat.xls on the book's CD-ROM. In the SearchAnExternalWorksheet tab, you will see a cell with a transaction ID. Select this cell and then click Format⇨Conditional Formatting from the Excel menu (see Figure 7-3). The conditional formatting takes this transaction ID, performs a lookup on the remote table, and if the respective gain on the transaction exceeds 1000, the transaction ID is colorized in green and the font appears in italics. If the gain is lower than a -1000 (that is, a loss that exceeds 1,000), then the transaction ID is colorized in red and the font appears in boldface.

Figure 7-3: Conditional formatting formula can make use of the named reference MyLookupTable (which resides on a separate worksheet).

Part III

The remote table is located on another worksheet (see Figure 7-6). This remote table is given the name `MyLookupTable`. The important feature here is that conditional formatting can directly make use of cell values from other worksheets.

Conditional formatting is not the only Excel component that works this way (that is, suffering from an apparent limitation and having a clever workaround). The same seems to happen with the Validation feature of Excel.

Situations in which a formula can reference itself

Conventional programming languages such as Java, C++, and Basic allow the construct of incrementing or adjusting the value of a variable based on itself. You can typically write something like this:

```
MyValue=MyValue+1
```

So, if `MyValue` happens to be 4, it will be bumped up to the value 5 the next time the program instruction `MyValue=MyValue+1` is run. You can create such constructs in Excel's VBA (Visual Basic for Applications). This is available to you if you get involved in VBA/macro programming.

You can't nominally do this with Excel worksheet formulas. The closest you can come is to place in a spreadsheet cell such as A1 the formula:

```
=A1+1
```

Upon doing so, you will immediately be prompted with a `Circular Error` warning. You can get around this problem by setting the calculation options to iterative (click Tools⇨Options and then click the Calculation tab). You can limit the number of iterations using the Maximum iterations option.

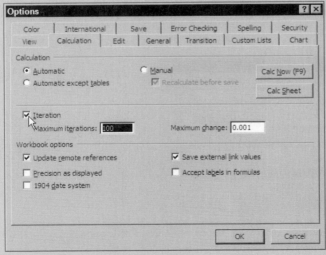

Circular references are permitted if you enable iterative calculations.

Iterative calculation is especially useful for simulations. If you need to single step through a simulation, set your calculation to Manual and the Maximum iterations to 1. A good example of a spreadsheet simulation can be found in the file `ch07_02ForestFireSimulation.xls` on the book's CD-ROM.

Restart	
Cycle	1000
Month	25-Mar
Fires	24
Live Trees	553
Total Trees	577
Pctg Tr burn	4%
Min tree density	22%
Cur tree density	42%
Max tree density	69%
Expected life	50.00
Average life	10.59
birth rate	0.05000
death rate	0.02000
fire rate	0.00010
Oldest Tree	44
Std Dev	7.17

Spreadsheet simulation of a forest fire using iterative calculations

You may want to set the calculation mode and install a special "Fire" font before opening the spreadsheet.

Because the simulation makes use of a circular reference, you need to set your calculation mode to iterative. Pressing the F9 key forces recalculations.

To get maximum enjoyment from the simulation, you need to have the `FireFont2` font installed in your system. This particular font makes the value 1 look like a tree and 9 look like a flame (these are the values that are displayed in the simulation window).

To load a font on your computer, open the Fonts Control Panel in your Windows operating system. On the File menu, click Install New Font. In the font directory of your book's CD-ROM, locate the font file (as shown in the next figure).

Remember to select Copy Fonts to Fonts Folder. After you are done with the simulation, remember to set your calculation mode back to Automatic and disable the iterative computation mode.

continued

Part III

continued

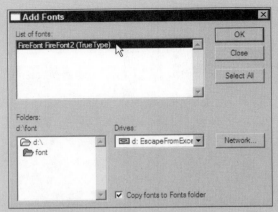

Adding the FireFont to your computer system

In case you think you can't have a formula reference itself without iterative or circular calculations, think again. There are certain circumstances in which a spreadsheet function can reference itself. Here are some examples:

```
=CELL("color",A5)          (computed from cell A5)
=OFFSET(A6,7,0)            (computed from cell A6)
```

The first formula can directly reference itself. The second formula can use itself as a starting point but can run into circular references if the row and column offsets are both set to zero.

Another situation in which it is perfectly legitimate to construct a spreadsheet formula that references the cell's own value occurs in conditional formatting. As shown in Figure 7-2, you can construct a formula that references itself. Notice that the pull-down condition type is set to `Formula Is` and that the conditional formatting formula for `B7` refers to itself:

```
=VLOOKUP(B7,MyLookupTable,6,FALSE)<-1000
```

The caveat with a conditional formatting formula is that the formula must return either a `TRUE` or a `FALSE`. The result returned does not affect the cell's value.

In addition to formulas for conditional formatting, you can use formulas for the Excel Data Validation feature in much the same way.

Data Validation

Sometimes you may prepare a spreadsheet that requires users to enter values. The values entered may need to be restricted to specific items or according to some criteria. The way to access the data validation facility is to click Data⇨Validation from the Excel menu.

In terms of restricting the data that can be entered into a cell, you have a variety of options. These include choosing whole numbers, decimals, date, time, and text length. For each of these you can choose values between, not between, equal to, not equal to, greater than, less than, greater than or equal to, and less than or equal to a given minimum or maximum number. Additionally, you can choose a custom formula or a list. I show both of these.

If, for instance, you are entering a series of values on expenditures, you may want to limit the individual amount to the maximum available balance or credit limit. This amount is dependent upon all your previous entries. You can use a custom formula to set this. The ch07_03SimpleValidation.xls file shows how (see Figure 7-4).

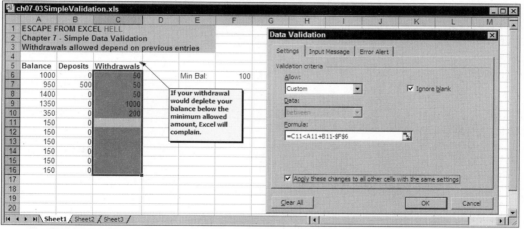

Figure 7-4: Withdrawals allowed depend on previous entries and the initial balance.

Notice that your validation formula is based on both relative and absolute cell coordinates:

```
=C6<A6+B6-$F$6
```

A validation formula structured this way allows you to easily copy the cell with validation and paste it to other spreadsheet locations.

NOTE
The Excel data validation facility is not foolproof. *After* making valid entries, a user can alter some cell, such as the initial balance or minimum balance, causing one or more entries to become invalid.

"I want to prevent duplicate numbers from being entered into a column."

Click Sheet2 of the `ch07_03SimpleValidation.xls` file (see Figure 7-5).

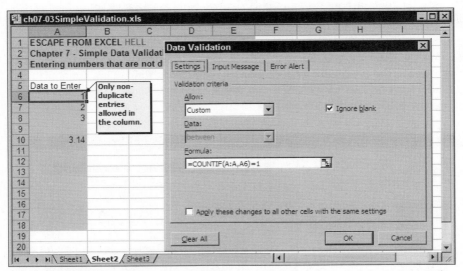

Figure 7-5: Validation can prevent duplicate entries from being placed into a column.

Notice that the formula for cell A6 is

```
=COUNTIF(A:A,A6)=1
```

and *not*

```
=COUNTIF($A:$A,A6)=1
```

The effect of using purely relative cell coordinates (from the first of these two formulas) is to allow you to replicate the Validation feature to cells in other columns.

"I am trying to create a drop-down list and am using the Excel Validation feature. My problem is that I can't seem to click a list that resides on another worksheet. Every time I try to do so, Excel complains with a warning sound but no message is displayed. If I enter the cell references exactly, such as =Sheet2!A1:A3, I get a warning message that says 'You may not use references to other worksheets or workbooks for Data Validation criteria.'"

As with conditional formatting, using defined names gets around this problem (see Figure 7-6).

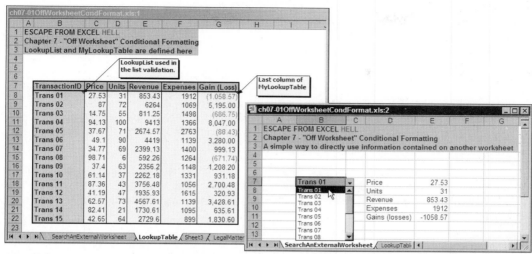

Figure 7-6: You can use a defined name (LookupList) to retrieve a list from another worksheet.

NOTE

"Is there any way I can view two worksheets from the same spreadsheet at one time?"

When you open the `ch07_01OffWorksheetCondFormat.xls` file, you see two windows open instead of one and they both seem to be for the same spreadsheet. This is a feature of Excel that you can easily use. The way to create these multiple views is to click Window⇨New Window from the Excel menu. While I have your attention on this topic, I want to alert you to a couple of features. You may be looking at two worksheets that are identically structured and may want to scroll through them synchronously. You can do so by going to the Excel Window menu and clicking Compare Side by Side With. If you happen to have multiple views of a single workbook or, for that matter, two parts of a single worksheet, you can perform synchronous scrolling. Obviously, you can scroll separate workbooks as well.

One of the validation criteria you can specify is a `List` (see Figure 7-7). Using this option, you can specify the `Source`, which is `LookupList` and happens to reside on a separate worksheet.

Notice that the data validation feature is tag teamed with conditional formatting, so that options you pick for gains or losses beyond 1000 are colorized.

"I would like to use the validation feature to retrieve a list from a remote workbook."

Because both data validation and conditional formatting can use defined names in their formulas, is it possible to use validation criteria or formatting criteria from another workbook? The answer is yes, but there is a potential issue of creating a hard link, which will cause problems after you save the files and decide to change the filename of the remote workbook. You can use a cleaner approach.

It is complex to understand its inner workings, but it is easy to use (see Figure 7-7):

1. Open a spreadsheet containing the list of items you want to restrict your data entry to. For this example, I want you to open the file ch07_04RemoteDataWorkbook.xls on the book's CD-ROM. It contains a list of accident causes on the SourceData worksheet. The very first item to be retrieved from the list of accident causes is in cell B5. This location is given the user-defined name Anchor01FirstDataPoint.

2. Open the ch07_05RemoteDataValidation.xls file. In cells A6 through A8, place the remote workbook name, worksheet, and location of the starting point of the data for the remote workbook of your choice (it is already populated with the correct data for this example).

   You can use a cell coordinate such as B5 instead of a defined name, but a better practice is to use a defined name for this "anchor cell." You do this so that you then won't need to worry if you insert or delete rows or columns on the remote workbook.

   I discuss anchor cells at length in my book *Excel Best Practices for Business* (Wiley Publishing, Inc.).

3. Notice that a line of text appears immediately above the list of data you want to retrieve. This text line will throw off the count for the number of rows in your list. Because the number of excess rows is 1, that is the number you place in A14 of the ch07_04RemoteDataWorkbook.xls file.

4. Click cell A22 to pick a value from the list of items from your remote workbook.

There are several key advantages of this framework:

- As you add new items to, or remove items from, the list on your remote workbook, the drop-down list grows or shrinks accordingly. You don't need to worry about redefining the cell boundaries of the list.

- The values in your list that reside on the remote workbook can be computed by formulas. They do not have to be static values.

- The pointers on the ch07_04RemoteDataWorkbook.xls file that tell it where to retrieve the list can be determined by a formula. Remember from Chapter 2 that you can create a dispatching formula using CHOOSE and MATCH. The formula for cell A6 can be something like the following:

```
=CHOOSE(MATCH(UnitsSold,A11:A13),"file1.xls","file2.xls","file3.xls")
```

- There are no hard-wired links involved in retrieving the data.

- No use of macros or VBA is involved.

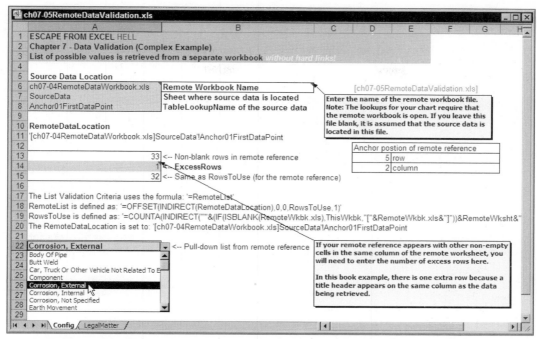

Figure 7-7: Point your file to a remote workbook and automatically retrieve a list of items from that workbook without using any hard links.

In general, data validation has some very powerful features. These come into play when you're constructing complex spreadsheets. As stated earlier, it is not foolproof, but if you have disciplined users who are looking to use rather than bypass the controls, this facility can serve your needs well.

Workbook, Worksheet, and File Protection

Depending on your needs, restricting all or parts of your spreadsheet may be important. I won't beat around the bush: The protections available using Excel's native facilities are based on a model of trust and therefore may not be secure enough for your needs. Given that you are sending your spreadsheets to casual users who are not intent on bypassing controls and safeguards, there is plenty you can do. There is also plenty to be perplexed about.

One thing that gets confusing is that Excel's file protection is not the same as its workbook-level protection. The former has to do with the physical access to the document. The latter concerns itself with attributes and structure of the spreadsheet. Workbook protection is not the same as protection at the sheet or cell level.

Protection at the Workbook Level

"We have a worksheet that has somehow become locked in a strange way. There is no way to maximize it, and it has lost its upper-right min, max, and cancel buttons. It is difficult to work with because we cannot move it, either. Any suggestions?"

From the Excel menu, click Tools⇨Protection⇨Unprotect Workbook. With any luck, you won't be asked for a password (see Figure 7-8).

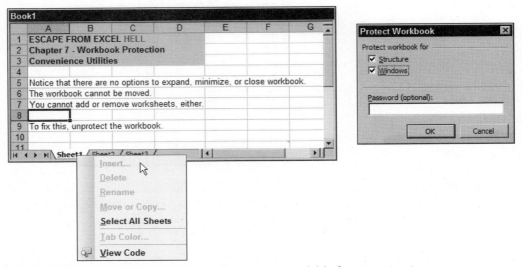

Figure 7-8: A protected workbook and the options available for activating it.

Workbook protection allows you to lock things such as adding or removing worksheets, or resizing and positioning a workbook window. Using these features makes sense when doing so in conjunction with macros in a spreadsheet-based application.

Workbook protection should not be confused with protecting individual worksheets.

Setting Protection for Individual Cells and at the Worksheet Level

"I want to distribute a spreadsheet that prevents users from viewing or altering the underlying formulas of certain spreadsheet cells."

The way you go about setting cell properties is by "formatting" the protection attributes. Press Ctrl+1 and click the Protection tab (see Figure 7-9). The default mode of Excel is to format its protection attributes as `Locked` only. If you don't want someone viewing the formula, you also have to place a checkmark next to the `Hidden` attribute.

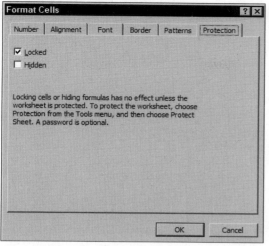

Figure 7-9: Formatting a cell's protection properties

When a spreadsheet cell is locked only, the underlying formula is perfectly visible but cannot be altered. If you want, you can make cells in your worksheet hidden but not locked. You might, for instance, be presenting a financial projection and don't want to reveal the formulas you are using. If the cells are hidden but not locked, it becomes possible to alter the original formulas for a set of cells during the course of a meeting.

NOTE

Because the protection attributes in individual cells are a part of their formatting, it is very easy to copy and paste cell formatting from one part of a spreadsheet to other locations.

TIP

It is good practice to color code cells protected differently than unprotected cells. This will help you to keep track of what you have changed. It also makes the experience easier for the user of your spreadsheet, because he or she will quickly acclimate to what can be changed and what cannot.

"I feel as though I'm going around in circles. I set my cell protection attributes. I turn on protect workbook, but nothing happens. My formulas still remain unlocked and visible."

Because of the way Excel handles protection, you have to activate the protect sheet property. You do this by clicking Tools⇨Protection⇨Protect Sheet (see Figure 7-10).

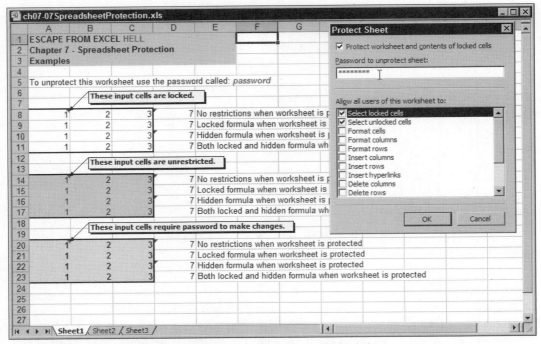

Figure 7-10: Activating the Protection Properties of an individual sheet

TIP

Whenever you're preparing a spreadsheet in which a password is involved in some aspect, be it a worksheet, workbook, or for file protection, always keep a backup version of the file without the password protection.

When you activate protection for the sheet, you can control a wide diversity of properties on a sheet-by-sheet level, including the ability to insert or delete rows and columns, or enable and disable AutoFilters, sorting, and PivotTables.

Disabling features doesn't always work the way you want or expect. You would expect that disabling the AutoFilter capability would also disable Advanced Filters, but it does not. Further, there is no option to disable Advanced Filters.

There are several other things to consider when protecting worksheets:

- When using the Tab key on a protected worksheet, the navigation path gets altered.

- Some spreadsheet add-ins do not work properly when the worksheets are protected.

- You are not restricted to setting a protection feature for the entire spreadsheet. You have the option of applying settings to selected cell ranges or individual cells.

"I want to distribute a spreadsheet with multiple passwords so that accounts payable personnel can modify only one set of spreadsheet cells and the accounts receivable personnel can modify a different set."

Before protecting a worksheet, click Tools⇨All Users to Edit Ranges (see Figure 7-11). You'll find this worksheet and the previous example in the `ch07_07SpreadsheetProtection.xls` file on the CD-ROM.

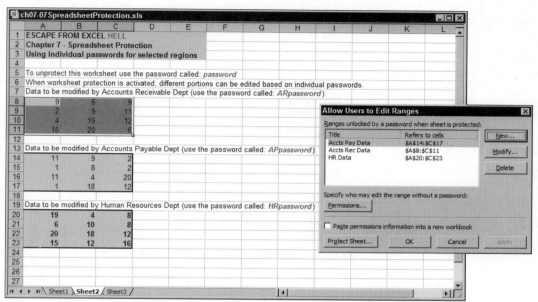

Figure 7-11: Individual passwords can be assigned to selected cell ranges.

"Worksheet protection is fine for one or two sheets, but I've got 17 sheets in my workbook! Is there any easier way to protect and unprotect the sheets in one step?"

You can protect all your workbook sheets in one step:

1. On the book's CD-ROM, locate the spreadsheet called `Utilities.xls`. Open this file.

2. Open the spreadsheet for which you want to protect all the sheets, activating that spreadsheet.

3. Press Alt+F8 (see Figure 7-12). This will display a list of macros you can run. Select `Utilities.xls!ProtectAllWorksheets` and click the Run button.

   You will be prompted for a password (see Figure 7-13).

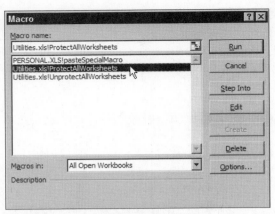

Figure 7-12: Select and run the ProtectAllWorksheets macro.

Figure 7-13: Assign the same password for all worksheets in a workbook.

There is a routine in this workbook called `UnprotectAllWorksheets` that works the same way but unprotects the sheets of your active workbook, provided that you have the password.

> *"My workbook has protected sheets and cells. I don't remember or know the password. How do I unprotect the spreadsheet?"*

It is always advisable to keep an unprotected backup copy of the workbook when it involves passwords. If you have a spreadsheet that you created but don't remember the password used, you have a number of options available. As stated earlier, Excel is not very secure (see the next sidebar, "An 'under the covers' look at Excel protection"). Some macro routines can be run using a "brute-force" technique to obliterate the existing passwords. Although there is no law in the United States prohibiting the recovery or removal of passwords from your own spreadsheet files, some issues may exist outside the United States, or when the situation involves other people's spreadsheets. Because these routines can be used to bypass the protections of someone else's intellectual property, I am not publishing such routines here. Suffice it so say that they are relatively easy to find using an Internet search engine such as Google.

An "under the covers" look at Excel protection

When you instruct Excel to protect a worksheet or a workbook, you are giving instructions to Excel as to how users should be allowed to interact with the spreadsheet. Excel doesn't change or encrypt the spreadsheet itself. It merely listens to permissions you give it. Two things should be inferred:

- Because the spreadsheet content is unencrypted, the contents of the spreadsheet can be examined by anyone. As a practical matter, unless you happen to work for Microsoft, the National Security Agency, or you are a hacker, it won't be so easy to read the underlying contents of the spreadsheet file.

- The easier way to get around the protection settings is just to change or remove the settings! Essentially, the only protection Excel provides is password protection.

When you supply a password, Excel converts your password, regardless of how short or long it is, into a special sequence of 12 characters and stores this converted password with the spreadsheet. You can examine this sequence of 12 characters, but it will be hard for you to correctly guess the original password.

Excel assumes that if you supply a password that, when converted, matches this 12-character sequence, then you are allowed to revise the permission settings for the spreadsheet. There's just one catch: These 12 characters, because of the way they are structured, can comprise only about 200,000 unique sequences (to be precise, it is $95*2^{11}=194,560$ unique sequences). It doesn't matter what you enter as a password. The sequence that gets stored with the spreadsheet will be one of these 200,000 distinctly known sequences. Given the speed of computers, a brute-force macro can easily unlock the spreadsheet in a matter of seconds!

This renders the Excel facilities for password protection inherently insecure.

The following piece of VBA code will give you an idea of how a brute-force algorithm works. The one here is purposely oversimplified and will not work, but you should get the basic idea.

```
Sub OverlySimplifiedUnprotectRoutine()
    Dim k1, k2, k3 As Integer
    n As Integer
    For k1 = 48 To 49
      For k2 = 48 To 49
        For k3 = 48 To 49
          For n = 32 To 126
            ActiveSheet.Unprotect _
                Chr(k1) & Chr(k2) & Chr(k3) & Chr(n)
      If ActiveSheet.ProtectContents = False Then
        MsgBox "Found the password: " & _
                Chr(k1) & Chr(k2) & Chr(k3) & Chr(n)
        Exit Sub
      End If
    Next: Next: Next: Next
End Sub
```

Part III

Physical File Access

"I'm not worried about protecting the formulas inside my spreadsheet. I just want a password to protect my file from being viewed by someone other than the intended recipient of the spreadsheet."

When you save your workbook, save it using File⇨Save As. In the Save As window, click Tools⇨General (see Figure 7-14).

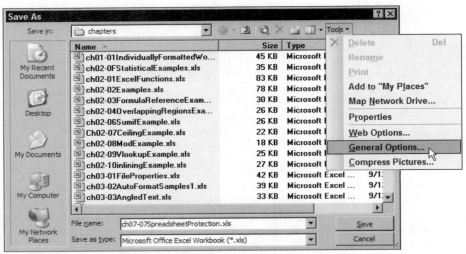

Figure 7-14: Navigation path for saving workbook with passwords

You are presented with two options: a password to open and a password to modify the workbook (see Figure 7-15). You can choose a separate password for each of these two options.

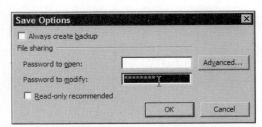

Figure 7-15: Setting password options

In case you happen to lose the password for your file, there are commercial services that will unlock the passwords, including those for file protection. More information about such services can be found on my site for this book: www.EscapeFromExcelHell.com.

"When I try to open a protected file, I get this message: 'This workbook has been password protected with an encryption scheme not available in this region. This workbook cannot be opened.'"

This problem has been known to appear in certain countries. At one point there was a legal restriction in France on the use of high-grade encryption standards, such as RC4. The workaround was for the user to set in his or her control panels a country other than France and then restart Excel.

As a practical matter, you need to be aware that older versions of Excel don't necessarily support all the different encryption schemes that may be available to you. When you save your file with password protection, clicking the Advanced button allows you to set the encryption scheme (see Figure 7-16). For backward compatibility, Microsoft recommends that you use Office 97/2000 Compatible.

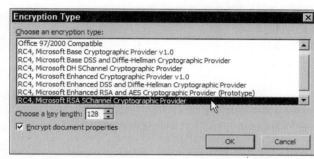

Figure 7-16: Setting Encryption Type when password protecting an Excel file

 CAUTION

The encryption types that are available to a user you are sending a password-protected file may not be same as the ones on your machine. Verify that the encryption type you plan to use is supported by the recipient.

Although you can use encryption schemes to protect the file password, the spreadsheet file is left open to inspection. Figure 7-17 illustrates this point very clearly. It shows in Notepad the plain-text content of a spreadsheet that uses Excel's password-protected file. The spreadsheet has this formula:

```
=2*foobar
```

and the following macro code:

```
Sub AVeryNonSecureMacro()
'
' AVeryNonSecureMacro Macro
' Macro recorded 11/6/2005 by Loren Abdulezer
'


    Range("A11").Select
```

```
    ActiveCell.FormulaR1C1 = _
        "If You Can Read This Macro From a Password Encrypted File Then The
File is NOT SECURE!!!"
    Range("A12").Select
End Sub
```

See whether you can spot in this code the file from the so-called password-encrypted file (see Figure 7-17).

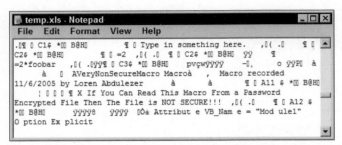

Figure 7-17: Password-encrypted spreadsheet file using one of the high-grade encryption schemes viewed with a plain-text editor

The reason all this is visible is that the encryption scheme encrypts the password, but doesn't do much about the content. This is downright scary! Short of using Microsoft's Information Rights Management technology or separate commercial-grade encryption software, you have no file security if someone has physical access to your spreadsheet file. Think about this the next time you e-mail your spreadsheet, even if it has Excel password protection.

> *"I want to securely e-mail a spreadsheet to someone and prevent anyone who intercepts the spreadsheet from opening it, unless they have been provided the password."*

The key to safely and securely transmitting spreadsheet files is to encrypt the *entire* spreadsheet file, not just the password and file properties. A quick Internet search reveals plenty of commercial grade encryption tools. If you need to securely encrypt your files with no-cost or very low-cost software, you may want to explore tools such as PGP (Pretty Good Privacy) and its derivatives. Information resources and links are posted on www.EscapeFromExcelHell.com.

With such tools, you can drag and drop a group of files, and not only encrypt them but also digitally sign them (see Figure 7-18).

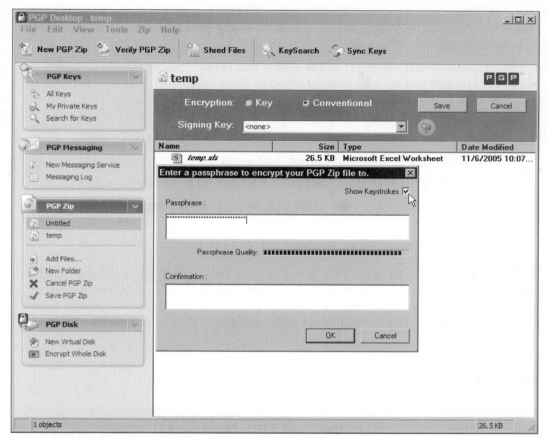

Figure 7-18: Encrypting files using commercial-grade software

When you inspect the resulting encrypted file, you can quickly tell that a casual glance at the contents does not reveal details about the original spreadsheet (see Figure 7-19).

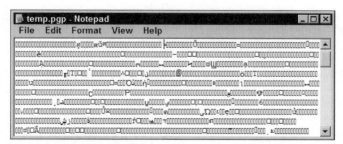

Figure 7-19: Details from the spreadsheet content are securely encrypted.

"Because of new regulations and reporting requirements, my office is now collecting and integrating hundreds and, eventually, thousands of spreadsheets every week. I need to set permissions and access privileges based on corporate policies and defined roles."

Welcome to the world of document and workflow management. Although the topic is beyond the scope of this book, Information Rights Management is a Microsoft technology that's designed to address these needs. IRM has facilities to

- Set file permissions at different levels and change the level for specific users.

- Assign permissions according to roles and responsibilities.

- Restrict file printing so that circulation of hard copies can be better managed.

- Set expiration dates to provide a time limit, which could prevent a file from being opened after the time limit is expired.

- Help restrict forwarded files from being opened by an unauthorized recipient.

IRM presupposes a certain level of infrastructure. As you can imagine, a file that times out has to synchronize against an authentication and reliable timekeeping source. IRM is a technology that is targeted to medium and large organizations because its security controls are specified as policies that would be applied organization wide or department wide.

Auto and Advanced Filters

Many spreadsheet users use filters. The essential notion behind filters is to retrieve a set of records that conform to certain criteria. In effect, filters serve as a sort of stand-in for a database. The filter works well because it can help you wade through lots of data when there's too much to easily peruse manually. Filters excel (no pun intended) at drilling down to a set of data.

Some might say that filters give users a poor man's database. In some respects this is true. However, filters accomplish things that you typically don't enjoy with a database:

- Traditional databases require that the datasets be highly structured. There may be a requirement that certain fields in a table be numeric, whereas others must contain a certain number of characters. Aside from the possible enforcement of certain data types, there may be some relational structures or constraints. By comparison, filters don't need to set such restrictions.

- One of the magical features of a filter is that the data retrieved by a filter can be cells with a spreadsheet formula. This feature allows you to change your data very fluidly. Of course you have to run a filtering process any time you retrieve records, but in the bigger scheme of things, you have a tremendous amount of flexibility. Your data can contain VLOOKUPs or other kinds of formulas to gather useful information.

- As you retrieve records in a filter, you can easily do all sorts of calculations on the returned data, including AVERAGE, SUM, MIN, MAX, and others.

Working with Auto Filters

"I would like to have a filtered list in which it would be easy to show things such as AVERAGE, SUM, MIN, MAX, and so on."

It is not uncommon to have a large portion of data, want to show pieces of it, and perform descriptive statistics such as mean value or standard deviation for a limited portion. The file `ch07_08Filters.xls` on the book's CD-ROM shows one such example (see Figure 7-20). It shows economic data from the U.S. Census Bureau for the year 2003.

	A	B	C	D	E	F	G	H	I	J
1	ESCAPE FROM EXCEL HELL									
2	Chapter 7 - Filters									
3	Validation and filters taken together				=SUBTOTAL(VLOOKUP($C8,Table01,2),D$12:D$62)					
4										
5			Average	82.64444	28.18889	67.08889	153310.8	670.7778	1171.556	25.41111
6			Count	9	9	9	9	9	9	9
7			Max	86.8	44.2	73.9	248171	817	1482	30.2
8			Min	78.3	17	42	85709	432	783	22.5
9			Average Count CountA	.837301	7.859619	9.603443	45983.66	114.42	204.9793	2.56293
10										
11		Region	Max	tg Co	Pctg Co	Pctg Oc	Median	Median	Median	Average
43		South Atlantic	Min	86	27.6	72.8	165739	718	1184	22.5
44		South Atlantic	Product Stdev	81.7	44.2	42	248171	721	1482	28.4
45		South Atlantic	Stdevp	84	25	70.2	144507	724	1151	24.8
46		South Atlantic	Georgia	80.9	25.7	68.3	140734	687	1155	26.1
47		South Atlantic	Maryland	86.8	34.5	69.4	186139	817	1395	30.2
48		South Atlantic	North Carolina	80.1	24.3	68.3	125428	601	1079	23.2
49		South Atlantic	South Carolina	81.5	23.2	69.8	121290	586	1037	23
50		South Atlantic	Virginia	84.5	32.2	69.1	162080	751	1278	25.8
51		South Atlantic	West Virginia	78.3	17	73.9	85709	432	783	24.7
63										
64										
65										
66		Source:	American Community Survey/US Census Bureau							
67			http://www.census.gov/acs/www/Products/Ranking/index.htm							
68										
69										

Figure 7-20: Performing statistics on filtered data

Setting up an AutoFilter is easy. Select the column headers of your source data (in this spreadsheet, the source data would be cells `B11:V11`). In the Excel menu, click Data⇨Filter⇨AutoFilter. When you click the triangular notch appearing on the right side of the column headers, you will have a list of options (see Figure 7-21).

Figure 7-21: Filtering your data

When you select the data you want filtered, such as the economic data for the South Atlantic region, you can use the function SUBTOTAL to obtain various kinds of statistical measures. As you may recall, SUBTOTAL uses a function number and a range of cells to produce the result. Truthfully, this would be a pain to manually adjust. Fortunately, you can make use of the Excel Validation technique shown earlier in this chapter. The key is to set up a remote list and lookup table (see Figure 7-22).

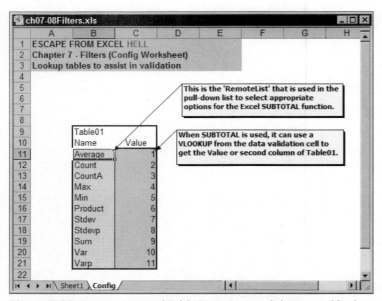

Figure 7-22: RemoteList and Table01 assist in validation and lookups.

After you have defined a RemoteList, you can use it for data validation (see Figure 7-23).

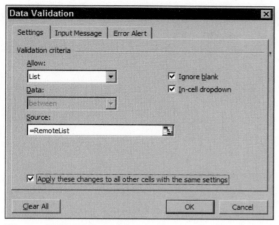

Figure 7-23: Using a remote list to choose the function you want

From here, it's just a matter of using VLOOKUP to retrieve the function number inside SUBTOTAL. Your formula may look something like the following:

```
=SUBTOTAL(VLOOKUP(ChosenLookupName,Table01,2),ColumnOfData)
```

"There are unique data values that should appear in the drop-down list of the AutoFilter. I know for a fact that they exist in the data, but they never make their way into the filtered data."

In Excel 2003, the Filter drop-down list will display, at most, 1,000 unique or distinct members. The items displayed will be the first thousand unique items the AutoFilter finds. If there are more than 1,000 unique items, you will not be warned that the filtered drop-down list is truncated.

 NOTE
Operations such as sorting or using custom selection criteria operate on all the data, not just the first 1,000 members that appear in the drop-down list.

"I need to drill down on a combination of data selection criteria."

This capability is what filters were designed for. Just select each independent criteria for the individual columns. It may be in your interest to use custom filtering. For instance, you may want to select information such as "Show me the data for the states where the percentage of people who completed high school is greater than 80% and the Median Housing Value of Specified Owner-Occupied Housing Units With a Mortgage is less than $100,000." Clicking Custom in the AutoFilter drop-down menu will bring up a window similar to Figure 7-24.

Part III

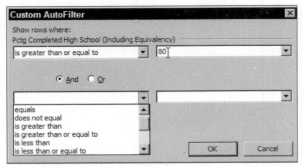

Figure 7-24: Custom filters allow you to specify ranges of values.

If you are trying to do a drill-down, you may have to apply custom filtering on multiple columns of data.

"I want to view the bottom 10% of my data."

Click the AutoFilter triangular notch and select "(Top 10)" as shown on the left side of Figure 7-25. In the Top 10 AutoFilter window, change Show "Top" to "Bottom" in the first pull-down option and select Percent instead of Items in the rightmost pull-down option.

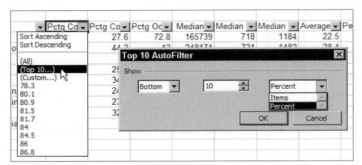

Figure 7-25: Selecting the bottom 10% of data using AutoFilters

Advanced Filters

"I need to filter records from a large list using complex criteria, and AutoFilters don't seem to be sufficient. When I try to use Advanced Filters, I find it baffling."

It is baffling because Advance Filters is one of the less polished features of Excel. A few things are worth mentioning and will help you to put this feature's facilities to use. Running an Advanced Filter requires that you specify a `List Range` and a `Criteria Range`. The Advanced Filter window appears when you click Data⇨Filter⇨Advanced Filter (see Figure 7-26).

NOTE

Though the regions specified when running an Advanced Filter can be set by pointing and clicking a mouse, the `Criteria Range` must be prepared in advance.

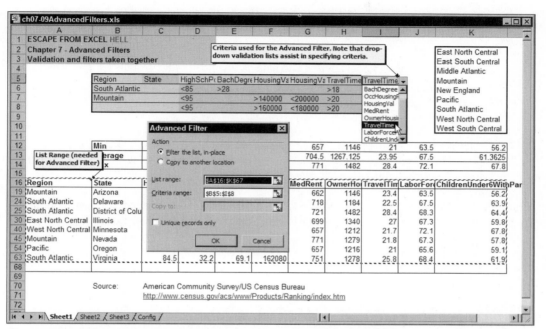

Figure 7-26: Selecting the Criteria and List ranges for an Advanced Filter

The `ch07_09AdvancedFilters.xls` file on the book's CD-ROM shows you how this can be handled. For the most part, Advanced Filters are not very friendly. Keep the following in mind.

- The `Criteria Range` should be specified in advance. As shown in Figure 7-26 and the example file, the `Criteria Range` appears in cells `B5:I8`.

- The first row of the `Criteria Range` (called the `Criteria Label`) specifies which fields from the `List Range` are to be used to retrieve data. The remaining rows immediately below specify the actual criteria used for each field.

- Each row in the `Criteria Range` spells out a specific query. For instance, the current example asks:

  "Give me the records for which the Region is South Atlantic, the percentage of high school graduates is less than 85 and the percentage of adults who have graduated with a Bachelors Degree exceeds 28." The next line in the `Criteria Range` asks another query. The same can be said for the third line. The results of all these queries are combined to produce a filtered list.

Part III

- Each additional column you add to the `Criteria Range` specifies an additional AND criteria.

- Each additional row you add to the `Criteria Range` specifies an additional inclusive OR criteria.

- The easiest way to interpret the `Criteria Range` is to think of the AND criteria running horizontally across and the inclusive OR criteria running vertically down the `Criteria Range`.

- The filtering action happens when you select Advanced Filter from the Excel menu.

- The `List Range` is the range of data that you normally would be filtering if you were using an AutoFilter. In this example, the `List Range` happens to comprise the cells `A16:K67`.

- When you run the Advanced Filter routine, you need to first select the `List Range` or select a cell in the first row of the `List Range`. In this example, it suffices to click the cell `A16` before running the Advanced Filter.

All this sounds as though it's a lot of work to go through for an Advanced Filter. It is, but the benefits come in when you incorporate formulas in your Advanced Filter.

"I want to produce a list of the records for which the housing value is 25% higher than the average housing value and the percentage of high school graduates is less than 85 and the percentage of adults who have graduated with a Bachelor's degree exceeds 28."

This situation is depicted in Figure 7-27. You have the ability to use formulas in place of static criteria, something you cannot do with AutoFilters. As with conditional formatting and validation, the formulas must evaluate to a TRUE or FALSE. The filtering formula should be pointing to the first data record in the `List Range` using a relative reference. Other cell references such as the average of all the data would be specified using absolute cell references.

One of the advantages of using Advanced Filters is that there is really no limit on how complex a set of queries you can create. A disadvantage of Advanced Filters is that they are not so user friendly. You may have noticed that I try to compensate for this by incorporating the drop-down cell validation feature in the `Criteria Range`, where appropriate. I should also mention that Advanced Filters can easily find their way into VBA applications. VBA programming can tap into the power of advanced filtering without inconveniencing the user.

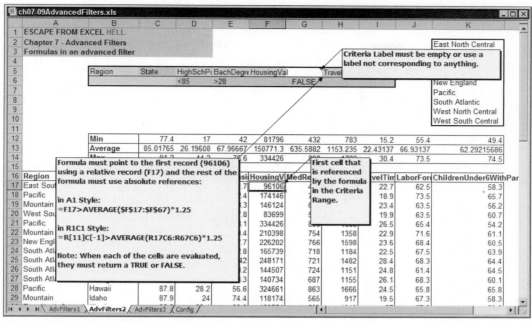

Figure 7-27: Advanced filtering involving formulas

Closing Thoughts

This chapter has exposed you to many issues on spreadsheet security, finding implicit and subtle relationships in a mass of data through filters, and controlling how you enter and view data.

Some of the topics covered include experiences that frustrate spreadsheet users who have to figure out how to perform various tasks (especially frustrating when working under hard deadlines). Other topics, such as the security issues, are likely to frustrate some users even more after they learn that their spreadsheets can be so vulnerable.

This chapter is part of your gathering arsenal of techniques. All this is a prelude to some very interesting and useful data analysis techniques in the chapters to follow.

Chapter 8

Involved Data Analysis

In This Chapter

◆ Data scrubbing techniques

◆ Sorting techniques (ZIP Codes, block sorting, and much more)

◆ Comparing spreadsheets

Overview

This chapter outlines some important and useful techniques in working with data. I cover many topics that will help get you heavily steeped in analyzing and presenting data, especially when you're under pressure at the eleventh hour. The first step in clearing the way to doing some decent data analysis is to scrub the data. All the remaining work is vastly simplified when you do this.

To better understand the concept of scrubbing the data, think of what is involved in managing a mailing list campaign. All your volunteers who collect and enter the data may not adhere to uniform standards. Sometimes information is missing. Other times you could end up having multiple records for the same person. If you plan to do some demographic analysis of your data, you need it to be accurate and don't want to be caught second-guessing your results.

The bottom line is that when you want to pounce on the data, the last thing you want is to be distracted by searching and exterminating misbehaving data. You also want to be as close as possible to having your data airtight so that your analytical results are packed with reliability.

Data Scrubbing

The first thing you may want to do when you have data and lots of it is to clean it up. You can start with some of the easier and obvious things.

"I have a list of names and want to make sure that the names are identically structured."

Consider a simple list like the following:

```
John Doe
Mary Smith
John A. Doe
Jane Doe
John A Doe
J Doe
john A   Doe
George Washington
   John      A  Doe
John B Doe
```

You have two kinds of problems going on at the same time.

One of these relates to the structure of the list, taking into account troublesome things such as excess spaces or inconsistent use of periods. A reasonable assumption would be to treat `John A Doe` and `John A. Doe` as one and the same person. Therefore, you could adjust the data so that all the middle initials have no period symbols appearing in them. Some names might have extra spaces between words. These can be safely eliminated, too.

The other problem involves a human interpretation of the data and specific knowledge that may not be encoded in the spreadsheet. Is `John Doe` the same person as `John A Doe`? Should the name `John Archibald Doe` and `John A Doe` be presumed to be the same person? If your list is composed of 10 people, you may know the answer right away because you personally know the individuals (and the computer does not). If the list of names has 400 or 4,000 records, the answer is not so clear.

In any case, the preferred approach is to employ a divide-and-conquer strategy. Deal with one problem at a time and eliminate it entirely from the picture (or at least "tag" the troublemakers) before taking on the next challenge. The ListCleanup worksheet of the `ch08_01DataScrubber.xls` file, on the book's CD-ROM, shows one way to do this (see Figure 8-1). Notice how each problem is addressed separately and removed from the picture. It's kind of like peeling the layers of an onion.

First, the nasty gremlins are zapped from the list using the Excel CLEAN function. In column C, TRIM is applied to column B to remove unneeded spaces. In column D, UPPER is used to convert the text in column C to uppercase. Column E removes the period appearing after the middle initial. Remaining names with periods in the text are highlighted. The highlights alert you that some action might be required. Column F displays two additional alerts; names having no spaces (such as first or last names only), and redundant appearance of a name (should you want names to appear only once).

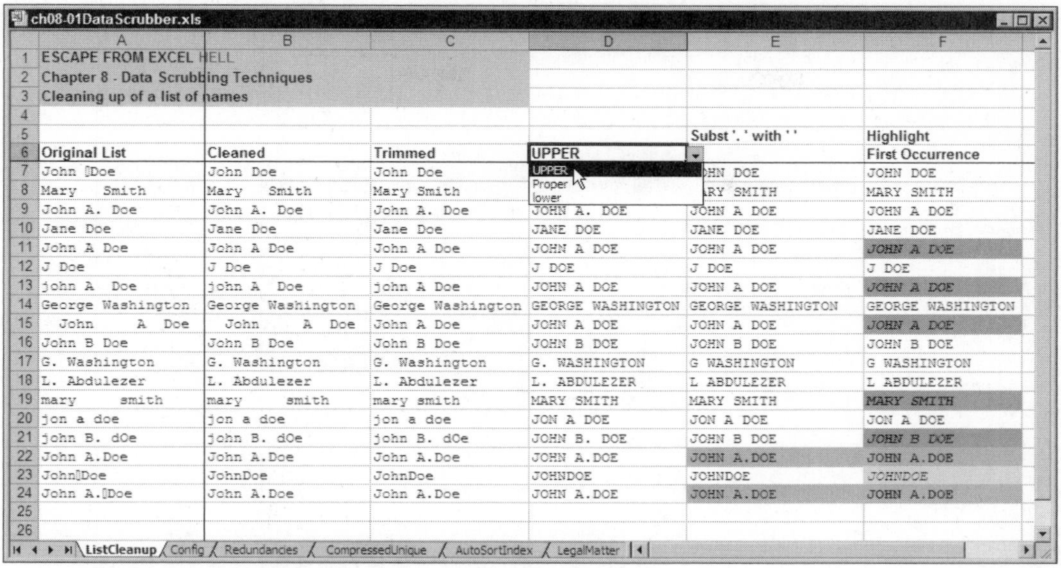

Figure 8-1: Cleaning up a list through successive changes

The spreadsheet shows columns:

Original List	Cleaned	Trimmed	UPPER	Subst '.' with ' '	Highlight First Occurrence
John Doe	John Doe	John Doe		JOHN DOE	JOHN DOE
Mary Smith	Mary Smith	Mary Smith		ARY SMITH	MARY SMITH
John A. Doe	John A. Doe	John A. Doe	JOHN A. DOE	JOHN A DOE	JOHN A DOE
Jane Doe	Jane Doe	Jane Doe	JANE DOE	JANE DOE	JANE DOE
John A Doe	John A Doe	John A Doe	JOHN A DOE	JOHN A DOE	JOHN A DOE
J Doe	J Doe	J Doe	J DOE	J DOE	J DOE
john A Doe	john A Doe	john A Doe	JOHN A DOE	JOHN A DOE	JOHN A DOE
George Washington	George Washington	George Washington	GEORGE WASHINGTON	GEORGE WASHINGTON	GEORGE WASHINGTON
John A Doe	John A Doe	John A Doe	JOHN A DOE	JOHN A DOE	JOHN A DOE
John B Doe	John B Doe	John B Doe	JOHN B DOE	JOHN B DOE	JOHN B DOE
G. Washington	G. Washington	G. Washington	G. WASHINGTON	G WASHINGTON	G WASHINGTON
L. Abdulezer	L. Abdulezer	L. Abdulezer	L. ABDULEZER	L ABDULEZER	L ABDULEZER
mary smith	mary smith	mary smith	MARY SMITH	MARY SMITH	MARY SMITH
jon a doe	jon a doe	jon a doe	JON A DOE	JON A DOE	JON A DOE
john B. dOe	john B. dOe	john B. dOe	JOHN B. DOE	JOHN B DOE	JOHN B DOE
John A.Doe	John A.Doe	John A.Doe	JOHN A.DOE	JOHN A.DOE	JOHN A.DOE
John Doe	JohnDoe	JohnDoe	JOHNDOE	JOHNDOE	JOHNDOE
John A. Doe	John A.Doe	John A.Doe	JOHN A.DOE	JOHN A.DOE	JOHN A.DOE

NOTE

Using data validation in conjunction with the use of CHOOSE allows you to select between UPPER, PROPER, and LOWER. The trick is to use two named ranges that overlap: RemoteList and RemoteTable. RemoteList is just the list of options you want to pick from. The picked item MyLookupValue is used by VLOOKUP to select the action you want using the formula:

```
=CHOOSE(VLOOKUP(MyLookupValue,RemoteTable,2,FALSE),
        UPPER($C7),
        PROPER($C7),
        LOWER($C7))
```

If you don't have the time or the inclination to work through formulas this way, just use the function directly, like this:

```
=UPPER($C7)
```

If your data resides on another worksheet, you can copy it onto this ListCleanup worksheet (or any similar tool of your own). Then copy the cleaned-up, or scrubbed, data and paste the values back to your original location (using Paste Special... Values).

"I have this list of names and would like to split it into separate columns for first, middle initial, and last name."

First, make sure that the data is cleaned up, as previously described. In the file ch08_01DataScrubber.xls, go to the NameParser worksheet (see Figure 8-2).

	A	B	C	D	E	F	G
	ch08-01DataScrubber.xls						
1	ESCAPE FROM EXCEL HELL						
2	Chapter 8 - Data Scrubbing Techniques						
3	Cleaning up of a list of names						
4							
5							
6	Cleaned List	spaces	1st sp	2nd sp	FirstName	MiddleName	Remainder
7	JOHN DOE	1	5		JOHN		DOE
8	MARY SMITH	1	5		MARY		SMITH
9	JOHN A DOE	2	5	7	JOHN	A	DOE
10	JANE DOE	1	5		JANE		DOE
11	JOHN A DOE	2	5	7	JOHN	A	DOE
12	J DOE	1	2		J		DOE
13	JOHN A DOE	2	5	7	JOHN	A	DOE
14	GEORGE WASHINGTON	1	7		GEORGE		WASHINGTON
15	JOHN A DOE	2	5	7	JOHN	A	DOE
16	JOHN B DOE	2	5	7	JOHN	B	DOE
17	G WASHINGTON	1	2		G		WASHINGTON
18	L ABDULEZER	1	2		L		ABDULEZER
19	MARY SMITH	1	5		MARY		SMITH
20	JON A DOE	2	4	6	JON	A	DOE
21	JOHN B DOE	2	5	7	JOHN	B	DOE
22	JOHN A.DOE	1	5		JOHN		A.DOE
23	JOHNDOE	0					JOHNDOE
24	JOHN A.DOE	1	5		JOHN		A.DOE
25							

ListCleanup \ NameParser \ Config \ Redundancies

Figure 8-2: Splitting names into their appropriate columns

Your specific needs in splitting a single column into multiple columns may involve very complicated criteria impossible to anticipate in this book. So, in this example, pay attention to how this problem is addressed so that you can adapt it to your own needs.

Notice the three "helper" columns (B, C, D). These aid in the computations for determining FirstName, MiddleName, and LastName. As you can see from the list, some of the names appear with middle initials or names; others show first and last name. A couple of cases even lack a first name. To determine what portion of the name goes into which column, you have to know how many words are contained in each line of column A. Because this is a "cleaned" list, counting the number of spaces accomplishes the same thing (column B). You also need to know where the first and second words begin and end. Again, locating the first and second space characters accomplishes this.

NOTE

There is a shortcut taken in the formula for counting the number of spaces:

```
=LEN(A7)-LEN(SUBSTITUTE(A7," ",""))
```

This formula is hardwired to the fact that the separate between words is a character space and happens to be one character long. If you have a more involved application in which the separator uses multiple characters, this formula will not work. Instead you would have to use a formula like the following:

```
=(LEN(A7)-
LEN(SUBSTITUTE(A7,WordSeparator,"")))/LEN(WordSeparator)
```

My preference is to build the spreadsheet with the full-featured formula from the get go; this way, there is less to reengineer later on and the chances of making an error are reduced.

NOTE

The formula for the finding the first space (column C) could have been written as follows:

```
=IF(ISERROR(FIND(" ",A7)),"",FIND(" ",A7))
```

This handles the exception of there being no space in A7, but it is not particularly elegant and it wastefully repeats a computation. It also contributes to the formula's becoming unwieldy. Column B (the number of spaces) already has information sufficient to avoid having to trap the error. The logic is, "if there are no spaces in A7, don't even bother trying to find it." This formula becomes:

```
=IF(B7<1,"",FIND(" ",A7))
```

When you get to the very hairy and computationally heavy formulas, a technique such as this helps immensely.

It is certainly possible to eliminate the helper columns (B, C, and D) so that the spreadsheet appears cleaner. Unless doing so is absolutely necessary, you're better off avoiding this practice. Here's why: The formulas for the "compactified" columns are far more complex. Instead of computing the first name as:

```
=IF(B8<1,"",LEFT(A8,C8-1))
```

you would have to write the formula for the FirstName as:

```
=IF(LEN(A7)-LEN(SUBSTITUTE(A7," ",""))<1,"",LEFT(A7,IF(LEN(A7)-
LEN(SUBSTITUTE(A7," ",""))<1,"",FIND(" ",A7))-1))
```

These very quickly turn into "megaformulas" that are hard to understand and manage. Unless you want to purposely obfuscate the formulas, I do not recommend any regular use of megaformulas.

TIP

If you must use a megaformula, it is best to keep it out of harm's way by defining it as a formula name.

"I am importing data into Excel from a data file with delimiters appearing in each data record or line. I need these broken out into separate columns."

There are several ways you can do this. If you have a delimited text file, you can open the file as you regularly would with an Excel spreadsheet. There may be special requirements, in which case you could make use of the file import wizard or the TextToColumn toolbar.

When you open the text file (such as `ch08_03TxtImportFile.txt`) from Excel, you are presented with an import wizard (see Figure 8-3):

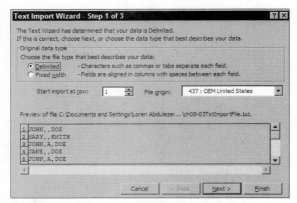

Figure 8-3: Choose between delimiters or fixed width.

Select the type of delimiter you want to use to separate words into columns (see Figure 8-4).

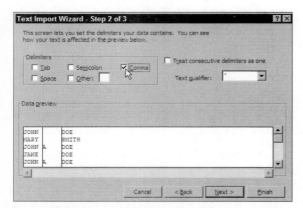

Figure 8-4: Select Comma as the delimiter.

NOTE

If you have some other kind of delimiter, such a vertical pipe "|" symbol, you can place it next to Other.

Be sure to place also place a checkmark next to the Other option; otherwise, the symbol you specify will be ignored!

In the third step of the Text Import Wizard, you can choose how you want the data for each column treated. You can specify General, Text, or Date. You also have the option to skip any column so that it does not get imported. This Skip feature can be useful when you're importing fixed-width data.

"I have a .csv (Comma Separated Variable) file that contains first, middle, and last names. I want to import only the first and last names. When I open the file, all the comma-separated fields are automatically imported. It seems I can't pick and choose."

You can. The quick way to do so is change the filename suffix from `.csv` to `.txt`. When you open the file from Excel, the Text Import Wizard will kick in, and you can adjust the import settings. The other option is to select from the Excel menu Data⇨Import External Data⇨Import Data and navigate to the `.csv` file.

Importing Log Files

"I have a Web log file for which I want a listing of Web pages requested along with the date and time of the page requests."

Many log files can present some interesting challenges. Consider a log file with content like the following:

```
192.168.0.1 - LoggedInUser [17/May/2006:00:05:32 -0400] "GET
/WebSite/nonWebMap/customerPath02_09.html HTTP/1.1" 304 -
192.168.0.1 - LoggedInUser [17/May/2006:00:05:33 -0400] "GET
/WebSite/nonWebMap/customerPath02_10.html HTTP/1.1" 304 -
192.168.0.1 - LoggedInUser [17/May/2006:00:12:06 -0400] "GET
/WebSite/customerFacing.html HTTP/1.1" 200 11959
257.223.2.14 - - [17/May/2006:21:10:39 -0400] "GET /pix/t/backup.gif HTTP/1.1"
200 94
257.223.2.14 - - [17/May/2006:21:10:39 -0400] "GET /pix/t/restore.gif
HTTP/1.1" 200 94
```

For the sake of showing how data can be extracted using Excel, I make no assumption that you have such tools available to you (even though the reality is that if you're working with Web log files, you may already have at your disposal some data analysis software for extracting specific data from the Web logs).

As with the example before, you'll need to peel the layers of the onion one at a time. The strategy is to first break the data into columns. Next, remove the columns you won't need. In the remaining columns, eliminate the portions you don't need, and finally, do any necessary cleanup.

From Excel, open the file ch08_04WebLog.log on the book's CD-ROM. You are presented with the Text Import Wizard. Select the Delimited option (fixed width does not work because the IP addresses are variable length). For the delimiter, choose Space.

When you get to the third step of the Import Wizard, you have the option to skip any of the columns. Unless you're about to run out of columns in your worksheet, you may want to hold off on skipping them here. It is usually better to bring them into Excel and leisurely inspect and delete what you don't need.

When the file opens in Excel, resize the column widths as appropriate (see Figure 8-5).

Gut out columns G and H (click the G and H column labels above the data for the respective columns; see Figure 8-5). With the columns selected, press the Del key.

Gut out column E, but insert two additional columns between columns D and F (you will need these two columns to hold date and time values).

Remove columns A, B, and C altogether.

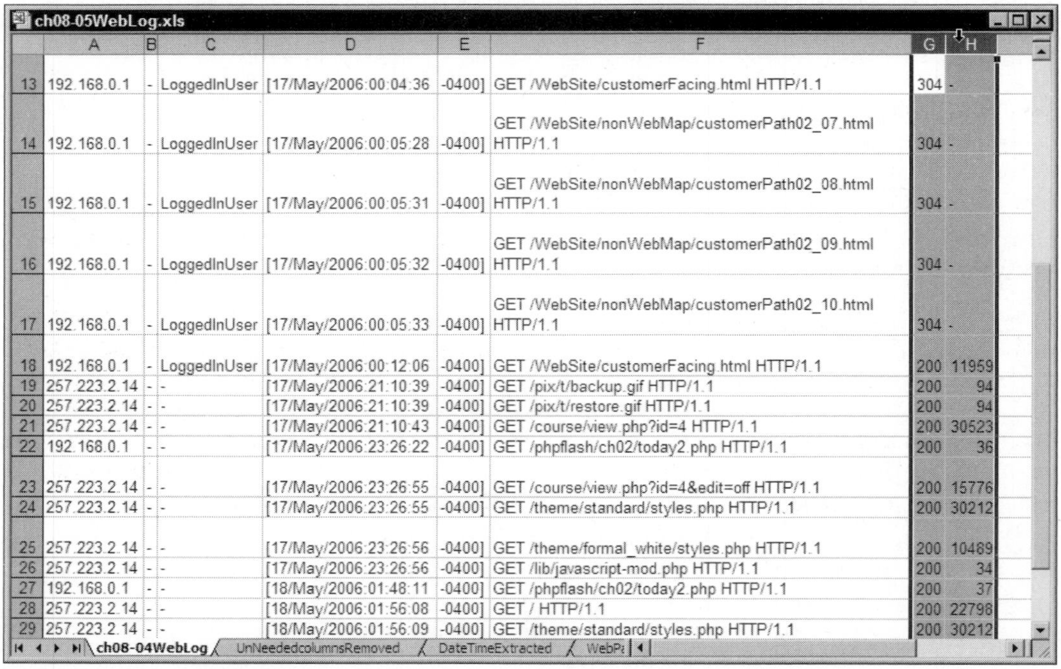

Figure 8-5: Raw log file data

What appears in column D for the raw date and time in Figure 8-5 becomes column A. If you want, you can insert a row at the top to place descriptive labels. For instance, column A could be labeled `RawDateTime`. The first such item in column A appears as:

```
[17/May/2006:00:01:36
```

If you try to extract a date value from this (that is, `=DATEVALUE("[17/May/2006:00:01:36")`), you will run into two problems. The left open bracket will confuse DATEVALUE. So will the slash (/)between `17,` `May,` and `2006.` You need to strip out the left bracket and substitute a hyphen (-) wherever a / appears. Assuming that A2 is

```
[17/May/2006:00:01:36
```

a formula in column B like the following will do this:

```
=SUBSTITUTE(MID(A2,2,100),"/","-")        returns 17-May-2006:00:01:36
```

You can go ahead in the empty columns C and D place formulas like:

```
=DATEVALUE(MID(B2,1,FIND(":",B2)-1))
=TIMEVALUE(MID(B2,FIND(":",B2)+1,100))
```

The first three lines of computations in Figure 8-6 show the numeric computations with no formatting applied. Beginning in row 6 and lower, the date and time values are formatted as dates and time.

The next step is to clean up column E and extract the filename or Web page that is being requested. Here you can use the TextToColumn feature. Select column E. If you have taken the opportunity of adding the TextToColumn icon to your toolbar, you can immediately click on this icon. Otherwise, click Data⇨Text To Columns from the Excel menu. For the Original Data Type, choose Delimited and after pressing the Next button place a checkmark next to Space (see Figure 8-7). This divides the data into three portions, for which you need only the middle column.

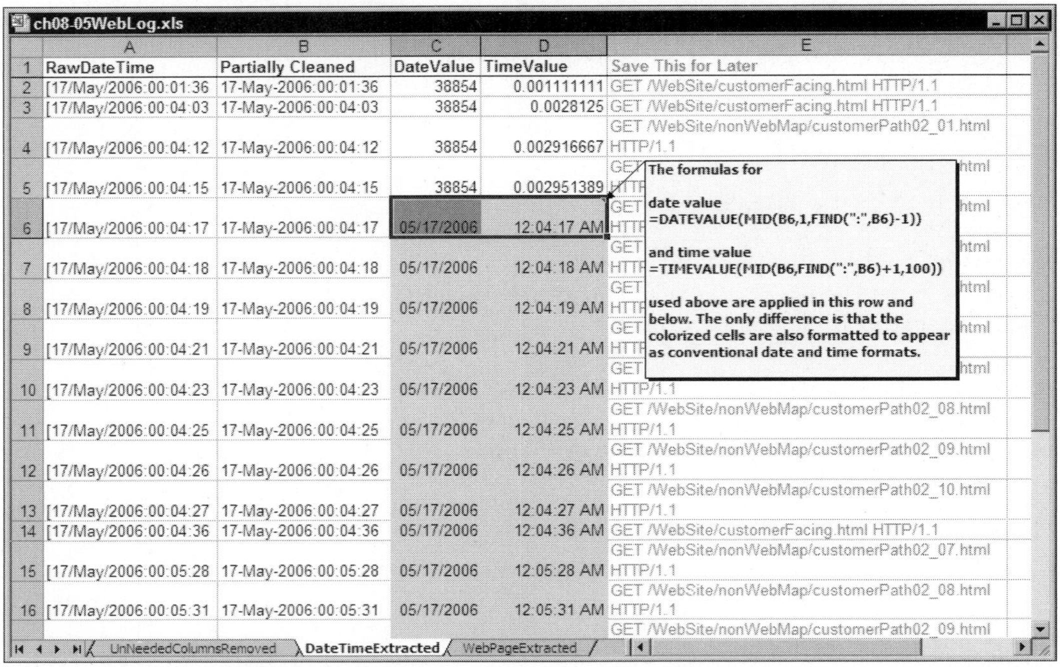

Figure 8-6: Date and time values separated into isolated columns

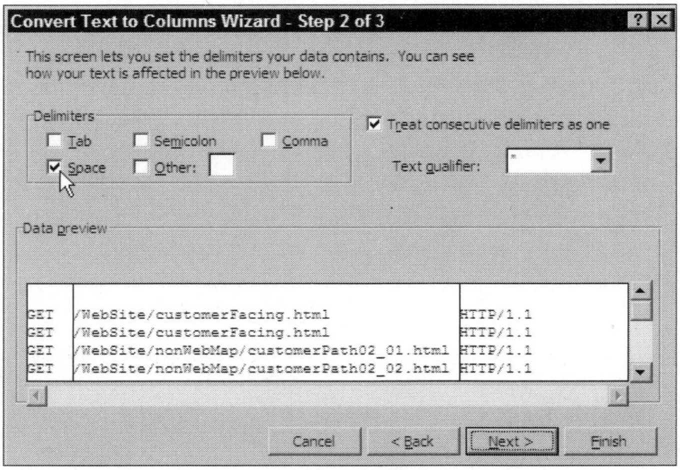

Figure 8-7: Separating by Space as the delimiter

In the third step of the Convert Text to Column Wizard, click the first column and then select Do not import column (skip). Do the same for the third column (see Figure 8-8).

Figure 8-8: Skip the excess columns you don't need.

Column E displays data such as:

```
/WebSite/nonWebMap/customerPath02_03.html
```

The last occurrence of / happens to occur at position 19. There's a clever way of figuring this out. The first step is to count the number of occurrences of /. That number is determined in column F of Figure 8-9 (this is the WebPageExtracted worksheet of ch08_05WebLog.xls), using the formula:

```
=(LEN(E6)-LEN(SUBSTITUTE(E6,F$1,"")))/LEN(F$1))      returns 3
                                                     (in cell F6)
```

Given the number of occurrences of /, the task is just a matter of substituting the last occurrence / with a unique string, and then finding its position (see Figure 8-9).

The formula used is:

```
=SEARCH(E6&"X",SUBSTITUTE(E6,"/",E6&"X",F6))      returns 19
                                                  (in cell G6)
```

The unique string I use is E6&"X". Here' is the reason why. I could use any unique string that doesn't occur in E6. A set of strings representing the value Pi ("3.14159265358979") is not likely to occur. This depends on my specific knowledge that the content is not going to have "3.14159265358979" appear anywhere inside it. I don't want to have to take personal responsibility for this every time I am going to import the Web logs. There could be thousands of lines of Web log entries. What's to stop one of them from having "3.14159265358979" in it? To make matters more complicated, I am mathematically inclined, so using the value of Pi in a Web page for one of my Web sites is not entirely out of the question.

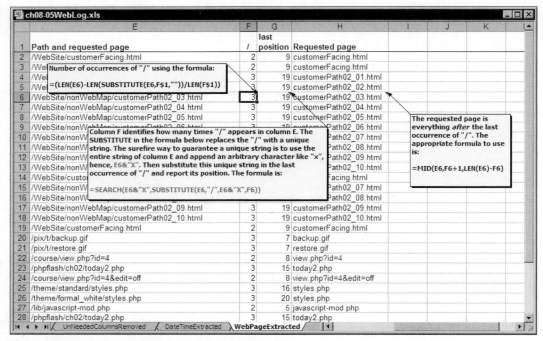

Figure 8-9: Computing the last known position of /

Finally, I am giving you a solution, and I don't want to have to guess something not likely to appear anywhere in your Web logs. The only way I can is to take your whole string (which appears in E6) and add one or more arbitrary characters to it. Because it is bigger than any text that appears in E6, it has to be unique. There is no way you can locate E6&"X" (or "/WebSite/nonWebMap/customerPath02_03.htmlX") inside E6, because the length is already exceeded. You can't argue with that logic!

Because E6 is a relative cell reference, this feature of generating a unique string remains true for every line it is replicated to. When you get to a formula using a complicated piece of logic, it is a good idea to use the Evaluate Formula toolbar icon. If you do not happen to have this icon in your toolbar, add it now because it is very useful. From the Excel menu, click Tools⇨Customize and, in the Commands tab, click Tools in the Category list. Look for the Evaluate Formula item in the right panel (see Figure 8-10) and drag it onto your toolbars.

As long as you're installing features of this kind, you should also add the toolbar icons for Trace Precedents, Trace Dependents, and Remove All Arrows (all of which are located on the same list as the Evaluate Formula icon). When you're done adding the icon to your toolbar, click OK.

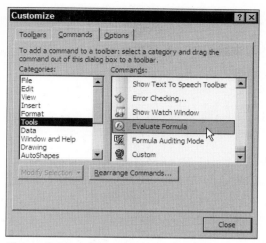

Figure 8-10: Adding the Evaluate Formula icon to your toolbar

Click any cell, such as G6, to see how the formula is evaluated (see Figure 8-11).

I leave you to explore the Evaluate Formula tool (as well as Trace Precedents and Trace Dependents) on your own. I recommend that you spend a little time figuring out how the value 19 is obtained in G6, the last position.

After the last position is known (19 in cell G6), the final step is a matter of using an Excel function such as MID to extract the requested page. For H6, the formula happens to be:

```
=MID(E6,G6+1,LEN(E6)-G6)          returns
                                   customerPath02_03.html
```

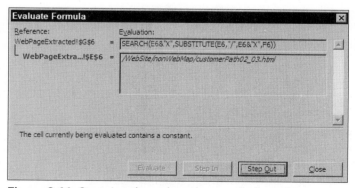

Figure 8-11: Stepping through each part of a formula

Testing for Data Types and Cell Properties

"I know that both ISERR and ISERROR test for errors. What's the difference between them?"

ISERR traps most types of errors but does not guard against a #VALUE! error. The #VALUE! condition does occur from time to time and frequently comes up with errors involving array formulas, such as:

```
=SUMPRODUCT({1,2,3},{1,2,3,4,5})
```

Figure 8-12 summarizes various data types and their properties. On the book's CD-ROM, you can open ch08_06DataTypesAndErrors.xls and input computations of your own choosing.

Computation	ERROR.TYPE	ISBLANK	ISERR	ISERROR	ISLOGICAL	ISNA	ISNONTEXT	ISNUMBER	ISREF	ISTEXT
abc	#N/A	FALSE	FALSE	FALSE	FALSE	FALSE	FALSE	FALSE	TRUE	TRUE
123	#N/A	FALSE	FALSE	FALSE	FALSE	FALSE	TRUE	TRUE	TRUE	FALSE
1234		FALSE	FALSE	FALSE	FALSE	FALSE	FALSE	FALSE	TRUE	TRUE
123.00		FALSE	FALSE	FALSE	FALSE	FALSE	FALSE	FALSE	TRUE	TRUE
TRUE		FALSE	FALSE	FALSE	TRUE	FALSE	TRUE	FALSE	TRUE	FALSE
12/23/2006		FALSE	FALSE	FALSE	FALSE	FALSE	TRUE	TRUE	TRUE	FALSE
0.000260089		FALSE	FALSE	FALSE	FALSE	FALSE	TRUE	TRUE	TRUE	FALSE
12/23/2006	#N/A	FALSE	FALSE	FALSE	FALSE	FALSE	FALSE	FALSE	TRUE	TRUE
	#N/A	FALSE	FALSE	FALSE	FALSE	FALSE	FALSE	FALSE	TRUE	TRUE
	#N/A	TRUE	FALSE	FALSE	FALSE	FALSE	TRUE	FALSE	TRUE	FALSE
#NULL!	1	FALSE	TRUE	TRUE	FALSE	FALSE	TRUE	FALSE	TRUE	FALSE
#DIV/0!	2	FALSE	TRUE	TRUE	FALSE	FALSE	TRUE	FALSE	TRUE	FALSE
#VALUE!	3	FALSE	FALSE	TRUE	FALSE	TRUE	TRUE	FALSE	TRUE	FALSE
#REF!	4	FALSE	TRUE	TRUE	FALSE	FALSE	TRUE	FALSE	FALSE	FALSE
#NAME?	5	FALSE	TRUE	TRUE	FALSE	FALSE	TRUE	FALSE	TRUE	FALSE
#NAME?	5	FALSE	TRUE	TRUE	FALSE	FALSE	TRUE	FALSE	TRUE	FALSE
#NUM!	6	FALSE	TRUE	TRUE	FALSE	FALSE	TRUE	FALSE	FALSE	FALSE
#N/A	7	FALSE	FALSE	FALSE	FALSE	FALSE	TRUE	TRUE	TRUE	FALSE
14	#N/A	FALSE	FALSE	TRUE	FALSE	TRUE	TRUE	FALSE	TRUE	FALSE
#N/A	7	TRUE	FALSE	FALSE	FALSE	FALSE	TRUE	FALSE	TRUE	FALSE

Tooltip in figure: **Number converted into text.** =TEXT(123,"#,##0.00")

Figure 8-12: A table to help distinguish various data types and their properties

Having a table like this is useful to gain a perspective on how data is treated in Excel computations. It would be a bit academic if all you could do is predict how a computation would appear on a table like the kind shown in Figure 8-12.

There are more important, but less obvious, things you can do. Take, for instance, the function ISNUMBER. It takes some input and tells you whether the input is a number. What could be more obvious than that? When ISUMBER is used in conjunction with other Excel functions, its value becomes more relevant. You could have a formula like:

```
=IF(ISNUMBER(SEARCH(A1,A2)),SEARCH(A1,A2),A1&" is not found in: "&A2)
```

If you look at the table in Figure 8-12, you can see that a #N/A can indeed be a truly blank cell. What's the difference between an empty string (such as using ="") and an #N/A, other than the fact that the #N/A mars the cell with something visually unintelligible? The following example should make clear why it is important.

"I have a chart where I am displaying some trendlines. I have missing data that is retrieved using a formula. I want the chart to ignore the empty values rather than treat them as zeros."

Figure 8-13 shows two column charts with data and the trendlines generated by Excel. In the lower chart, the missing data is treated as zeros. This drastically affects the trendline. You can go to the actual worksheet (Sheet2 of ch08_06DataTypesAndErrors.xls). Incidentally, using an empty string (calculated using ="") is not correctly interpreted by the chart as blank data.

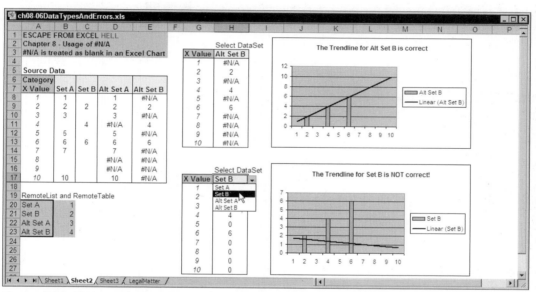

Figure 8-13: #N/A can be used to treat the empty data points in a chart as truly blank.

In the upper chart, blanks are represented by #N/A and are a signal for the Excel chart to ignore the empty data point. Accordingly, the trendline produced matches the column chart.

Eliminating Unneeded Data

Excel allows you to use plenty of rows in a spreadsheet. Sometimes you can wind up with a lot of empty space, so it takes a long time to navigate back and forth in a worksheet. Also, the formulas may be more difficult to interpret when you start getting to the double-letter columns. Excel 12 allows you to have data stretching across thousands of columns instead of just hundreds. At some point or another, you will want to coalesce the data so that it forms a contiguous block. I point out some methods for accomplishing this.

"I need to consolidate some of my data, which happens to be arranged in groups of two rows by two columns, but is separated by rows."

As long as the cells happen to be straight data, are the same shapes, and are aligned in the same columns, you can select these regions and then copy and paste them. The intervening rows will be automatically removed from the pasted contents. To select multiple regions, you can Ctrl+click the regions. Alternatively, you can press Ctrl+G to open a Go To window, click the Special button, and select Constants, as illustrated in Figure 8-14.

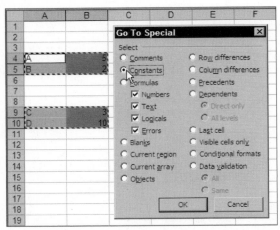

Figure 8-14: Selecting Constants in the Go To Special window

After the text is selected (as shown in the background of Figure 8-14), you can copy and paste the values to a contiguous region.

 NOTE

If your regions do not line up exactly, you will get a warning stating, `That command cannot be used on multiple selection.` Apparently, Excel is very finicky when it comes to copying from multiple rages in one step. Also, you cannot use this technique for cutting and pasting, just copying and pasting.

The one situation for which this technique really works well is when you're copying multiple ranges of data that reside in a single column.

Empty regions of a spreadsheet are not the only things you want to eliminate:

> *"I have a list of data and want to identify the repeated items, and if possible, eliminate them."*

The central function that allows you to accomplish this is COUNTIF. To see how this function is used, go to the Redundancies worksheet of ch08_01DataScrubber.xls (see Figure 8-15).

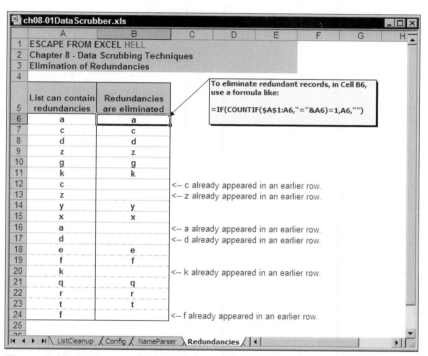

Figure 8-15: Basic use of COUNTIF to track occurrences

The formula going from B6 downward is

```
=IF(COUNTIF($A$1:A6,"="&A6)=1,A6,"")
```

You are in effect asking how many occurrences of the value of A6 are there starting from A6 up through the current row. And when the count exceeds 1, just eliminate it.

If you want to eliminate the empty rows, you can just copy the items in column B and paste them to another part of the spreadsheet. If doing so is a one-time proposition, it's easy to apply. But what if your data is changing regularly? You could easily end up doing a lot of electronic pencil pushing. An alternative is to automate this task using standard spreadsheet formulas. You can find the technique in the CompressedUnique worksheet of ch08_01DataScrubber.xls (see Figure 8-16). In the 451 items listed in column B, there are 133 unique names. These are displayed in column I.

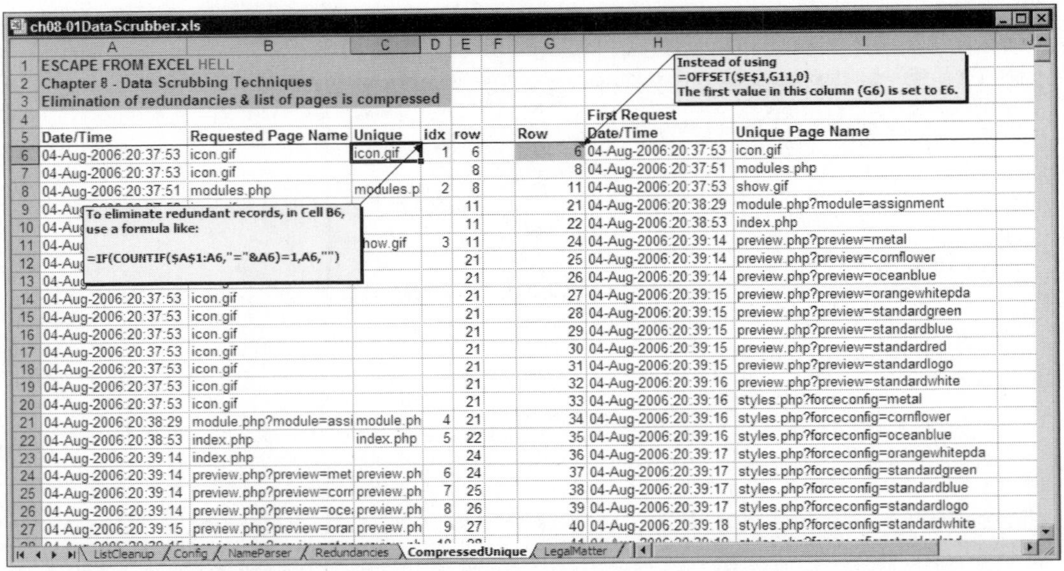

Figure 8-16: Redundancies in column B are eliminated and displayed in column I.

You can just use this tool directly, without understanding much about it. Simply place the data that needs to be "compressed" in column B. The compressed list is automatically produced in column I. It is worth your while to explore and understand worksheet; it can be readily adapted for many other purposes.

Getting Acquainted with Sorting Techniques

To discuss sorting techniques, I begin with the very simplest of sorting issues and then address more challenging problems.

Understanding Sort Order

"When I sort a list of data, I find that the sort order doesn't behave consistently between sort ascending and sort descending."

First it is important to understand the pecking order when it comes to which gets sorted first in a list with hybrid data types. When you are sorting in ascending order, even though the sort goes from smallest to largest value, certain data types appears before others. The order is as follows:

1. Numbers appear first, starting with the most negative value.

2. Text starting with alphanumeric values appears in the following sequence:

   first by digits treated as text:

   ```
   0 1 2 3 4 5 6 7 8 9
   ```

   then by space, punctuation, and special symbols:

   ```
   (space) ! " # $ % & ( ) * , . / : ; ? @ [ \ ] ^ _ ` { | } ~ + < = >
   ```

   and finally by letters of the alphabet (case insensitive):

   ```
   A B C D E F G H I J K L M N O P Q R S T U V W X Y Z
   ```

   Apostrophes (') and hyphens (–) are ignored, with one exception: If two text strings are the same except for a hyphen, the text with the hyphen is sorted last.

3. Booleans (the logical values TRUE and FALSE) come next. FALSE appears before TRUE.

4. Errors such as #VALUE! and #DIV/0! follow the Booleans; however, there are no shades of gray or distinctions among errors.

5. Blanks always appear last in any sort, regardless of whether you are using an ascending or descending sort.

In a descending sort, the sequence is essentially:

```
Errors (though not rearranged) ➪ Booleans (first TRUE, then FALSE) ➪ Text
(Z-A, special symbols and punctuations, 9-0) ➪ numbers (largest values
followed by most negative values).
```

Figure 8-17 helps to visualize this sequencing.

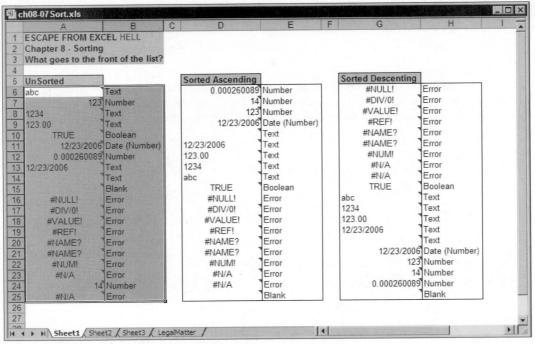

Figure 8-17: Sorting follows a specific sequence.

You may be confronted with several issues when sorting.

- Excel senses adjacent cells it thinks should be included in your sort. It asks you for permission to expand the selection. Instead of identifying what cells should be added, it immediately proceeds to add what it wants (without telling you which cells) and does the sort. You risk losing control.

  If you are sure about your selection, select Continue with the Current Selection. If you think that Excel may be correct and you may need to expand your selection, click the Cancel button and adjust your selection manually. All too often, Excel does a poor job of mind reading.

- Sometimes, a sorted list doesn't seem to be correct.

  If you use the Sort Ascending and Sort Descending toolbar icons to perform your sorts, you may find that they are a little trigger happy. They will make certain assumptions without alerting you. The tell-tale sign that some of your data has been mistakenly treated as a (nonsorted) header is that the selected range of cells is one shorter after the sort.

  If the region you are selecting (such as cells A6:B25 of Figure 8-17) has text on the top row and numbers in the second row, the Sort Ascending and Descending icons will treat the top row as a header and exclude it from the sort. This will not happen if you click Data⇨Sort from the Excel menu. Though Excel will automatically choose a setting with headers in it, you at least have the option of choosing No Header before continuing with the sort.

- Excel can sense when there is text that looks like a number. For instance, you may have a set of five-digit ZIP Codes. Some of these may start with a leading zero, such as 07782. If you type 07782 into a spreadsheet cell, Excel will convert it to 7782. To keep the leading zero, you have two options: format the cell to display five digits no matter what; or, enter an apostrophe before the five-digit number, so that you enter '07782. The apostrophe effectively turns the ZIP Code into text. Generally, this does not cause problems. After all, you not likely to multiply or add ZIP Codes. It does, however, become an issue when sorting. Excel will sense that you have a list of numbers and text that look like numbers, and ask you what you want to do (see Figure 8-19).

Excel can still surprise you. Say that you treat this list of text that looks like numbers and actual numbers as a pure set of numbers. Excel starts to adapt and automatically treats other, similar lists as though they are composed of just numbers when sorting. This behavior may not be what you want. If you find Excel behaving this way and you can't get it out of this mode, you have to quit Excel and then reopen the spreadsheet (see Figure 8-18).

Figure 8-18: If you are unsure about the selection to sort, click Cancel, reselect manually, and sort.

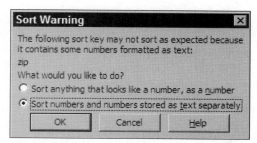

Figure 8-19: You need to determine whether text that looks like a number should be treated like one.

Converting Text That Looks Like a Number into a Number

Sometimes the data you want sorted as a number is in the form of text. You may have a list of such numbers and want to convert them into numbers.

"When I import data from a financial application, negative numbers appear with a minus symbol or dash at the end of the number. How do I convert this to a number?"

You can use a simple formula like the following:

```
=-1*MID(A1,1,LEN(A1)-1)
```

This formula strips the minus symbol from the end of the text and then multiplies the text by minus 1. In Excel you can have a piece of text like =`"123"` in cell G1 and, in G2, use a formula such as =`G1+3` to get the number `126`.

Though the simple formula does convert the text into the correct negative number, you need to add a little meat to the bones to make the formula behave when you need it to. Chances are, if you're getting data from an external program, you need to refresh the data on a recurring basis. Some numbers will always be negative; others will vacillate between positive and negative. Also, you have to handle blank cells. Figure 8-20 shows how to handle both the trailing minus symbol and blanks. If your data is in column B, a formula for handling this could be:

```
=IF(OR(B6="",B6="-"),"",(IF(RIGHT(B6)="-",-1*MID(B6,1,LEN(B6)-1),1*B6)))
```

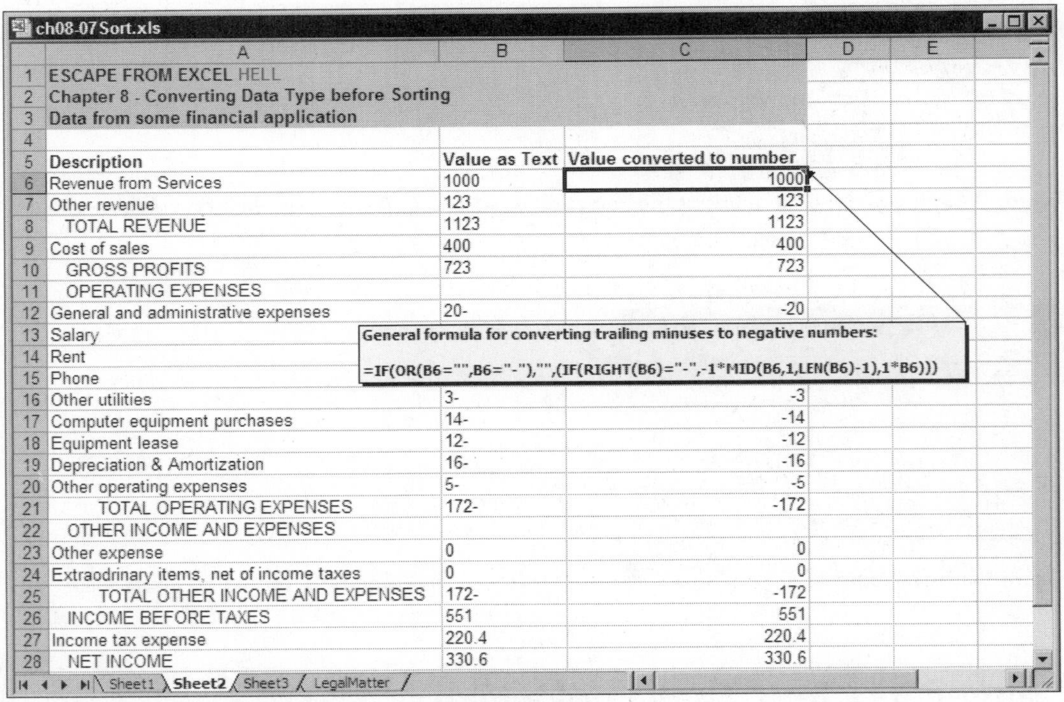

Figure 8-20: Negative text values are properly converted

Sorting ZIP Codes

"When I sort ZIP Codes, they don't seem to sort correctly. Particularly, I have problems when ZIP Codes appear in both five- and nine-digit codes."

Sorting ZIP Codes is a problem that constantly plagues people. If you have a series of ZIP Codes like the following:

```
10021
10021-0012
10029
90210
```

it will be sorted to:

```
10021
10029
90210
10021-0012
```

As far as Excel is concerned, five- and nine-digit ZIP Codes live on different planets. There is, however, a simple way out of this problem. There are two variations and I give you both.

The first way is to convert all your ZIP Codes into text. Because you won't generally need to perform arithmetic operations on ZIP Codes, you don't need Excel to treat them as numbers. Follow these steps.

1. In your list of data, insert a new column next to the ones containing ZIP Codes. If your ZIP Codes are shown in column E, your empty column will be column F.

2. If your ZIP Codes start appearing in cell E11, place the following formula into cell F11:

   `=IF(LEN(E11)<=5,TEXT(E11,"00000"),TEXT(E11,"00000-0000"))`

3. Replicate this formula as far down the column as you need. For argument's sake, assume that the list goes down to F14.

4. Select cells F5:F14 and copy them using Ctrl+C. Click cell E11. From the Excel menu, click Edit⇨Paste Special... Values.

5. Delete column F (click the column label F so that the whole column is selected; then, from the Excel menu, click Edit⇨Delete).

6. Column E is now replaced with ZIP Codes in their proper five- and nine-digit appearance, and they are treated by Excel as text. This means that the column's content can be sorted correctly. Note that when you sort using this column, you will be prompted to tell Excel whether you want to sort text appearing as numbers like a number. Don't choose this option. Choose instead the Sort Numbers and Numbers Stored As Text Separately option.

Part III

Overall, this method works well, but it can have some hitches, as outlined next.

"My list of ZIP Codes is determined using formulas and the numbers are not static values. So, I cannot just simply overwrite the ZIP Codes with static text values."

In this case, don't delete column F. Keep it and use it for your sorting. It is important to remember that you need to include in your sort all the data needed in the sort column F. Figure 8-21 shows how this is handled.

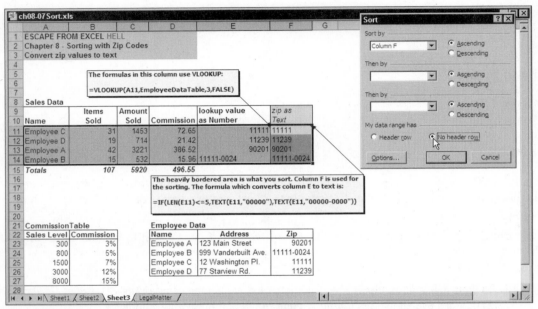

Figure 8-21: Sorting based on text values of ZIP Codes instead of their numeric values

Block Sorting

"I have a mailing list retrieved from a word processing or tab delimited text file. It shows the Member ID on one line, name on another, followed by street address, city, state, and ZIP. I would like this list sorted by Member ID. Any suggestions?"

The technique you can use is to erect a "scaffolding" that binds all the supplementary information (Name, Address, City, State, ZIP) to the Member ID. When the scaffold is built, do the sorting using the scaffold as the sort key.

Figure 8-22 shows what the scaffolding looks like.

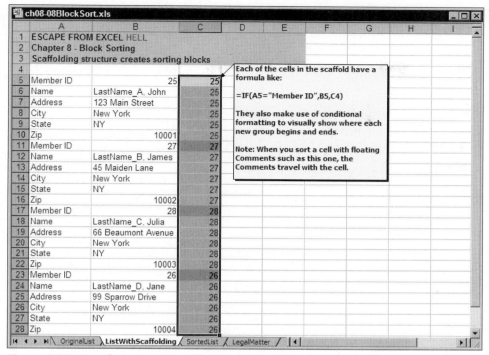

Figure 8-22: List of names with scaffolding on the side

The formula for each of the numbers appearing in the "scaffold" (column C) is straight forward:

```
=IF(A5="Member ID",B5,C4)                    (for cell C5)
```

Follow these steps:

1. Create your scaffold formula (from the top).

Start at the top of the scaffold, which is at row 2, column C. Retrieve the value of the label two cells over to the left. Depending on which row the calculation is being done in, you will get either Member ID, Name, Address, City, State, or ZIP. If you get Member ID, it signals the start of a new record; in which case, grab the actual Member ID number that happens to be one cell over to the left. If the label you just retrieved is not the Member ID, then you're still on the same record number as that of the cell one row above you on the scaffold.

NOTE

Before I forget, because your scaffolding formula looks at the value of the cell immediately above it, you cannot start the formula for your scaffold on row 1. If the data you want to block sort begins on row 1, insert a new row so that the data begins on row 2; then, start your scaffolding.

2. Replicate the scaffolding formula by copying and pasting the formula.

   The scaffolding formula is replicated down the column. Note that nothing has been sorted yet. The sequence of records is 25, 27, 28, 26.

3. Select both your data and scaffold for sorting.

   Select all your data from the top-left corner all the way down to the bottom-right of your scaffold.

TIP

Remember, if you have a large amount of data, use the navigation techniques provided in Chapter 1.

4. Perform the sort.

   After your data is selected, go to the Excel Data menu and click Sort.

   Make sure that you specify No Header Row.

   After you have specified No Header Row, select the scaffold column (in this case, column 3) for your Sort By Criteria. Then click OK.

Keep in mind that the Member IDs (or whatever you want to sort by) do not have to be numbers. They can be labels of any kind, just as long as you can use them as your basis for sorting.

Sorting with More Than Three Sort Keys

In Excel 2003 and earlier editions, you can use, at most, three columns (or rows) as your basis for sorting. This is fine when you have a simple list consisting of, for example, name, age, and ZIP Code, but what if you need more criteria?

Although Excel limits how many columns you use as criteria for sorting, an easy workaround exists. It basically boils down to multiple passes for sorting.

"I have some economic data with many columns and I need to sort all the data on four sort keys in descending order. I want to see all the data sorted in descending order by the high school data, then Bachelor's degree, then by percentage owner occupied, and finally by housing value."

Though it sounds complicated, this sort is basically doable. The key is to break this into multiple passes of three sort keys at a time; and, most important, *to apply the passes in reverse sequence.*

To make this very simple: If you need to sort a list using multiple criteria A, B, C, D, with A being the most important, followed by B, and then C, and finally D, then sort by B, C, D in one pass. After this sort is complete, sort by A.

As an example, open the file called ch08_09MultiColumnSort.xls, on the book's CD-ROM. In Sheet1, select the data for all the states (51 rows because the District of Columbia is included). From the Excel menu, click Data⇨Sort and choose the three sort keys B, C, and D as shown in Figure 8-23. Don't forget to select descending order.

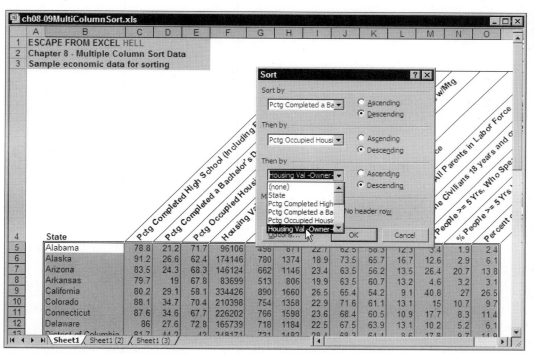

Figure 8-23: Sort on keys B, C, D with housing value on the bottom rung

After the B-C-D sort is complete, perform the A sort in the next pass (see Figure 8-24).

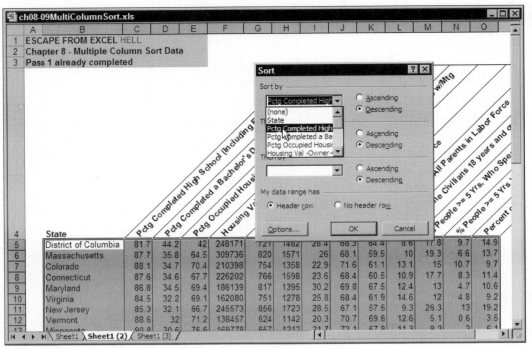

Figure 8-24: Perform the A sort.

The file `ch08_09MultiColumnSort.xls` has three worksheets. These show the sort in successive stages of completion.

Sorting by Cell Number Format and by Cell Color

"We use color codes to help keep track of project status; Red, Amber, and Green. How can we sort our projects by color?"

Excel has no preexisting function sort by color. This type of sorting requires some VBA coding. I give you three ways to accomplish what you need:

1. The code for a function called `getColorIndex` that does this is already written into the Escape Excel Hell Utility Pak. If you already have the utility pack installed, you can use it in any of your spreadsheets.

2. I give you the VBA code so that you can write it into any spreadsheet you want and make any improvements you see fit.

3. If you are not familiar with VBA programming and want to incorporate `getColorIndex` in your other spreadsheets, open the file `ch08_10SortBycolor.xls` and save it to a filename of your choice. This file has the VBA code in it, so you can retrofit it with content from other worksheets you may have created elsewhere. Remember, you can right-click worksheet tabs from another spreadsheet and copy or move your existing worksheets to this one.

Open the file called `ch08_10SortByColor.xls` (see Figure 8-25).

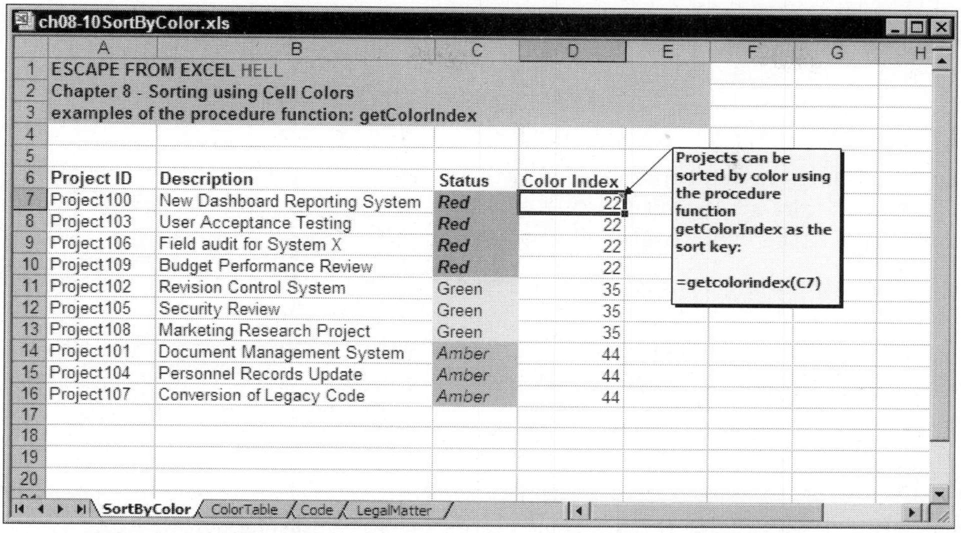

	A	B	C	D	E	F	G	H
1	ESCAPE FROM EXCEL HELL							
2	Chapter 8 - Sorting using Cell Colors							
3	examples of the procedure function: getColorIndex							
4								
5								
6	Project ID	Description	Status	Color Index				
7	Project100	New Dashboard Reporting System	Red	22				
8	Project103	User Acceptance Testing	Red	22				
9	Project106	Field audit for System X	Red	22				
10	Project109	Budget Performance Review	Red	22				
11	Project102	Revision Control System	Green	35				
12	Project105	Security Review	Green	35				
13	Project108	Marketing Research Project	Green	35				
14	Project101	Document Management System	Amber	44				
15	Project104	Personnel Records Update	Amber	44				
16	Project107	Conversion of Legacy Code	Amber	44				
17								
18								
19								
20								

Projects can be sorted by color using the procedure function getColorIndex as the sort key:

=getcolorindex(C7)

Figure 8-25: You can use `GetColorIndex` to retrieve the color of a cell background or its font color.

The procedure function `getColorIndex` has the following syntax:

```
getColorIndex(CellCoordinate)
getColorIndex(CellCoordinate,InteriorOrFontSelector)
```

If only the cell coordinate is provided, `getColorIndex` returns an integer that corresponds to the cell's background color.

If you want the color index of the cell's font instead of the cell's background color, use `getColorIndex` with two arguments: the cell's coordinate and the interior/font selector with a value of 2. A value of 1 for the interior/font selector does the same thing as it would if you don't supply a second argument (that is, it returns the color index of the cell's background).

The VBA code for this procedure function is the following:

```
Option Explicit
Function getColorIndex(myCell As Range, Optional iArg As Integer = 1)

Application.Volatile True

Select Case iArg
    Case 1
        getColorIndex = myCell.Interior.ColorIndex
    Case 2
```

```
        getColorIndex = myCell.Font.ColorIndex
End Select

End Function
```

Those of you who like to dabble in VBA coding may find this a nice example of how to define a procedure function with optional arguments.

As previously stated, if you don't want to play with VBA code but still want this functionality, you can start with the spreadsheet ch08_10SortByColor.xls file and add to it worksheets and formulas based on spreadsheets you already have.

Sometimes you may want to sort data in a worksheet based on how the values in a cell are formatted. This type of facility does not require use of any VBA or macro. It has nothing to do with color but rather with the type of number format use in a cell. You can create a sort key based on numeric format by using:

```
=CELL("format",A1)                    (returns numeric
                                       cell format for A1)
```

Examples of various cell formats and the value of the "format" returned by CELL are shown in Table 8-1.

TABLE 8-1   NUMERIC "FORMAT" TYPES USING THE EXCEL CELL FUNCTION

If Cell Format Is...	CELL Returns...
General	G
0	F0
#,##0	,0
0.00	F2
#,##0.00	,2
$#,##0_);($#,##0)	C0
$#,##0_);[Red]($#,##0)	C0-
$#,##0.00_);($#,##0.00)	C2
$#,##0.00_);[Red]($#,##0.00)	C2-
0%	P0
0.00%	P2
0.00E+00	S2
# ?/? or # ??/??	G

If Cell Format Is...	CELL Returns...
m/d/yy or m/d/yy h:mm or mm/dd/yy	D4
d-mmm-yy or dd-mmm-yy	D1
d-mmm or dd-mmm	D2
mmm-yy	D3
mm/dd	D5
h:mm AM/PM	D7
h:mm:ss AM/PM	D6
h:mm	D9
h:mm:ss	D8

Sorting by IP Block

"I have a list of IP addresses that I need sorted."

The world is becoming increasingly Web-centric. As it does, a term such as an IP address is spoken in larger circles. In this regard, I repeatedly come across many colleagues who have a list of IP addresses and need to sort them. Typically, these IP addresses are the network server addresses, or addresses of firewalls.

Whatever the network addresses happens to be, it becomes a drudgery to sort the IP addresses. The reason is simple. Excel interprets an address like 95.243.188.67 as text. You could sort the text address 95.243.188.67 with other IP addresses, but doing so would not give a correct result. For a sort to work, these digits would need to be placed on equal footing. Basically, you would have to place leading zeros so that all of the IP blocks have three digits. In this case, the address 95.243.188.67 would be converted to 095.243.188.067.

The general convention with IP addresses is not to have leading zeros in the IP blocks. There's an alternative way that works quite well. This involves converting the IP addresses to hexadecimal code. This hexadecimal address is precisely eight characters wide and is perfect for use as a sort key.

The ch08_11SortByIPBlock.xls file does this conversion for you (see Figure 8-26).

 NOTE

The ch08_11SortByIPBlock.xls and in particular the function DEC2HEX require that you have the Excel Analysis ToolPak.

Understanding IP addresses

IP addresses are kind of an Internet ZIP Code. When you look at an IP address, you see that it has four blocks of numbers, separated by periods. A good way to think about this is as an IP address in the form of:

```
region.country.state.city
```

The world has various regions such as the Americas, Europe, and Asia. Within the Americas are the countries Canada, the United States, Mexico, Central America, and South America. Within the United States are 50 states, starting alphabetically with Alabama and Alaska. Within the state of Alabama are cities such as Montgomery and Huntsville.

Instead of specifying an address as:

```
Americas.UnitedStates.Alabama.Montgomery
```

you could use a numeric scheme so that each block in the address is assigned a number. This makes it easier for computers to use. The preceding address might be replaced by a numeric sequence like:

```
01.001.001.00001
```

There is a fundamental difference between the made-up scheme of world addresses I just presented and true Internet IP addresses. In the geographic scheme, you start off with just a few regions in the first block in the geographic IP. In the second block, you could have a few dozen countries. In the third block for states, you could have plenty more. Finally, in the forth block for cities within states, you could have thousands of cities and towns within a state.

By contrast, the Internet model of IP addresses is uniformly distributed. Each of the blocks in an IP address varies between 1 and 255. The lowest value for an IP address is 1.1.1.1 and the highest is 255.255.255.255, making for a total of 4,228,250,625 (= 255 times 255 times 255 times 255). Right now there are more people on the planet than there are assignable IP addresses! As IP addresses become more of a scarce commodity, keeping track of them becomes increasingly important.

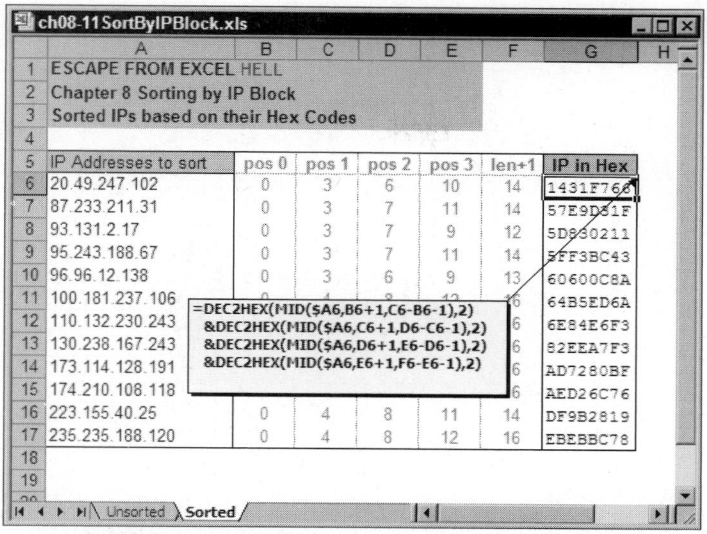

Figure 8-26: DEC2HEX is used to convert the IP address to its hexadecimal form.

Auto-Sort (Using Arrays)

"I have a list of numbers that is constantly being updated. Is there any way I can have the numbers automatically sorted?"

The answer is yes, but it involves using array formulas. Open the spreadsheet called `ch08_12AutoSort.xls` (see Figure 8-27). It contains a section called Randomly Generated Numbers. As numbers within this section are changed, they are automatically sorted in columns C and D. This sorting uses array formulas and does not entail any macros or VBA programming whatsoever.

Every time you press the F9 key or do something to force recalculation, a new set of numbers for sorting is generated in column A. I use this number generation scheme to illustrate that sorting occurs automatically. In reality, the numbers to be auto-sorted would typically be updated manually.

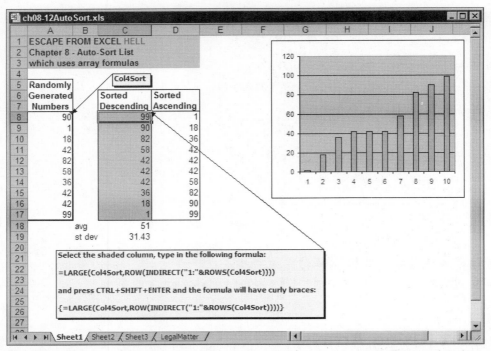

Figure 8-27: As numbers are changed in column A, they are automatically sorted in descending and ascending order in columns C and D.

This kind of facility becomes particularly useful when you have a larger number of items to sort, instead of just ten items as illustrated here.

The formula used in this sort is as follows:

```
{=LARGE(Col4Sort,ROW(INDIRECT("1:"&ROWS(Col4Sort))))}
```

To get this formula to work correctly, first select the region where you want the cells to be sorted. In this case, select cells C8:C17. Press F2 to go to the edit mode and type in the following formula in the Formula Bar (without the curly braces):

```
=LARGE(Col4Sort,ROW(INDIRECT("1:"&ROWS(Col4Sort))))
```

While still in the edit mode, press Ctrl+Shift+Enter. This will create an array formula that does the auto-sorting.

The formula works by returning the *n*th largest value in a selection of cells. The selection of cells is the user-defined range of Col4Sort. If you want, you can substitute it with the cell range $A8:$A17. Additionally, it cycles from 1 through the total number of rows in Col4Sort and places the values in order, within the selected range. To see this process in action, you can use the Evaluate Formula toolbar icon (see Figure 8-28) discussed earlier in this chapter.

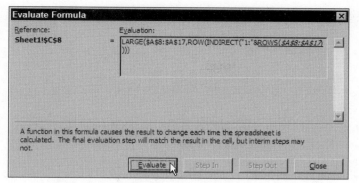

Figure 8-28: The Evaluate Formula toolbar icon helps to understand how array formulas are computed.

The descending auto-sort works the same way except that it picks the nth smallest values. The formula used for this is as follows:

```
{=SMALL(Col4Sort,ROW(INDIRECT("1:"&ROWS(Col4Sort))))}
```

Comparing Spreadsheets

"I need to compare two very similar spreadsheets to see where they differ."

There are several ways to compare spreadsheets. You can compare two spreadsheets side by side as described in the "Data Validation" section of Chapter 7. Another approach might be to subtract the values from each cell in a worksheet with those of another. If there are no differences, every subtraction should return a zero value. This works, but it's clumsy at best. It will not permit you the freedom of quickly specifying which worksheets you want to compare or the range of cells to analyze.

A third approach exists that will help make your job easier in this kind of task. If you had a wish list, what would you want to see?

- You might want to look at worksheet A over a range of cells in one region, see its values, and if it differs from a second worksheet, highlight where they are different.

- You might want to switch your view and look at the equivalent set of cells in worksheet B.

- When there are differences between the worksheets, it would certainly be nice to know by how much they differ on a cell-by-cell basis.

- Rather than look at a range of cells for a fixed set of coordinates, you might want to scroll across or down a spreadsheet.

- As long as you can scroll, it makes sense to have row and column cells move along with it.

- Also nice would be to see the range of cell coordinates you are currently examining listed.

- You should easily be able to specify a new workbook to examine by just changing the reference to the file location.

- As long as file and cell coordinates can be specified, it would be nice to have the option of doing everything in A1 style or R1C1 style cell coordinates.

Does having all these capabilities sound too good to be true? See for yourself: Open the ch08_13DataCompare.xls spreadsheet on the CD-ROM (see Figure 8-29).

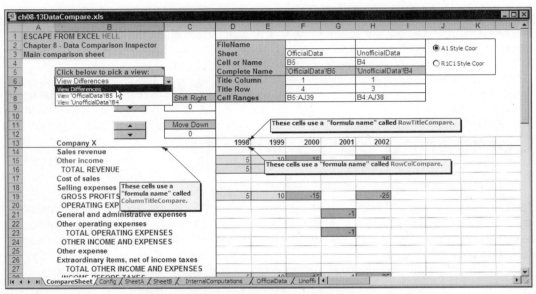

Figure 8-29: Tool for comparing differences between spreadsheets

There are several things to notice in this spreadsheet:

- The data compare spreadsheet shows a swatch of 35 × 35 rows and columns of any two remote spreadsheets of your choosing. Any difference in value or text in the range of cells is highlighted using conditional formatting.

- You can select from among three views: the differences between the two remote worksheets, the first worksheet, and the second worksheet. When a worksheet is displayed, any cells that are different are automatically highlighted. Notice that the names of the remote spreadsheets are automatically displayed in the drop-down list. (This feature relies on the validation feature described in Chapter 7.)

- Using the spinner control arrows, you can scroll left/right and up/down.

- As you scroll, the row and column headers are automatically kept in synch.

- Notice that formula names are used. For instance, cells in the 35×35 compare sheet use the formula

```
=RowColCompare
```

This technique of presenting information keeps the spreadsheet clean in appearance, and the underlying definition for RowColCompare is kept out of harm's way. The name RowColCompare happens to be defined as:

```
=CHOOSE(
   ViewListValue,
   IF(SheetA!RC=SheetB!RC,"",
      IF(ISNUMBER(SheetA!RC),SheetA!RC-SheetB!RC,
         T(SheetA!RC))),
   IF(ISNUMBER(SheetA!RC),SheetA!RC,T(SheetA!RC)),
   IF(ISNUMBER(SheetB!RC),SheetB!RC,T(SheetB!RC)))
```

This formula is shown in the R1C1 notation because it appears as precisely the identical formula regardless of which cell you happen to view the definition from. This notation style makes the formula much easier to understand because you don't have to mentally translate the formula based on the current cell position.

- When you reference the remote worksheet, you have the option of using A1 or R1C1 style cell coordinates in the remote worksheets.

This tool requires that the remote spreadsheets be open; otherwise, it cannot read the values. A benefit of this tool is that the remote worksheets can be "live," that is, you can be comparing two spreadsheets, a baseline and an alternate spreadsheet, make changes in the alternate, and see the differences.

Closing Thoughts

This chapter might make you feel as though you're in boot camp and training to become a data artisan. If you are constantly working with data, chances are you have to clean it, manipulate it, analyze it, and sometimes look at it sideways. This chapter shows you a number of techniques. My hope is that you can harvest the variety of sorting techniques outlined here and put them to use in your own situation.

Regardless of the venue, the emphasis is placed on how to apply techniques in analyzing data.

Part III

When problems are difficult, it is often because many things are happening simultaneously. The lynchpin to solving these problems involves isolating and resolving each issue one at a time, without the distraction of the others. You saw this up front in the ListCleanup worksheet (refer to Figure 8-1), in which each column in succession performs a specific task and removes it from the picture. I want you to take this way of approaching problems to heart.

This notion of "peeling the onion" is applied, in this chapter, to data analysis, for which the focus is on specific formulas and small chunks of data. What happens when you apply this to the structure of very large spreadsheets? Well, that's the topic addressed in Chapter 9, in which you'll see how to apply the Layered Approach to some very, very large spreadsheets.

Chapter 9

Very Large Spreadsheets

In This Chapter

- ◆ Changing control and documentation strategies for large spreadsheets
- ◆ Managing complexity through the Layered Approach
- ◆ Scaling strategies for spreadsheets that get big
- ◆ Random number generation
- ◆ Common spreadsheet errors and how to fix them

Overview

In this chapter I address the subject of very large and complex spreadsheets. This chapter differs from others in the book, for good reason. Instead of my trying to show small, self-contained examples and solutions, I felt that attacking problems with very big spreadsheets would be more instructive. In the process, I also show solutions and methodologies relating to smaller pieces. Along the way I cover a variety of important topics.

Many people shy away from attempting large spreadsheets, largely because such spreadsheets become too unwieldy. This situation doesn't have to be the case. You just need to be armed with certain techniques, and be disciplined in how you go about building such spreadsheets.

Interestingly enough, many of the problems that plague big spreadsheets also infest their smaller cousins.

Very large spreadsheets should be approached from two angles: preventing spreadsheets destined to become large and unmanageable from fulfilling that destiny; and dealing with spreadsheets that are already unwieldy and too complex. As you will soon see, large quantities of data may make reducing the size of a spreadsheet hard, but much can be done to improve its manageability.

In this chapter, I begin with some rather drab concepts that are all too often neglected or overlooked but are, nonetheless, important. These concepts pertain to filenaming and change control. I then introduce some preliminary notions about splitting the functional components of a spreadsheet into separate worksheet layers. I skip long explanations and jump into a full-blown example of building and handling a very large spreadsheet to illustrate basic techniques and point out the kind of practical considerations that come into play.

Next, I discuss a variety of miscellaneous problems and their solutions that are central to simplifying large and complex spreadsheets. Those of you who can't get enough of the topic of large spreadsheets may want to pick up a copy of my book *Excel Best Practices for Business* (Wiley Publishing, Inc.).

Keeping Your Documents in Order

When you start having numerous files and many changes occurring in them, you can easily lose track of all your changes and versions. You might remember things clearly today, but three months from now it might take a little doing to recall all your changes. To help get around these issues, I outline two approaches. The first deals with the practice of filenaming. Because it feels trivial and there are no safeguards to ensure that the practice is conscientiously applied, it winds up being forgotten or belatedly enforced. Another feature that is important to manage is change control.

Filenaming Strategy

If you're about to overhaul a large and complex spreadsheet, chances are that multiple kinds of changes to your spreadsheet may be needed. You might want to tidy up the appearance of a spreadsheet. At the same time, there may be some changes to the logic in a number of formulas. There may be some charts to adjust. You may also need to weed out extraneous data. Rather than make all these changes in a jumbled up manner, you might benefit by dividing these changes into stages. Filenaming is one of the easiest ways to accomplish this.

I almost never hear anyone worry about how to name a file. After all, filenaming is almost trivial. However, when you have several dozen or hundreds of files in a directory (or across multiple directories), the practice of consistently naming files can go a long way toward eliminating confusion.

Here are some simple suggestions:

- Choose filenames that convey what is contained in the spreadsheet. Otherwise, it becomes very hard to figure out what the files contain. Filenames like `N939C.xls` and `N5579.xls` are cryptic. You can't tell what they're for by looking at their names. Furthermore, when you see the two files together along with others, do the filenames help you to figure out which file belongs to what?

- Choose a filename that makes it easy to discern the "what" part (for example, BalanceSheet as opposed to IncomeStatement) from the version. An underscore symbol makes it easy to visually separate these. For example, consider these three spreadsheets:

  - `BalanceSheet2006_01.xls`

  - `BalanceSheet2007_01.xls`

  - `BalanceSheet2007_02.xls`

  The two digits at the end of the name can be used to designate a version number. The base part of the name is composed of what appears to be a financial statement type (Balance Sheet) and a year. The underscore helps to visually separate the base part of the name from the version number.

- Pick a naming convention that makes sense when sorted alphabetically. Specifically, when you serialize the version number, you may want to consider using two digits rather than one. If you don't, your file directly might appear as:

```
MyFinancialForcast_1.xls
MyFinancialForcast_10.xls
MyFinancialForcast_11.xls
MyFinancialForcast_12.xls
MyFinancialForcast_13.xls
MyFinancialForcast_2.xls
MyFinancialForcast_3.xls
MyFinancialForcast_4.xls
MyFinancialForcast_5.xls
MyFinancialForcast_6.xls
MyFinancialForcast_7.xls
MyFinancialForcast_8.xls
MyFinancialForcast_9.xls
```

If you use a two-digit sequence, you won't run into this problem until you surpass 99. If you have that many versions of a file, it may be time to consider a new sequence altogether.

- Make it a principle to never apply changes to your original file or a baseline, but rather work on a copy. If your baseline file is `MyWorkbook_01.xls`, save it as `MyWorkbook_01A.xls` and make your changes there (you might, for instance, have improvements to your formulas). You may later decide to add two new worksheets to it and concentrate your changes to these new worksheets. You save the workbook as `MyWorkbook_01B.xls`. You then go through some testing and validation and are now satisfied that the changes you made are working, and save a new baseline `MyWorkbook_02.xls`.

  Notice that there is no confusion between what is a baseline and what is an experimental version of your spreadsheet.

  The benefit of separating baselines from the variations is that you always have a fallback position. If at some point you discover a fundamental design flaw in the spreadsheet, you can rollback the changes to the previous baseline and rework your changes. It may not matter much with ordinary spreadsheet, but it can make a critical difference when you are working with a very large and complex spreadsheet.

I know that I seem to be spending many words for something as simple as the filename. It's for a good reason. Apply these practices and they'll will save you some heartache in the long run. I guarantee it.

Change Control

One of the best things you can do when you're working with a complicated spreadsheet is to document changes. It may occur to you to insert hovering comments in spreadsheet cells. This may be useful for giving a person a hint as to what to enter or avoid entering in a spreadsheet, but it may be of limited value as a tool for documenting changes over the life cycle of your spreadsheet. One of the reasons that it may be hard to apply is that the details get buried inside the spreadsheet.

I don't want to suggest that comments are ineffective for documenting spreadsheet changes. When coupled with macros, they can be a very effective tool.

Another technique that is sometimes useful is to embed a comment inside a formula. Here is an example:

```
=SUM("I chose to sum the first ten instead of twelve rows",A1:A10)
```

Because the quoted expression evaluates to zero, the outcome is the same as SUM(A1:A10).

You can pepper your spreadsheet with annotations, but you are missing several important ingredients:

- As already stated, the annotations are deep inside the spreadsheet and are not so easy to corral.

- There is no automatic way to document changes to your changes. This is an important feature and is also known as an audit trail.

- There is no sense of a chronology—of tracing through changes in the order they were made.

- There may be limited ability to identify what changes are associated with different versions of the spreadsheet.

- There is no automatic provision for identifying who made the changes.

For these and other reasons, I provide a `RevisionHistory.xlt` template for your use. When you open the file from the CD-ROM, click Save As, and specify the file type as an `.xlt` template. Its use is shown in Chapter 3 (see Figure 3-2). This tool addresses most of the features just outlined. Note that the tool is macro based. Because it is open source, you are free to extend it. Also, the tool does not automatically capture changes as they happen. It requires you to document the changes, but makes it easy to do so. The tool is an integral part of the spreadsheet, which makes it easy to establish an audit trail.

Form a change control standpoint, it may become necessary, after your spreadsheet comes close to being production ready, to enable the Track Changes feature. You do so from the Excel Tools menu. This will track all your changes and should be enabled when you've pretty much finalized a spreadsheet and need to keep track of all changes made from then on.

One final note before I leave the topic of change control: Change control is based on a model of trust. It is very easy to bypass controls without leaving a proper audit trail.

Managing Complexity Through the Layered Approach

You may notice that throughout this book I frequently resort to using multiple worksheets within a workbook. You may see them typically having labels such as: SourceData, Config, Analysis Engine, and one or more Presentation Layers. This layering of functionality into separate worksheets is intentional. It is a very powerful mechanism for managing flexibility.

In the following sections, I briefly describe the goals for what each of these layers are and then show how to apply the Layering Approach.

The Source Data Layer

When you have a very large spreadsheet, you would do well to keep the bulk data separated from the rest of the spreadsheet. The idea to keep in mind is that within the Source Data layer, no computations are being performed. If you start tacking on calculations for each and every row of data, you may soon find yourself in computational quicksand.

Two issues to avoid at all costs are a dramatic drop in calculation performance and the commingling of data with the analysis and presentation.

Look at the picture logically. After you open a spreadsheet with large amounts of data, how much effort is spent by Excel to keep the spreadsheet open as you jump around to different parts of various worksheets? Obviously, the answer is not much. If you can, you should have the spreadsheet perform as few calculations as possible. In the best of all possible worlds, a spreadsheet with 60,000 rows of data should crunch numbers almost as well as one with 1,600 rows of data. The only difference should be that one of them is bigger. It might take more disk space and time to save a file, but performance-wise there shouldn't be much difference. That's the theory, anyhow. You're about to see how close we can get to theory. In the example shown a little later, you'll encounter a spreadsheet with close to 120,000 rows of data.

If you design things correctly, you'll be able to push the envelope pretty close to the limit.

To avoid the nightmares in managing the spreadsheet, keep any formulas and custom formatting as far away as possible from the source data. Just make sure that the source data you need to work with is properly structured so that the analysis on limited portions can be done without having to worry about the data structure. For example, if you'll be looking up countries based on a two-letter code or some other kind of index, and you have 60,000 rows of raw data, you need to make sure that all 60,000 rows possess valid codes.

I want to provide one more compelling reason to separate your computational formulas from your data. When they are separated, it becomes an easy process to update your data without touching the rest of the spreadsheet. In terms of reliability, time, and cost, the results are a major economic savings.

The Analysis Layer

Again, imagine that your spreadsheet contains 60,000 rows of data. You may need to perform some kind of computation, such as a moving average, on this data. Do you want to perform the computation of all 60,000 rows at one time? More important, if you are working with only a month's worth of data at a time, why bother trying to perform calculations on every piece of data? Just compute those values that you need to examine and nothing else. Don't even bother making the results of the calculations look pretty. Save that for the Presentation Layer.

The analysis engine shouldn't have to worry which data to analyze. It should just be given a small morsel of data, perform the computation, and be done with it.

The Configuration Layer

The Config worksheet layer should house information about where the data is located, how it's structured, and other housekeeping information necessary for the spreadsheet model to run properly. It can also include some brief lookup tables. Mostly, the Configuration layer serves as a relay station.

The Presentation Layer

The Presentation Layer (or sometimes layers) takes the analysis results and transforms it into a presentable report or graphic. In theory, the Presentation Layer should not be performing any computations; those should be left for the Analysis Layer.

Applying Layered Approach

To show the Layered Approach in action, I am using some meteorological data obtained from the U.S. National Weather Service. This is data collected from 152 weather stations during World War II. The goal is to make a spreadsheet for which it's easy to view temperature and precipitation data by country, over time. To make this work, a number of simplifying decisions will have to be made. I point these out along the way.

File Organization

The data is contained in the Spreadsheets directory of the book's CD-ROM; alternatively, you can obtain it from:

```
http://www.ncdc.noaa.gov/oa/climate/online/ww-ii-data.html
```

The files for this data set include:

- `ww-ii-data.txt`—The main data file in fixed-width delimited format; this is in excess of 15 megabytes in file size.

- `station-list.txt`—A list of weather station locations for the dataset, which identifies station name, country code, map coordinates, and station elevation.

- `country-id.txt`—Shows the country identifiers (two-character ID).

- `format.txt`—Describes the format of the data, principally identifying units used.

You'll also find a `readme.txt` file and a `map.gif` file on the CD.

The Game Plan

Here are the basic steps that follow:

- Bring the main data into Excel.

- Determine what, if any, changes you need to make to the data.

- Map the data to quickly find information you may need to view.

- Create a mechanism that uses the map to retrieve the data.

- Set up the analysis engine to work on the retrieved data.

- Create a Presentation Layer to view the data.

In the steps that follow, I include all the problems you are likely to encounter along the way and how to deal with them. I also include the spreadsheet at various stages of completion so that you can skip ahead or rework some specific step.

Setting Up the Source Data

A quick glance at the files reveals that the file `ww-ii-data.txt` is comparatively large (in excess of 15MB). This is nothing to sneeze at. When you first try to import the data by opening the text file from Excel (remember to select all files in your file options to select a `.txt` file), you quickly discover it is large. To be precise, it contains 119,041 rows (see Figure 9-1).

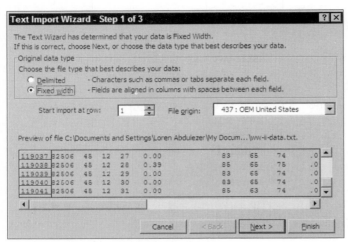

Figure 9-1: Almost 120,000 rows to import

Worksheets in Excel 2003 (and earlier) max out at 65,536 rows. Clearly, not all the data can be imported from the single file. It will have to be split into two files. You will need a suitable text editor to perform this task. For a file of this size, you would need something more than Notepad. Actually, you can use Word because it is capable of displaying line numbers. Any industrial-strength text editor will do the job.

Although Notepad is not designed for a file of this size, you can use it. In fact, I use it just to prove that you can get by with an inadequate tool such as Notepad. I also use Notepad because not all readers would have an alternative text editor readily available to them.

To get started, open a new text file in Notepad or the text editor of your choice. In addition, open the `ww-ii-data.txt` file in Notepad (or again, your favorite text editor). Because of the file size, it may take a while to open. Be patient. When it is open, select and copy the first line of the `ww-ii-data.txt` file, which is the header row, and paste it into the empty text file.

For good measure, insert a blank line immediately following the pasted content. You can do this by pressing the Enter key after you paste the content.

Next, select the `ww-ii-data.txt` file and scroll down to about the middle of the file. Click at the start of any line near this halfway point. If you are unsure of exactly where one line ends and another begins, try to enable your text editor to display normally invisible characters such as carriage returns and tabs. Notepad is truly low end, so it will not display invisible characters. In this case, look back at Figure 9-1. Notice that there is a five-digit number followed by a two-digit year number, month number, and then day number. If you select just before the five-digit number on the left side of the window, you should be okay. Now scroll down to the end of the ww-ii-data.txt file and Shift+click at the tail end of the document. This action selects everything in the second half of the text file. Cut and paste it to the effectively empty text file you created earlier. Save this file as data2.txt. Save the ww-ii-data.txt file, which is now half its original size, as data1.txt.

You are now ready to import both of these files. Instead of starting with a blank workbook, you can use the RevisionHistory.xlt template and record changes to your spreadsheet with it.

With a new file created based on the template, insert two empty worksheets and rename them as SourceData1 and SourceData2. Click cell A1 of the SourceData1 worksheet. From the Excel Data menu, click Import External Data⇨Import Data. Though you'll see numerous database and Web query options, you can just open the data1.txt file. Excel will show you the appropriate options for the text file in a Text Import Wizard. When you apply the Fixed Width options, make sure that the vertical separator lines reside between each of the column headers. Sometimes Excel fails to insert them. This can happen if Excel didn't find data directly underneath a particular column header. Remember, the data is split into two files, so the appropriate date might not be evident until you get to the second file.

After you complete the three steps of the Text Import Wizard, you will get to an Import Data window. Although you can just go ahead and click OK to place the imported data into the SourceData1 worksheet, you may want to peruse the data query's properties (see Figure 9-2).

Figure 9-2: Setting the External Data Range Properties

No action is required here at this time. I just want to show options available to you. Finish the import so that the data is now displayed in the SourceData1 worksheet. Do the same for data2.txt, but import it into the SourceData2 worksheet.

NOTE

You may be wondering why I had you import two smaller files instead of repeating the import on the large file and specifying a Start Row of 65,537 in place of the default value of 1 (see Figure 9-1). The reason is that the largest value accepted for the Start Row is 32,767, so it becomes impossible to choose a higher start row.

After the files are imported, you can redistribute the data between the two sheets so that they are roughly balanced between the two source data sheets. Before moving the content, make sure that the column headers between the two worksheets are identical. Recall my suggestion that you insert a blank line between the headers in data2.txt and the data below it. There are two reasons for doing this. One has to do with cleanly separating the data from the header. The second reason is that this row can be used to verify that the columns of both charts are identical.

At this stage, you may want to record some of your key changes made to the spreadsheet (which should be easy to do if your starting spreadsheet is based on the Revision History template). You can open the file ch09_LargeSpreadsheet_01.xls to see how the spreadsheet currently looks.

A Preliminary Assessment of Your Data

Now that you've got all this data, you have to assess its state and determine whether you need to perform any actions.

To gain a perspective of what the data means, open the format.txt file. If you open this text file using Excel, you will see three columns: the abbreviated header label, the full description, and units used.

The fields you may want to turn your attention to are the following:

```
STA -  Station Number
YR     Year
MO     Month
DA     Day
PRCP   24 Hour Precipitation
MAX    Maximum Temperature
MIN    Minimum Temperature
MEA    Mean Temperature
```

FINDING ANOMALIES

Something is curious. In the columns of data with column headers for the weather station, year, month, day, and so on, there is a column header TSHDSBRSGF. It seems to be a combined column that identifies whether thunder, sleet, hail, dust or sand, smoke or haze, blowing snow, rain, snow, glaze, or fog was reported. Though it is a combined column of zeros and ones, the way the data came into Excel is inconsistent. It sometimes shows up as a number like 1 or 0, or blank (same as a 0).

The problem is that when it shows up as an isolated digit like 1, you can't clearly tell which of these classifications it belongs to. If you go back to the source data, you can see that the appearance of an isolated 1 is almost always associated with rain. This makes sense. Unfortunately, the entries as imported in this column are largely ambiguous. You are faced with your first conundrum: either report the data with each column individually separated, or forego the use of the data in the column altogether.

As a general practice, I try to salvage useful data, if I may have a use for it later on. To make life a little easier for you, I have already re-imported, breaking out the TSHDSBRSGF into individual columns (see Figure 9-3).

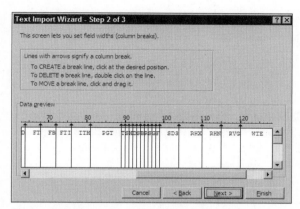

Figure 9-3: Re-importing with individual columns separated

You can open the ch09_LargeSpreadsheet_02.xls with the correctly structured data.

SORTING YOUR DATA

Another key decision to make concerns how to sort your data. You can keep it more or less the way it is, sequenced by station number and then date, or by date and then station number. Personally, I think the first of these two makes more sense and is easier to handle.

Notice that the date info is broken out into three columns (year, month, and day), so there are four columns for your sort key. To sort the data, you can apply the technique outlined in Chapter 8 for sorting with more than three sort keys. Basically, you would first sort by year, month, and day. Then you would sort again by station number.

I want to point out an easier way that involves only one sort. It involves adding a temporary column based on the composite date. There are some good reasons for wanting to use a composite date column for the sort instead of the individual columns of year, month, and date. It permits error checking. You may have data like a February 29th occurring on a non-Leap Year or something equally spurious. In such situations, you may have to eliminate the data, or revise it (and, of course, document this in your revision history log).

In column AG, add a formula like the following and replicate it down to the last row of data for each of the source data worksheets:

```
=DATE(1900+B2,C2,D2)                        (cell AG2)
```

After you have the date values computed by formula, you can select the AG column, copy it (Ctrl+C), and use Paste Special... Values to overwrite itself. This will remove the formulas and just keep the values. Now you can perform a single sort based on the station number and the date value in column AG. Remember to apply these steps to both the SourceData1 and SourceData2 worksheets.

Incidentally, the data as you originally imported to the spreadsheet is almost properly sorted. A small number of records are out of sequence. The data for station number 34149 on June 21st, 1945, appears approximately 10 rows earlier than it should.

Before leaving the topic of the preliminary assessment of data, you should note that the precipitation data has a bunch of "T" and TRUE values in it. For now, keep this in the back of your mind.

Mapping the Data

At this point, you have a large amount of data and it appears to be structured in an organized pattern by station number and date. It would be nice to just pluck out the data for any desired station number and date. To do this, you need to create a map that Excel formulas can use to locate the data in an instant.

CREATING A STATION LIST MAP

To create a Station List Map, you need to obtain a list of all the unique station IDs. A quick way to do this is to use the Row Compression Technique, described in detail later in this chapter. Because the station numbers and station data are already sorted, you need only to track where the station numbers change. If you know these locations, you can retrieve every station number and starting row. This is handled in columns AH, AI, and AJ of the source data worksheets (of the ch09_LargeSpreadsheet_03.xls file). This is enough to create a basic map. Copy the starting row numbers and place the values onto a Map worksheet (see Figure 9-4).

After the location values are kept in the Map worksheet, you can discard the computations in columns AH, AI, and AJ of the source data worksheets.

TIP

I constantly prune redundant or unneeded calculations and data when I know they won't be needed. This pruning is an important practice that helps to keep large spreadsheets from becoming unwieldy. Try to make this practice a habit when you're working with large and complex spreadsheets.

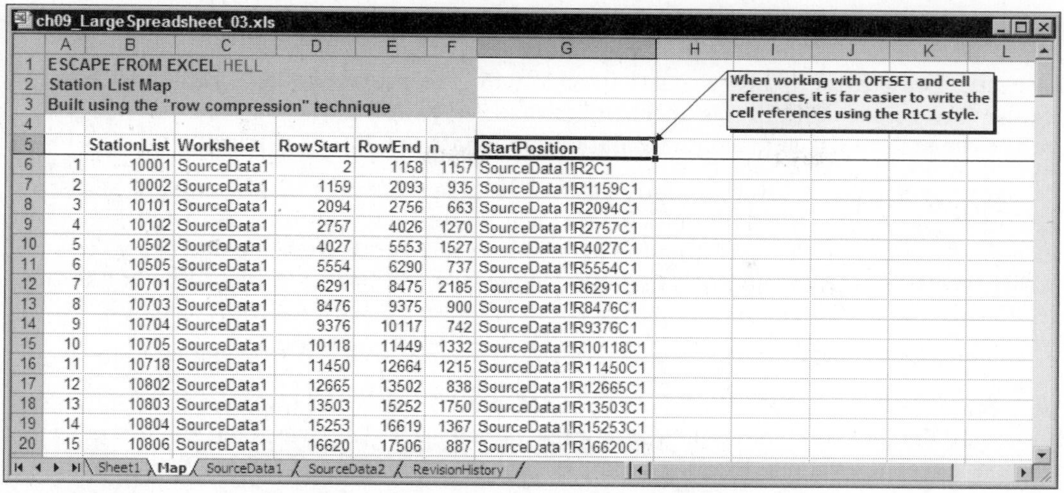

ch09_LargeSpreadsheet_03.xls

ESCAPE FROM EXCEL HELL
Station List Map
Built using the "row compression" technique

	StationList	Worksheet	RowStart	RowEnd	n	StartPosition
1	10001	SourceData1	2	1158	1157	SourceData1!R2C1
2	10002	SourceData1	1159	2093	935	SourceData1!R1159C1
3	10101	SourceData1	2094	2756	663	SourceData1!R2094C1
4	10102	SourceData1	2757	4026	1270	SourceData1!R2757C1
5	10502	SourceData1	4027	5553	1527	SourceData1!R4027C1
6	10505	SourceData1	5554	6290	737	SourceData1!R5554C1
7	10701	SourceData1	6291	8475	2185	SourceData1!R6291C1
8	10703	SourceData1	8476	9375	900	SourceData1!R8476C1
9	10704	SourceData1	9376	10117	742	SourceData1!R9376C1
10	10705	SourceData1	10118	11449	1332	SourceData1!R10118C1
11	10718	SourceData1	11450	12664	1215	SourceData1!R11450C1
12	10802	SourceData1	12665	13502	838	SourceData1!R12665C1
13	10803	SourceData1	13503	15252	1750	SourceData1!R13503C1
14	10804	SourceData1	15253	16619	1367	SourceData1!R15253C1
15	10806	SourceData1	16620	17506	887	SourceData1!R16620C1

Figure 9-4: Station List Map based on row compression technique

The starting cell position of each of the stations is displayed as a cell reference in column G of the Map worksheet. The cell coordinate is displayed using the R1C1 cell referencing style. When you start working with OFFSET, INDIRECT, and Excel formulas involving cell references, it is far easier to keep track of things in the R1C1 cell reference style than it is to use the A1 style.

Integrating the Station List and Country ID Data

The data as it stands is good, but more things need to be done. For one thing, a station number by itself is not very informative. The `station-list.txt` and `country-id.txt` files provide the missing information.

Two avenues are available to you. You can:

- Create separate worksheets in your main spreadsheet that contain a country list and descriptive information about each of the states.
- Embed this information directly into the Map worksheet.

Both approaches are valid, so there's no wrong choice here. The correct choice is dependent upon your future needs.

When data regularly changes, such as geographic locale (for example, Myanmar used to be called Burma) it would make sense to track regions and country separately. In database terminology, the general practice would be to *normalize* the data.

Part III

In this particular example, the data was prepared in commemoration of the 50th anniversary of World War II. Therefore, no expectation exists that the data will be updated. It just covers the five-year period between 1940 and 1945. The geographic designations won't change. The point is that in this specific situation, very little harm can take place in integrating the station-list and country-id data directly into the Map worksheet.

You can copy and paste values directly into the Map worksheet. That way is slow and error prone, though. A more efficient and effective way to retrieve the values is to use a VLOOKUP to retrieve the data from the external spreadsheets. Remember, when you use VLOOKUP, be sure to specify the FALSE parameter. You will end up with a formula like this:

```
=VLOOKUP($B6,'station-list.txt'!$A$7:$F$167,2,FALSE)
```

After you have the data retrieved and in your Map worksheet, kill the links and formulas by copying the looked-up data and pasting the values back. This wipes out the formulas and just leaves the values. Pruning formulas that are no longer needed is a way of keeping the potential number of computations at a minimum.

When you work with large datasets, you are bound to come across gaps or holes in the data. This dataset is no exception. When I perform a VLOOKUP, I get some #N/A results. It seems that the country-id.txt file does not have a listing for the country code PI. Fortunately, this problem is easily resolved through a search on the Web. It turns out to be the Paracel Islands.

For your information, the Paracel Islands are in Southeastern Asia. It is a group of small islands and reefs in the South China Sea, about one-third of the way from central Vietnam to the northern Philippines. I never cease to be amazed about the things I can find on the Internet.

Because the data is historical in nature and is not changing in the source data worksheets, you can map some data locations within the spreadsheet, as well as take care of some preprocessing.

Assembling the Config Information

The Config worksheet contains two parts. The first is to be used as the list of countries that can be scrolled and selected from a Validation list. The second uses the country picked to retrieve all the weather stations associated with the selected country.

Of these two parts, the first is relatively easy to understand; the second is not.

THE FIRST PART: THE LIST OF COUNTRIES

This is just a list of two-letter country codes in alphabetical order, an index number, the country name, the row information retrieved from the Map worksheet, and a count of the number of stations per country. The last item is computed using a formula like the following:

```
=COUNTIF(Map!$I$6:$I$157,Config!A6)        (cell E6)
```

The A6 cell holds a two-letter country code, and I6:I157 contains all the occurrences of country codes appearing in the Map data.

Look at the count of the number of weather stations for each of the countries. It is as low as a count of 1 and as high as 14. If you want to display all the information for a given country, you need to account for at least 14 or 15 sets of data at any time.

THE SECOND PART: THE LIST OF STATIONS IN A COUNTRY

The goal here is to identify the data for all of the stations in a single country regardless of where it resides in the 120,000 rows spread across two source data worksheets. The Map worksheet provides hooks into the starting location of every station listed, but it is silent about which ones to choose. The Config worksheet takes this one step further. For any selected country, it identifies the entry points into each of the stations associated with the selected country.

I need to clarify a point. Up until now, there has been no actual drop-down list of countries that you can pick from. This is reserved for a later stage when a user picks from a list in the Presentation Layer. Because that layer hasn't been created, no list exists to pick from. When a drop-down list is created and a person selects an item from it, a lookup value within the Config worksheet will be revised. Right now, you can manually adjust that lookup value in cell H4 on the Config worksheet of ch09_LargeSpreadsheet_04.xls (see Figure 9-5).

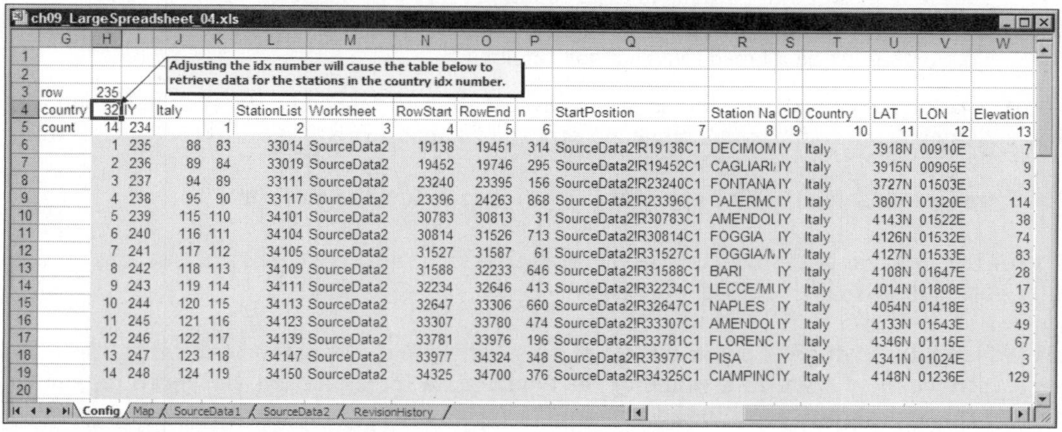

Figure 9-5: Individual station data for a given country number

The Analysis Layer

Notice that each step of the way, I try to solve a specific problem without getting involved in others. The Map provides hooks into the all of the spreadsheet cell coordinates of where to find station data. Config solves the problem of which station data to select from. The

Analysis Layer tackles a different problem altogether. It picks the actual data and must place them in tabular format by date so that data from different stations line up chronologically.

First, the Analysis Layer grabs the table data from the Config worksheet. Actually, it flips the data around, transposing rows into columns, and vice versa. This makes it easier to work with. Each of the columns from c through r represent data retrieved for individual weather stations. Rows 23 and 24 display the earliest and latest dates where there is data for the particular weather station. These dates are important, as you will soon see.

There is a timeline of dates in cells B31:B61. These dates form the category value that will appear in a chart. The cell values that are to appear in the presentation chart reside in cells C31:R61.

The job of the Analysis Layer is to populate cells C31:R61 with the appropriate chart data. It has to address the following:

- It has to retrieve the appropriate kind of data, which may be precipitation, recorded temperature, or whatever is accessible from the source data. This is essentially handled using a column offset in cell C26.

- The data appearing in cells C31:R61 need to work over a timeline. This is done by adjusting the starting period of this group data by an increment number (cell C28).

- It has to align the chronologies for each of the stations. Just because you have half a dozen or so weather stations in a particular country doesn't mean that they all started recording data from the same starting date. If you want to graph them all at one time, the data must be aligned to a common timeline.

- Data for each weather station has an earliest starting date and a latest date. If your timeline falls outside this range, no data should appear in C31:R61.

The formula for the cell values appearing in C31:R61 follow the pattern:

```
=IF(OR($C31<D$23,$C31>D$24,D$23=""),#N/A,OFFSET(INDIRECT(D$16,FALSE),$B31+$C$2
8-D$25-2,$C$26-1))
```

It is essentially saying: "If dates are out of range or there is not data, do nothing; otherwise, retrieve the station data value for the type of data (precipitation, temperature, and so on), for the appropriate point in the timeline."

It suffices to say that the column offset for the type of data (cell C26), and the increment number for the timeline (cell C28), which controls the data produced in the Analysis Layer, are all driven by actions of the user in the Presentation Layer.

Before I move on to discuss the Presentation Layer, notice that everything here is driven by computations on a limited amount of data. Moreover, almost no effort is spent on making the Analysis Layer a presentation showpiece. That job is left to the Presentation Layer.

Presentation Layer

Believe it or not, all the hard work has been done. Now it's time to reap the benefits. Figure 9-6 shows how a presentation layer can be structured. There are three pull-down lists: one for the country, another to tell Excel whether to display dates for the available data, latitude/longitude data of the weather stations, or their elevation, and finally, the type of data that is to appear in the line chart.

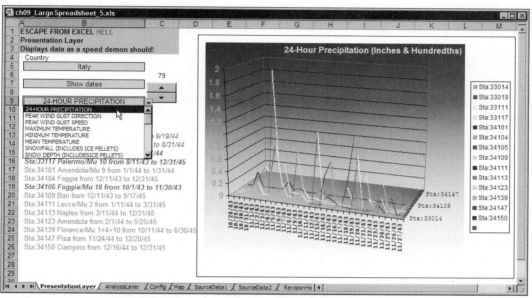

Figure 9-6: The Presentation Layer puts all the data at your fingertips.

After choosing the country, display mode, and type of data to plot, you need only to increment the timeline with the spinner control arrows on the worksheet.

Keep in mind that this spreadsheet exceeds 13.5MB in size and has more than 119,000 records. From the way the spreadsheet performs, you would never know that the spreadsheet is so big. This spreadsheet literally flies!

An important feature of the Presentation Layer is that no computations are performed in it. It just retrieves the results from the Analysis Layer. It also tells the Analysis Layer what data to work on. Because no computations are performed here, you are free to concentrate on making the best possible presentation without worrying about breaking delicate or complex formulas.

Dealing with Large and Complex Spreadsheet Issues

When it comes to large and complex spreadsheets, not everything is centered on the Layered Approach. There are many techniques for simplifying spreadsheets and improving formulas. I walk you through a range of them because they are important and straightforward to apply. Some of these relate to specific problems; others focus on what to do in certain situations.

Scaling Strategies

Many times a spreadsheet is designed for a specific purpose that is limited in scope. If a spreadsheet is successful, it continues to be used even when the needs change. Some of these needs have to do with scaling. It's one thing if you are tracking information within your department; it's entirely another when the same spreadsheet has to accommodate all the departments in your organization.

All sorts of things come into play as a spreadsheet grows. For one thing, it takes on an air of formality. Familiar name references such as Bob and Charlie give way to formal versions following a pattern of Salutation, Surname, MI, First Name, or whatever may be required. Rather than have a single column for a name, you have multiple columns. You may have to enter department and budget authorization codes where there were previously none. Because of a corporate merger, everything in your spreadsheet is topsy-turvy. Suddenly, the spreadsheet you've been comfortably working with is no longer simple. You can't just *casually examine* the spreadsheet and know that from the spreadsheet standpoint, everything is fine.

I want to address some challenges you might find along the way. I call these challenges "growing pains." I begin with date arithmetic and then move onto managing spreadsheets that are getting unwieldy.

Date Arithmetic

"I have been preparing a weekly expense report. My manager has asked me to summarize this by month."

It's a simple enough task to do on pencil and paper, and it's asked often enough. Automating this kind of accounting on a spreadsheet is all but obvious. The big challenge is not in the splitting of the dates, but in splitting an amount that is reported for a specific week whose start date is in a prior month.

The `ch09_02DateSummarization.xls` on the book's CD-ROM shows how to handle this (see Figure 9-7).

The principal approach in this worksheet is to calculate how many days of each week should be allocated for the prior month and how many should be allocated for the current month (relative to the week ending date). After you have this split, you can take the quantity, whether it is expense or whatever, and split it between the prior and current month.

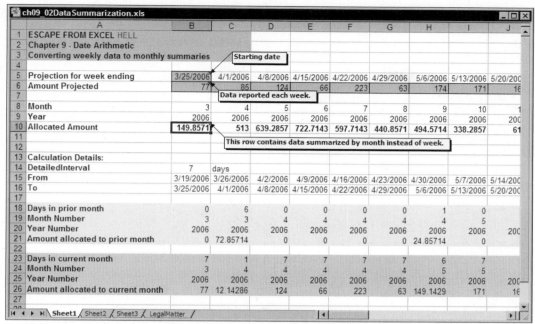

Figure 9-7: Spreadsheet for converting weekly data to monthly data

The next step is to sum up these quantities for each month and year combination. The following formula shows how this is done in for cell B10 of the worksheet.

```
=SUMPRODUCT(AllocationPriorMonth,--($B$19:$BA$19=B8),--
($B$20:$BA$20=B9))+SUMPRODUCT(AllocationCurrentMonth,--($B$24:$BA$24=B8),--($B
$25:$BA$25=B9))
```

The double minus operators on the equality operations converts the TRUE values into 1 and FALSE values into 0. This has the effect of walking across the intermediate calculations and matching them to a specific month and year, and summing all the matched items.

TIP
You can adjust the DetailedInterval in cell B14 from 7 to 14, if your reporting interval is every two weeks instead of one.

DECISIONS ABOUT HOW TO STRUCTURE FORMULAS

Perhaps this discussion is somewhat of a best practices style guide. When you work with spreadsheets, questions for which you get no real resolution. The issues may be hovering in the back of your mind, but you move on. I'd like to throw my two cents in on one of these nagging questions. It has to do with replicated use of a formula versus picking a value from one location.

Have you ever come across the situation in which you enter a value like 25 in cell A1 and want that value to appear in all the cells immediately below? There are two ways you can do this. One of these is replicate the cell through a series of cascading references like the following:

=A1	(cell A2)
=A2	(cell A3)
=A3	(cell A4)

The alternative would be to have them all reference a common cell, like so:

=A$1	(cell A2)
=A$1	(cell A3)
=A$1	(cell A4)

From a performance standpoint, the speed of calculation with both these options is so quick that it hardly makes any difference which way you structure the formula. There are some pros and cons on these methods. The first method offers convenience, because it is just a simple formula replication. You can change the value in one of the middle cells and have it continue down the list. (If you know that you need to do this, I suggest you make use of conditional formatting to signal that the cell has been changed.)

The first method has a disadvantage as well. If you need to change the value of A1 and its descendents, you may find yourself having to make sure that the chain hasn't been broken anywhere. This can be easy to do if the list of cells concerned is short, such as when the complete list of cells in question is all simultaneously visible. If you have to scroll through a list, it means you're spending time wading through a spreadsheet when you may need to be focusing on other tasks. This is something you probably want to minimize.

The Capabilities of RAND as a Pseudo Random Number Generator

Every now and then you may need to generate a set of random numbers. Using conventional computers or any kind, it is virtually impossible to generate *true* random numbers. The best that can be done is to generate pseudo random numbers that are statistically similar to true random numbers. Excel provides a pseudo random number generator called RAND.

RAND is a suitable for many purposes, but it is a rudimentary function. Basically, it simulates a Uniform probability distribution. It will return a decimal number between 0 and 1. It gives no preference to choosing any specific number. If you apply RAND to 1,000 cells, you will find that roughly 25 percent of those cells will have numbers less than or equal to 0.25. Similarly, close to a quarter of the cells will have numbers that fall between 0.25 and 0.5. You will get similar results for the third and fourth quarters of the cells. The fact that it has essentially no weighting or bias is what is called "uniform."

There are some issues you need to be aware of when working with RAND, especially for a large spreadsheet, or more to the point, large samples.

RAND is not exactly uniform. If you are generating something like a million or several hundred thousand pseudo random numbers, you will find that the numbers are not so evenly spaced and there is a certain amount of bunching. There is also another important issue. If you have a large number of cells using RAND, depending on the version of Excel you are using, RAND can produce negative numbers. This is not supposed to happen, but it does. For instance, it's a known bug in early versions of Excel 2003.

Another critical point is that RAND is implemented differently for different versions of Excel. The way it behaves on your machine may differ from how it does on someone else's.

For purposes of generating a small set of pseudo random numbers, RAND is perfectly fine. "Small" can be interpreted as several hundred or less. I would not generally trust numbers generated by RAND when the sample size exceeds a thousand items. If you need to generate a large number of pseudo random numbers and need them to be "sufficiently random," I suggest that you have them generated outside Excel using industrial-strength tools. Then import the data into Excel.

Approximating Probability Distributions Other Than Uniform

Given that you are working with only small samples but need to generate pseudo random numbers that approximate various probability distributions, there are some techniques you can use.

"I need to generate a set of numbers with a mean value of 100 and standard deviation of 15, which approximates a normal distribution."

A normal distribution is a bell-shaped curve with numbers clustering around the mean value, and the standard deviation provides an estimate of how tight or loose that clustering is. Here is a formula you can use:

```
=NORMINV(RAND(),100,15)
```

You can replicate the formula down a column or across a row to produce many values simultaneously. The numbers generated may be something like:

```
89.94325304
109.7067120
53.87176760
101.9848605
100.8420070
95.40942430
97.55789961
122.5657179
106.7168462
96.56469258
100.3304455
```

This is a very small sample of 11 items. Even with such a small sample size, the mean or average value is 97.77 and the standard deviation is 16.9. These are pretty close to the idealized mean of 100 and standard deviation of 15. As the sample size increases, the sampled mean and standard deviation will get closer to 100 and 15.

"I manage a Help Desk operation and need to project incoming calls, based on an average of 5 calls per day."

Nowadays, whenever you call customer service, you almost never get a real person. If you're thinking of setting up an operation in which people can actually talk to a person instead of a machine, how many people are required to staff it? These are problems relating to capacity planning. Though the scenarios can get quite complex, they start out with relatively simple approaches.

The file ch09_03PoissonDistribution.xls shows a simplified spreadsheet that uses RAND to drive a simulation and generate a histogram for a Help Desk operation (see Figure 9-8). It is based on the Poisson Distribution. As does the previous example involving the Normal distribution, it uses RAND to generate a pool of probabilities. This time, it uses a lookup table to translate this into counts. These counts are then tabulated and shown in an Excel chart in the form of a histogram.

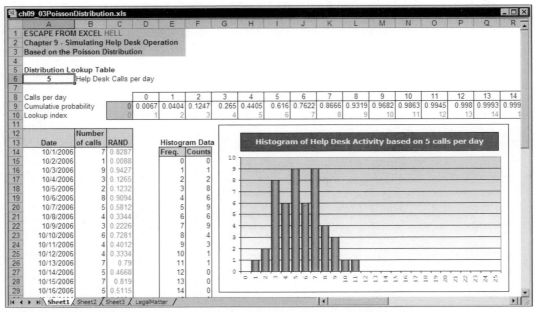

Figure 9-8: Histogram of incoming calls simulation using Poisson Distribution

 CAUTION
Remember, RAND is not an industrial-strength random number generator. When running simulations using RAND, you need to independently verify results and conclusions that you may obtain from such simulations!

Fixing Common Spreadsheet Errors

Spreadsheets often miss their mark because of silly things. Those are the worst kinds of mistakes because they are so easily glossed over. A simple rounding error can change the outcome of some complex decision logic. Digits in a number can be easily transposed. A formula has an error hidden in it that isn't manifested until other data in the spreadsheet changes a certain way. When spreadsheets are small and easy to examine, problems can be spotted and fixed right away. As the spreadsheets grow in size and complexity, such errors become easier to miss and their consequences can be grave.

Horror stories about spreadsheet errors go on all the time, but most don't manage to make the press. There's a well-known case about a company that made a $24 million spreadsheet error. Because the company entered into a nonnegotiable contract and the error was discovered after the fact, the company paid more than it needed to with this amount.

Table 9-1 outlines common formula errors that work their way into spreadsheets.

TABLE 9-1   COMMON FORMULA ERRORS

Situation	Description
Overspecified formulas	A situation that usually manifests itself in the form of a SUM of a SUM. Sometimes you'll be able to spot a formula that appears to be more complicated than you know it ought to be. Another telltale sign is when there's a group of cells that should be using identical or similarly structured formulas and you find out they are not. For example, if you were to replicate the formulas across a range of cells and you find that doing so breaks the spreadsheet when it shouldn't have, then clearly some formulas are in need of fixing.
Missing logic	Assumptions built into formulas that lack the logic that determines why they are what they are and how they should change.
Incorrect ranges	Formulas that might specify incorrect ranges. Sometimes a formula might take a range that extends too far. You might, for instance, have a sum of the values in the next 12 rows when Excel should be summing only the next 10 values. If the two remaining cells are blank, then no is harm done. Right? Wrong! It's just a time bomb waiting to explode. One day, one or both of those empty cells may be populated with a value or formula. Oops, there goes the correctness of your original SUM formulas, and out the window goes your spreadsheet.

continued

TABLE 9-1　COMMON FORMULA ERRORS *(continued)*

Situation	Description
Census-type errors	A tendency to group or sum numbers incorrectly.
Apples-and-oranges errors	Apples are grouped with oranges when the two groups should remain completely separate.
Normalization errors	Everything should add up to 100 percent but doesn't because some things are under- or overrepresented. This usually happens with two groups: logical errors and rounding errors. By far the more common of the two is rounding errors.
Comparison errors	These arise when two independent sets of data are on a spreadsheet that should add up to the same total but don't. Because they are assumed to add up to the same number, only one set is actually added. The total of the alternate set is never added, hence the error goes undetected.

Clerical Errors

"I have a financial report that indicates that the total assets of the XYZ division are $255,234,912 (rounded to the nearest $100). When I total the list of assets I track in my spreadsheet, I find the total to be $255,243,912. How do I account for this discrepancy?"

There can be any of a number of reasons for the two sets of numbers to differ. A common one is a transposition of digits. If there is only one transposition error, it can be pretty easy to spot. Subtract one number from the other. If this difference is divisible by 9, the chances are pretty good that two digits next to one another are transposed; in this case, it's `255243912 - 255234912 = 9000`. Look in the list of assets in the spreadsheet to see whether there are any items for which the transposing of digits in the appropriate range would account for this $9,000 difference.

Removing Hardwired Dependencies

It is commonly acknowledged that roughly 80 percent all the spreadsheets in the world have errors in them. Even if the rate were a half or a third of this figure, that is a staggering amount. Probably the single biggest contributor to error-prone spreadsheets is that they have hardwired dependencies that need to be fixed.

You can have a formula that applies a sales tax rate to a given amount, such as the following:

```
=A2*1.08375
```

The tax rate of `8.375%` is a hardwired value. If possible, this hardwired dependency should be removed from the formula. Why? Consider this: On another worksheet, you might have a formula like:

```
=G24*1.08375
```

On another worksheet, you might have the formula:

```
=H18*1.09375
```

Oops! A mistake in the formula! How will you guard against that? That's one of the reasons to stay away from hardwired formulas. When the day does come to revise the sales tax rate, you can do a global search and replace using Ctrl+H. In this case, you'll easily find all the instances of `1.08375`. You may not be aware that one of your formulas uses the value `1.09375`, so it goes undetected and uncorrected. It would be a whole lot easier, safer, and less time consuming if you had designed your formulas this way:

```
=A2*(1+SalesTaxRate).
```

You need to update only one number and all your work is done. There's another reason that it's in your interest to remove the hardwired dependencies; doing so allows you to conduct what-if scenarios.

Does this mean that you must absolutely avoid all hardwired dependencies? Absolutely not! If you track ongoing compute monthly expenses and want to project them as an annual estimate, nothing is wrong with using a multiplying factor of `12` directly in the formula:

```
=12*SUM(MyMonthlyExpenses)
```

The number of months in a year will not change.

 NOTE

You still may want to remove the dependency on a hard number, `12`, because you might want to vary the time frame from a year to some other interval.

Working with Data Validation and Formula Auditing

"I can use the data validation feature to control the entry of data, but these validation features are not fool-proof. For instance, I can overwrite cells that use validation using Copy and Paste Special Values. If the value pasted doesn't match the validation rule, Excel doesn't complain."

Although cell validation feature allows its controls to be bypassed, there are some things you can do. The very first is to see whether there is any invalid data, and to find it. You can use the formula-auditing facilities of Excel. Excel has a Formula Auditing toolbar that can be made to appear by clicking Tools⇨Customize on the Excel menu and then, in the Toolbars tab, placing a checkmark next to Formula Auditing (see Figure 9-9).

Figure 9-9: Activating the Formula Auditing toolbar

From the Formula Auditing toolbar, you can click the Circle Invalid Data icon (see Figure 9-10). In the file ch09_04SpreadsheetValidation.xls, on the book's CD-ROM, information is originally entered in a correct manner. At a later point, something happens to data that would cause the data, if reentered as is, to be flagged as invalid. In this case, the minimum balance level for an account is changed from 200 to 500. The spreadsheet won't yell at you the instant it happens. But you can use the Circle Invalid Data icon to signal violations in the data validation rule that you may have set up.

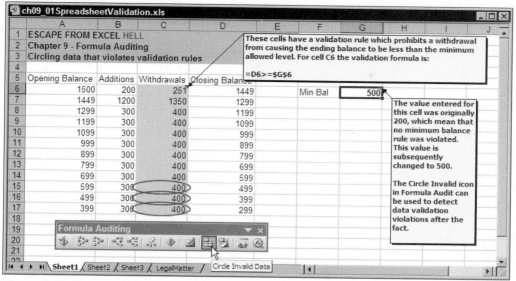

Figure 9-10: Spotting invalid data after the fact

NOTE

The data validation rule is testing for something that is changed *after* the data is entered. It is a lot simpler to say:

```
Ending balance must be greater than or equal to the minimum
allowed level
```

than it is to say:

```
Opening balance + deposit - withdrawal must be greater than or
equal to the minimum allowed level
```

Suppose that the ending balance happens to be a very complicated formula and not the simple case of `opening balance + deposit - withdrawal`. There is no need to dredge up that complicated formula in the validation criteria. Instead, you can just use the ending balance after the calculation and compare it to the minimum level directly. This is a subtlety not often appreciated.

Consolidating Data

"I have a big spreadsheet with lots of data widely dispersed across many rows and columns. How can I consolidate it?"

Several methods are available to you for consolidating data. The best technique depends upon your specific situation. The techniques include consolidation through copy and paste, and dynamic row compression.

Consolidating Through Copy and Paste

If you have plenty of empty space between your data and need to move it to one location, a simple copy and paste may do the trick. Note this series of restrictions:

- You can copy separated selections and paste them all to a single consolidated region, but you cannot cut separated selections.

- The regions you select from need to be identically structured in terms of their shapes, and they need to be similarly positioned.

- The way you select a region can make a difference in the ability to copy and paste.

- Only values and formats are pasted. The formulas can be pasted but they may not work the way you might expect.

Excel allows you to select cells in a worksheet that can be physically separated by one or more cells. You can do this by Ctrl+clicking the individual cells. For instance, you can select A1:A3 and C1:C3 in this manner. With this group selected, you can format all the selected cells, such as italicizing them. If all the rows and columns of the selected regions are aligned, you can do other things. Using Ctrl+C, you can copy the "extended selection" and paste it. When you paste it, all the intervening empty cells are eliminated. You can use this feature to your advantage and consolidate vast amounts of data.

You have a couple of challenges to understand. The data has to be identically structured and aligned. It may be a chore to Ctrl+click all the individual cells.

TIP

If you need to repeat the extended copy and paste several times, you can give your extended region a user-defined name of your choosing. The next time you need to select that range, you can press Ctrl+G and select the name in the Go To window. After selecting it, you can press Ctrl+C to copy the extended selection and paste elsewhere.

"I have three columns of data, and need to consolidate them. The problem is that the cells with data are not aligned in any manner."

Select a single column at a time; for instance, select only column B. With the individual column selected, press Ctrl+G and click the Special button in the Go To window. For your special select, choose Constants. The constants selected (i.e., your data) now includes only those cells selected before you pressed Ctrl+G (see Figure 9-11).

Because you now have an extended selection of the appropriate cells in a single column, you can press Ctrl+C to copy and paste the consolidated cells to another region using Ctrl+V. Of course, you have to repeat this process for each of the columns in your source data; but applying this technique is relatively simple and straightforward.

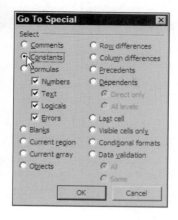

Figure 9-11: Selecting constants a single column at a time

NOTE

When you paste from an extended selection, only the values and formats are transferred. If you need to paste the formulas, you can do so. Here's how: Copy your extended selection as before. Instead of pressing Ctrl+V for a regular paste procedure, apply Paste Special Formulas. The formulas get pasted, but they may not work the way you expect. You can run into trouble with formulas that contain relative or hybrid cell references. They will work just fine for cells that don't depend on cell references, such as

```
=TODAY()
=RAND()
```

Dynamic Row Compression

"I have a long list of data that changes often. I need to filter and consolidate the list on a regular basis."

In certain situations, copying an extended selection and pasting it is not the right prescription. Consider having thousands upon thousands of rows of data that contain mostly zero values (not empty cells) and some nonzero cells.

You can easily get some elementary statistics on the nonzero cells. The average value of cells in column B given that they are greater than zero would be computed by the following:

```
=SUM(B:B)/COUNTIF(B:B,">0")
```

What if you want to find the average value of all cells if they have a value greater than 2500? You can use a formula like this:

```
=SUMIF(B:B,">2500")/COUNTIF(B:B,">2500")
```

or

```
=SUMIF(B:B,">"&SomeThreshold)/COUNTIF(B:B,">"&SomeThreshold)
```

What if you want to find the standard deviation of these values? There is no STDEVIF function in Excel. You might create some kind of filter, but you would have to rerun your filter every time your data changes. There's a way to get around this. From the book's CD-ROM, open the file ch09_05RowCompression.xls (see Figure 9-12). In this spreadsheet, I break out each of the steps into separate worksheets. The OrigData worksheet shows a series of dates in column A and Expenses in column B. Note that most of the expenses have zero value. In the MarkedForCompression worksheet tab, a test is performed in column C. The result returned is the row number of the next successful test.

```
=IF(B9>C$5,ROW(),C10)                    (cell C9)
```

This idea of reporting the next successful location is known as the Sentinel LookAhead Technique and is described in my book *Excel Best Practices for Business* (Wiley Publishing, Inc.).

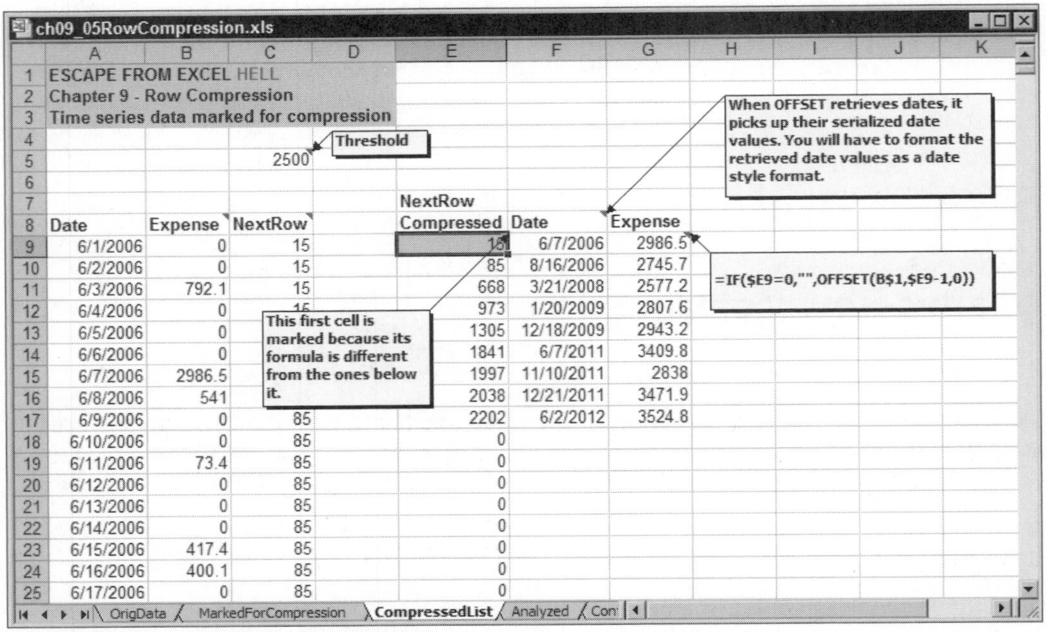

Figure 9-12: Time series data tested for certain criteria and "compressed"

The next piece of formula magic is to collapse the long list of NextRow items (column C) into a short list (column E). Each item in column E contains the next row number in the LookAhead list. The formula for this is as follows:

```
=OFFSET($C$1,E9,0)                              (cell E10)
```

When the list of rows is assembled, it is just a matter of retrieving the respective date and expense values in columns F and G.

NOTE

By definition, the very first cell in the short list uses a different formula than all those below.

Now that the list is condensed to only what is needed, it is simply a matter of doing the needed statistical analysis. The size of this list is based on the number of nonzero entries in column E. A formula that produces this result is the following:

```
=COUNTIF(E:E,">0")
```

To give you the option of picking from any of a variety of statistical functions, you can use the SUBTOTAL function.

SUBTOTAL, as you may recall, relies on a function number as its first argument. Because most people probably won't bother with memorizing function numbers, I generate a drop-down list in cell I8 (see Figure 9-13) and perform a VLOOKUP to retrieve the function number. So basically, this formula is applying a SUBTOTAL function on a list of size n (found at cell J7), starting from cell G9.

```
=SUBTOTAL(VLOOKUP(I8,RemoteTable,2),OFFSET($G$9,0,0,J$7,1))
```

Figure 9-13: Choosing from a selection of statistical functions on the compressed data

The reason I use $G$9, and J$7 instead of G9 and J7, respectively, is that you can easily replicate this formula (in cell J8) and the function selector (in cell I8) into cells below. This would enable you to compute several of these functions at one time.

Improving Your Formulas

Aside from removing hardwired dependencies, the clarity of spreadsheet formulas can be improved. The result is a formula that is generally easier to read, reduces risk of errors, and results in calculation performance gains.

Formula Simplification

Many formulas are needlessly overspecified. Consider the following:

```
=IF($A2=LEFT($A3,LEN($A2)),TRUE,FALSE)
```

```
=IF(RC1=LEFT(R[1]C1,LEN(RC1)),TRUE,FALSE)
```

This can be reduced to:

```
=$A2=LEFT($A3,LEN($A2))
```

There is no need for an IF test here; it is redundant. The logical testing for equality inside the IF expression already produces the appropriate TRUE or FALSE response.

Unused Formulas

Many spreadsheets grow organically. During the process of building a spreadsheet, there may be a need to weed out formulas that compute things but are not used anywhere else. An easy way to find out whether a formula is being used anywhere is to make use of the Trace Dependency features of Excel. Excel has a Formula Auditing toolbar. This facility allows you to trace how numbers feed into a particular formula (see Figure 9-14).

 NOTE
You can click the toolbar icon multiple times to trace back or forward through successive levels.

As stated earlier, you may have a formula on a spreadsheet and you may not know whether it is used anywhere. Using the Trace Dependents icon, you can see which cells use the formula. If it is not used anywhere, you will receive a message: The Trace Dependents command found no formulas that refer to the active cell.

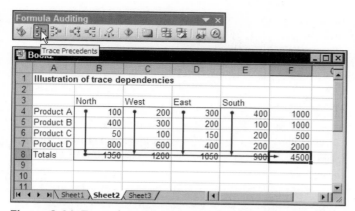

Figure 9-14: Trace dependencies show how numbers flow through a spreadsheet.

 CAUTION

The trace facilities don't detect formulas that use cell references in them with functions such as INDIRECT or OFFSET. If you use such types of functions in your formulas, you may need to independently track the dependencies.

Cell Colorization

Colorizing cells can greatly facilitate the clarity of a spreadsheet. Here are three simple rules to apply:

1. Colorize input cells to signal into which cells a user is expected to enter something.

2. Colorize cells with special formulas you need to draw attention to.

3. Don't go overboard in colorizing everything in your spreadsheet.

The first rule is appropriate when you have lots for formulas on a worksheet and you want the user to adjust the values in certain cells only. It might be an interest rate or principal in some complicated loan calculation. Although you can use worksheet protection, which can force users to tab through specifically designated cells, the whole user experience is more pleasant if the input cells are colorized, anyway.

The second rule is an aid for you, the spreadsheet designer, to avoid accidentally wiping out cell formulas when replicating cells in a spreadsheet. Look back at Figure 9-8. The cells C9 and C10 are colorized in gray to help distinguish them from the POISSON formulas to its immediate right.

The third rule (don't go overboard) is at least as important as the previous two.

Many spreadsheet and formula errors can be found in Appendix A.

Closing Thoughts

Managing large and complex spreadsheets requires that you be vigilant in every formula or change you make. If you handle it well, your spreadsheet won't have to be sluggish or difficult to manage as it gets large. This fact is clearly illustrated in the Layered Approach example (ch09_LargeSpreadsheet_05.xls) presented earlier in this chapter.

You may have read through the change logs in the RevisionHistory worksheet tab of that spreadsheet and noticed that all the comments from beginning to end were made in the space of 24 hours. Those are the actual dates and times, and the spreadsheet was done in a day (which includes writing the manuscript portions for the Layered Approach in this book). The point I want to get across is that if you arm yourself with the right techniques and utilize effective practices, you can maintain sanity in your spreadsheets and your state of mind.

Chapter 10

Other Challenging Topics

In This Chapter

- ◆ Non-volatile RAND
- ◆ Effective practices in VBA/macro programming
- ◆ Code signing with digital certificates
- ◆ Useful PivotTable techniques
- ◆ Spreadsheet in a dashboard

Overview

This chapter is a mixture of shorter, involved, but important problems, some of which you'd expect, such as PivotTables, and some you may not have come across previously in an Excel book, such as obtaining and installing commercial-grade code-signing digital certificates.

The chapter begins with a discussion on recalculation in Excel and shows how to turn some of its features into a surprising advantage. One of the recalculation examples is a simulation model that involves manually configuring Excel settings. VBA/macro programming is introduced as a way to understand the process of automatically making configuration changes when the simulation workbook is opened and restoring settings when it is closed. The emphasis is on how to retrofit Excel spreadsheets by using effective and best practices.

Many spreadsheet developers commonly distribute spreadsheets that incorporate VBA/macro programming code. Developers and users alike would be much more comfortable if the code that's distributed could be digitally signed, thus providing assurances of the authenticity of code and receiving verification that it hasn't been altered by third parties while in transmission. Self-signed certificates offer a no-cost solution but do not provide reliable assurances that commercial-grade certificates offer. Although knowledge abounds about the self-signed certificates, little is widely circulated about obtaining and setting up commercial-grade code-signing certificates. I provide information that helps to bridge this apparent gap.

PivotTables are used by plenty of users. They're a powerful facility, but they can easily frustrate spreadsheet users who have to construct them the hard way. I show some tips on smoothing this process.

A popular trend in the spreadsheet community is to build dashboards to spot important patterns and highlight key information. This chapter introduces a tool called Crystal Xcelsius (a product of Business Objects, S.A.) that generates highly interactive and visual dashboards by simply importing the whole spreadsheet model. When the visual dashboards are exported to PowerPoint, Acrobat PDF, and Flash, all the formulas are fully live. This capability of distributing spreadsheet models in the form of a portable and highly interactive dashboard is a milestone and pivot point that the industry is starting to revolve around. It will colorize spreadsheet technology for years to come, and readers should have early access to these new and important tools.

A Few Rabbits Out of the Hat with Recalculation

There are subtleties that are involved when Excel handles recalculation. Recalculation is intended to be transparent to the user. There are some circumstances in which the specifics on how recalculation is handled become important. Rather than discuss *problems* of calculation that get in the way, I want to talk about *opportunities* for its being put to use.

Incremental Counters

For most users, Excel is reasonably fast. However, Excel Data Tables are notoriously slow, especially Two-Way Data Tables. To bypass this issue, the designers of Excel built in a calculation mode called Automatic Except Tables. This allows users to build spreadsheets involving Data Tables without having to endure their sluggish behavior, except when it is necessary to refresh the table. This alternative mode of computation confers an unexpected and useful behavior. It can be used to create iterative structures, as well as halt the volatile nature of functions such as RAND and NOW.

> *"I want to run a spreadsheet in which I can increment or decrement a date, but with no macro involved."*

In certain situations, a user may have a requirement that spreadsheets are not permitted to run macros of any kind. The Control Toolbox spinner button relies on macros, and accordingly is not permitted. The older-style Forms Spinners can be used to increment values without requiring macros. They have some problems. The minimum value they can increment is 0 and the maximum value is 30000. Also, the incremental changes must be integer values.

What if you need to go beyond the 30000 limit? If you wanted to use the incremented value to represent dates, you would find that the limit of 30000, if converted to a date format, would represent February 18, 1982. Unless you happen to be an historian working with an earlier part of the twentieth century, you could be out of luck.

The spreadsheet file ch10_01IncrementCounter.xls allows you to go past these limitations without the use of any macros (see Figure 10-1). It relies on using Excel tables and setting the Calculation mode to Automatic Except Tables.

To increment the counter, you would press the keystroke sequence Ctrl+Shift+Alt+F9 to force a full recalculation. All the other spreadsheet cells, other than those of the Counter table, update immediately. You can choose between incrementing or decrementing. When you want to reset the counter to the starting point, select Reset (increment disabled) in the drop-down list in row 9. You may be prompted to press the F9 key. Do so if instructed.

If you want, you can change the incrementing and decrementing periods from daily to weekly by setting the values from 1 day to 7 days in cells B26 and B27. Remember to preserve the negative sign in the decrementing value!

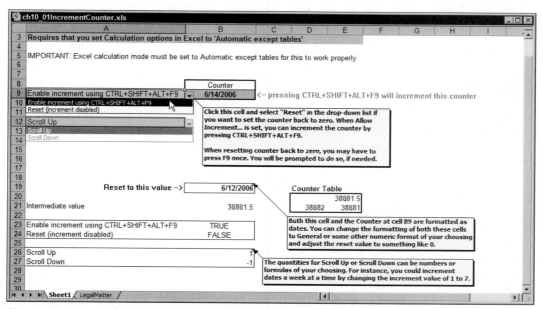

Figure 10-1: Incrementing dates and values without macros and without the limitations of the older-style spinners.

Date Arithmetic and Formula Replication

As long as I am discussing dates, I want to cover a date arithmetic problem:

> *"I issue invoices to monthly subscribers based on the date they started their subscription. This is easy to compute when the subscription date falls during the middle of the month. When the subscription date starts on a day such as January 31st, I run into problems calculating the next date for the invoice. There is no February 31st date. I would want the new invoice date to be February 28th or 29th depending on whether it is a leap year. In the following months it would be March 30th, April 30th, May 31st, and so on."*

To compute the same day next month, you could use a naive formula like this:

```
=DATE(YEAR(A1),MONTH(A1)+1,DAY(A1))
```

This formula would take a date like January 15th, 2007, and return a date like February 15th, 2007. When you start with a date like January 31st, the formula would return a date in the beginning of March. From a chronological perspective, this is correct, but it opens a can of worms for things such as monthly invoicing. A revision to this formula that addresses this issue is as follows:

```
=MIN(DATE(YEAR(A1),MONTH(A1)+2,0),DATE(YEAR(A1),MONTH(A1)+1,DAY(A1)))
```

This formula behaves correctly for purposes such as invoicing. A date of `2/28/2007` is returned when `A1` is `1/31/2007`. If `A1` is `1/15/2007`, the date returned is `2/15/2007`. The structure of this formula opens certain problems when you try to replicate it down a column.

> *"I have a formula that computes the equivalent date next month. I start with a date of 1/31/2007 and get 2/28/2007; so far, so good. I replicate this formula down to the next row and get 3/28/2007. When I replicate it again, the data I get back is 4/28/2007. Somehow the dates have all switched tracks and are now pegged to the 28th of the month. This is not what I want."*

When you replicate formulas, you may have the choice of referencing the immediately preceding cell or the very first one in a long chain of cells. This topic is brought up in Chapter 9. Most of the time this is not an issue. Here is one case in which this choice really makes a difference. Instead of picking the immediately preceding cell, you can reference the starting date and count the number of months. Open the file `ch10_02SameEquivDateNext Month.xls` to see how this is done (see Figure 10-2).

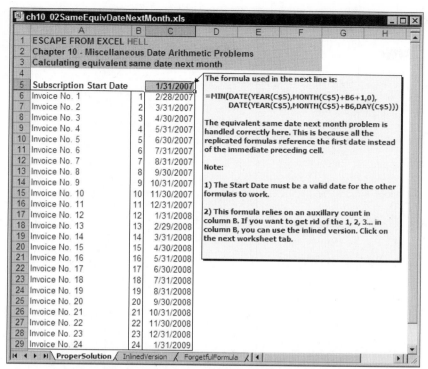

Figure 10-2: Equivalent date next month is correctly calculated.

Freezing Random Numbers

"I want to have a set of random numbers generated and not have to worry about their values constantly changing."

The common solution to this problem is to generate a set of random numbers using RAND and paste the set's values onto another set of cells. This will freeze the values, but it definitely hampers the interactivity of a spreadsheet.

The second common solution is to use macros to automate this process, either by clicking a button or using some kind of event macro to detect when a change occurs, and then paste the values. This solution requires a certain level of knowledge, familiarity, and skills in VBA programming that not everyone has.

Though it is not too difficult to go the VBA route, I want to show you a third approach that is really quite easy, and is easy to integrate into spreadsheet simulations. The key is to use RAND inside an Excel Data Table and set the calculation mode to Automatic Except Tables.

Excel data tables explained

You may have noticed that the Excel Data menu contains an option called Tables; however, its use is not altogether evident. The Table feature of Excel happens to be very powerful. Here are the basics of what it does and how to get it working.

The Table feature of Excel allows you to harness the what-if power of Excel in a systematic manner. You can follow along with this example with the file `ch10_03TableExamples.xls` from the book's CD-ROM.

Start with a simple compound calculation, based on three inputs (opening balance, interest rate, number of periods), and two results (ending balance and gain). Don't get caught up in the details of the calculations; just focus on how Data Table is set up.

The formula for computing the ending balance is as follows:

`=OpeningBalance*(1+InterestRate)^Periods`

It is easy to compute the ending balance for this formula. If you start with an open balance of `1,000` and an interest rate of `2%`, you will have an ending balance of `1061.21` at the end of `3` years. What happens at the end of `4` years? That's easy enough: Punch in the number `4` in place of `3` and the new value is automatically computed. How about `5` years, or maybe `6`? Now the process of tinkering with all these individual test values is starting to get tedious.

Instead of manually redoing all these variations one at a time, you can tabulate all your test values in one step using an Excel Data Table. The first step is to designate an input cell. In this example, the number of periods is the input cell. This is what you vary. The next step is to identify the results you want tabulated in the table. In this example, the results would correspond to the ending balance and the gain (numerical difference between the closing and opening balance).

Place the opening balance, interest rate, periods, ending balance, and gain in cells `B7`, `B8`, `B9`, `B10`, and `B11`, respectively.

Somewhere on your worksheet, specify result values you want to appear in your table. If you want to show the ending balance and gain in your table, place a reference to them at the top of where the table is to appear. In cell `E9`, you could reference the ending balance at `B10` by entering the formula:

`=B10`

Similarly, in cell `F9`, you could reference the gain at `B11` by entering the formula:

`=B11`

The next step is to specify the values you want to use in place of your input cell. You may want to use values `1` through `10` for the period. In a vertical column to the immediate left and below the reference to the results, enter the numbers `1` through `10` vertically downs the column. Don't worry about adjusting the values now. Later on you'll be able to change them, including using formulas of your choosing (this turns out to be an important feature). The table headers result in an inverted "L." Notice that the intersection of these cells is empty.

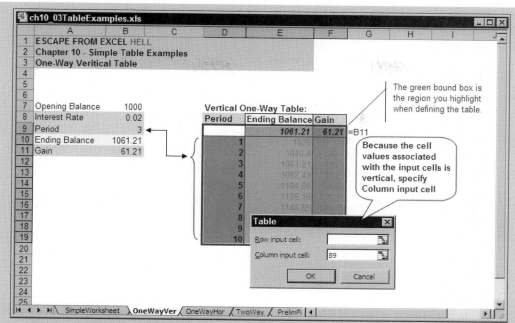

Setting up a One-Way Vertical Table

Select the region bounded by the inverted L. From the Data menu, click Tables and, in the Table dialog box, specify the input cell to be used for the table column. The Period value is located in cell B9. Enter the cell reference:

B9

When you click the OK button, the table is populated. Notice that there is no need to place an equal sign (=) symbol in front of the cell reference B9.

You can do the equivalent for a Horizontal One-Way Table and for a Two-Way Data Table. In a Two-Way Data Table, you specify two input cells, one for the rows and the other for the columns. The reference to the result value now occupies the empty cell of the inverted L structure. The top row and the column both contain reference to input cells.

This workbook provides an example of each of these three types of tables.

Notice that in a Two-Way Data Table, you can specify only a single result value reference. For instance, you cannot specify both the ending balance and gain within an individual table. Of course, you can create two separate data tables, one for the ending balance and the other for the projected gain.

Now we come to the crux of the interest in tables. Spreadsheets, as you know, tend to be very fast. This speed is in part owing to the fact that much of any spreadsheet is nonchanging and static. Excel tracks formula dependencies in the spreadsheet and computes only what it needs. There is one exception: tables. The default behavior of tables is to calculate everything in it, whenever there's a change of any kind in the spreadsheet. As a result, tables can really slow down an otherwise speedy spreadsheet. To get around this problem, Excel provides a semiautomatic mode in which tables are manually calculated while the rest of the spreadsheet is automatic.

You can harness this feature. It can be used to preempt the volatile nature of Excel functions such as RAND. Set up a table that uses RAND while table calculations are set to manual.

From the Excel menu, select Tools⇨Options and, in the Calculation tab, select the option for Automatic Except Tables. Open the file ch10_04FreezableRandSimulation.xls from the book's CD-ROM and click the NonVolatileRandomGenerator worksheet tab (see Figure 10-3).

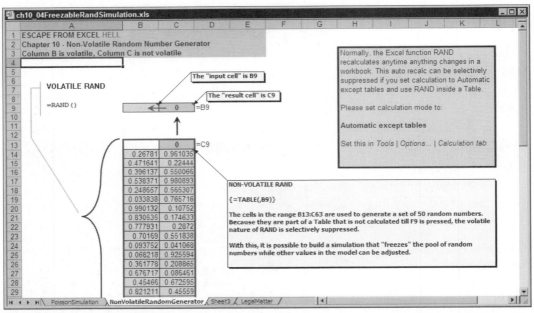

Figure 10-3: Freezable random numbers

This worksheet sets up a table in much the same way as is discussed in the earlier sidebar "Excel data tables explained." The input cell in this worksheet is located in cell B9. The result value in cell C9 is simply =B9. It just copies the value of whatever is in the input cell. These two template cells are replicated into the table below. Instead of using a deterministic pattern to populate the table, such as 1, 2, 3, ... or 0.02, 0.04, 0.06,... use the RAND function. The cells on the right side of the table are based on the RAND pattern, but they get updated only when you press F9 (remember, calculation mode needs to be set to Automatic Except Tables). The cells in column C stay frozen during normal spreadsheet activity. For instance, enter anything in cell A4 such as the formula =2+3. When you press Enter, you see that the cells with the RAND functions in column B are automatically updated, but their counterparts in column C are not. Now press F9. The cells in column C are all refreshed with new values.

NOTE

Generating random numbers in this nonvolatile manner is even more nonvolatile than you might think. Within the Data Table where the numbers are being generated, you can't just click an individual result cell, overwrite it with a new formula, and press Enter. Excel will stop you. This will help to keep your table formulas from being accidentally clobbered.

If you do need to erase these TABLE formulas, you can select the whole range of them simultaneously and press the Del key.

There is an additional advantage of generating RAND. Freezing a sequence of random numbers can be very useful, especially in spreadsheet simulations.

Applying Frozen Random Numbers in a Simulation

"I have a simulation that uses a pool of (pseudo) random numbers. I can't get the random numbers to sit still long enough for me to tweak other parameters in the model."

If you already have `ch10_04FreezableRandSimulation.xls` and set the calculation mode to Automatic Except Tables, click the PoissonSimulation worksheet tab (see Figure 10-4).

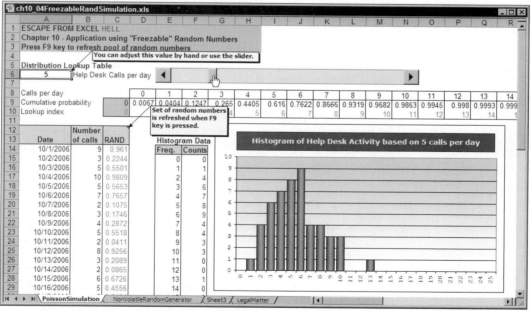

Figure 10-4: The slider can be adjusted without random numbers being reset.

This is almost exactly the same worksheet as the `ch09_03PoissonDistribution.xls` file introduced in Chapter 9. There are two key differences. There is a slider that allows you to adjust the expected number of incoming calls per day, and the values used to generate the histogram are all driven by the table on the NonVolatileRandomGenerator worksheet. You can now adjust the slider without altering the pool of random numbers. When you want to refresh the pool of numbers, simply press F9. Pretty cool, huh?

Some Practical Issues with Macros

To use spreadsheets without macros can at times be a significant handicap. When you use them, there are certain things you may want to do. I outline some of these here. Particularly, you want macros to behave a certain way. They should at least obey the following rules:

- They should be polite.
- They should not disrupt other things already in your spreadsheet environment.
- Their behavior should be well determined.

I explain some examples, but I want you to focus on how macros are brought in and not so much on the details of the macro code. In the next sections, I walk you through two examples; one of these involves calculation settings and the other involves customizing charts.

There is another topic I want to address, which relates to using digital certificates for signing your macro code. I show you how this process works.

Modifying the Behavior of Spreadsheets

"I have this spreadsheet I want to distribute. To get it to work properly, I have to instruct users to configure Excel a certain way. This creates a support problem. Is there a simple way around this?"

If your spreadsheet requires custom settings, such as the calculation settings for the random number simulation of the previous section, you can't avoid having to make the settings somewhere. However, you can do things to help it from becoming cumbersome, disruptive, or unreliable. This is where macros appropriately enter into the scene (see the "A quick primer on macros" sidebar).

I want to explain a little about how to use macros for modifying spreadsheet behavior. In this case, the macros are being used as *facilitators*.

NOTE

This discussion assumes that you already have some familiarity with macros. If this whole discussion is terra incognita, you may want to consult some other books on VBA. There's a smattering of VBA in my book *Excel Best Practices for Business* (particularly Chapters 12 and 13, which introduce macros and applies them innovatively). If you really need a book that covers the topic comprehensively, consult *Excel 2003 Power Programming with VBA* by John Walkenbach (Wiley Publishing, Inc.).

"When my spreadsheet opens, I want certain things to happen automatically. I can record a macro for these actions and edit them. I'm not sure how to make them run automatically."

Basically, what you're looking for is a special macro called `Workbook_Open()`. Here's the oversimplified version of how this process works. Your macro code travels with your spreadsheet and acts behind the scenes. To get to the code, you can summon the Visual Basic Editor from Excel by pressing Alt+F11. Pressing Alt+F11 again brings you back to Excel. This allows you to toggle back and forth.

When you're inside the Visual Basic Editor (or VBE), you should see a number of panes (see Figure 10-5). It is a good idea to keep several of these panes open. Start with the Project Explorer, which is generally docked to the left side of the VBA. If you don't see it, press Ctrl+R. The Project Explorer is to the VBE what the Windows Explorer is to the Windows operating system environment. As does the Windows Explorer, it displays a list of the open VBA projects in a hierarchical fashion.

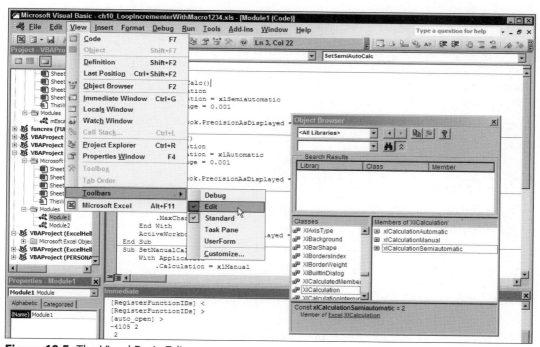

Figure 10-5: The Visual Basic Editor

TIP

I recommend that you add the Edit toolbar in addition to Standard to appear on-screen. From the VBE menu, select View⇨Toolbars and place a checkmark next to Edit (as illustrated in Figure 10-5).

Also from the VBE menu, click Tools⇨Options and click the Editor tab. Make sure that a checkmark appears next to both Auto Syntax Check and Require Variable Declaration. It is a good idea to check all the items for Code Settings and Window Settings.

A quick primer on macros

Macros can serve many purposes, including:

- Task automation: Performing tasks such as copying and pasting data from one spreadsheet to another

- Behavioral modification: Altering the way a spreadsheet behaves in some manner that is consistent with user expectations

- Function procedures: Creating custom functions that can be used in spreadsheet formulas like regular Excel functions

- Add-ins: Groups of VBA/macro code that can be used in all your spreadsheets

- Professional application: A complete application running on top of a spreadsheet engine replete with all the features of things such as a defined user interface, an initialization process, a close-out process, robust error and exception handling, optimized algorithms, persistence, and statefulness management.

Most people who use macros have at one time or another been exposed to using them for the purpose of task automation. The ability to record macros is a major feature that greatly simplifies task automation. After a macro is recorded, it is saved and the steps recorded can be reenacted. Before reenactment, you have the opportunity to view and modify the code.

Even if you're not familiar with VBA (Visual Basic for Applications), you can glean a lot by inspecting the code. Here is an example of recorded macro code that pastes the formulas from already copied cells to a new range of cells:

```
Sub PasteFormulasMacro()
'
' PasteFormulasMacroMacro
' Macro recorded 6/9/2005 by Loren Abdulezer
'


    Selection.PasteSpecial Paste:=xlPasteFormulas, Operation:=xlNone, _
        SkipBlanks:=False, Transpose:=False
End Sub
```

Notice that the code is created by recording an action. The action has a name: PasteFormulasMacro. The name is preceded by the keyword Sub, which tells Excel where the code begins, what its name is, where the code ends, and how to treat all the "inside stuff" between the Sub beginning and End Sub.

The empty parentheses in the first line tells Excel that nothing special has to be specified to run the code for it to run. Everything needed to run PasteFormulasMacro can already be found in Excel's environment. The single apostrophe at the start of the line allows commentary to be embedded within the code. The actual code that performs the task can be one or many statements. In this case, it is a single statement broken out into two separate lines. The underscore appearing at the end of the first line signals that the statement continues onto the next line.

Within the statement, you can see items that you can easily recognize, such as the values `False` or `True`. Though you may not be familiar with all the syntax, you can guess at some of the meaning. For instance, in the context of pasting something, you can see that the property of `SkipBlanks` is set to `False`.

As you can see, it is possible to glean much from looking at the code even if you are not familiar with VBA. There is nothing really hard about it. You can easily discern that `SkipBlanks` is set to `False`, and you don't even need a manual to figure out what `SkipBlanks` means. If I asked you to write code like this from scratch, how would you know that you might need to specify `SkipBlanks`? Even if you know you need it, how would you know the correct syntax for it? The good news that is you really don't have to know these things dead cold. You can just record your actions and Excel creates the macro with the proper syntax. Let Excel do the hard work for you! Afterward, you can tweak the code. This flexibility is one of the reasons that Excel VBA programming is so popular.

Modifying the behavior of a spreadsheet is a specific variation on task automation. Instead of performing some tasks actively, actions happen behind the scenes, and often in subtle ways. The objective behind behavior modification is to get a spreadsheet to work in a more fluid manner.

Function procedures are user-definable functions that work the same way as regular Excel functions. These custom functions serve the principal purposes.

The first purpose is to make available some feature of Excel that is not regularly accessible. As an example, Chapter 8 illustrates a function procedure `getColorIndex` (found in the `ch08_10SortByColor.xls` file) that returns a numeric code based on the color of a specified cell's pattern or font.

The second purpose is to define some mathematical or algorithmic construct used in a computation. Here are two such examples:

```
Function IncrementByOne(myValue)
'    Add 1 to myValue and return it.
     IncrementByOne = myValue + 1
End Function



Function ExceptionHandle(myComputation, myAlternate)
'    Evaluate myComputation
'    If it works, return it
'    otherwise evaluate myAlternate and return it.
     ExceptionHandle = myComputation
     If IsError(myComputation) Then ExceptionHandle = myAlternate
End Function
```

Function procedures begin with the word `Function` instead of `Sub`. Function procedures return a value back into the spreadsheet cell.

Projects are typically organized into virtual folders, which include Microsoft Excel Objects and Modules.

For each project, there is an object called `ThisWorkbook`. There's also an object for each individual worksheet, named Sheet1, Sheet2, Sheet3, and so on. These collections of objects are effectively event objects and are used to write specific code for event procedures.

Whenever you record a macro, it gets placed into a new module.

NOTE

If you don't see folders for Microsoft Excel Object and Modules in the Project Explorer, you can toggle the view by clicking the folder icon that appears at the top of the Project Explorer pane.

If you wish to place your Project Explorer in a different location, you can "undock" it by clicking and dragging its title bar.

If you want to view properties of any object in the Project Explorer, select it and press the F4 key. As you click the various objects in the Project Explorer, the properties are displayed in the Properties window. At least for now, don't worry too much about the Properties pane. You can close it now, knowing that you can summon it back at any time.

As can the Project Explorer, the Properties sheet can be undocked. If you want to park it back underneath the Project Editor, and the VBE is "fighting" with you when you try to dock it, drag the Properties window to the very bottom edge of the Project Explorer.

Elementary Techniques for Developing Code

Rather than trying to outline and explain the purpose of each and every portion of the VBE, I think it is better to show how they're used in action. During this session, you'll develop a lot of "throwaway" code. The strategy is to go through the steps in rapid succession, first creating some sample code to pick from, moving on to refinement and reliability, and then on to achieving tightly defined control.

NOTE

This style of preparing code is far different than it would be if you were well versed in VBA programming. It is really meant for the beginner who does not have a wealth of experience to draw upon when coding, but who nonetheless needs to put together something that basically works.

"I need to develop code that automatically sets the calculation mode in Excel when I open a specific spreadsheet."

First, let me outline the big game plan. If your spreadsheet will be changing the settings on someone else's computer, you have to do several things:

- Give the user fair warning that a change is about to be made.
- Give the user the option to opt out.
- Restore the original settings when you're done.

You don't want to be breaking things on somebody else's machine. I once received a spreadsheet on CD-ROM from a government agency; the spreadsheet worked fine but unilaterally hijacked my Excel settings. When I exited the VBA application, my settings did not return to their original state. I later inspected the code and saw that no provision had been made for changing back the settings. Needless to say, I was not happy.

TIP

If you have a spreadsheet with macros and are uncertain of what it will do, either don't open it at all or launch it with the macros disabled. Holding down the Shift key while opening the spreadsheet generally disables the macros in the workbook. You can then view the code by pressing A+F11 to enter the Visual Basic Editor.

NOTE

Some developers password protect their VBA projects, which prevents the code from being viewed. Incidentally, all the VBA projects in my book are either totally open for viewing or use the password named `password` so that you can inspect all the code. Password protecting a VBA project with a publicly known password can help prevent an accidental change or alteration to the code. I also add another layer of assurance by digitally signing the VBA/macro code. If my signed code is altered, Excel alerts you that the code has been altered and disables it.

The first step is to create some throwaway code. Follow with me in these steps. Launch Excel as you normally do. At this point, the only workbook open should be Book1. From the Excel menu, click Tools⇨Macro⇨Record New Macro and give it the name ThrowAwayMacro. In the drop-down list of the Record Macro window, select This Workbook and click OK. Now your every action should be recorded in your ThrowAwayMacro.

Click cell A1 and type a short but descriptive sentence of your next action. Press Enter and then perform the action. For instance, you might type the sentence:

```
Setting calc mode to Manual
```

And then, from the Excel menu, click Tools⇨Options, click the Calculation tab, select Manual, and click OK. Apply the same kind of sequence for your next action. In the next line (A2), you might enter:

```
Setting calc mode to Automatic
```

And then set the calculation mode to Automatic.

Go through the process a third time, entering in A3:

```
Setting calc mode to semi-automatic
```

And then setting the calculation mode to Automatic Except Tables.

Click the stop record button, press Alt+F11, and look at the Project Explorer. You should see a VBA project called Book1. Double-click Module1 inside the Modules folder of this project. You should see code similar to the following:

```vba
Option Explicit

Sub ThrowAwayMacro()
'
' ThrowAwayMacro Macro
' Macro recorded 12/4/2005 by Loren Abdulezer
'


    Range("A1").Select
    ActiveCell.FormulaR1C1 = "Setting calc mode to Manual"
    Range("A2").Select
    With Application
        .Calculation = xlManual
        .MaxChange = 0.001
    End With
    ActiveWorkbook.PrecisionAsDisplayed = False
    ActiveCell.FormulaR1C1 = "Setting calc mode to Automatic"
    Range("A3").Select
    With Application
        .Calculation = xlAutomatic
        .MaxChange = 0.001
    End With
    ActiveWorkbook.PrecisionAsDisplayed = False
    ActiveCell.FormulaR1C1 = "Setting calc mode to semi-automatic"
    Range("A4").Select
    With Application
        .Calculation = xlSemiautomatic
        .MaxChange = 0.001
    End With
    ActiveWorkbook.PrecisionAsDisplayed = False
End Sub
```

NOTE

If you don't see Option Explicit on the very first line, it means you did not follow my earlier suggestion to actively enable Require Variable Declaration. This option instructs the VBE to automatically insert an Option Explicit statement at the start of your code.

Option Explicit tells VBE that anytime you use a new variable within your code, you must specify whether that variable is a string, a number, a range, or whatever.

Now take all the code starting with Sub ThrowAwayMacro and ending with End Sub and make three copies of it by copying and pasting. Change the name of the Sub in the first copy from ThrowAwayMacro to SetManualCalc, the second copy to SetAutoCalc, and the third to SetSemiAutoCalc. Notice that a line separator appears between each procedure. Start stripping out the unneeded code for each of these. Your entries created during the macro recording session should be broken out into individual procedures. For example, the first of the three procedures could be written as:

```
Sub SetManualCalc()
    With Application
        .Calculation = xlManual
        .MaxChange = 0.001
    End With
    ActiveWorkbook.PrecisionAsDisplayed = False
End Sub
```

Now test this code to make sure that it works. Press Alt+F11 switch back to your Excel workbook. Check your current calculation setting. Then, run one of the macros to set it to a different setting. If your current setting is Automatic Except Tables, try running SetManualCalc. Run the macro by pressing Alt+F8 and selecting SetManualCalc (or, though a little slower, you could navigate through the Excel menu clicking Tools⇨Macro⇨ Macros to get to the same macro window). After running this macro, you should see that the current calculation mode is now set to manual. Test this for all three of the macros to make sure that they are working correctly before you move on.

This code can be simplified further. The statement

```
    ActiveWorkbook.PrecisionAsDisplayed = False
```

looks as though it is not needed. You can eliminate the line, but it is wise to convert it to a comment by placing an apostrophe symbol at the start of the line.

```
'    ActiveWorkbook.PrecisionAsDisplayed = False
```

Run the code again to make sure that it works. After you've verified that it is working with this statement, see whether you can further simplify the code. If you look in the code, you see a line that says:

```
    .MaxChange = 0.001
```

Does there appear to be anything that the three procedures you created are doing differently with respect to MaxChange? The answer appears to be no. Take one of the procedures and comment out the statement. Now try running it again to verify that you haven't broken anything. After you've verified all three procedures this way, eliminate the extraneous comments.

Your `SetManualCalc` should look like:

```
Sub SetManualCalc()
    With Application
        .Calculation = xlManual
    End With
End Sub
```

The `With` construct works well when you specify multiple properties within an object. Because the latest version of the procedures is actually specifying just one property, you could reduce the code of all three procedures to the following:

```
Sub SetManualCalc()
    Application.Calculation = xlManual
End Sub

Sub SetAutoCalc()
    Application.Calculation = xlAutomatic
End Sub

Sub SetSemiAutoCalc()
    Application.Calculation = xlSemiautomatic
End Sub
```

This is quite a reduction in code. I'm sure some readers are probably thinking, *"Why did he make me go through all that, when he just could have given me shortened version in the first place?"* There's a very good reason. The object is not the programming code, but rather the process and methodical nature that enable you to tackle the harder problems. In the words of a very wise person, slow and steady wins the race!

Now that you have some simple and clean code, copy the code to a workbook in which the calculation settings really need to be adjusted. In Excel, open the file `ch10_CalcExperiment_00.xls` (on the book's CD-ROM) and press Alt+F11 to switch to the Visual Basic Editor. Notice that this project has no modules. You will have to insert a module into this VBA project to copy the code. Right-click this project and click Insert⇨ Module in the context menu (see Figure 10-6).

 NOTE

With the new module created, paste the code of the three procedures into the module. Press Alt+F11 to switch back to your regular Excel environment. Now test the three macros. You may ask," *What?! Again?"* The answer is yes, again. When the programming starts to truly get complex, how do you know that the code is solid unless you're vigilant about testing as you make changes?

After verifying that it works, save your file as `ch10_CalcExperiment_00A.xls` and throw away the Book1 spreadsheet in its entirety.

The With construct

The `With` construct is a bit curious. It follows the syntax of:

```
With SomeObject
    .aProperty = aValue
    .anotherProperty = anotherValue
    .yetAnotherProperty = yetAnotherValue
End With
```

This is the same as saying:

```
SomeObject.aProperty = aValue
SomeObject.anotherProperty = anotherValue
SomeObject.yetAnotherProperty = yetAnotherValue
```

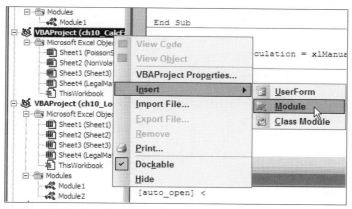

Figure 10-6: Inserting a module

POLITELY MODIFYING THE BEHAVIOR

You have an interesting problem. You can modify the calculation mode, but how do you return it to its original state? You need to define some kind of variable or container to hold the value. Remember, when using `Option Explicit` you need to declare the variable, stating what kind of data it is going to hold.

To help organize your code, insert a second module.

Within the module, declare a variable that will hold the original settings. Immediately underneath `Option Explicit`, enter the following:

```
Public vOriginalUserCM As Variant
```

The variable you are declaring is called `vOriginalUserCM`. Alternatively, you could call it `vOriginalUserCalcMode`. This variable is directly accessible throughout the whole module.

A word about naming conventions

At first glance, a name like `vOriginalUserCM` looks a little cryptic. When you're looking at a massive amount of code, especially out of context, you'll come to appreciate a naming convention like this. The `v` at the start of the name is a signal to you that the variable is being declared as a `Variant`, which is a catchall for all kinds of data types. It is a customary practice in Visual Basic to precede a name with an abbreviated data type descriptor. For instance, an Integer counter might be called `iCounter`; the value of a `True`/False test result for similarity might be called `bTestSimilar`; and so on. Here are some commonly used prefixes you may want to use:

b	Boolean	obj	Object
cht	Excel.Chart	rng	Excel.Range
dte	Date	s	String
dec	Decimal	u	User-defined type
d	Double	v	Variant
i	Integer	wkb	Excel.Workbook
l	Long	wks	Excel.Worksheet

VBA allows you up to 255 characters for a variable name. Normally, the first letter of each word in the variable name is capitalized. You can make a variable name verbose, but it gets to be unwieldy. Although it is in your interest to keep the names short, if you go overboard, you'll be spending too much time guessing what the name means six months after you walk away from the code.

Define a procedure called `InitGlobalVariables`:

```
Sub InitGlobalVariables()
vOriginalUserCM = Application.Calculation
Debug.Print vOriginalUserCM
SetSemiAutoCalc
Debug.Print Application.Calculation
End Sub
```

This code is saying is the following:

1. Store the current calculation mode in `vOriginalCM`.

2. Display the value of `vOriginalCM` in the Immediate window (to verify that the variable has captured the needed information).

3. Set the calculation mode to Automatic Except Tables.

4. Display the value of the new calculation mode to the Immediate window (to verify that the setting has been changed).

You can run this code directly from the VBE. Just click your mouse anywhere inside this code and press F8. The very first statement in your procedure is highlighted in yellow with an arrow pointing to the left of the code. Continue pressing F8 to execute a statement at a time. When you get to the Debug.Print statements, the evaluated result is displayed directly inside the Immediate window (if the window isn't already open, press Ctrl+G). Remember to continue pressing F8 until you reach the end of the procedure or press the Reset icon on the VBE Standard toolbar (it's a little blue rectangular box), or click Run⇨Reset from the VBE menu. Don't just leave this run mode turned on and hanging!

After the SetSemiAutoCalc is run, the second Debug.Print statement should output the value 2 to the Immediate window. If you're not sure whether this is the correct value, press F2 to make the Object Browser visible (look at the lower-right corner of Figure 10-5). This displays all the known objects that can be referenced, and there are plenty of them. Scroll down till you get to xlCalculationSemiautomatic, and click it to view the value of the constant returned.

After you verify that the correct values are being returned, you can comment out or delete the Debug.Print statements. Your code in Module2 should look something like:

```
Option Explicit

Public vOriginalUserCM As Variant

Sub InitGlobalVariables()
vOriginalUserCM = Application.Calculation
SetSemiAutoCalc
vCustomUserCM = Application.Calculation
End Sub
```

The code in Module1 should look something like:

```
Option Explicit

Sub SetManualCalc()
    Application.Calculation = xlManual
End Sub
Sub SetAutoCalc()
    Application.Calculation = xlAutomatic
End Sub
Sub SetSemiAutoCalc()
    Application.Calculation = xlSemiautomatic
End Sub
```

In the VBE Debug menu, click Compile VBAProject. If you have any glaring errors in your code, they will be identified. If there are no compile errors and you haven't modified your code, the Compile VBAProject option in the Debug menu is grayed out.

Now would be a good time to save your file. With your code currently active, you can just press Ctrl+S.

> ## Understanding the difference between compilation and runtime errors
>
> Certain kinds of errors happen in code. If you try to call a procedure that doesn't exist, your Visual Basic environment will be unable to compile the code and run it. If you get this kind of compilation error, look to see whether you misspelled the procedure or a variable name.
>
> If the code you are running is trying to locate a nonexistent file, you will, of course, get a runtime error. You can't detect runtime errors by looking at your code.

EVENT PROCEDURES

Your next step is to call this code whenever you open (and to restore the original settings just before you close) the workbook. Actually, this step is very easy. In the VBA project, double-click the `ThisWorkbook` object to view its code (alternatively, you can just right-click it and click `View Code` in the context menu). Either way, you get to the same pane where you enter code. Notice the two drop-down lists. The one on the left allows you to choose between `(General)` and `Workbook`. Click `Workbook`. When you do this, the drop-down list on the right changes to a variety of event procedures you can select.

In addition to the `Option Explicit` statement, you are provided a stub to insert code for the `Workbook_Open` event procedure. You can stuff code that you want run in the empty line between the beginning and end of this procedure. In this case, the code you would want to stuff it with is the `InitGlobalVariables` you previously created. Your code should look like the following:

```
Option Explicit

Private Sub Workbook_Open()
    InitGlobalVariables
End Sub
```

TIP

As you enter the first few letters, such as `InitG`, you can press Ctrl+Space and the rest of the name will be automatically inserted so that `InitGlobalVariables` appears. This auto-completion saves time and helps to prevent spelling mistakes and the errors they cause.

TIP

When you are looking at code in the VBE, selecting the procedure (such as `InitGlobalVariables`) or variable name and pressing Shift+F2 opens the code in which that procedure or variable is defined, thereby allowing you to navigate the code. Make it a habit to regularly use this facility. It will come in handy when you work with large or complex VBA projects.

This code sets the calculation mode when you open the workbook. You need to handle the flip side: restoring your original settings just before you close the workbook.

In the pull-down list of event procedures at the top-right side of the code pane, click BeforeClose (see Figure 10-7).

In the `Workbook_BeforeClose` procedure, you need to insert only the following line of code to restore the original calculation settings:

```
Application.Calculation = vOriginalUserCM
```

At this stage, save the file, switch to your regular Excel environment (press Alt+F11), and close the file. From the Excel menu, click Tools⇨Options and, in the Calculation tab, set the calculation mode to Manual.

Now open the `ch10_CalcExperiment_00A.xls` file you just saved and click the PoissonDistribution worksheet tab. Observe how the column chart appears when the calls per day is at a certain value, such as 6. Move the slider so that the number of calls per day changes. Move it back to the original value. If you did everything correctly in the coding, the shape of the histogram is restored. Now press F9 to force the pool of random numbers to be refreshed.

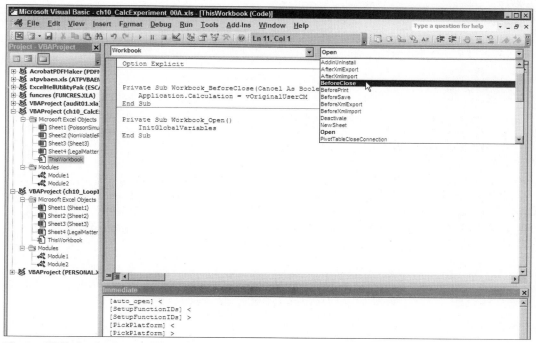

Figure 10-7: Setting event procedures

Part III

If this behavior is occurring, you know that the `Open_Workbook` and the `InitGlobalVariables` procedures are working.

To test the second half, just close this spreadsheet. After it is closed, see whether your calculation mode is restored to its original setting.

When everything works the way you expect and you've tested it to your satisfaction, save your "_00A" file to a new version, "_01," as your official backup and a "_01A" working copy (keeping in practice with the filenaming strategy outlined in Chapter 9).

SOMETHING IS STILL MISSING

One of the cardinal rules when writing VBA code is that if you will be changing the settings, you need to alert the user of this and allow him or her to opt out.

At a minimum, the user should be alerted about pending actions. In your `Open_Workbook` procedure, insert code for a message box, as in the following:

```
MsgBox "Changing calculation mode to SemiAutomatic. " & vbCrLf & _
       "Your original settings will be restored " & vbCrLf & _
       "when this workbook is closed."
```

In your `Workbook_BeforeClose` procedure, insert a simple message such as this:

```
MsgBox "Restoring your original calculation settings."
```

 NOTE

vbCrLf is a preset Visual Basic constant that signifies a carriage return/linefeed line terminator. The vb should not be confused with a Variant data type. Plenty of these vb constants are defined in Visual Basic. In the VBE, open the Object Browser (press F2) and scroll through the list.

Now it's time to put a little more oomph into the message box. Instead of supplying it with a single quoted expression, you can make use of a more complex series of prompts with multiple buttons and other features. Figure 10-8 shows how the Visual Basic Editor automatically provides assistance in constructing the code.

```
Private Sub Workbook_Open()
MsgBox ("I want to temporarily change calculation settings." & vbCrLf & _
        "The calculation mode will be set to SemiAutomatic. " & vbCrLf & _
        "Your original settings will be restored when this" & vbCrLf & _
        "this workbook is closed.", vbY
MsgBox(Prompt, [Buttons As VbMsgBoxStyle]    vbOKCancel              xf]) As VbMsgBoxResult
End Sub                                       vbOKOnly
                                              vbQuestion
                                              vbRetryCancel
                                              vbSystemModal
                                              vbYesNo
                                              vbYesNoCancel
```

Figure 10-8: Automatic VBE code assistance

NOTE

There are two ways of constructing a message box. In a simple message box without the enclosing parentheses, you can enter something like the following:

```
MsgBox "This is a simplified message"
```

In a more complex type of message box in which the enclosing parentheses are used, MsgBox expects to feed its answer to some variable or serve as the argument used in an evaluated expression. Here is an example:

```
iMsgBoxResponse = MsgBox("Give me your answer.", vbYesNo)
```

MsgBox in this form complains if it doesn't have a variable such as iMsgBoxResponse to send it to.

The way the message box is used in Open_Workbook is a bit more sophisticated. It is necessary to use a variable in which the message box response can be held. When MsgBox returns a value, it is an integer. Use the variable iCalcMsgBoxResponse to store the response. Underneath your variable declaration for vOriginalUserCM, add the following line of code:

```
Public iCalcMsgBoxResponse As Integer
```

The original message box just alerts the user of a pending action instead of giving an option to opt out. The following message box code prompts the user to make a decision:

```
iCalcMsgBoxResponse = _
    MsgBox("I want to temporarily change calculation settings." & vbCrLf & _
        "The calculation mode will be set to SemiAutomatic. " & vbCrLf & _
        "Your original settings will be restored when this" & vbCrLf & _
        "this workbook is closed.", vbYesNo)
```

NOTE

If you're curious about what the various "vb" constants are, just write a procedure such as this:

```
Sub ThrowAwayTest()
Debug.Print vbYesNo
Debug.Print vbYes
Debug.Print vbNo
Debug.Print vbOKCancel
Debug.Print vbOKOnly
End Sub
```

Though you can use an If Then clause to decide what to do with the value stored in iCalcMsgBoxResponse, using a Select Case construct is actually quite elegant. Here is what the code might look like:

Part III

```
Select Case iCalcMsgBoxResponse
   Case vbYes
       InitGlobalVariables
   Case vbNo
       MsgBox "OK, I won't change any settings"
End Select
```

If the answer is yes, `InitGlobalVariables` is run. If it is no, a reply of acknowledgement is sent back to the reader and no other action is taken till the workbook gets closed.

Using a similar `Select Case` structure, the original settings are restored if `iCalcMsgBoxResponse` is set to the value of `vbYes` (which happens to be an `Integer` of the value 4).

```
Private Sub Workbook_BeforeClose(Cancel As Boolean)
   Select Case iCalcMsgBoxResponse
      Case vbYes
          MsgBox "Restoring your original calculation settings."
          Application.Calculation = vOriginalUserCM
      Case vbNo
'         Nothing to apply here.
   End Select
```

Try working through the code and testing it.

We're almost done. First, however, is an important lesson to learn. One of the steps was overlooked that should have been noticed and addressed a while ago. When a spreadsheet is saved, it is usually recalculated. You may want to disable this capability while your spreadsheet is open so that you can save it without having to force a recalc unless you want to do so. When your workbook is closed, all the original settings are restored.

Ignoring for the moment the specific changes you would make, can you guess where in your code you'll be making changes? Pause a moment before reading ahead.

There are three logical places, and they correspond to the major activities in your code. The first is when you're declaring global variables. The second is when you set the initial values for the settings. The third is when you get around to restoring them.

Fortunately, you need to insert only a grand total of four lines of code and you're done! This is an important point. If the code is designed reasonably well and is largely modular, your code will suffer very little disruption. This translates to software that is more reliable, less expensive to maintain, and, in terms of the cost of supporting the software over the product lifetime, far cheaper.

Here are the four lines of code:

```
Public bOriginalUserCBS As Boolean
bOriginalUserCBS = Application.CalculateBeforeSave
Application.CalculateBeforeSave = False
Application.CalculateBeforeSave = bOriginalUserCBS
```

The variable name `bOriginalUserCBS` refers to Calculate Before Save property. The `b` in front signifies that the variable is a Boolean `True` or `False` value.

Before moving on to the next topic (using authenticated certificates for digitally signing VBA code), I want to point out that there still is a wide margin of difference between this code and a commercial VBA application. The reason for the wide margin is that commercial applications need to take into a far greater amount of complexity.

The completed file of this application is `ch10_CalcExperiment_02.xls`.

Signing Digital Certificates

"I want to distribute my spreadsheets with macros so that they can be loaded without all the security alerts."

You may have noticed that all the spreadsheets with macro code in this book have a verifiable digital signature. This means that they're extraordinarily hard to forge. It also means that after you designate the signer (me) as a trusted publisher, you can open spreadsheets with macros without having Excel wave a red flag every time the file is opened.

If you plan on professionally distributing spreadsheets with macros, you should consider using verifiable digital certificates. Of course, it costs money to obtain a digital certificate from a Microsoft Trusted Certificate Authority, but it's well worth the expense. The certificate provides a layer of protection for both you and your customers or clients. It also makes it easier for people who use your spreadsheets to load them up without always having to go through alert screens.

 NOTE

If you don't want to spend the money, you can create self-signed digital certificates and use them to sign and distribute your spreadsheets with macros. The process is not as elaborate, but they don't provide the layer of protection and conveniences that you get with a commercial-grade certificate.

I outline a few things about self-certified digital signatures but don't go on at length because your attention should really be focused on commercial-grade certificates. You can find abundant information on the Internet regarding self-signed certificates, but relatively little clear-cut information on how to obtain and set up a commercial-grade certificate. I imagine that many of you who have reason to use digital signing would opt for this capability if it weren't such an obscure art. My aim is to make this process accessible and concrete.

Primer on digital code signing

When you download software that contains programming code such as a VBA project or a spreadsheet with macros, how can you know with certainty that it came from a specific developer? Remember, there are all sorts of scams and schemes such as phishing to fool you into thinking you're connecting to an authentic Web site. Even if the programs you receive originate from the party you believe them to be, how do you know they haven't been tampered with by somebody else after they were created? This is a problem that commercial-grade digital signing solves. It doesn't guarantee that the macros are harmless, but it gives you reliable assurance of who created the macros and that nothing has been altered since the signing.

To make use of the digital signature protection mechanism, you have to do one thing in your Excel environment: Set your security level above Low. If you don't do this, Microsoft's protection mechanism won't kick into action. The default macro security level for Microsoft Excel is High. If you frequently receive spreadsheets with macros from colleagues you work with, chances are they will not have digital certificates attached to them (at least not until your colleagues buy this book!). You will not be able to run the macros in your spreadsheet unless you lower the security level to Medium or Low (and I strongly recommend that you never use the Low security level!). Using a Medium security level is fine for most purposes. That setting always gives you maximum versatility. Whenever you receive a spreadsheet that is not listed by you as a trusted publisher, you have the option of deciding whether to enable the macros. You are given this option every time you load the spreadsheet.

Here are the basic steps involved in enabling your system to digitally sign documents or code:

- The software developer/publisher (you) requests a digital certificate from a trusted certificate authority. The developer/publisher has to supply all sorts of information, such as proof of its corporate identity, location of business, ownership of its domain name (for example, evolvingtech.com), the code signer's identity, and so on.

- This information is assembled and used to generate a public and private key. The public key is something you submit to the Certificate Authority and the private key is something you never share with anyone else. The public key is used as your certificate request that is submitted to the Certificate Authority.

- The Certificate Authority does a background check to verify your identity and information. If all checks out, the agency will issue to you a certificate that is valid for a set period of time.

- The file you receive from the Certificate Authority must be paired with your private key for the certificate to be usable. Using an import utility, the combined pair is installed in your system.

- After you've properly installed the certificate, you can start making use of digital signing.

Self-Signed Digital Certificates: The "No Cost" Solution

There's a saying that you get what you pay for. Self-signed digital certificates are no exception. They are easy to set up but provide virtually no real benefits. Here are the setup steps:

1. From the Windows Start menu, click Program⇨Microsoft Office⇨Microsoft Office Tools⇨Digital Certificates for VBA Projects. Please note that this path may vary by operating system and its configuration.

2. You are presented with a screen that allows you to create a self-signed certificate right on the spot (see Figure 10-9).

Figure 10-9: Creating a self-signed digital certificate

That's it; you're done. There's no verification, no passwords, no nothing. Now you have a digital certificate that can be used to sign your VBA projects. To view your certificate, open your Internet Explorer Web Browser and in its menu click Tools⇨Internet Options, click the Content tab, and click the Certificates... button (see Figure 10-10).

You can immediately put it to use. Launch Excel and open one of your spreadsheets that has a VBA/macro code. With the spreadsheet open, press Alt+F11 to open the Visual Basic Editor. Within your VBA project, go to the Tools menu and click Digital Signature (see Figure 10-11).

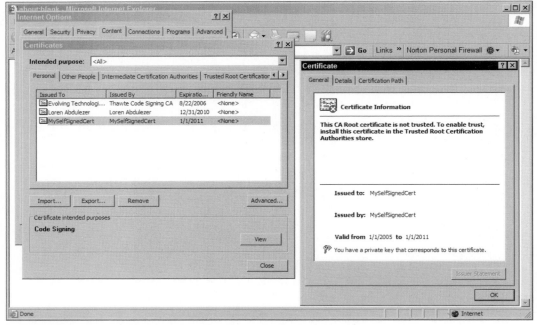

Figure 10-10: Information about your self-signed certificates

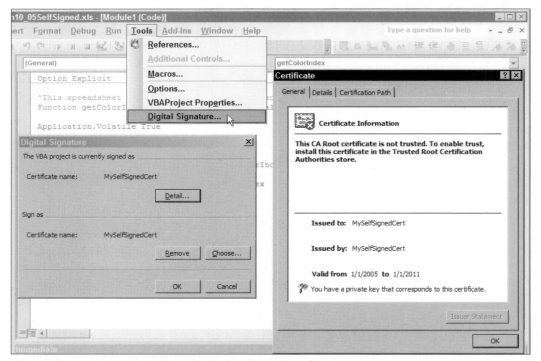

Figure 10-11: VBA project signed with the chosen certificate

So far, everything looks wonderful. Now comes the rub. When you send this file to a colleague or a client, he or she opens the file and is alerted that the file has macro code, *but there is no provision to trust the publisher!* (see Figure 10-12).

This feature is grayed out with self-signed documents.

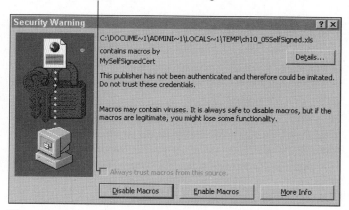

Figure 10-12: Self-signed documents can't be trusted!

Commercial Grade Certificates: From No Cost to Low Cost

Although information abounds about self-signed certificates, relatively little information exists that outlines clearly the steps involved in obtaining and installing commercial-grade certificates for code signing.

There are plenty of commercial CAs (certificate authorities) that are equipped to issue code-signing certificates. Figure 10-9, shown previously, shows a link that says Click here for a list of commercial certificate authorities. Follow this link for a list of companies and turn your attention to those that provide code-signing certificates.

NOTE

The specific procedures involved in obtaining certificates vary from CA to CA. Space does not permit me to outline all of them. For a concrete example, I show how it's done with Thawte. Regardless of which CA you choose to use, the basic steps should be similar to those illustrated in this example.

"When I go to a Web site of a Certificate Authority, I am presented with an astounding diversity of certificates and services. How do I find the kind that I need?"

Look for anything that says "code signing." Most of these Web sites have a site map or provide a search facility on their home page. If you do use the Web site search engine, try searching for the term *code signing*. Often you will find that code signing covers a variety of specific types of program code, such as Java. Select the one for VBA and Office applications.

Understanding code signing

It is important to understand what is meant by VBA code signing and what kind of protection it provides.

In principle, a spreadsheet composed of just worksheets and no macros should be "harmless." The moment you add programming code, the potential exists for the spreadsheet to do some damage. No ironclad assurance can be given that a spreadsheet with macros will do no damage. I am sure you would feel a lot more comfortable to know that you are receiving the spreadsheet from someone you trust, and to know for a fact that it hasn't been tampered with by anybody else. This is the kind of assurance that a digital certificate can provide.

Spreadsheets present an interesting problem. By their very nature, spreadsheets are interactive documents and are constantly being updated with new data and formulas. So if users will be making changes to a spreadsheet and saving them, wouldn't that be changing the file? So then, how is it possible to preserve the digital certificate?

Despite this seeming conundrum, the answer turns out to be surprisingly simple: Provide assurances on the assets you're worrying about, not the whole file. In this case, it just happens to be the VBA code. All that gets digitally signed is the VBA project. This permits end users to make (data and formula) changes to the signed spreadsheet without compromising the digital signature.

TIP

To obtain the code signing certificate, stay within the list of Microsoft Root Certificate Program Members (which you can find by clicking the link identified in Figure 10-9). Don't be afraid to do some price and comparison shopping. You'll quickly find that some companies are considerably less expensive than others even though they provide the same product/service. Because all these companies are equally certified by Microsoft, choose the one that matches your needs and pricing constraints most closely.

Almost all the CAs have some kind of data sheet or white papers that gives semi-technical information about the features of their code signing offering and the process of obtaining certificates.

TIP

If the data sheets, white papers, or articles are not giving you clear information (they're more sales pitch than straight talk), go to the support pages of the Web site and look at items such as troubleshooting guides and other info that would be relevant to existing customers.

The quick road to getting the pricing, selecting the type of certificate, and requesting a certificate is to find the "Buy" link and start the process. Following are some details of what happens when you do that.

GENERATING A PRIVATE KEY

"I have seen many software utilities for generating private keys. I'm not seeing any information on the CA's Web site that tells me what software I should be using to generate a private key file."

That's because you fill out a form on the Certificate Authorities Web site that uses information you provide to create a key file (with a name of your choosing but having a .pvk suffix) that gets saved to your hard disk along with a password known only to you. The type of information you are asked to provide includes:

- Certificate duration (typically, a one- or two-year duration)
- Organization name
- Organization unit (the department responsible for the certificate)
- Country code
- State or province
- City or town
- Web server domain name

A private key file is generated and you save it on your hard disk. When you save it, you attach a password to the file; this password is known only to you (see Figure 10-13).

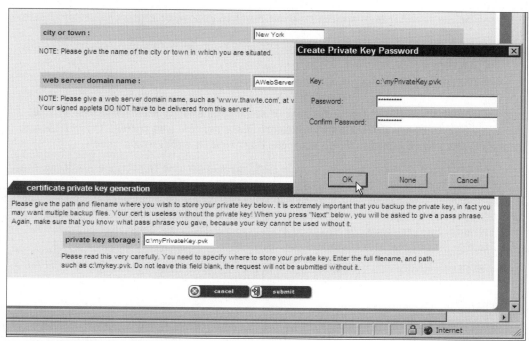

Figure 10-13: Saving a private key file to your local hard drive

THE CERTIFICATE REQUEST

To kick off the actual request, you have to supply a bunch of information. Not surprisingly, this includes how you intend to pay for the certificate:

- Currency to be quoted (that is, whether you're paying in dollars, euro, yen, and so on)
- Terms of payment (generally, payment is by credit card but other methods of payment are generally available)

You also have to provide contact details, including the corporate contact. This person's name would actually be embedded in the certificate. The CA performs a standard background check about the company and will likely contact this person before issuing the certificate.

Information is also requested about the technical contact (which can be the same person as corporate contact).

As you can imagine, other kinds of information is also requested, such as the street address of the main corporate offices of the organization being certified. You'll run into problems if you give the CA a P.O. Box address.

When you're requesting a Class 3 certificate (generally suited for commercial retail channels), you need to provide more information, such as your organization type, be it a public company, private company, nonprofit organization, university, government department, or other.

Before sending off all this information, you are asked to provide a password so that you can access online the status of your certificate request, renew, or replace your certificate.

CAUTION

Do not supply the same password as the one you use for your private key.

When you complete your certificate request or some time shortly afterward, you will be given a login ID to check the status of your certificate request and receive the certificate. It typically takes the CA two to three business days to do a background check.

When the certificate is ready, you are notified and should be able to retrieve it online. This file is in effect a rehash of the information you already sent the CA but is signed by the CA attesting that the information you provided in your certificate request checks out and that it has independently checked other information (such as assuring that your organization meets minimum requirements for financial stability; the CA may check your company rating on Dunn & Bradstreet, for instance).

Because of the formality of all this, the process may appear daunting; it's not.

INSTALLING THE CERTIFICATE

Now comes the real challenge. The certificate file you get back is useless to anyone unless someone happens to have your private key file and the password to your private key. For everything to work, you need to pair the two files. Just putting these two files in the same directory doesn't do anything. They really need to be joined at the hip. Doing so requires the use of a special utility (called `pvkimprt.exe`) that you download from Microsoft at:

```
http://www.office.microsoft.com/downloads/2000/pvkimprt.aspx
```

NOTE

Information about updates and changes related to `pvkimprt.exe` (including changes in the URL and revisions in the software) is posted, along with other information about obtaining and using digital certificates, on my Web site:

```
www.EscapeFromExcelHell.com
```

When you download the `pvkimprt.exe` file (which is about 275K in size), you will encounter a couple of complications. The first is that you have to expand the `pvkimprt.exe` file (by double-clicking it).

The part that gets especially confusing is that the name of the expanded file is also called `pvkimprt.exe`! It gets expanded into a comparatively large End User License Agreement and a miniscule `pvkimprt.exe` file (about 14K). You may have to reboot your computer.

After you go thorough this process, you can pair the file you receive from the Certificate Authority with your private key file. Your private key is a .pvk file and the other is a .spc file.

NOTE

For your information, an SPC file is also known as a PKCS#7 signed data object that contains X.509 certificates. This typically includes the signer's certificate and the root certificate, which forms a certificate chain.

Here is the code usage for this routine:

```
PvkImprt [options] <SPC File> <PVK File>
   options:
      -IMPORT (default) Imports the Key, and Certificate to a System Store
      -PFX     Exports the Key, Certificate and Chain to a PFX File
      -RSA     (default) Use the System Default PROV_RSA_FULL Provider
      -DSS     Use the System Default PROV_DSS Provider
```

Not much other documentation exists for this routine, except for a readme file that identifies a known issue and a workaround. You should get a screen similar to Figure 10-14 when you run the utility from the command or DOS prompt.

```
C:\pvkimprt.exe C:\cert\mycert.spc C:\cert\myPrivateKey.pvk
```

A small window pops up to request a password of your private key. The next screen shows a `Welcome to the Certificate Import Wizard` message, and the screen after that is as shown in Figure 10-14.

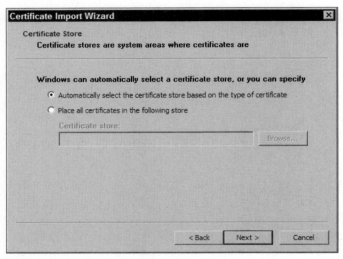

Figure 10-14: Setting certificate stores

When you complete this process, you should be able to sign your VBA projects using your new certificate.

NOTE

There is an issue you may need to troubleshoot. The machine on which you generated the private key may not use the same operating system as the one you plan to use for signing. Different Windows OSs may have different default key lengths. The workaround is to run the `pvimprt` routine as follows:

```
C:\pvkimprt.exe -pfx C:\cert\mycert.spc C:\cert\myPrivateKey.pvk
```

This is used to generate a PFX file (personal information exchange file defined in the PKCS#12 standard). When this file is generated, it can be imported into the certificate store using conventional software such as Internet Explorer.

ON THE HOME STRETCH

Your work is done in setting up the certificate. Now you can sign all your VBA projects.

"How easy is it for my signed spreadsheets to be loaded without having the users go through a security alert every time?"

When you distribute your signed spreadsheets, users will have to identify you as a trusted publisher at least once. This is relatively easy to do. The little box that was grayed out in Figure 10-12 is no longer grayed out. If the user's security setting is at High, the user can just place a checkmark in that box and click the Enable button. You are added to the list of trusted sources and from this point onward the spreadsheets digitally signed with your certificate will automatically load without requiring permission to execute macros.

NOTE
Keep in mind that the digital signature applies only to the code in your VBA project and not the spreadsheet formulas and data. Both you and your users need to be aware of this subtlety.

"What happens to a spreadsheet if someone alters the VBA code and attempts to save the spreadsheet without digitally signing it?"

The user who is altering the VBA code is notified that the existing digital signature is being discarded in its entirety. The altered file containing VBA code is then saved as though an authenticated digital signature were never applied. If the code is tampered with in some way, say, by someone trying to hack the code, the user who tries to open the spreadsheet is immediately alerted that the code has been altered; provided, of course, that the user's security setting is at least Medium.

"I receive spreadsheets that have been digitally signed by a specific publisher. My security settings are set to High. The only way I can open a spreadsheet with macros is if I add the publisher to my list of trusted sources. This effectively eliminates my ability to selectively pick and choose which spreadsheets I would allow macros to be enabled for when opening. I don't like this all-or-nothing situation."

Ironically, a security setting of Medium provides more flexibility than does High. With a security setting of Medium, you are prompted every time you open a spreadsheet as to whether to enable macros for each spreadsheet containing macros; you receive this prompt until you identify the publisher as a trusted source. In this mode, you can inspect the certificates.

Before moving on to the topic of PivotTables, I want to leave you with one thought on why, aside from security reasons, it makes sense to digitally sign your VBA code. That is, it provides a mechanism that helps to protect your intellectual property.

Useful PivotTable Techniques

In this section I outline some practical issues with PivotTables to show some techniques for working with them. Additionally, I address how to "reconstitute" Web content that was obviously created using a PivotTable but now appears as static text inside an HTML page.

Part III

PivotTables with Varying-Size Import Data

"I have a PivotTable whose source data changes very often. After the data is updated, there may be more rows or fewer rows. My problem is that when I perform a Refresh Data action in my PivotTable, the additional rows are not automatically picked up."

Normally, when you create a PivotTable you define a region of data that gets imported. Actually, The PivotTable Import Wizard generally does a good job of guessing the boundaries. This is fine when the total number of rows and columns is not changing. If your data is being exported from some database every week or several days, and the number of rows exported changes, you may have to spend some time reworking your PivotTable to accommodate the resized data instead of just clicking the refresh button (the red ! on the PivotTable toolbar).

There's an easy way around this, which is to define a formula name whose range is dynamically resized as data is added or removed.

Define a name that's pegged to the worksheet where your data resides. In Figure 10-15, the worksheet where the data resides is called SourceData. Define a name called `DynamicTableImport`. Instead of giving it a specific fixed cell, give it a dynamically resizable definition:

```
=OFFSET($A$1,0,0,COUNTA($A:$A),COUNTA($1:$1))
```

When you import your data in the PivotTable Wizard, specify `DynamicTableImport` as shown in Figure 10-15, instead of a fixed cell range.

NOTE

Even though you defined the name `DynamicTableImport` without reference to a specific worksheet, Excel automatically inserts the sheet name. At a later time, if you decide to change the sheet name, the defined name may still reference the sheet name as it was at the time that the name was created. Because it refers to the underlying object and not the worksheet tab label, the original object name may still exist in the definition. This should cause no problem computation-wise, but it can definitely cause some confusion!

More information about this topic and some VBA code for handling these issues can be found on www.EscapeFromExcelHell.com.

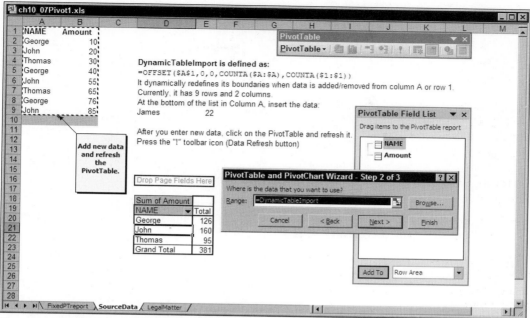

Figure 10-15: PivotTable based on dynamic cell range

Reconstituted PivotTables

A wealth of data is accessible online, and it continues to grow at an astonishing pace. Although there is plenty of data, the form it takes may not be so convenient. As you surf the Internet on your Web browser, you are bound to come across pages that were obviously prepared with Excel PivotTables but are saved and distributed as static HTML. This kind of page is just text, and there is no ability to pivot the data whatsoever.

I want to show you a way to reconstitute the PivotTable. Although it would lack the underlying formulas and detailed data of the original spreadsheet, you can at least pivot it to restructure the data already there.

FILLING IN THE BLANKS

"I have a Web page that looks as though it came from a PivotTable. I saved it and brought it into Excel. I'm having a heck of a time converting it to a PivotTable. Excel won't even let me create a PivotTable. It says: 'The PivotTable field name is not valid. To create a PivotTable report, you must use data that is organized as a list with labeled columns. If you are changing the name of a PivotTable field, you must type a new name for the field.'"

You have several dragons to slay. First, you may need to clean up the data. The formulas you'll need later will be much easier to manage if you get rid of things such as Merged Cells (see Figure 10-16). The headers should all be properly labeled; otherwise, you get a message saying that the PivotTable field is not a valid field. You may want to follow along by opening the `ch10_08Pivot2Reconstituted.xls` file on the book's CD-ROM.

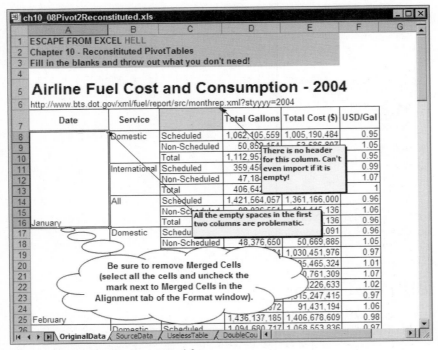

Figure 10-16: Data in its original form

These are things you can quickly clean up and generate a PivotTable. When you do, you'll find some problems (see Figure 10-17).

You have two big challenges:

- Filling in the blanks
- Not overcounting the data because of totals

Filling in the blanks is easy. If your first piece of data begins in cell A8, you can use a formula like this:

```
=IF(A8<>"",A8,H7)
```
(cell H8
in SourceData worksheet)

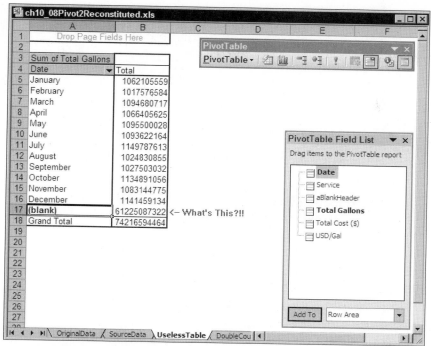

Figure 10-17: PivotTable lumps all the empty cells into a "(Blank)" field.

This formula immediately solves the problem of the blank cells. The data (cells H8:M115 of the SourceData worksheet) recast in this manner easily goes into a PivotTable and has no blank fields to speak of. This is too easy (hint, hint). Unfortunately, there is a problem. The totals are mixed in with the data and cause a double counting.

ONCE IS ENOUGH!

"The data going into my PivotTable is double counted because it includes totals."

Actually, the situation is not all that bad. Before creating a PivotTable, you can sort your data to aggregate all the rows with totals and remove them. This is a very low-tech approach and is easy to do. I want to show you another way. The idea is to filter out any rows with the totals and then use the filtered data to generate the PivotTable.

AutoFilters don't seem to do the trick; at least not directly. Though you can select (Custom) and exclude rows with totals, they still make their way into the PivotTable. The way around this is simply to copy the visible filtered data and paste the values to another set of rows that are not hidden. This row can then be used to generate a correct PivotTable.

I believe this approach is highly reliable and I recommend this as an effective way to eliminate the totals from a list.

"The data that gets fed into my PivotTable has totals and formulas and is constantly updated. I don't want to mess around with filtering and manually pasting data to get a proper PivotTable. I just want to click the Data Refresh button."

At this point, it may be time to start thinking about some serious VBA coding. If you are totally averse to VBA/macro coding, I have a very clean solution that just involves conventional Excel formulas, with no copy/paste involved.

Interested? Read on.

It is based on the Row Compression technique introduced in Chapter 9. Look at the data in cells O8:T55 and the cells in columns V through Z (see Figure 10-18).

Date	Service	SchedType	Total Gallons	Total Cost ($)	USD/Gal
January	Domestic	Scheduled	1062105559	1005190484	0.95
January	Domestic	Non-Scheduled	50852154	53586807	1.05
January	International	Scheduled	359458498	355975516	0.99
January	International	Non-Scheduled	47184400	50558329	1.07
February	Domestic	Scheduled	1017576584	979782091	0.96
February	Domestic	Non-Scheduled	48376650	50669885	1.05
February	International	Scheduled	332166929	335465324	1.01
February	International	Non-Scheduled	38017022	40761309	1.07
March	Domestic	Scheduled	1094680717	1058553836	0.97
March	Domestic	Non-Scheduled	52730168	54944157	1.04
March	International	Scheduled	354966361	376775200	1.06
March	International	Non-Scheduled	32016877	33675087	1.05
April	Domestic	Scheduled	1066405625	1059874838	0.99
April	Domestic	Non-Scheduled	50388896	55356320	1.1
April	International	Scheduled	365635649	376172110	1.03
April	International	Non-Scheduled	26767407	29607966	1.11
May	Domestic	Scheduled	1095500028	1174562079	1.07
May	Domestic	Non-Scheduled	46673322	55547468	1.19

Figure 10-18: Automatic shortened list based on conventional spreadsheet formulas

It's already starting to look like a PivotTable when you glance at it. Part of the reason for this is that the cell borders help to frame the data. Do you think I would spend the time to manually edit the cell borders; knowing full well that this spreadsheet will be used by you with other data that's structured differently? If you've gone this far through the book, you know that I don't do that. The borders automatically wrap themselves around the data for enhanced visual presentation.

"Smart" Borders and conditional formatting

When data is structured in some ordered fashion so that all of January's data is together, followed by all of February's data and so forth; it becomes easy to use conditional formatting to sense when a crossing over is occurring from one group to the next. It's just a matter of each cell to apply a formula to detect this change. As shown later in this sidebar, three conditions are tested. If the first test succeeds, a border is drawn above and below the cell. If it fails but the second succeeds, a border is drawn above the cell. If neither of those makes the grade, but the third test succeeds, a border is placed at the bottom of the cell.

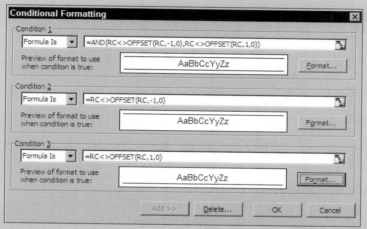

Formulas and settings for conditional format

Two observations are worthy of notice:

- I present the formulas here in the R1C1 cell reference style. Formulas in the R1C1 style have the advantage of being independent of the cell they are defined in. For instance, the formula in the second test is

  ```
  =RC<>OFFSET(RC,-1,0)
  ```

  When you look at the same conditional formatting applied to a cell 20 rows below, you see that the formula for this test is *exactly identical*. This duplication makes it much easier to work with formulas that don't change, especially when working with OFFSET.

- The formula OFFSET(RC,-1,0) simply says, "give me the value of the cell one row above my current row and column." The reason OFFSET is used is that it is perfectly behaved when you insert or delete rows and columns. This gives you maximum flexibility in redesigning the layout of your spreadsheets.

continued

continued

This conditional formatting is applied to columns 15, 16, and 17 (or O, P, Q in the A1 notation) from rows 8 through 55. You can switch back and forth between both cell reference styles. The spreadsheet is equally happy with either mode. When in the A1 style, every conditional formula will look different and is tethered to the cell it is defined in. In the R1C1 style, there are three unique formulas as shown in the preceding figure, and never change as you inspect each cell.

Smart Borders and conditional formatting is useful and underutilized feature of Excel. To learn more about this topic, check out Chapter 7 in my book *Excel Best Practices for Business*.

Spreadsheets and Dashboards

There have been significant advances in spreadsheets over the years. The number of rows might increase, calculation speed is faster; but on an overall basis, the spreadsheet metaphor has arguably been evolving at a snail's pace.

I want to outline a new kind of metaphor that's emerging. Let me give you a scenario. You are at a meeting presenting your operating budget for next year, presenting the various charts in PowerPoint slides. It's a nice presentation and everybody is in agreement with your assessment, except one person. That is a vice president who always plays devil's advocate no matter who is speaking. I'm sure you know him or her very well. In any case, he puts you on the spot with a scenario that's not included in your PowerPoint slides. You're prepared for this situation, and in your PowerPoint slide you have a hidden spreadsheet that's connected to one of your charts. You go to the chart, click and drag a couple of sliders and dials, and wham! Your graphs are instantly updated, reflecting the new set of assumptions (see Figure 10-19).

You leave everyone in the room, the vice president included, with their jaws hanging wide open (open the file `ch10_09SpreadsheetInASlide.ppt` on the book's CD-ROM).

Making a Dashboard

I am including on the book CD-ROM a free trial version of the software tool used to make this presentation. It is called Crystal Xcelsius Professional and is a product of Business Objects, SA (the same people who produce Crystal Reports).

NOTE

Crystal Xcelsius allows you to generate full-fledged dashboards in the following formats: Macromedia Flash files, Adobe .PDF documents, PowerPoint slides, and HTML Pages. This free trial software and the dashboards produced by it never time out, which is great news. Being that it is a demo software, it does have a big DEMO notice overlaid on the dashboard. Also, the source .XLF files cannot be saved.

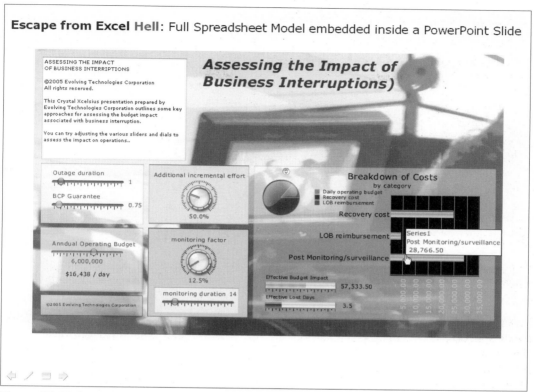

Figure 10-19: Digital dashboard as a PowerPoint slide

 NOTE
Dashboards generated as .PDF documents require Adobe Acrobat Reader 6.0 or later for proper viewing.

The process of preparing a portable dashboard is easy:

1. Create a spreadsheet as you normally do in Excel and save it.
2. Open the Crystal Xcelsius software and import it.
3. Drop visual components on a "work area" and hook them to your imported spreadsheet data and formulas.
4. Export the visual model to your desired format.

That's it. There's quite literally nothing else to do, and everything is point and click. I want to walk you through an example. Open the spreadsheet file called `ch10_09CrystalXcelsius .xls` (see Figure 10-20). Notice that the colorized values in the spreadsheet are just plain numbers and the noncolorized portions are formulas, such as SUM or SUMPRODUCT.

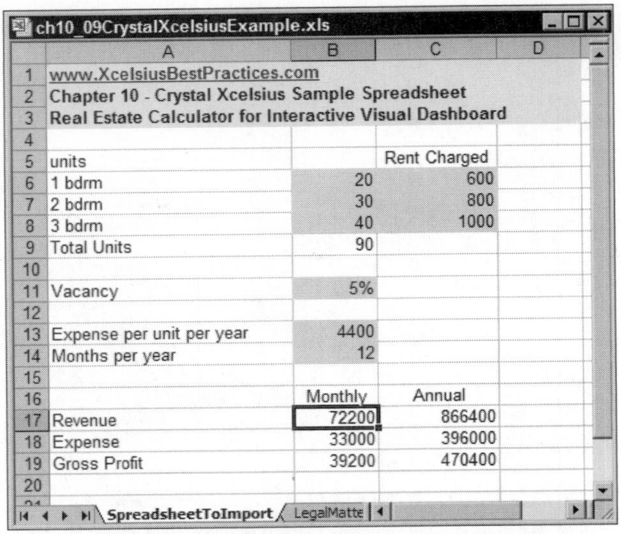

ch10_09CrystalXcelsiusExample.xls

	A	B	C	D
1	www.XcelsiusBestPractices.com			
2	Chapter 10 - Crystal Xcelsius Sample Spreadsheet			
3	Real Estate Calculator for Interactive Visual Dashboard			
4				
5	units		Rent Charged	
6	1 bdrm	20	600	
7	2 bdrm	30	800	
8	3 bdrm	40	1000	
9	Total Units	90		
10				
11	Vacancy	5%		
12				
13	Expense per unit per year	4400		
14	Months per year	12		
15				
16		Monthly	Annual	
17	Revenue	72200	866400	
18	Expense	33000	396000	
19	Gross Profit	39200	470400	
20				

SpreadsheetToImport / LegalMatte

Figure 10-20: Spreadsheet prior to import of Crystal Xcelsius

This is your ho-hum, garden-variety spreadsheet that is sure to set everyone's eyes glazing if it is presented in a boardroom meeting.

Your next step is to open Crystal Xcelsius. If you haven't installed it, now would be a good time (instructions for the installation are given in Appendix D).

Launch Crystal Xcelsius and open the file called `ch10_09XcelsiusStep1.xlf` (see Figure 10-21).

Several windows or panels should visible. The Components window contains a catalog of drag-and-drop widgets that you can place onto the work area (the central part of the screen). When you place a component onto the work area, it gets added to the list in your Object Browser, which you can see at the bottom-left corner of Figure 10-21. Notice that three components are listed (a rectangle, gauge, and horizontal slider), which match the object visible in the work area.

You can turn off the visibility of an item in the work area by checking the box next to the appropriate item in the Object Browser. Double-clicking the item (either in the Object Browser, or the actual component in the work area) causes the component's Properties window to appear.

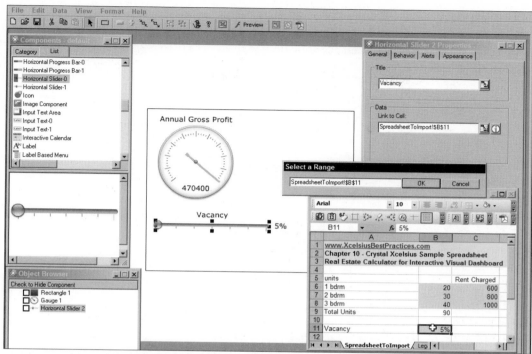

Figure 10-21: Crystal Xcelsius designer workbench

The Properties window typically has four tabs for different kinds of settings:

- General

- Behavior

- Alerts

- Appearance

Depending on the kind of component, the General tab may have a data link to the imported spreadsheet.

Figure 10-22 shows how to import an Excel spreadsheet into Crystal Xcelsius. Click the Excel Import button and an Import Model window opens to locate the file.

NOTE

When Crystal Xcelsius imports a spreadsheet, it literally imports the whole spreadsheet file, with its formulas, data, and formats. If you never have to re-import the spreadsheet, you can throw away the original spreadsheet, and the Xcelsius file and its generated dashboards will be none the wiser.

Each Xcelsius file keeps its own private copy of the spreadsheet. It also keeps track of where the spreadsheet was located at the time of import—for instance, in the examples where the path is set:

```
c:\spreadsheets
```

If you update the underlying spreadsheet, you need to re-import the file.

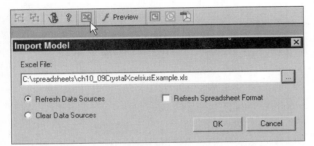

Figure 10-22: Importing an Excel workbook

If you click the Preview button next to the Excel import button, the model comes alive. You can move the slider and the gauge adjusts. However, its behavior does not seem to be correct. Click the Preview button again to go back to your designer mode. Double-click the slider component to open its Properties window and then click the Behavior tab. Remember, the slider is using percentages between 0 and 100. In reality, the vacancy percentage should never be more than about 15 percent, so change its maximum value to 0.25 (for 25 percent) and set the increment to 0.001.

Now create a second slider. You can drag one from the components panel and drop it onto the work area. Link it to the data for monthly expense (this is the 4400 amount that appears in the spreadsheet). In the Behavior tab, limit the upper value to 10000.

 TIP

If you have several similar components with the same kind of attributes, you can save time by creating an initial component, adjusting its size, appearance, and behavior, and then selecting it; next, press Ctrl+C to copy and Ctrl+V to paste it. Afterward, you can tweak the duplicated component for further refinement.

Do something similar for the gauge component. Set its upper and lower limit to plus and minus one million. Click the Alerts tab, place a checkmark next to Enable Alerts, and click High Values Are Good (see Figure 10-23).

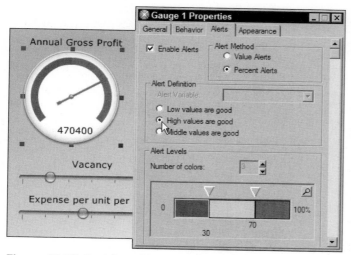

Figure 10-23: Enabling alerts in your dashboard

Preview your dashboard. By this point, you should be getting the hang of producing dashboards.

Publishing Your Dashboard

You have one step remaining: to export the dashboard to your desired format. When the dashboard is exported, the exported file is no longer tethered to the original spreadsheet. This means that you can e-mail the file, distribute it on a CD-ROM, or post it to a Web site for live viewing. To see some sample files, you can go to the following sites:

www.xcelsius.com
www.XcelsiusBestPactices.com

Using a Spreadsheet in a Dashboard

There are plenty of components and widgets in Crystal Xcelsius. One definitely worth mentioning is the Grid component. The Grid can link a swatch of spreadsheet cells to your dashboard (see Figure 10-24). Aside from displaying values, you can enter and change values by clicking and dragging over input cells of the spreadsheet, and instantly have the spreadsheet dashboard recalculate.

Part III

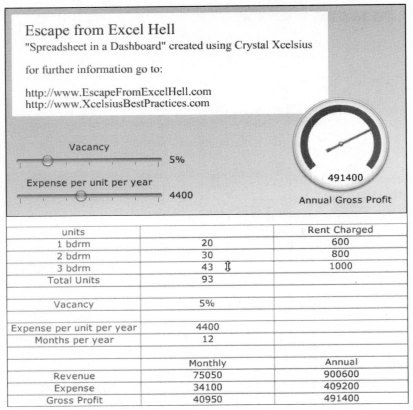

Figure 10-24: A Grid can put a whole spreadsheet on a dashboard.

TIP

A user asks: "Is there any way of distributing a live Excel spreadsheet without requiring the user to be running Excel?"

Microsoft provides a free Excel viewer software package, but you can't do any live calculations with it. Xcelsius has a Grid component that allows you to take swatches of spreadsheet cells and place them directly in your dashboard. You can then double-click a cell to change its value or click and drag the dashboard cell to "nudge" its value up or down. With this feature, you can post live Flash spreadsheets on a Web site and have people interact with this using only a Web browser!

There are plenty of other components worth mentioning, such as the Calendar component. For what it's worth, this technology has extensions that allow the dashboard to connect to the backend database, exchange XML information, and utilize Web Services.

This is a technology that warrants serious exploration.

Closing Thoughts

This chapter addresses a mixture of practical problems that not everybody voices as an "Excel Hell" problem. I don't have people stopping me in the hallway and saying, "How can I get myself a digital certificate to sign my code?" However, I also don't come across serious VBA programmers who say they're not interested in using digital certificates. I don't generally hear people volunteering requests for taking static published information and reverse engineering it into a PivotTable. When I speak about it, they start clamoring for the tools.

I think these are important problems that people want to know about. When you get to problems like the kind discussed in this chapter, you can't gloss over the details. At the risk of sounding cliché, the devil truly is in the details.

I know that when I am challenged by difficult problems, and someone has some information, I appreciate getting every ounce of detail that I can. I somehow believe that if I am shedding some light on a problem that's vexing you, you would appreciate the extra information and attention, and maybe something I said is that critical element that helps you to break that logjam.

One of the things I've tried to do throughout this book is to not only solve problems but also crystallize methodologies and winning strategies to solving problems. Much of this approach falls in line with best practices. Throughout this book, but especially in the later chapters, I wanted to bring into focus some of these best practices through practical examples.

This chapter appropriately ends in a high note, because it shows how easy and productive it can be to think outside the box, *and thereby escape from Excel Hell*.

Appendix

Miscellaneous Solved Problems

The topics discussed throughout the chapters in *Escape from Excel Hell* have been organized along the lines of major themes. There are plenty of problems that didn't make their way into the chapters that are worth knowing about. Accordingly, they're presented here. Some of these are just very brief notes; others are more involved discussions.

 NOTE

To save you the trouble of typing formulas manually, you can find many of the formulas for this appendix in the `takeaway.txt` file on the book's CD-ROM.

Counting Data

COUNTIF is a versatile function that can be used in many ways. Though used throughout this book, it can never hurt to have more examples of it.

Counting How Many Cells Have a Particular Word in Them

```
=COUNTIF(A:A, "*EXCEL*")
```

Finds how many cells in column A have the word "EXCEL" in it.

COUNTIF with Multiple Criteria for a Single Range

```
=COUNTIF(A2:A10,">10,<=100")
=COUNTIF(B:B,">10,<=100")
```

The first formula counts how many cells in the range A2:A10 have values that exceed 10 but are less than or equal to 100. The second formula does the equivalent for all of column B.

COUNTIF with Two Criteria for Multiple Ranges

```
=SUMPRODUCT(--(A2:A10="FirstMatch"),--(B2:B10="SecondMatch"))
```

COUNTIF with N Criteria for Multiple Ranges

```
=SUMPRODUCT(--(A2:A10="FirstMatch"),--(B2:B10="SecondMatch"),...--(N2:N10="NthMatch"))
```

Unless you want to specify cell coordinates, you cannot use whole columns (for example, A:A).

COUNTIF with Compound Criteria

```
=SUMPRODUCT(--(A2:A10>55),--(B2:B10<=75)) SUMPRODUCT(--(A2:A10>55),--(A2:A10<=75))
```

Computing with Rows and Columns

Knowing your way around a spreadsheet can be aided by specific functions.

Finding the Column Letter of the Current Cell

```
=LEFT(ADDRESS(ROW(),COLUMN(),2),FIND("$",ADDRESS(ROW(),COLUMN(),2))-1)
```

Formula for Computing A1 Status

```
=INFO("origin")="$A:$A$1"
```

Important in conjunction with INDIRECT.

Formula for Worksheet Name

```
=MID(CELL("filename",B25),FIND("]",CELL("filename",B25))+1,LEN(CELL("filename"
,B25))-FIND("]",CELL("filename",B25)))
```

Formula for Filename with Full Path

```
=CELL("filename")
```
returns filename with full path for this spreadsheet

or

```
=CELL("filename",RemoteSavedWrkbk!A1)
```
returns filename with full path for another workbook

Controlling Macros

There are things you can do to adjust the behavior of macros. One of them is external to the macro itself; the other is from within the macro at the programming code level.

Suppressing the Workbook_Open Macro

Spreadsheets have a specially defined event routine called `Workbook_Open`. Any code inside this routine is automatically run whenever the spreadsheet file is opened. This makes it immediately useful for many purposes, such as opening to a particular worksheet and cell location, or adjusting calculation settings.

There are times, however, when you may not want the `Workbook_Open` routine to automatically kick in. Holding down the Shift key while opening the file disables this routine.

 WARNING

If you are opening a spreadsheet containing a valid digital certificate from a trusted source, holding down the Shift key while opening the spreadsheet file does not suppress the `Workbook_Open` routine!

"I am able to suppress the Workbook_Open routine using the Shift-key' technique. Though I suppress this action, are all the macros disabled, or only the Workbook_Open routine?"

Using the Shift key suppresses the `Workbook_Open` macro only when the file is opened. After it's opened, none of the macros are disabled. If they are from an untrusted source, they'll be sitting there like landmines waiting to explode.

Optional Arguments in Macros

"How do I set up function procedures in my macros that have optional arguments?"

Here is an example of setting up function procedures in macros that involves an optional argument.

Suppose that you have a custom function you can use inside your spreadsheet that increments a number by some value:

```
Function IncrementMe(iSomeInteger, Optional iArg As Integer = 1)
    IncrementMe = iSomeInteger + iArg
End Function
```

In your spreadsheet, you can enter a formula like:

```
=IncrementMe(24,3)                    returns 27
=IncrementMe(24)                      returns 25
```

Converting Data

Though these are covered earlier in the book, it is convenient to have a summary of a couple of techniques for converting data.

Quick Way of Turning a Text Representation of a Number into Its Numeric Value

```
=--MID("A1234",2,3)
```

Converting 20060616 to the Date 6/16/2006 (as a serial date)

If `A1` contains the number `20060616`, the following formula is used:

```
=DATE(LEFT(A1, 4),mid(A1,5,2),right(A1,2))
```

Miscellaneous Calculations

These are useful tasks that can come in handy.

PASTE SPECIAL — CALCULATOR BUTTONS

"I want to increase the values in a range of cells by adding 23 to each of them."

Copy a cell having the value `23` (using `Ctrl+C`), select the range of cells you want to modify, and then click Paste Special Add.

You can also multiply, subtract, or divide by a factor. To reverse the sign of a group of cells, you can multiple by a factor of -1. To increase their value by 10 percent, you can apply a multiplication factor of 1.1.

HYPERLINK MISCHIEF

"When I click a hyperlink inside an Excel spreadsheet, instead of opening the file in the local directory of my hard drive, my browser suddenly searches for the file on the Internet."

You may need to adjust the spreadsheet's Properties Hyperlink Base option (which is set in the Summary tab). If your link should be pointing to a file that is co-located in the same directory of your current directory path, then make sure to clear out any URL in the Hyperlink base.

> *"I need to generate a repeating sequence 1, 2, 3, ... , 11, 12, 1, 2, ...*
>
> *When I use the MOD function, I can get a repeating sequence, but the starting number is always zero (1, 2, 3, ... , 11, 12, 0, 1, 2, ...). How can I get rid of the zero in the sequence?"*

```
=MAX(1,MOD(1+B8,13))                          (cell C8)
```

Arrays

Array formulas are always confusing. The formulas with the curly braces look confusing. Entering them correctly can be confusing. Following are some examples you can use as models.

NOTE
Array formulas require you to enter the formula without the curly braces, and while you're still in Edit mode, press Ctrl+Shift+Enter instead of just the Enter key. The surrounding curly braces appear after pressing Ctrl+Shift+Enter.

Find If 1, 2, 3, 4, 5, 6, 7, 8, 9, 10 in Any Permutation Is Completely Accounted for in a Range of Cells

```
{=COUNT(MATCH(ROW(INDIRECT("1:10")),A2:A11,0))=10}
```

Reference an Array Inside a Formula
In some situations, an array doesn't surround the whole formulas but is a small piece inside a formula. Here are some examples:

```
=HLOOKUP("a",{"a","b","c";1,2,3},2,FALSE)
=VLOOKUP("c",{"a",1;"b",2;"c",3},2,FALSE)
```

Sorting by *Numeric* Cell Format
You may need to group cells based on their numeric format. For instance, you may want to group cells displayed as percentages, or dates, or whatever. This is not the same as grouping by font or cell color.

You can create a sort key using CELL("format",TheCellReference), such as:

```
=CELL("format",A1)
```

You can then use the value returned by this as a sort key.

Character and Text Manipulation

It helps to have on a printed page examples of character symbols generated by the CHAR function. The examples and the Map of ASCII Characters that follow should serve as a convenient reference. Also, check out the file ch02_02Examples.xls on the book's CD-ROM for formulas and more examples.

Producing Single Digits from 0 Through 9

```
0        =CHAR(48)
1        =CHAR(49)
. . .
9        =CHAR(57)
```

Producing UpperCase Characters A Through Z

```
A        =CHAR(65)
B        =CHAR(66)
. . .
Z        =CHAR(90)
```

Producing LowerCase Characters a Through z

```
a        =CHAR(97)
b        =CHAR(98)
. . .
z        =CHAR(122)
```

Producing Special Characters

A character space is CHAR(32) and a tab is CHAR(9).

Following is a listing that shows a "map" of ASCII character codes. This list can also be found in the ch02_02Examples.xls file on the book's CD-ROM.

Map of ASCII Characters

! =CHAR(33)	~ =CHAR(126)	£ =CHAR(163)	Â =CHAR(194)	á =CHAR(225)	
" =CHAR(34)	€ =CHAR(128)	¤ =CHAR(164)	Ã =CHAR(195)	â =CHAR(226)	
# =CHAR(35)	, =CHAR(130)	¥ =CHAR(165)	Ä =CHAR(196)	ã =CHAR(227)	
$ =CHAR(36)	ƒ =CHAR(131)	¦ =CHAR(166)	Å =CHAR(197)	ä =CHAR(228)	
% =CHAR(37)	„ =CHAR(132)	§ =CHAR(167)	Æ =CHAR(198)	å =CHAR(229)	
& =CHAR(38)	... =CHAR(133)	¨ =CHAR(168)	Ç =CHAR(199)	æ =CHAR(230)	
' =CHAR(39)	† =CHAR(134)	© =CHAR(169)	È =CHAR(200)	ç =CHAR(231)	
(=CHAR(40)	‡ =CHAR(135)	ª =CHAR(170)	É =CHAR(201)	è =CHAR(232)	
) =CHAR(41)	^ =CHAR(136)	« =CHAR(171)	Ê =CHAR(202)	é =CHAR(233)	
* =CHAR(42)	‰ =CHAR(137)	¬ =CHAR(172)	Ë =CHAR(203)	ê =CHAR(234)	
+ =CHAR(43)	Š =CHAR(138)	– =CHAR(173)	Ì =CHAR(204)	ë =CHAR(235)	
, =CHAR(44)	‹ =CHAR(139)	® =CHAR(174)	Í =CHAR(205)	ì =CHAR(236)	
- =CHAR(45)	Œ =CHAR(140)	¯ =CHAR(175)	Î =CHAR(206)	í =CHAR(237)	
. =CHAR(46)	Ž =CHAR(142)	° =CHAR(176)	Ï =CHAR(207)	î =CHAR(238)	
/ =CHAR(47)	' =CHAR(145)	± =CHAR(177)	a =CHAR(208)	ï =CHAR(239)	
: =CHAR(58)	' =CHAR(146)	^{2} =CHAR(178)	Ñ =CHAR(209)	ð =CHAR(240)	
; =CHAR(59)	" =CHAR(147)	^{3} =CHAR(179)	Ò =CHAR(210)	ñ =CHAR(241)	
< =CHAR(60)	" =CHAR(148)	´ =CHAR(180)	Ó =CHAR(211)	ò =CHAR(242)	
= =CHAR(61)	• =CHAR(149)	µ =CHAR(181)	Ô =CHAR(212)	ó =CHAR(243)	
> =CHAR(62)	– =CHAR(150)	¶ =CHAR(182)	Õ =CHAR(213)	ô =CHAR(244)	
? =CHAR(63)	— =CHAR(151)	· =CHAR(183)	Ö =CHAR(214)	õ =CHAR(245)	
@ =CHAR(64)	~ =CHAR(152)	¸ =CHAR(184)	× =CHAR(215)	ö =CHAR(246)	
[=CHAR(91)	™ =CHAR(153)	^{1} =CHAR(185)	Ø =CHAR(216)	÷ =CHAR(247)	
\ =CHAR(92)	š =CHAR(154)	º =CHAR(186)	Ù =CHAR(217)	ø =CHAR(248)	
] =CHAR(93)	› =CHAR(155)	» =CHAR(187)	Ú =CHAR(218)	ù =CHAR(249)	
^ =CHAR(94)	œ =CHAR(156)	¼ =CHAR(188)	Û =CHAR(219)	ú =CHAR(250)	
_ =CHAR(95)	ž =CHAR(158)	½ =CHAR(189)	Ü =CHAR(220)	û =CHAR(251)	
` =CHAR(96)	Ÿ =CHAR(159)	¾ =CHAR(190)	Ý =CHAR(221)	ü =CHAR(252)	
{ =CHAR(123)	=CHAR(160)	¿ =CHAR(191)	Þ =CHAR(222)	ý =CHAR(253)	
	=CHAR(124)	¡ =CHAR(161)	À =CHAR(192)	ß =CHAR(223)	þ =CHAR(254)	
} =CHAR(125)	¢ =CHAR(162)	Á =CHAR(193)	à =CHAR(224)	ÿ =CHAR(255)	

Approximations

With 15 decimals of precision, Excel can be quite accurate. However, you may be applying some formula to estimate a quantity, or using some technique in Numerical Analysis. The formula itself may lack the precision.

As an example, you might be applying some decision criteria based on three pieces of information. In reality there are 13 pieces of information that could affect the outcome. The other 10 that you skipped might affect your estimate by only 1 or 2 percent. Incorporating them would make the formula too complex. When working with problems like this, you may need some type of rounding technique.

The technique that follows gives you a way to handle this kind of problem. It uses the ABS function in a clever way.

Replacing Approximate Values with Exact Values

"If a number is extremely close to a 0 or 1, I want it to return exactly 0 or 1, or otherwise signal some exception."

Say that you have a calculation in the cell A1 that should return exactly a 0 or 1. It might be a logic switch telling the rest of your Excel calculations to do something such as Buy or Sell. The problem is that the switch may be a faulty switch; returning a value close to a 0 or 1, such as 0.999998. To get around this problem, create a new switch with a formula like:

```
=if((ABS(A1-0.5)-0.5)^2<0.000000001),ROUND(A1,0),9999)
=if((ABS(FaultySwitch-0.5)-
0.5)^2<SmallDelta),ROUND(FaultySwitch,0),ErrorValue)
```

If the value of A1 is very close to 1, then the ABS(A1-0.5) will be very close to ABS(1-0.5) or 0.5. If the value of A1 is very close to 0, then the ABS(A1-0.5) will be very close to ABS(0-0.5) or ABS(-0.5), which is 0.5. In either case, you'll get to a number close to 0.5. If you subtract exactly 0.5 from this number, you'll wind up with a number like 0.00001 or -0.00001. If you square this number, you'll wind up with something like 0.000000001. When you're within this range, it is fairly safe to assume that A1 is sufficiently close to a 0 or 1. Return A1 rounded to zero decimal places to get *exactly* a 0 or 1.

Formula Simplification

Every time you simplify a formula, your spreadsheet gains in terms of better performance, higher reliability, and manageability. This section presents some practical examples to follow.

Formula Simplification Examples

In the example of AppendixA_04FormulaSimplification.xls (see Figure A-1), the last name is being extracted.

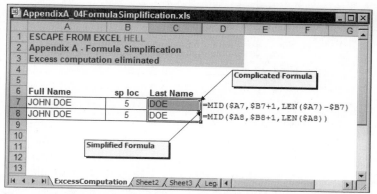

Figure A-1: Simplified formula eliminates excess computation.

This formula has two versions:

```
=MID(A7,B7+1,LEN(A7)-B7)                     (formula in row 7)
=MID(A8,B8+1,LEN(A8))                        (formula in row 8)
```

MID, as you may recall, extracts a string of a given length from a starting position. Here is how both formulas are computed:

```
=MID("JOHN DOE",6,3)                         (row 7 computation)
=MID("JOHN DOE",6,8)                         (row 8 computation)
```

The row 7 formula calculates the exact size of the last name DOE (which happens to be 3) and returns exactly that many letters.

The row 8 formula is simpler. It doesn't bother with calculating the exact size. It starts from position 6 and tries to extract eight characters, even though only three are available.

Both formulas produce the same result. One formula is simpler, the other is more formal. Which is the better formula to use? Well, that's your choice. Here's my suggestion. All other things being equal, the simpler formula has fewer computations or moving parts. Usually, this state of affairs leads to easier maintenance and better performance. If you want to use the simpler formula, you will do well to document it somewhere.

Some Simple Formula Modification Issues

"I opened a financial report that is in tab delimited form. The text descriptions are not indented using spaces, but rather by indenting being set to individual columns. The report name and main headings appear in the first column, item headings in the second, and sub-item headings in the third column. Although I can resize the columns, it would be much easier for me to put these all in a single column and indent them with spaces."

Columns A, B, C, and D, as shown in Figure A-2, show labels appearing in various columns. Column E shows the equivalent information consolidated to a single column.

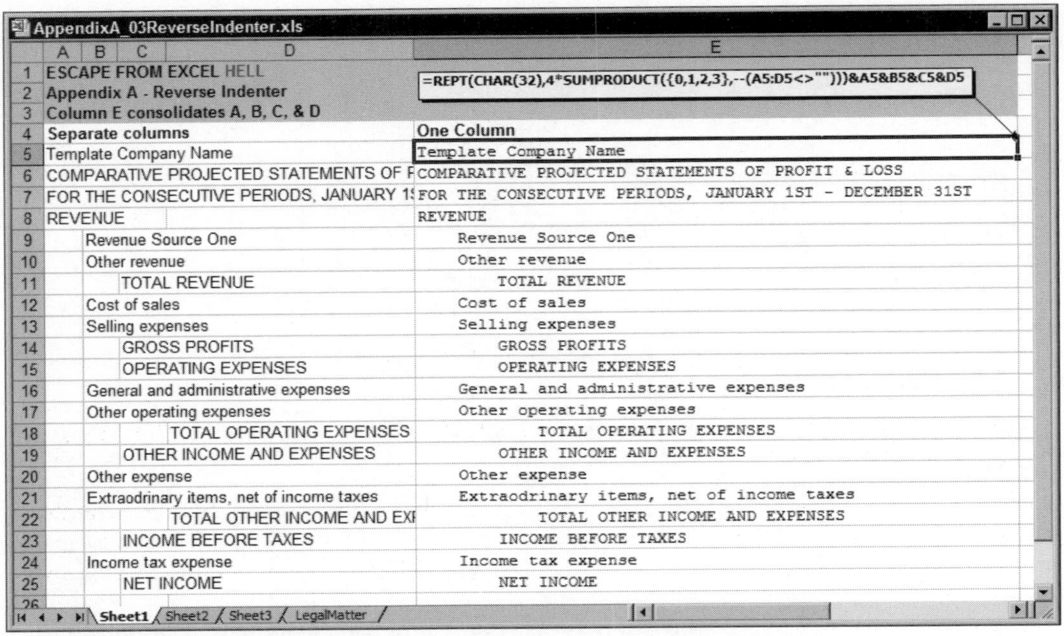

Figure A-2: Consolidated column simplifies spreadsheet handling

Here is how you convert it. Assuming that your data starts in cell A1, with the text on any row but only in a single column, and you want to indent by four spaces, type the formula in cell E1:

```
=REPT(CHAR(32),4*SUMPRODUCT({0,1,2,3},--(A1:D1<>"")))&A1&B1&C1&D1
```

Select the results in column E, copy the results (Ctrl+C), and go back to your original spreadsheet and click Paste Special Values. If you paste the results in column A, be sure to clear out columns B, C, and D.

You can tweak this formula. The CHAR (32) function generates a character space. You can choose an alternative character such as a decimal point using CHAR(46). You may want to refer back to the character codes table for other character symbols. You can change the number 4 to however many spaces or symbols you want for each level of indenting. To make all this easier for you, you'll find the preceding formula in the takeaway.txt file on the book's CD-ROM and the file AppendixA_03ReverseIndenter.xls has a sample of this.

Formula Replication Without Alteration

"I want to copy a formula in a cell and paste it to another cell without altering the formula."

Select the cell you want to copy and press the F2 key to go into the edit mode on the Formula Bar. Press Ctrl+A to select the whole formula, and then press Ctrl+C followed by the Esc key. Select the cell you want the identical formula to appear in, press the F2 key followed by Ctrl+V to paste the formula, and press Enter. You may also need to copy and paste the cell formula.

Formula Replication and Table Making

"I have a formula for cell C5 which happens to be =C4, and when I drag the cell to a different location such as E7, the formula is still =C4, but I would like it to be =E6 instead. How can I do this without manually editing the formula?"

Select both cells `C5` and `C4` and move them in one step to your desired location. By the way, it is a lot simpler to do a straight cut and paste.

Basic Table Making

"I want to construct a conversion table that reads the row and column headers, and uses a formula to compute the value in the intersection."

Figure A-3 shows you how to do this. Cell `C10` is composed of `$A10` and `C$6`. The formula has to reference the row labels appearing in column A, and the column labels running across row 6. If you are trying to construct a table based on units, here is the formula to use:

```
=CONVERT(1,$A10,C$6)                          (cell C10)
```

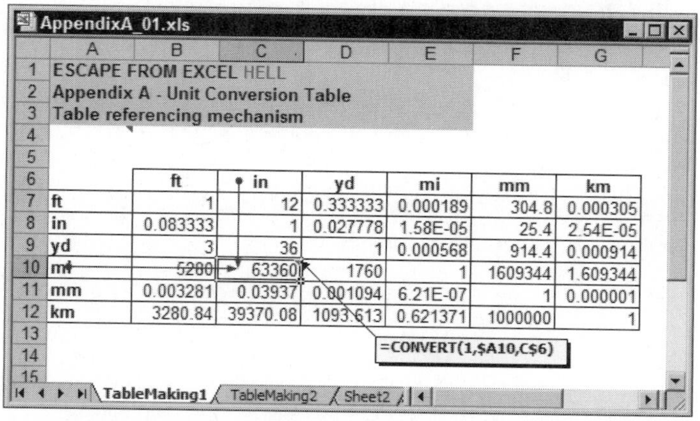

	ft	in	yd	mi	mm	km
ft	1	12	0.333333	0.000189	304.8	0.000305
in	0.083333	1	0.027778	1.58E-05	25.4	2.54E-05
yd	3	36	1	0.000568	914.4	0.000914
mi	5280	63360	1760	1	1609344	1.609344
mm	0.003281	0.03937	0.001094	6.21E-07	1	0.000001
km	3280.84	39370.08	1093.613	0.621371	1000000	1

Figure A-3: Row and column headers are ready to construct the table.

Notice that the use of the `$` symbol causes column `A` and row `6` to be treated as absolute makes it easy to construct a table just by replicating the formula.

Also note that this table uses the CONVERT function, which requires the Analysis ToolPak to be loaded. If the ToolPak is not loaded, a warning message appears in cell `A4`.

The formula for the warning error is

```
=IF(ISERROR(DEC2HEX(1)=1),"YOU NEED TO HAVE THE EXCEL ANALYSIS TOOLPAK ADD-IN
INSTALLED!","")
```

Advanced Table Making

"I want to build a table with color bands for my data."

The TableMaking2 worksheet does this using conditional formatting (see Figure A-4). The quick way to use this table is to just right-click the worksheet tab and, in the context menu, select Move or Copy and place the table in your spreadsheet. After this is done, you can change the formulas inside the colorized table and adjust the conditional format settings for colors, borders, and so on.

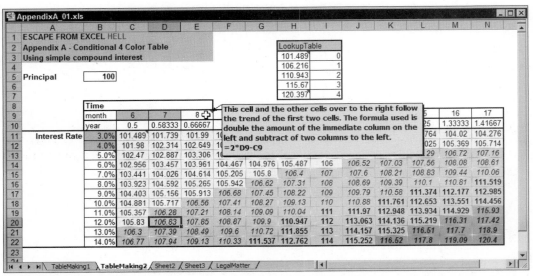

Figure A-4: Advance table creates colored bands and automatically increments row and column headers.

 NOTE

Conditional formatting in Excel 2003 and earlier supports at most three conditions, yet this table shows four colored bands. This fourth band is possible because a *phantom condition* is used. The fourth condition is a predefined format that is applied when the first three conditional tests fail.

"When I set up a table, I want to continue a progression of numbers based on the first two numbers of the sequence. For instance, if I have the numbers 5, 7, I would like to see the sequence continue with 9, 11, 13..."

The formula is to multiply the first cell in the sequence by 2 and subtract from it the second cell. This action gives you the third cell in the sequence. You can continue this progression using the two previous cells:

```
5                                  (cell C9)
7                                  (cell D9)
=2*D9-C9                           (cell E9 returns 9)
=2*E9-D9                           (cell F9 returns 11)
=2*F9-E9                           (cell G9 returns 13)
```

Although this can be done across a row, it is just as easily performed down a column. The following shows how this is done from column B to generate the sequence 4, 5, 6...

```
4                                  (cell B11)
5                                  (cell B12)
=2*B12-B11                         (cell B13 returns 6)
=2*B13-B12                         (cell B14 returns 7)
=2*B14-B13                         (cell B15 returns 8)
```

NOTE

This technique of using row and column progressions is very useful for constructing tables. This is shown in the TableMaking2 worksheet. In actual practice, you don't need to colorize the starter cells in the progression.

Annotating and Decorating Spreadsheets

Not everything in spreadsheets revolves around formulas. Comments are useful for annotating a spreadsheet. You may want more control over how a comment appears.

Controlling Boldface in Cell Comments

"I often see spreadsheets with 'hovering' comments appearing only in boldface. When I create comments, they always appear with my user name in boldface. When I type my comment immediately below the name, they appear without boldface. How do I get everything to be completely in boldface?"

When you insert a comment, select the user name that is already in boldface and just start typing over it.

"How do I control comments so that they are always visible versus automatically visible whenever I pass my mouse over the cell?"

Right-click the cell in question and click Show/Hide Comments or Hide Comments in the context menu.

> *"I normally enter my dates in Excel with a "m/d/yyyy" pattern. For example, April 5, 2006 would be entered and should appear as "4/5/2006," but Excel changes it to a "4/5/06." This never used to happen and I don't know what caused it. Right now, I want to make it work the way it always has."*

Some other program on your computer may have changed the operating system's regional settings without your knowing it. You can fix the regional settings by making an adjustment directly in the operating system. When you make the adjustment, Excel will revise its behavior. Follow these steps:

1. From the Windows Start menu, click Start⇨Settings⇨Control Panel.
2. Double-click the Regional Settings or Regional Options icon.
3. In the Short date format list, click a format that uses four digits for the year ("yyyy").

Recalculation

Table A-1 shows recalculation keystroke sequences.

TABLE A-1   **FORCING RECALCULATION**

Press F9	Calculates formulas changed since the last calculation, and formulas dependent on them, in all open workbooks. When calculation settings are set to Automatic, you do not need to press F9.
Shift+F9	Calculates formulas changed since the last calculation, and formulas dependent on them, in just the active worksheet.
Ctrl+Alt+F9	Calculates all formulas in all open workbooks, regardless of whether they have changed.
Ctrl+Shift+Alt+F9	Rechecks dependent formulas, and then calculates all formulas in all open workbooks, regardless of whether they have changed.

To halt a long calculation, try pressing Ctrl+Break or the Esc key.

Analysis ToolPak

The Analysis ToolPak is supplied with every licensed copy of Excel. It is not always installed.

What do you do when you're distributing a spreadsheet that uses a function based on the Analysis ToolPak? Also, it is sometimes a mystery as to what functions are provided by the Analysis ToolPak. I provide a basic list.

Distributing Spreadsheets That Use the Analysis ToolPak

"I am distributing a spreadsheet that uses the RANDBETWEEN function. This requires that the Analysis ToolPak be installed. How do I alert the user if the ToolPak is not installed?"

Use a formula that requires a ToolPak function. If it causes an error, have it display a message that tells the user to install the ToolPak. That's much better than a cryptic error message. A formula such as the following will work well:

```
=IF(ISERROR(DEC2HEX(1)=1),"YOU NEED TO HAVE THE EXCEL ANALYSIS TOOLPAK ADD-IN
INSTALLED!","")
```

My suggestion is that you place this in a prominent location in the spreadsheet. You may also want to format the font in a red color and in boldface, or something that is sure to gain the attention of the user.

```
=INT(CONVERT(H1,"m","ft"))&" feet  "&INT(MOD(CONVERT(H1,"m","ft"),1)*12)&"
"&CHOOSE((ROUND((((H1*3.2808-INT(ROUND(H1*3.2808,2)))*12-TRUNC((H1*3.2808-
INT(ROUND(H1*3.2808,2)))*12))/0.125,0)),"1/8","1/4","3/8","1/2","5/8","3/4","7
/8")&" inches"
```

Analysis ToolPak Functions

Base Conversion Functions

```
Bin2Hex(number [, places])
Bin2Oct(number [, places])
Bin2Dec(number)
Dec2Bin(number [, places])
Dec2Oct(number [, places])
Dec2Hex(number [, places])
Hex2Bin(number [, places])
Hex2Dec(number)
```

```
Hex2Oct(number [, places])
Oct2Dec(number)
Oct2Bin(number [, places])
Oct2Hex(number [, places])
```

Engineering Functions

```
Erf(lower_limit [, upper_limit])
Erfc(X)
Factdouble(number)
IsOdd(number)
IsEven(number)
SqrtPI(number)
Quotient(numerator, denominator)
MRound(number, multiple)
Delta(number1 [, number2])
GeStep(number [, step])
BesselI(X, n)
BesselJ(X, n)
BesselY(X, n)
BesselK(X, n)
Convert(number, from_unit, to_unit)
```

Complex Functions

```
ImSub(inumber1, inumber2)
ImDiv(inumber1, inumber2)
ImConjugate(inumber)
ImSin(inumber)
ImCos(inumber)
ImExp(inumber)
ImLog10(inumber)
ImLog2(inumber)
ImLn(inumber)
ImSqrt(inumber)
ImAbs(inumber)
ImArgument(inumber)
ImReal(inumber)
Imaginary(inumber)
ImPower(inumber, number)
Complex(real_num, i_num [, suffix])
```

Functions with 1..29 Arguments

```
SeriesSum(X, n, m, coefficients)
ImSum(inumber1 [, inumber2, ... inumber29])
```

```
ImProduct(inumber1 [, inumber2,, ... inumber29])
Lcm(number1 [, number2,, ... number29])
Gcd(number1 [, number2,, ... number29])
Multinomial(number1 [, number2,, ... number29])
Date manipulation functions
Weeknum(serial_number [, return_type])
EoMonth(start_date, months)
Workday(start_date, days [, holidays])
Networkdays(start_date, end_date [, holidays])
```

Financial Date Functions

```
Edate(start_date, months)
Yearfrac(start_date, end_date [, basis])
```

Coupons

```
Coupdaybs(settlement, maturity, frequency [, basis])
Coupdays(settlement, maturity, frequency [, basis])
Coupdaysnc(settlement, maturity, frequency [, basis])
Coupncd(settlement, maturity, frequency [, basis])
Coupnum(settlement, maturity, frequency [, basis])
Couppcd(settlement, maturity, frequency [, basis])
```

Extended Excel Financial Functions

```
Cumipmt(rate, nper, pv, start_period, end_period, type_payment)
Cumprinc(rate, nper, pv, start_period, end_period, type_payment)
FvSchedule(principal, schedule)
XNpv(rate, values, dates)
XIrr(values, dates [, guess])
```

Add-In Functions

```
Randbetween(bottom, top)
IsShared(OutputBook As String) As Boolean
```

French Financial Functions

```
Amorlinc(cost, date_purchased, first_period, salvage, period, rate, Function
Amordegrc(cost, date_purchased, first_period, salvage, period, rate [,
year_basis])
```

Compound Interest

```
Effect(nominal_rate, npery)
Nominal(effect_rate, npery)
```

Fractional Quotation

```
Dollarde(fractional_dollar, fraction)
Dollarfr(decimal_dollar, fraction)
```

Fix Income Securities

```
Accrint(issue, first_interest, settlement, rate, par, frequency [, basis])
Accrintm(issue, settlement, rate [, par , basis])
Price(settlement, maturity, rate, yld, redemption, frequency [, basis])
Yield(settlement, maturity, rate, par, redemption, frequency [, basis])
Pricemat(settlement, maturity, issue, rate, yld [, basis])
Yieldmat(settlement, maturity, issue, rate, pr [, basis])
Pricedisc(settlement, maturity, discount, redemption [, basis])
Yielddisc(settlement, maturity, pr, redemption [, basis])
Disc(settlement, maturity, pr, redemption [, basis])
Received(settlement, maturity, investment, discount [, basis])
Intrate(settlement, maturity, investment, redemption [, basis])
Tbillprice(settlement, maturity, discount)
Tbillyield(settlement, maturity, pr)
Tbilleq(settlement, maturity, discount)
Duration(settlement, maturity, coupon, yld, frequency [, basis])
MDuration(settlement, maturity, coupon, yld, frequency [, basis])
OddFPrice(settlement, maturity, issue, first_coupon, rate, yld, redemption,
frequency [, basis])
OddFYield(settlement, maturity, issue, first_coupon, rate, pr, redemption,
frequency [, basis])
OddLPrice(settlement, maturity, last_interest, rate, yld, redemption,
frequency [, basis])
OddLYield(settlement, maturity, last_interest, rate, pr, redemption, frequency
[, basis])
```

Statistical Calculations Involving Frequencies

Excel supports a wealth of statistical functions, ranging from Hypergeometric distributions to correlation coefficients to simple averages. With all the functions, it would be nice to have a self-contained approach to grouped data (that is, data with frequencies).

If I said that there are 10 people with salaries of 40K, 13 people with salaries of 55K, 17 people with salaries of 67K, 12 people with salaries of 89K, and 3 people with salaries of 102K, and I ask you what is the median, average, and standard deviation of this data, how would you compute this?

You have three approaches:

- Run the computations in Excel.

- Run the computations on the Graphing Calculator you used for your college-level course in statistics.

- Work it out with pencil and paper using formulas from a text book.

Actually, there's one more: Ask a friend.

At first glance, you would think that the computation should be automatic with the functions in Excel. MEDIAN, AVERAGE, and STDEV are standard Excel functions. However, they don't provide a way of directly entering grouped data such as in the above example. In the file ch02_0FStatisticalExamples.xls (on the book's CD-ROM), I show you how to handle this problem (see Figure A-5).

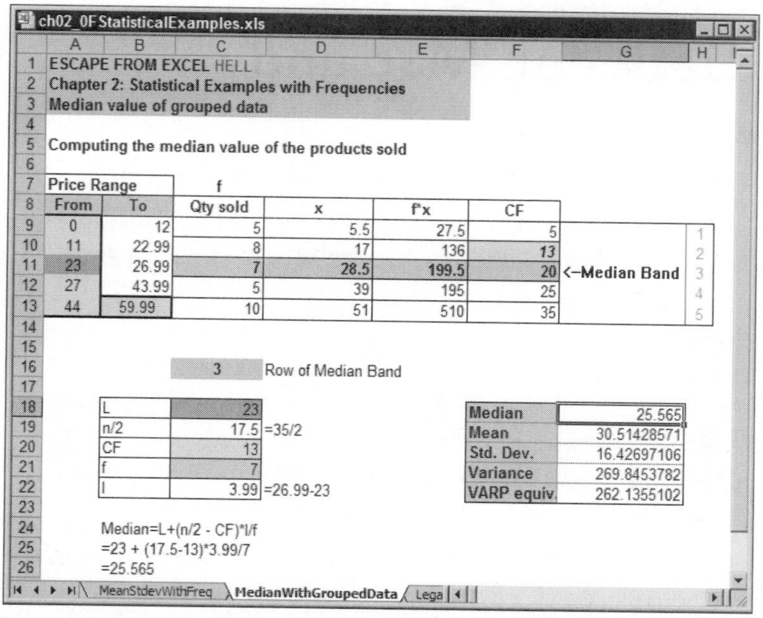

Figure A-5: Calculating a median with grouped data

Incidentally, the answer to my earlier questions are as follows:

```
Median = 63,706
Average = 65,964
Standard Deviation = 18,552
```

Windows and Office

The Old Copy-to-Notepad-and-Back Routine

"Sometimes I need to copy a bunch of spreadsheets cells and paste the text only into my Web-based e-mail program. The problem is that my e-mail program pastes the cell values and formats together. There is no way to paste just the values without the formatting."

Here's a very simple solution to this problem. Paste your spreadsheet content into Notepad. Then, select and copy the content from Notepad and paste it into your e-mail program.

Differences between Mac and Windows

Some keyboard differences exist between the Mac and Windows versions of Excel.

- Recalculation of the workbook is accomplished by pressing ⌘+= (Command + equal) instead of F9.

- On the Mac, spreadsheet options are set by clicking Excel Preferences from the application menu (on Windows, click Tools Options). On pre-OS X–based Macs (System 9 and earlier), you click File⇨Preferences. The Preferences window appears when you press ⌘+, (Command+comma).

- When editing a formula in the Formula Bar, you can press ⌘+T instead of F4 to cycle through the various permutations of absolute, relative, and hybrid cell references.

- To toggle back and forth between Excel and the Visual Basic Editor, press Option+F11 instead of Alt+F11.

- There are some apparent difference between the Microsoft documentation that accompanies Excel for the Mac and the software itself. On a system running Tiger (OS X 10.4.3) with Excel 2004, the documentation says that to create names using row and column labels, you press Ctrl+Shift+F3. This key combination does not seem to work, but ⌘+Fn+Shift+F3 does. I can't even find in the documentation the keystroke sequence for defining a single name over a range of cells. I found that pressing ⌘+Fn+F3 does the trick.

- Add-in files in OS X are generally located in the following folder:

```
Applications/Microsoft Office 2004/Office/Addins
```

On the Windows platform, the Add-In directory is usually found in:

```
C:\Documents and Settings\{your user name}\Application Data\
Microsoft\Excel\AddIns
```

Ten Easy Rules to Remember

I want to leave you with some helpful guides. Feel free to add another ten of your own!

1. Remove the hardwired values from your formulas.

2. Keep your chart series data and the heavy data analysis it depends on separate (preferably on separate worksheets).

3. Keep the data analysis and the source data it draws from separate.

4. It is better to have several cells doing pieces of a complex calculation than to have one spreadsheet cell with a massive formula.

5. For every detailed worksheet that has tons of detailed schedules and subschedules, make sure that there is a quick summary of its salient features.

6. Every worksheet should be able to, at a quick glance, answer who, what, and when (that is, you've placed identifying information in A1:A3).

7. Every time you use an existing spreadsheet to create a new one (such as going from last month's expense report to this month's), make it a habit to add at least one improvement to the spreadsheet.

8. Don't be afraid to experiment and try a new formula or Excel function you've never used before.

9. If you are doing a calculation that looks too complicated, and you think it ought to be simpler, chances are you're right. Try to find a way to make your formulas simpler.

10. Don't think that everything numeric has to be spreadsheet based. There are plenty of other ways and software tools that work better than spreadsheets within a specific context. Don't be afraid to explore your options.

Appendix

Installing the Escape Excel Hell Utility Pak

A number of routines are provided in this book in the form of an add-in called Escape Excel Hell Utility Pak. This appendix outlines steps in installing and uninstalling this add-in, along with a description of the routines and some additional information that may be useful.

 NOTE
From time to time, updated versions of the installer and Escape Excel Hell Utility Pak are posted on my Web site at `www.EscapeFromExcelHell.com`.

Within the `spreadsheets` directory is a file called `ReadMe.xls`. Double-click this file and click the button called Install EscapeExcelHell.xla (see Figure B-1).

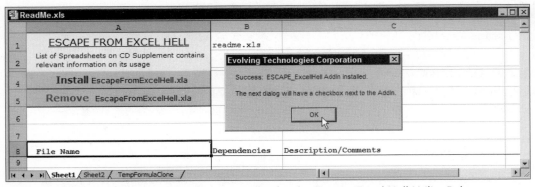

Figure B-1: Launching the installer and uninstaller for the Escape Excel Hell Utility Pak

The appropriate file is placed into the Excel Add-In directory. During the process of this install, you should see the list of installed add-ins (see Figure B-2).

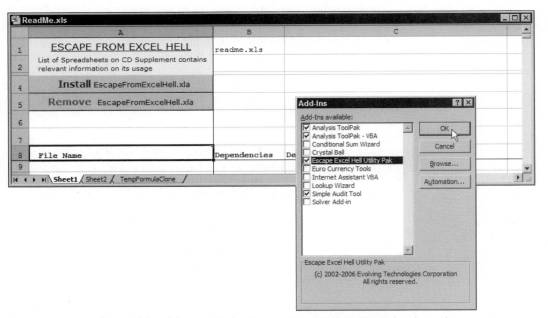

Figure B-2: List of available add-ins with the Escape Excel Hell Utility Pak selected.

Click OK and the routines should be installed.

To uninstall, simply click the button called `Remove EscapeExcelHell.xla` and uncheck the utility as instructed.

List of Routines in the Escape Excel Hell Utility Pak

The Escape Excel Hell Utility Pak contains macro routines and function procedures.

MACRO ROUTINES

The following is a description of the macro routines that can be run:

Summary of Contents	Description	Comments
SortAscendByDate	Sorts worksheet tabs by date	If contiguous groups of worksheets are selected, only they will be sorted. *Note:* Dates should conform to something like 'mmm-yyyy' ('mmm-yy' structured tabs will work; organize the months but not the year).
SortAscend	Sorts worksheet tabs by alphabetical order	If contiguous groups of worksheets are selected, only they will be sorted.
SortDescend	Sorts worksheet tabs by reverse alphabetical order	If contiguous groups of worksheets are selected, only they will be sorted.
NextWorksheetMacro	Goes to worksheet tab on the right while preserving same cell selection as in previous worksheet	Ctrl+Shift+L
PriorWorksheetMacro	Goes to worksheet tab on the left while preserving same cell selection as in previous worksheet	Ctrl+Shift+J

FUNCTION PROCEDURES

Three procedure functions are included in the Utility Pak.

MYWEEKDAY accomplishes the same as the Excel WEEKDAY function, except that it uses a string expression instead of a serialized date. The syntax usage for this function is

```
MYWEEKDAY(strDayOfWeek As String, Optional iArg As Integer = 1)
```

MYWEEKDAY returns day number that matches day of week according to the following table:

Default (No Optional Argument Supplied)	Optional Argument Supplied = 1	Optional Argument Supplied = 2	Optional Argument Supplied = 3	Value Returned
			"Monday"	0
"Sunday"	"Sunday"	"Monday"	"Tuesday"	1
"Monday"	"Monday"	"Tuesday"	"Wednesday"	2
"Tuesday"	"Tuesday"	"Wednesday"	"Thursday"	3
"Wednesday"	"Wednesday"	"Thursday"	"Friday"	4
"Thursday"	"Thursday"	"Friday"	"Saturday"	5
"Friday"	"Friday"	"Saturday"	"Sunday"	6
"Saturday"	"Saturday"	"Sunday"		7

 NOTE

The usage of optional arguments in MYWEEKDAY matches the usage of the Excel WEEKDAY function.

The function `getColorIndex` returns the color index of the cell. The syntax usage of `getColorIndex` is

```
getColorIndex(myCell, Optional iArg As Integer = 1)
```

If no optional argument is supplied or the value of the optional argument is 1, the color index value of the cell's shading is returned. If the value of the optional argument is 2, the color index value of the cell's shading is returned.

`ExceptionHandle` is designed to handle errors in the evaluation of an expression by computing an alternative computation. The syntax usage for ExceptionHandle is

```
ExceptionHandle(myComputation, myAlternate)
```

This function evaluates `myComputation` and returns it, unless there is an error; in which case it returns the evaluation of `myAlternate`. The following example should make this clear:

```
=EXCEPTIONHANDLE(2/0,5)                        returns 5
```

Troubleshooting and Other Useful Information

On occasion, it may be necessary to manually install or uninstall an add-in. Some quick steps are outlined next.

MANUALLY INSTALLING AN ADD-IN

Install the add-in using these steps:

1. From the add-in file, the filename should have an .XLA suffix. Move it over to the directory:

   ```
   C:\Documents and Settings\{your user name}\Application
   Data\Microsoft\Excel\AddIns
   ```

   You can do this using the Windows Explorer to drag and drop the file.

2. Launch Excel. From the Excel menu, click Tools⇨Add-Ins.

   Look to see whether the add-in is available. Place a checkmark next to it. If you don't see it in the list, click the Browse button. You should be viewing the contents of the AddIns directory, and the specific Add-In file should be visible. Select this file and click OK. This time, you should see it in your list. If there is no checkmark to its immediate left, check it now.

   Click the OK button of the Add-Ins window.

CHANGING THE NAME OF AN ADD-IN

"I want to be able to change the name that appears for an add-in."

When you click Tools⇨Add-Ins you are able to check and uncheck available Add-Ins. From all outward appearances, it doesn't seem as though the name can be revised.

There's a quick solution. First quit Excel (actually, this is very important).

Next, locate your add-in file in the Windows Explorer.

When you see the file you want to adjust, right-click it and select Properties, and go to the Summary tab. Within the Summary tab, there should appear a list of property attributes such as Title, Subject, Category, and Keyword (see Figure B-3). Click the actual title, edit it, and click first the Apply button and then OK. The next time you launch Excel and examine the list of available Add-In names, you should see the revised name appear correctly.

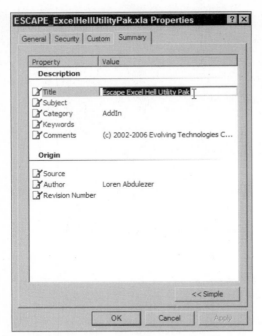

Figure B-3: Setting properties in the file's Properties tab

Appendix

Escape From Excel Hell Techniques and Hip Pocket Tips

Escape From Excel Hell is filled with a substantial amount of information. To make this information convenient and readily accessible, selected techniques and tips from this book are provided here (see Table C-1). You can use this reference to quickly locate information you may need.

From time to time, be sure to check for updated information from my Web site: www.EscapeFromExcelHell.com.

TABLE C-1	**LIST OF ESCAPE FROM EXCEL HELL SOLUTIONS, TECHNIQUES, AND TIPS**		
No.	**Problem, Solution, Technique, or Tip**	**Ch.**	**Section**
1	ACTIVATING SPREADSHEET PROTECTION	Ch 3	Setting Numeric and Text Representation
2	ACTIVIATING SHEET PROTECTION	Ch 7	Setting Protection for Individual Cells and at the Worksheet Level

continued

TABLE C-1   LIST OF ESCAPE FROM EXCEL HELL SOLUTIONS, TECHNIQUES, AND TIPS *(continued)*

No.	Problem, Solution, Technique, or Tip	Ch.	Section
3	ADD-IN LOCATION ON THE MACINTOSH PLATFORM	App A	Differences between Mac and Windows
4	ADDING A TRENDLINE TO A CHART	Ch 6	Adding a Trendline
5	ADDING HOURS TO A DATE WITHOUT THE ACTUAL HAVING EXCEL CHOP OFF SOME OF THE HOURS	Ch 5	Using Inlining with calendar arithmetic
6	ADDING NEW COLORS TO FONTS AND PATTERNS	Ch 3	Adjusting Cell Background Patterns
7	ADVANCING A DATE BY A GIVEN NUMBER DAY, MONTHS, AND YEARS	Ch 5	Using Inlining with calendar arithmetic
8	ALIGNING TEXT IN A COLUMN	Ch 3	Understanding Fonts and Formatting
9	ALLOCATING WEEKLY DATA ACROSS A MONTHLY TIMELINE	Ch 9	Date Arithmetic
10	APPLYING COMMON HEADER AND FOOTER SETTINGS ACROSS WORKSHEETS	Ch 3	Managing Headers and Footers
11	ARRIVAL RATE PROBLEM	Ch 9	Approximating Probability Distributions Other Than Uniform
12	ASCII CHARACTER SET	App A	Map of ASCII Characters
13	AUTO CORRECTION	Ch 3	AutoFormat and AutoCorrect Features
14	AUTOFILTER DOESN'T FIND EVERYTHING	Ch 7	Working with Auto Filters
15	AUTOFILTER SPECIAL SELECTION	Ch 7	Working with Auto Filters
16	AUTOMATING A PROGRESSION OF NUMBERS	App A	Formula Simplification
17	AUTO-OPEN SMARTLY	Ch 4	Managing the User Experience
18	AUTO-SORTING NUMBERS AS IT CHANGES	Ch 8	Auto-Sort (Using Arrays)

No.	Problem, Solution, Technique, or Tip	Ch.	Section
19	AVOIDING ERRORS WITH NEGATIVE TIME QUANTITIES	Ch 5	Using Inlining with calendar arithmetic
20	AVOIDING NEEDLESS SECURITY ALERTS WHEN MACROS ARE TO BE TRUSTED	Ch 10	Signing Digital Certificates
21	BACKING OUT OF A MISTAKEN DATE ENTRY	App A	Annotating and Decorating Spreadsheets
22	BUILDING YOUR CUSTOM TOOLBAR	Ch 1	Customizing Your Excel Software with Toolbars
23	CALCULATING DAY OF WEEK FOR A GIVEN DATE	Ch 2	NETWORDAYS, WORKDAY, and WEEKDAY
24	CALCULATING MEDIAN FOR GROUPED DATA	App A	Statistical Calculations Involving Frequencies
25	CAN'T CHANGE A SETTING: OPTIONS ARE GRAYED OUT	Ch 1	My Spreadsheets Have Gone Haywire — Help!!
26	CELL FORMATTING: ANGLED OR SLANTED TEXT	Ch 3	Creating Angled Text
27	CELL FORMATTING: WRAPPING TEXT	Ch 3	Wrapping Text
28	CHANGING SPREADSHEET PREVIEW	Ch 3	Previewing Your New Template
29	CHART REPLICATION PROBLEM AND HOW TO GET AROUND IT	Ch 6	Worksheet and Workbook-level Names
30	CHART TIME TO AUTOMATICALLY RETRIEVE VALUES COMPUTED IN A WORKSHEET	Ch 6	Dynamically Updated Text in a Chart
31	CHARTING: EXCEL TRENDLINES FEATURE AND NOT HAVING THEM SKEWED	Ch 8	Testing for Data Types and Cell Properties
32	CLEANING UP A LIST OF DATA	Ch 8	Data Scrubbing
33	CLONING A CHART, BUT WITH NEW DATA	Ch 6	Dynamically Updated Text in a Chart
34	COLORIZING INPUT CELLS	Ch 3	Adjusting Cell Background Patterns
35	COMPARING TWO WORKSHEETS FOR DIFFERENCES	Ch 8	Comparing Spreadsheets
36	COMPRESSING DATA	Ch 9	Dynamic Row Compression

continued

TABLE C-1 **LIST OF ESCAPE FROM EXCEL HELL SOLUTIONS, TECHNIQUES, AND TIPS** *(continued)*

No.	Problem, Solution, Technique, or Tip	Ch.	Section
37	COMPUTING TRIG FUNCTIONS WITH DEGREES (INSTEAD OF RADIANS)	Ch 5	Conversion Between Degrees and Radians
38	CONDITIONAL FORMATTING BASED ON CRITERIA FROM ANOTHER WORKSHEET OR ANOTHER WORKBOOK	Ch 7	Conditional Formatting Using Content from Another Worksheet or Workbook
39	CONSOLIDATING DATA	Ch 9	Consolidating Data
40	CONSOLIDATING DATA	Ch 9	Dynamic Row Compression
41	CONSOLIDATING DATA: COPY AND PASTE TECHNIQUE	Ch 3	Grabbing the Data You Want
42	CONSOLIDATING UNALIGNED DATA	Ch 9	Consolidating Through Copy and Paste
43	CONSTRUCTING LOOKUP TABLES	Ch 2	Relative, Absolute, and Hybrid Cell References and Replicating Formulas
44	CONSTRUCTING TABLES	App A	Formula Simplification
45	CONTROLLING WHEN RANDOM NUMBERS GET RECALCULATED	Ch 10	Freezing Random Numbers
46	CONVERSION OF DIGITS TO DATES	Ch 2	Working with Dates and Times
47	CONVERSION OF STANDARD UNITS	Ch 5	Converting Measures Using CONVERT
48	CONVERTING 20060616 TO THE DATE 6/16/2006 (AS A SERIAL DATE)	App A	Converting Data
49	CONVERTING A DATE INTO A DAY OF WEEK IN THE FORM OF A SINGLE DIGIT	Ch 5	Date and Time Functions
50	CONVERTING A DAY OF WEEK AS TEXT (SUCH AS "WEDNESDAY") THAT IS NOT A CALENDAR DATE INTO A CORRESPONDING SINGLE DIGIT NUMBER	Ch 5	Date and Time Functions
51	CONVERTING A REGULAR DECIMAL NUMBER INTO A ROMAN NUMERAL	Ch 5	Roman Numerals

No.	Problem, Solution, Technique, or Tip	Ch.	Section
52	CONVERTING A SET OF DIGITS INTO A SERIALIZED DATE	Ch 5	Date and Time Functions
53	CONVERTING APPARENTLY NEGATIVE NUMBERS INTO ACTUAL NEGATIVE NUMBERS	Ch 8	Converting Text That Looks Like a Number into a Number
54	CONVERTING COMPOUND QUANTITIES LIKE VELOCITY IN ONE SET OF UNITS TO ANOTHER	Ch 5	Converting Measures Using CONVERT
55	CONVERTING FROM BOOLEAN (TRUE/FALSE VALUES) TO NUMERIC	Ch 2	TRUE and FALSE
56	CONVERTING FROM NUMERIC VALUES TO BOOLEAN (TRUE/FALSE)	Ch 2	TRUE and FALSE
57	CONVERTING TO UNITS NOT DEFINED BY EXCEL'S CONVERT FUNCTION	Ch 5	Converting Measures Using CONVERT
58	COPYING A MACRO FROM ONE WORKBOOK TO ANOTHER	Ch 4	Those Pesky Macros
59	COUNTIF WITH COMPOUND CRITERIA	App A	Counting Data
60	COUNTIF WITH MULTIPLE CRITERIA FOR A SINGLE RANGE	App A	Counting Data
61	COUNTIF WITH N CRITERIA FOR MULTIPLE RANGES	App A	Counting Data
62	COUNTIF WITH TWO CRITERIA FOR MULTIPLE RANGES	App A	Counting Data
63	COUNTING HOW MANY CELLS HAVE A PARTICULAR WORD IN THEM	App A	Counting Data
64	CREATING A DYNAMIC DROP DOWN LIIST	Ch 7	Data Validation
65	CREATING A HISTOGRAM WITH REDEFINEABLE INTERVALS	Ch 6	Creating Histograms
66	CREATING CONDITIONAL CHARTS	Ch 6	Conditionally Formatted Charts
67	CREATING DYNAMICALLY UPDATED TEXT INSIDE A CHART	Ch 6	Inserting a Text Box into a Chart

continued

TABLE C-1 **LIST OF ESCAPE FROM EXCEL HELL SOLUTIONS, TECHNIQUES, AND TIPS** *(continued)*

No.	Problem, Solution, Technique, or Tip	Ch.	Section
68	CREATING A VALIDATION LIST FROM A REMOTE WORKBOOK	Ch 7	Data Validation
69	DATA CONSOLIDATION	Ch 8	Eliminating Unneeded Data
70	DATA REPLICATION ISSUES	Ch 10	Date Arithmetic and Formula Replication
71	DATE AND TIME VALUE CONVERSION	Ch 2	TIMEVALUE and DATEVALUE
72	DATE/TIME STAMPING AND CHANGE CONTROL	Ch 3	Saving Multiple Versions of a File Is Not Enough
73	DECIMAL POINT OF NUMBERS ENTERED IS CHANGED BY EXCEL WHEN IT IS ENTERED AND WITHOUT WARNING	Ch 1	My Spreadsheets Have Gone Haywire — Help!!
74	DESPLAYING A MONTH NUMBER AS A DATE (SUCH AS 1⇨JANUARY)	Ch 2	DAY, MONTH, and YEAR
75	DETECTING TRANSPOSITION ERRORS IN DATA	Ch 9	Clerical Errors
76	DIFF TOOL FOR WORKSHEETS	Ch 8	Comparing Spreadsheets
77	DISABLING AUTOMATIC HYPERLINKS	Ch 4	Text as a Hyperlink
78	DISABLING MACROS	Ch 1	Macro Security
79	DISAPPEARING ACT: RESTORING WINDOW CONTROLS TO RESIZE WINDOWS	Ch 7	Protection at the Workbook Level
80	DISAPPEARING COMPONENTS, THE FORMULA BAR IS GONE	Ch 1	My Spreadsheets Have Gone Haywire — Help!!
81	DISCRETE EVENT SIMULATION	Ch 9	Approximating Probability Distributions Other Than Uniform
82	DISPLAYING DATA THAT SPANS OVER MANY ORDERS OF MAGNITUDE	Ch 6	A little info about the source data used in this example
83	DISPLAYING ERROR BARS IN A CHART	Ch 6	Representing Data
84	DISPLAYING HIGH, LOW, AND CLOSING VALUES IN A CHART	Ch 6	Representing Data

continued

TABLE C-1   LIST OF ESCAPE FROM EXCEL HELL SOLUTIONS, TECHNIQUES, AND TIPS (continued)

No.	Problem, Solution, Technique, or Tip	Ch.	Section
103	FILTERING BASED ON FORMULA	Ch 7	Advanced Filters
104	FIND IF 1, 2, 3, 4, 5, 6, 7, 8, 9, 10 IN ANY PERMUTATION IS COMPLETELY ACCOUNTED FOR IN A RANGE OF CELLS	App A	Arrays
105	FINDING AND USING THE CATALOG OF .XLT TEMPLATES	Ch 1	Excel Workbooks, Worksheets, and Templates
106	FINDING THE COLUMN LETTER OF THE CURRENT CELL	App A	Computing with Rows and Columns
107	FIXING COLUMN LETTERS FLOWING FROM RIGHT TO LEFT	Ch 1	My Spreadsheets Have Gone Haywire — Help!
108	FLAGGING FOR DUPLICATES DURING DATA ENTRY	Ch 8	Eliminating Unneeded Data
109	FORMATTING A CHART COMPONENT TO APPEAR IN 3D	Ch 6	Creating 2.5 Dimensions
110	FORMATTING DATES TO ANY TEXT FORMAT	Ch 2	DAY, MONTH, and YEAR
111	FORMATTING REPORTS	Ch 3	AutoFormat and AutoCorrect Features
112	FORMULA FOR COMPUTING A1 STATUS	App A	Computing with Rows and Columns
113	FORMULA FOR FILENAME WITH FULL PATH	App A	Computing with Rows and Columns
114	FORMULA FOR WORKSHEET NAME	App A	Computing with Rows and Columns
115	FORMULAS GUIDE FOR NEWBIES	Ch 2	Formula Basics
116	GENERATING A RANGE OF DATE INTERVALS	Ch 5	Date and Time Functions
117	GENERATING REPEATING SEQUENCES WITHOUT A ZERO IN IT	App A	Hyperlink Mischief
118	GETTING A CHART TO ONLY SHOW NON-ZERO DATA FOR A RANGE OF CATEGORY VALUES	Ch 6	To Gap or Not to Gap

continued

TABLE C-1   LIST OF ESCAPE FROM EXCEL HELL SOLUTIONS, TECHNIQUES, AND TIPS (continued)

No.	Problem, Solution, Technique, or Tip	Ch.	Section
137	INFORMATION RIGHTS MANAGEMENT	Ch 7	Physical File Access
138	INLINING TECHNIQUES	Ch 5	Date and Time Functions
139	INSERTING LINE BREAKS IN CELLS	Ch 3	Wrapping Text
140	INTELLIGENT DATE ARITHMETIC	Ch 10	Date Arithmetic and Formula Replication
141	IRM AS A MEANS TO SET CORPORATE SECURITY POLICES AND PRACTICES	Ch 7	Physical File Access
142	LAYERED APPROACH	Ch 9	Managing Complexity Through the Layered Approach
143	LIMITATION: DATA VALIDATION FEATURE	Ch 9	Working with Data Validation and Formula Auditing
144	LIMITATIONS: AUTOFILTER	Ch 7	Working with Auto Filters
145	LOCATION WHERE .XLT TEMPLATES ARE STORED	Ch 1	Excel Workbooks, Worksheets, and Templates
146	LOGIC SWITCH: BOOLEAN NEGATION	Ch 2	Excel Logic Switches
147	MAC DOCUMENTATION AND EXCEL 2004 FOR MACINTOSH: APPARENT DISCREPANCIES	App A	Differences between Mac and Windows
148	MACRO: GETCOLORINDEX	Ch 8	Sorting by Cell Number Format and by Cell Color
149	MANAGING DATA LABEL VALUES	Ch 6	Creating 2.5 Dimensions
150	MANAGING DATA LABELS	Ch 6	Creating 2.5 Dimensions
151	MANUALLY ADJUSTING WORKSHEET SEQUENCE IN A WORKBOOK	Ch 4	Managing Multiple Worksheets in a Single Workbook
152	MATCHING ORDER	Ch 2	CHOOSE and MATCH
153	MISSING ICONS IN MY TOOLBAR	Ch 1	Toolbars and Toolbar Icons
154	MODIFYING BEHAVIOR OF SPREADSHEET	Ch 10	Modifying the Behavior of Spreadsheets
155	MULTIPLE PASSWORDS WITHIN A WORKSHEET	Ch 7	Setting Protection for Individual Cells and at the Worksheet Level

No.	Problem, Solution, Technique, or Tip	Ch.	Section
156	NAVIGATING THE MAZE OF DIGITAL CERTIFICATES	Ch 10	Understanding Code Signing
157	NAVIGATING THROUGH WORKSHEETS	Ch 1	Excel Workbooks, Worksheets, and Templates
158	NAVIGATING TO A SPECIFIC WORKSHEET	Ch 4	Oh, I've Got Plenty of Worksheets
159	NORMAL DISTRIBUTION: CREATING A SAMPLE BASED ON EXPECTED MEAN AND STANDARD DEVIATION	Ch 9	Approximating Probability Distributions Other Than Uniform
160	NUMERIC FORMAT: INVISIBLE DATA	Ch 3	Setting Numeric and Text Representation
161	NUMERIC FORMAT: SETTING CURRENCY SYMBOL	Ch 3	Setting Numeric and Text Representation
162	ONE STEP ACTION: PRINTING A GROUP OF WORKSHEETS	Ch 4	More Bells and Whistles
163	ORGANIZING SPREADSHEETS	Ch 3	Essential Spreadsheet Information Should be Upfront
164	PARSING COMPLICATED LOG FILES	Ch 8	Importing Log Files
165	PARSING DATA	Ch 8	Data Scrubbing
166	PHANTOM MACROS: SECURITY WARNING EVEN THOUGH THERE IS NO MACRO	Ch 4	Those Pesky Macros
167	PIVOTTABLES: AVOIDING DOUBLE COUNTED DATA	Ch 10	Once Is Enough!
168	POPUP COMMENTS: USEFUL COMBINATIONS OF COLORS	Ch 3	Maximizing the Benefits of the Comments Feature
169	PRACTICAL TIPS OF WHEN AND HOW TO APPLY ABSOLUTE, RELATIVE, AND HYBRID CELL REFERENCES	Ch 2	Relative, Absolute, and Hybrid Cell References and Replicating Formulas
170	PREPARING REPORTS: SLANTED TEXT IN TABLES	Ch 3	Creating Angled Text
171	PREVENTING AN AUTO-START MACRO FROM AUTOMATICALLY KICKING IN	Ch 4	Those Pesky Macros

continued

TABLE C-1 **LIST OF ESCAPE FROM EXCEL HELL SOLUTIONS, TECHNIQUES, AND TIPS** *(continued)*

No.	Problem, Solution, Technique, or Tip	Ch.	Section
172	PREVENTING DUPLICATE NUMBERS FROM BEING ENTERED INTO A COLUMN	Ch 7	Data Validation
173	PREVENTING ZERO VALUES OR EMPTY CELLS FROM SKEWING EXCEL TRENDLINES	Ch 8	Testing for Data Types and Cell Properties
174	PRINTING "&" IN THE SPREADSHEET HEADER/FOOTER	Ch 1	Introduction and Overview
175	PRINTING A GROUP OF WORKSHEETS IN ONE STEP	Ch 4	More Bells and Whistles
176	PROBLEMS AND CHALLENGES OF CLEANING UP A LIST OF DATA	Ch 8	Data Scrubbing
177	PROJECT MANAGEMENT: COUNTING DAYS	Ch 2	NETWORDAYS, WORKDAY, and WEEKDAY
178	PROJECT MANAGEMENT: ESTIMATING COMPLETION DATE	Ch 2	NETWORDAYS, WORKDAY, and WEEKDAY
179	PROTECTING ALL WORKSHEETS IN ONE STEP	Ch 7	Setting Protection for Individual Cells and at the Worksheet Level
180	QUICK WAY OF TURNING A TEXT REPRESENTATION OF A NUMBER INTO ITS NUMERIC VALUE	App A	Converting Data
181	RECALCULATION KEYSTROKE SEQUENCES	App A	Table A-1
182	RECONSTITUTED OR REVERSE ENGINEERED PIVOTTABLES	Ch 10	Filling in the Blanks
183	REFERENCE AN ARRAY INSIDE A FORMULA	App A	Arrays
184	REMOVING BLANK CELLS IN A RANGE	Ch 3	Grabbing the Data You Want
185	REMOVING EXCEL PROTECTION	Ch 7	Setting Protection for Individual Cells and at the Worksheet Level
186	REMOVING FORMATTING INFORMATION WHEN TRANSFERRING DATA TO AN EXTERNAL PROGRAM	App A	Windows and Office

continued

TABLE C-1   LIST OF ESCAPE FROM EXCEL HELL SOLUTIONS, TECHNIQUES, AND TIPS *(continued)*

No.	Problem, Solution, Technique, or Tip	Ch.	Section
204	SETTING UP OPTIONAL ARGUMENTS IN MACROS	App A	Controlling Macros
205	SETTING WORKSHEET PROTECTION	Ch 7	Setting Protection for Individual Cells and at the Worksheet Level
206	SETTINGS: ADJUSTING DEFAULT SETTINGS FOR GRIDLINES	Ch 3	Removing the Gridlines
207	SHOWING BOTH A SECONDARY X- AND SECONDARY Y-AXIS	Ch 6	A little info about the source data used in this example
208	SIMULATION: GENERATING NORMAL DISTRIBUTION TEST SAMPLE	Ch 9	Approximating Probability Distributions Other Than Uniform
209	SIMULTANEOUSLY VIEWING AND UPDATING TWO WORKSHEETS FROM A SINGLE WORKBOOK	Ch 7	Data Validation
210	SMART DATA: AUTOMATIC BORDERS THAT "BOXES" DATA AS THE DATA CHANGES	Ch 10	Once Is Enough!
211	SOME EXCEL MENU ITEMS ARE HIDDEN AND THEY KEEP CHANGING	Ch 1	Excel Menus
212	SORT ORDER BY DATA TYPES	Ch 8	Understanding Sort Order
213	SORTING BY IP ADDRESS	Ch 8	Sorting by IP Block
214	SORTING BY NUMERIC CELL FORMAT	App A	Arrays
215	SORTING BY SPREADSHEET CELL COLOR	Ch 8	Sorting by Cell Number Format and by Cell Color
216	SORTING DATA IN CLUSTERS	Ch 8	Block Sorting
217	SORTING FIVE- AND NINE-DIGIT ZIP CODES TOGETHER	Ch 8	Sorting ZIP Codes
218	SORTING ISSUES: FIXING PROBELMS CAUSED BY MERGED CELLS	Ch 3	Working with Merged Cells (and Handling the Problems They Cause)
219	SORTING ON MORE THAN THREE KEYS	Ch 8	Sorting with More Than Three Sort Keys

continued

TABLE C-1   **LIST OF ESCAPE FROM EXCEL HELL SOLUTIONS, TECHNIQUES, AND TIPS** *(continued)*

No.	Problem, Solution, Technique, or Tip	Ch.	Section
238	TOTALLY LOCKED UP FILE	Ch 7	Physical File Access
239	TURNING HEADERS AND FOOTERS ON AND OFF	Ch 4	More Bells and Whistles
240	UNDERSTANDING A SECONDARY CHART AXIS	Ch 6	A little info about the source data used in this example
241	UNDERSTANDING ABSOLUTE, RELATIVE, AND HYBRID CELL REFERENCES AND THEIR USE IN FORMULAS	Ch 2	Relative, Absolute, and Hybrid Cell References and Replicating Formulas
242	UNDERSTANDING CASE SENSITIVITY IN EXCEL FORMULAS	Ch 2	String Equality and Case Sensitivity
243	UNDERSTANDING DIFFERENCE BETWEEN ISERR AND ISERROR	Ch 8	Testing for Data Types and Cell Properties
244	UNDERSTANDING HOW ADVANCED FILTERS WORK	Ch 7	Advanced Filters
245	UNDERSTANDING HOW R1C1 WORKS	Ch 1	Understanding the R1C1 reference style
246	UNDERSTNDING THE PECKING ORDER IN SORT ORDER	Ch 8	Understanding Sort Order
247	UNDOING DATE FORMATS WHEN EXCEL WANT TO KEEP THE DATE FORMAT	Ch 2	Working with Dates and Times
248	USING A MACRO TO SET CALCULATION MODE	Ch 10	Elementary Techniques for Developing Code
249	USING A SEPARATE SORT KEY FOR ZIP CODES	Ch 8	Sorting ZIP Codes
250	USING A SUBSCRIPTS AND SUPERSCRIPTS IN HEADERS AND FOOTERS	Ch 4	More Bells and Whistles
251	USING COMPUTED VALUES IN HEARS AND FOOTERS	Ch 4	More Bells and Whistles
252	USING CONDITIONAL FORMATTING BASED ON CELL VALUE	Ch 7	Conditional Formatting
253	USING COPY AND PASTING TO CONSOLIDATE DATA	Ch 3	Grabbing the Data You Want

Appendix

About the CD

- ◆ Spreadsheets for the book
- ◆ Escape Excel Hell Utility Add-In
- ◆ takeaway.txt
- ◆ eBook
- ◆ Crystal Xcelsius Professional (Trial version that never times out!)
- ◆ Sample dashboards prepared with Crystal Xcelsius
- ◆ Adobe Acrobat Reader

System Requirements

Make sure your computer meets the minimum system requirements listed below. If your computer doesn't match up to most of these requirements, you may have problems in using the contents of the CD.

- A PC with a Pentium or faster processor, or a Mac OS computer with a PowerPC processor.
- Microsoft Windows 98 or later, or Mac OS X.
- At least 16MB of total RAM installed on your computer. For best performance, we recommend at least 32MB of RAM installed.
- A CD-ROM drive.

Using the CD with Microsoft Windows

The files on the CD are organized into four groups:

- A folder called spreadsheets, which contains all the spreadsheets described in Escape From Excel Hell.

- A folder called other_files, which contains a set of supplementary nonspreadsheet files.

- A folder called additional_software, which contains a nontimed trial version of Crystal Xcelsius Professional (this is Windows-only software), as well as Adobe Reader software (installers for both Windows and Macintosh platforms provided on disc).

- A folder called eBook, which contains a .pdf version of this book that you can view and search using Adobe Reader. Adobe Reader is also included on the CD in the additional_software folder.

At the root level of the CD there is a ReadMe.html file and a spreadsheets.zip file.

Installing the Spreadsheet Files

Your CD is designed for maximum convenience. All the spreadsheets on the CD (there are more than 75 of them) can be directly accessed in the spreadsheets directory. You should be able to double-click on any file. Many authors segment the spreadsheets into individual folders for each chapter. My approach is to label the chapter numbers and sequence within the chapter directly in the filename, and keep all the files in one common directory. Doing so allows you to rummage through the files without the inconvenience of opening and closing folders.

My strong recommendation is that you open the ReadMe.xls file first. This is your portal to all the spreadsheets. It contains hyperlinks for each file, an explanation of what the spreadsheet does, and lists any special dependencies or requirements (such as calculation settings).

A couple of key points are worth mentioning. When you open spreadsheet files directly from the CD, they all open in Read-Only format. It may be more convenient for you to place a copy of the spreadsheets.zip file directly onto your hard drive and expand it to a directory of your choice, so you won't have to deal with the Read-Only issues.

For your convenience, the ReadMe.xls file allows you to install (and remove) the Escape Excel Hell Utility Pak at the click of a button. More information can be found about this in Appendix B ("Installing the Escape Excel Hell Utility Pak").

 NOTE
If you try to install the Excel Hell Utility Pak directly from the CD-ROM, you will encounter difficulties uninstalling and reinstalling, due to permission settings. Instead, copy the spreadsheets.zip file to your hard disk, expand it there, and install the Utility Pak from your expanded ReadMe.xls on your hard disk.

Installing Crystal Xcelsius Professional

Crystal Xcelsius allows you to convert your Excel Spreadsheets to highly visual and inter-active standalone dashboards in the form of Flash (.swf) files, PowerPoint (.ppt) slides, and Adobe Portable Document Format (.pdf) files. These generated dashboards can be e-mailed or posted on a Web site for direct viewing within your Web browser.

The Crystal Xcelsius software is Windows only. To install the software, follow these steps:

1. Double-click InstallCrystalXcelsiusProTrial to open the installer.

2. Click "Next" to begin setup.

3. Check the radio button next to "I accept the agreement" to accept the EULA.

4. Click "Next."

5. Determine the location where you would like to install Crystal Xcelsius Professional. By default it is installed into "C:\Program Files\Business Objects\Crystal Xcelsius Professional 4 Trial." Click "Browse" and select a different location if you want to change this.

6. Click "Next."

7. Choose where you would like Setup to install the Crystal Xcelsius shortcuts into the Start menu. By default, they are installed in "Business Objects\Crystal Xcelsius Professional 4 Trial." Click "Browse" and select a different location if you want to change this, or select "Don't create a Start Menu folder" to bypass this step.

8. Click "Next."

9. Select the additional tasks you would like Setup to perform, including either: 1) Creating a desktop icon for Crystal Xcelsius, or 2) Always playing your flash files inside Internet Explorer. Both options are selected by default. Uncheck either box to skip that task.

10. Click "Next."

11. Click "Install" to begin the installation of Crystal Xcelsius Professional onto your computer.

12. After Setup has finished installing Crystal Xcelsius, you can choose to either install Macromedia Flash Player 7 (required by Crystal Xcelsius), and/or immediately launch the application. Select your options, then click "Finish" to complete the installation process.

The complete user guide for Crystal Xcelsius is in the form of a PDF file and can be found in the other_files directory. Also contained in the other_files directory, are a set of Crystal Xcelsius files and dashboards, article reprints, and a white paper.

Installing the Adobe Acrobat Reader

Adobe Reader is used to access the eBook version of this title. To install the software, fol-low these steps:

1. Double-click the "setup.exe" from the Adobe Reader folder.

2. Follow the prompts in the interface to install Adobe Reader.

How to Use the CD Using the Mac OS

First read through the information for the Windows users. There are a number of differences that are outlined here.

Installing the Spreadsheet Files

Within the ReadMe.xls file there is a worksheet tab called "ForMacUsers" which has specific usage notes relevant for Mac users. Though the details are provided within the worksheet, I summarize a few of them here:

- Add-in files in OS X are generally located in:

  `Applications/Microsoft Office 2004/Office/Addins`

- There appears to be some issues with referencing the Analysis ToolPak (on OS X) from a macro. I am looking into this and will have updates on my Web site:

  `www.EscapeFromExcelHEll.com`

- There are some keyboard differences. Recalculation of the workbook is accomplished by pressing ⌘+= (Command Equals) keys instead of F9. Excel Options on the Mac platform are called Preferences and pressing ⌘+, (Command Comma) opens the Preferences window. Toggle back and forth between Excel and the Visual Basic Editor, and press Option+F11 instead of Alt+F11.

Installing the Escape Excel Hell Utility requires a manual install. Follow the steps below:

1. Locate the Esape_ExcelHellUtilityPak.xla file in the spreadsheets directory and place a copy of it in:

   `Applications/Microsoft Office 2004/Office/Addins`

2. Launch Excel 2004 for Macintosh.

3. Click Tools⇨Add-Ins.

4. Look to see if the Escape Excel Hell Utility Pak is in the list of Add-Ins. If it is and it does not have a checkmark next to it, check it now. If it is not on the list, press the Browse button and locate the file, and then click OK.

5. The Escape Excel Hell Utility Pak should be listed and checked. Press OK to save and exit the Add-Ins window.

NOTE

Excel 2004 for the Macintosh does not provide some of the essential features that can be found in the Professional Edition of Excel 2003 for Windows, such as full XML support. A solution for many Macintosh users who need these capabilities, is to obtain Excel 2003 Professional for Windows and run it using Windows emulation software. If you are using Excel on the Mac in this mode, you can follow the installation information for the Windows platform, and should not be encumbered by the Mac limitations cited here.

Installing Crystal Xcelsius Professional

Crystal Xcelsius is a Windows-only product, but it runs with Windows emulation software such as Virtual PC. With the emulation software, follow the instructions as you would for Windows.

Installing the Adobe Acrobat Reader

Adobe Reader is used to access the eBook version of this title. To install the software, follow these steps:

1. Double-click the "Adobe Reader 7.0.5 Installer" from the Adobe Reader folder.
2. Follow the prompts in the interface to install Adobe Reader.

What You'll Find

Here's a summary of the software on this CD arranged by category.

- Spreadsheet files
- Trial Version of Crystal Xcelsius Professional

The Trial Version of Crystal Xcelsius Professional and the dashboards it generates never time out. The section on spreadsheets and dashboards in Chapter 10 explains how to use the software. The complete user guide in PDF form is supplied on this CD, along with article reprints and a white paper.

The Trial Version of Crystal Xcelsius Professional is the full product in all respects, except two:

- You cannot XLF files.
- The words "Trial Version" appears on the dashboards that are generated.

For further information about Crystal Xcelsius, go to:

```
http://www.xcelsius.com
http://www.XcelsiusBestPractices.com
```

NOTE

Shareware programs are fully functional, free trial versions of copyrighted programs. If you like particular programs, register with their authors for a nominal fee and receive licenses, enhanced versions, and technical support. Freeware programs are free, copyrighted games, applications, and utilities. You can copy them to as many PCs as you like — free — but they have no technical support. GNU software is governed by its own license, which is included inside the folder of the GNU software. There are no restrictions on distribution of this software. See the GNU license for more details. Trial, demo, or evaluation versions are usually limited either by time or functionality (such as being unable to save projects).

If You've Got Problems (of the CD Kind)

I tried my best to compile programs that work on most computers with the minimum system requirements. Alas, your computer may differ, and some programs may not work properly for some reason.

The two likeliest problems are that you don't have enough memory (RAM) for the programs you want to use, or you have other programs running that are affecting installation or running of a program. If you get error messages such as Not enough memory or Setup cannot continue, try one or more of these methods and then try using the software again:

- **Turn off any anti-virus software that you have on your computer.** Installers sometimes mimic virus activity and may make your computer incorrectly believe that it is being infected by a virus.

- **Close all running programs.** The more programs you're running, the less memory is available to other programs. Installers also typically update files and programs. So if you keep other programs running, installation may not work properly.

- **Have your local computer store add more RAM to your computer.** This is, admittedly, a drastic and somewhat expensive step. However, if you have a Windows 95 or later PC or a Mac OS computer with a PowerPC chip, adding more memory can really help the speed of your computer and allow more programs to run at the same time.

- **Remember to load both the Analysis Toolpak Add-In and the Analysis Toolpak - VBA Add-In.** Several of thespreadsheets use the CONVERT and RANDBETWEEN function. Be sure to load the Analysis Toolpak for your Excel Add-Ins. Instructions for loading add-ins is described in Appendix B. The option for the Analysis Toolpak in the list of available Add-Ins may not be displayed if you have not completed a full Excel installation.

Customer Care

If you have trouble with the CD-ROM, please call the Wiley Product Technical Support phone number at (800) 762-2974. Outside the United States, call 1(317) 572-3994. You can also contact Wiley Product Technical Support at **http://support.wiley.com**. John Wiley & Sons will provide technical support only for installation and other general quality control items. For technical support on the applications themselves, consult the program's vendor or author.

To place additional orders or to request information about other Wiley products, please call (877) 762-2974.

Index

Symbols and Numbers

continued

continued

continued

continued

Wiley Publishing, Inc. End-User License Agreement